GRACE NOTES

Russ —

Happy Parenthood —

Warm Wishes

GraceNotefully,

[signature]

Feb 12. 2010

GRACE NOTES

A story of Music, Trials and Unexpected Blessings

Sang-Eun Lee Bukaty

Library of Congress Control Number: 2009902833

ISBN: 978-0-578-01546-0

Printed in the United States of America

Author's Note

"Tell me the stories about when you were a little girl, Mommy."
My youngest daughter, Michelle, used to ask.
So I told her about the day my father took me to
An American restaurant and showed me how to use a knife
And a fork. I told her about the time I ran away.
I told her about the little girl who jumped rope in rubber shoes.
"Tell me more," she used to say. She always knew
There were more stories
I was not telling her.
Many more.
Stories millions of little Michelles would like to hear
So they can tell their little daughters and sons
So they can tell their daughters and sons.
The stories we hang on to because
Memories are becoming faint with each generation.
The stories of all the Korean mothers
Because it is everyone's story, yet unique.
The stories that would fill in and
Complete the identity of all the other
Terrys, Kimmys and Michelles
Like the last piece of a jigsaw puzzle.
The stories that make us grow and love and
Ultimately learn the true value of life in a foreign land,
Which is now our home.

This is the true story of my life. Every event is portrayed the way it remains in my memory. I have chosen to write it in English because, while I speak Korean fluently, my skills in Korean writing declined in over the four decades I have lived in America.

I would not be able to write it in Korean in a way that would impact readers as I intended. I am saddened by this fact, but it is an element of the natural process of becoming a Korean-American and of becoming a half-ripened American. It is a loss but also an advantage of living in both cultures, languages but most of all, the souls of each world.

This book is dedicated to my daughters,
Terry, Kimmy and Michelle
And
All the Korean-American mothers and their
second-generation children

Prologue

The Moo-Kung-Wha restaurant was full of Ewha high school girls in navy skirts and white blouses. Everyone turned to stare as my old Civics teacher, Mr. Park, and I walked in. The mere fact that I was no longer in the school uniform, but in a brightly colored summer suit – and walking in with a male teacher who was still single -- was enough to stop everyone from slurping their noodle soup. A dozen gazes followed us as we took a table in the far corner and sat across from each other.

"So, when are you leaving for America?" Mr. Park asked.

"In a couple of weeks, on the 14th of September," I replied. "I thank you for taking time to have lunch with me." I felt a little awkward but was honored that he took me to a restaurant off campus.

It had been two years since I graduated from high school, but I felt as though I had just snuck off campus for lunch. I could have sat with any of the young girls in the restaurant and felt right at home. All my memories from that time were so clear and alive.

In a society where the teacher-student relationship was rigid, we, students at the Music and Art high school were proud to be different. We were considered "emotional and free spirited artists." Some of the Ewha girls resented us for wearing the same uniform and being on the same campus without having to maintain the same high academic standards. They also envied our talents and the freedom we had, to study what we wanted.

Studying music so devotedly was a noble and elite thing to do. We felt truly special. We were living in a world that was unknown to outsiders, and only we had the privilege of sharing it with each other. Even the Ewha teachers, from whom we took morning classes, were inclined to joke with us casually and show an interest in the arts we were studying. Oftentimes, they would ask us to perform on the piano, cello, or violin, or ask a voice major to sing.

Most of the girls in our class were a little more attentive in the subjects taught by unmarried male teachers. Civics was one of them. Even though Mr. Park came into the class in suits with tattered cuffs day after day – there was nothing charming or attractive about him outwardly – most of us thought there was something decent, sincere, and sensitive about Mr. Park. For me, it was the day he rubbed his eyes with his fist as he told us the story of Dante, the medieval poet who was led to spiritual awakening by Beatrice, who greeted him with her angelic face after he had spent nine long years yearning for her. This was how Mr. Park got on my list of teachers to say goodbye to.

Mr. Park gazed at me from across the table. "So, I have been seeing you play the cello on TV quite a bit. Do you enjoy doing that?"

"Yes, I do, and it's pretty good money," I said proudly. "I don't ask my mom for spending money anymore."

"Music is really a big part of your life, isn't it?" He asked, looking straight at me. "How far do you think you will go with it?"

"How can you ask, how far?" I said in shock. "Music is my life. My teacher Mr. Kim told me that I couldn't even think of getting married unless I find someone who would understand that I am a musician and a performer. Everything else is insignificant."

"You really believe that, don't you? I hope you realize how lucky you are to study what you love, and that you are so good at it." He took a sip of his tea.

I twisted and adjusted my seat. "We heard that in Russia, talented music students are sent away to a camp far from their families and locked up so they will spend time and energy only to practice," I said.

"Oh, how horrible!" he exclaimed.

"Oh, not at all. We were saying how absolutely wonderful it would be to concentrate on music only."

Now he stared at me quizzically. "I want to tell you a story," he paused and put his locked hands under his chin.

"You know, the most valuable pearls come from the South Sea." He took a sip of the tea again and set his cup down. "They come in large oysters. The inside walls of those shells have the most beautiful mother-of-pearl you will ever see. For oysters, having a pearl in their stomach can give them the most God-awful pain." He grabbed his stomach and crunched his face. "Because it is a form of cancer – foreign material that collects and attaches to the flesh. The pain is so severe that the oyster has to make a decision. It can open its mouth, let it out, and become pain-free, or keep the pearl inside, enduring the pain, letting it grow bigger and more beautiful. All the while, the oyster polishes it with his flesh, trying to minimize the pain." Mr. Park looked far away before continuing.

"As it polishes harder, patiently, faithfully, the pain deepens, and then one day the pearl starts to gleam, indicating the value of this most beautiful object. The longer the oyster endures the pain and the more efforts put forth in producing the mysterious beauty, the more valu-able the pearl becomes. And the gleaming beauty radiates from the very core."

Mr. Park circled his fingertip around the cup and said firmly, "Only then does the pearl give peace and joy to its harboring oyster."

I was completely enthralled by his story.

"A lot of people live their lives never having anything to polish. They never experience the joy it could give them, just as there are lots of oysters that never have even the smallest worthless pearls in them. Doesn't mean they aren't happy," he added. "But they may never know the deepest joy that comes from acquiring the ultimate value within them. "You have a God-given gift. You have already planted the seed to grow and polish. There will be days you will want to scream from the pain and come close to giving up your music."

I sighed and closed my mouth as if I didn't want anything to escape. I knew then that I would never open my mouth and let out my pearl—my music.

His words rang in my ears as I walked all the way home. I was born to play the cello. I couldn't possibly imagine giving it up.

It was only decades later that I realized how those words from the man in the seedy suit remained in my heart, making a haunting connection to my life.

Then God said to me, "My grace is sufficient for you, for my power is made perfect in weakness." Therefore I will boast all the more gladly about my weaknesses, so that Christ's power may rest on me.

2 Corinthians 12:9

1

My mother used to cover my right eye, hold three fingers in front of my face and ask, "How many?" Then, she would move her fingers farther away and hold out only two of them. She did this so often, I didn't want to answer anymore. I knew that the impaired vision in my left eye was not changing, and it made me sad to know that she was constantly thinking about it.

One day when I was nine years old, Mother got teary and told me why. My birth had been a painful, grief filled experience for her. She said that she'd wanted to give me one of her eyes to replace my near useless one. I sensed that she wanted to tell me the story in detail, details of how much she loved me and how I saved our family.

As I listened to her tell me the story, I felt happy and sad, wanted and unwanted. But most of all, it made me feel loved. This was how the story went:

Mrs. Takahashi, the midwife, with her skilled moves, pressed and gently massaged my mother's engorged muscles around the birth canal—Mrs. Takahashi's well-known magical touch to keep it from tearing.

No one had ever met Mr. Takahashi, a Japanese man, and Mrs. Takahashi lived alone with her two young daughters, giving the impression that she was no longer married to him. Although she was Japanese, Mrs. Takahashi usually wore a traditional Korean dress, thus avoiding the silent, sneering looks. She delivered just about every baby in the neighborhood and developed a reputation for being the best and most skillful midwife, as well as the kindest.

Two maids were standing by waiting for signals from Mrs. Takahashi, each holding a hot towel in one hand and a cold towel in another. My father paced in the *sarang-bang* (outer room), the men's quarter. He wasn't allowed anywhere near the *an-bang* (inner room), the women's quarter, where Mom was laboring.

Because husbands went out to work and their wives stayed in and did housework, Mr. and Mrs. were often addressed as *nai-wae* meaning literally, "inner person and outer person." Husbands received business guests, played *Ma-jak*, read the newspaper, or simply relaxed in the *sarang-bang*. The *an-bang* was a combination family room and bedroom, and wives used it to receive their guests.

As with the previous four labors, Mother never screamed. She only moaned and bit her lower lip. One of the maids dabbed beads of perspiration from her forehead with a cold towel. The forehead was the only place where coldness was applied. It was thought that while delivering a baby, a mother should be kept warm at all times, even on the hottest day of summer.

"I will bear any kind of pain if you would only deliver a boy," Mother pleaded desperately.

"We all hope it will be a boy this time," Mrs. Takahashi smiled softly as she inserted her fingers into mom's vagina to measure her dilation.

"I simply wouldn't know what to do if it is another girl," Mother murmured. "I must never show the baby to my father-in-law if it's a girl. It would be grounds for divorce. I will get kicked out of the marriage," she said gasping. "For good." Her voice was weak with effort and hard to understand.

"Nonsense! Your first-born Sang-In is a boy," the midwife said. "I wouldn't worry a bit about it. Now push gently by breathing out. Don't push like you are going to the bathroom. We don't want any tears down there."

Mrs. Takahashi blew out her breath, demonstrating as if she was the one having the baby. Then she slipped another blanket under Mom to cover the wetness from the broken bag of waters. "Take a deep breath in, and then breathe out with all your might," said Mrs. Takahashi.

"Say pooh, pooh, and take short quick breaths in between. There, there, the head is crowning. Just a little more. Push," she spurred. "You are doing very well, a little more."

Finally, Mrs. Takahashi grabbed the top of my black head tight with her fingers and tried to turn it gently. "A little more," she urged my mother. Her fingers kept slipping on my slick black hair.

Mom's long, silk skirt was wet. It stuck to her thighs and wrapped around her legs, and the water seeped through the soft flannel fabric into the heavy cotton mat on which she laid.

All of a sudden, with tremendous urgency, as if surging out of an abruptly opened canal gate, I gushed out.

"There it is. The baby is out!" Mrs. Takahashi exclaimed. She grabbed me upside down by the ankles with one hand, and with the other hand she gave a quick swish through my mouth to clear out the mucus. Then she motioned for the maid to wipe my mother's lower lip, bloody from biting it so hard.

"Well, I'll be! It's another girl," she said. "*Uh-Chum-Joh-Ah*! Oh my goodness! What do you know? And she is beautiful," Mrs. Takahashi exclaimed. "Perfectly formed face, not a wrinkle, not a squashed nose. She will be the first lady one day."

There I was in Mrs. Takahashi's palm—the very first person I met. She then carefully placed me in my mother's arms.

The heaviness of my mother's heart outweighed the pain of just giving birth. The contractions in her uterus from her suckling baby, along with a dreadfully dull headache made her whole body feel numb. She rubbed her stomach slowly as she fell in and out of sleep, staring at the faint image of the paisley wallpaper on the ceiling in the streaks of moonlight coming through the cracks of the window curtains. The hard *on-dol* floor felt agonizing on her hemorrhoids, as if her bottom was lying on a board full of needles.

She knew she would be smiling and enduring the pain with pleasure if only the baby had been a boy. The reward would have been enormous. Tears ran down her cheeks from the guilt and disgrace of having a girl for the fourth time. She shook her head to get rid of the image of my grandfather's face, full of anger and disappointment.

"I will have to deal with it in the morning," she thought to herself, reflecting on the painful experiences of the past deliveries.

Mom remembered well the last three times she had brought her newborn baby girls into his room to be named. As far as my grandfather was concerned, girls had no value in life; however, he instantly adored my oldest sister, Sang-Soon, his first granddaughter.

"Good thing she is a girl with that curly hair and her skin so fair," he said with a sour smile, caressing her harshly. He wouldn't admit his love for her, yet he presented Mom with a box full of jewels, including his jade buttons and a heart-shaped 24-carat gold ring for the baby. He named her Sang-Soon, "Soon" meaning "good and well behaved."

When my second sister Sang-Hie was born two years later, mother wrapped the baby in a five-color striped *sak-dong* blanket and shuffled her steps slowly into his room. Two maids supported her on each side by her arms and slid my grandfather's door open. Even before they lowered her to sit and bow to my grandfather, he roared and hurled a thunderous insult at my mother and her precious second daughter in her arms.

"Get that thing out of my sight! I don't want to see her. Get her out of here. Who wants another girl in this house?"

He even refused to open the book of the family tree to name her. The *Jok-Bo*, the archive for family lineage, only records the names of boys. Even though girls' names weren't recorded in *Jok-Bo* (they are daughters only until they get married, because once married, they belong to the groom's family), they were entitled to be named following the already established lines of characters shared among the common generations.

Each generation's name had already been decided by the family tree. All of my siblings and cousins were named "Sang" as the first part of their first name, and only the second part of the first name, given by my grandfather was to be our very own.

"Name her Sang-Hie, for "Hie" means a girl. That's the best I can do," Grandfather said. "My time is too valuable to spend it researching and consulting a psychic to name a girl. Take her away."

He refused to even look at my second sister. One girl in the family was bad enough. One girl in the family was good enough. If only there had been a boy in between, she might have been more or less accepted. But two girls in a row would definitely chase the family luck away.

Then, three years later, my third sister was born. There was no greeting grandfather by my mother with this baby. My father delivered the sad news to my grandfather alone.

"Buy the best quality herbal medicine for her," my grandfather roared. "Pay any price for it to make her have a boy." He then named her Sang-Won. "Won" also means a girl.

Mother then drank the herbal medicine that was prescribed specifically to become impregnated with a boy baby.

"If only I had known it was a girl," Mom murmured faintly. A sigh followed. "Not only do I have to deal with that old goat, my whole family had to wait to escape from the war – all for another girl," Mother murmured again. But her worries were just beginning.

I was born in June of 1945, during the Pacific War. At the same time Mother's womb was growing heavy, the government was pressuring everyone in Seoul to evacuate. In the Japanese-occupied Korea, the capital city, Seoul, was the prime target for bombing, and my parents had been getting our family ready to escape to Kang-Ghe, my mother's hometown in northern Korea, where her father lived and practiced medicine.

Traveling long distances was becoming much too hard for Mother so they decided to wait until she delivered the baby. Neither situation was great, but she wanted to have the comfort of her own home for the delivery.

Orders urging people to evacuate were announced loudly several times a day. Bombing in the South Pacific was nearing hourly. Our bags were packed and plans to give a few family members a head start were made and changed daily. Everything hinged on how soon Mom would become strong enough to travel.

Back when my mom graduated from college in Japan, it was taboo for a girl to be so highly educated. When Mother came back to Korea, she found all the eligible bachelors were married through arrangements made by matchmakers. Educated women were considered career-bound and therefore only headaches to husbands. They had opinions about everything and wanted the world to hear their voices. This kept them off the "potentials list" in the matchmaker's book.

Even though my mother eventually married into a family with a high standard of education (my father went to Columbia University in New York for his Master's degree and my grandfather held a high position in the banking industry all his life), she couldn't help but feel that she was not the ideal daughter-in-law they'd expected for their oldest son. For one thing, she never took the dinner table into grandfather's room herself, which was expected from an obedient daughter-in-law.

She had not been afraid to show the world that she was different. She was not only a college graduate, she was also raised as the only and the most precious daughter of a prominent doctor in her hometown. When she had her first baby, my brother, she was proud and relieved. But after three girls in a row, she felt inadequate as the oldest daughter-in-law in the reputable Lee family. And now, during the war, the worst possible time to have a baby, while holding everyone in jeopardy, she delivered yet another girl.

"If only I had known it was a girl," she sighed again.

But for the first few days, Mother didn't dwell too much on the guilt she should have had for birthing this tiny bundle of misfortune. Nursing was an easy task for her. Milk was plentiful and Mom was fed calcium-rich kelp soup in beef and bonito broth three times a day to produce more milk. With plenty of help, she was able to rest. All I did was sleep and eat. At night, she lay in the dark caressing me. She rubbed her cheek against my cheek. My little forehead was puffed out a bit, and my turned-up nose had tiny white dots like pear skin. Mom felt the softness of my nose and kissed me. The warmth and the softness of the new bundle in her arms was sheer heaven.

She ran her fingers up and down my cheek as I sucked vigorously from her full breast and she felt the satisfaction of holding a little miracle. She was afraid to show her contentment but she couldn't deny her true feelings. "No way would I have had an abortion," she said through clenched teeth to no one. "That old crow is crazy to want a boy so much. I already gave him one." She wiped away her tears of anger. "This is my baby and I will love her no matter what the old man says." Mom kissed my head full of black hair and then she quickly straightened her face, afraid someone might see her smile at me.

My grandfather named me Sang-Eun. "Eun" means, "grace." Mom swore that he blurted it out without putting much thought into it. The following morning, my father showed his bit of interest by bringing a package of herbal medicine for mother to drink. The herbs were to promote her health and recharge her weakened body. My father acknowledged that I was the best looking baby so far. To my mom, her husband's acceptance of another female baby was enough to relieve her heavy heart full of guilt.

It was only the fifth night of my life when I cried all night and refused to take milk. All night, my mother held me close to her and guided my little mouth to her nipple while singing softly, but it was no use. When she finally turned the light on to take a closer look, her frail body trembled. Her heart nearly stopped from the horrifying sight. Both of my eyes were covered with something white.

With shaking hands, Mom pulled my eyelids apart wide to examine them.

"Oh my God! I can't see her eyeballs!" she cried out. "What is happening to my baby? Please, please, let it clear by morning. Don't let anything happen to this precious baby. I promise I will love her and never regret that she is a girl. Please God!" Mom repeated over and over. She then rang the bell for the maid to summon Mrs. Takahashi in the middle of the night.

"And wake up Sang-In's father," she commanded. My brother's name was Sang-In, "In" meaning "tiger." My father was referred to as "Sang-In's father."

She crawled and got the magnifying glass and started looking at my eyes. Both were white and there were no eyeballs to be seen.

"What happened?" Mother wailed. "She looked fine yesterday. What have I done? What do I do? What should I do?"

Panic stricken, mother put her hands together and started praying to God, and to the "Three-Spirits-Granny," a Korean legendary godmother. She watches over all newborns and even facilitates the slap on the baby's behind to shoot them out of the mother's womb. It was said that this was why all Korean babies were born with black and blue Mongolian marks on their behinds.

When Mrs. Takahashi arrived she examined my eyes and immediately started chanting to Buddha. "*Nami-ami-taa-bul. Guan-se-um-bo-o-sal.*"

"Please, we are not Buddhists," mother said. "Don't pray to Shuk-ga-moni. Not in this house. Please."

My father was surprisingly calm, "Don't worry. Take her to the Red Cross hospital first thing in the morning. She probably just has a little infection," he said calmly as he left the disturbed group of women and went back to the *sarang-bang*.

A week had passed since the eye doctor at the Red Cross hospital scraped the white off my eyes and wrapped them both in bandages. I screamed until my tiny vocal cords were hoarse. I would fall asleep from exhaustion from crying and then wake up, startled, as if I were having sharp pains, and scream again.

A week had also passed since my mother last ate or slept. Her days were filled with tears. The shame and regret of having a girl were long gone. She made a daily trip to the hospital carrying me on her back in a colorful blanket. Every day they changed the dressing on my eyes and applied more ointment.

"The right eye is clearing out nicely. I am not sure what is happening to the left eye," the Japanese doctor shook his head. "Well, at least she will have one perfect eye," he said without emotion.

"What do you mean one perfect eye? You mean she may lose the vision in the left eye?" Mother's voice was shaking. "But, will it heal eventually? Won't you please do everything you can to heal it? My husband is a government minister. He, he is the head of the food and housing ministry for all of Korea. And we can pay any amount of money. Please!"

"It isn't the money, ma'am," he said. "There isn't much I can do. We will just have to wait and see." Mom shuddered at his casual, matter-of-fact tone that sounded almost cruel.

"I am pretty certain she can see out of her left eye, though how much, I can't tell." He added, "Of course by the time she is grown, ophthalmology will so far advanced, they may be able to come up with some sort of solution, if in fact she loses the vision. Like even a transplant, maybe."

It was at this point that mother completely lost her dignity and got on her knees.

"What if it doesn't heal?" she cried. "Is there any way I can give my baby one of my eyes? I have lived nearly half of my life. My baby's life is just beginning."

"Ma'am, please don't do this." He pulled her up. "I don't know what's happening to her eyes. We will just have to wait and see."

The daily visits to the hospital eventually tapered down to once a week. Mother was not producing as much milk because of her own lack of nourishment. She learned to change the dressing and patch my left eye on her own in between trips to the hospital. The white film on my left eye was peeling away little by little, and showing more of the eyeball, so Mother was encouraged. She started playing games such as moving a brightly colored object back and forth over my face to see if both eyes were following it.

Now that mother was recovered, it was time for us to move to Kang-Ghe. The call to evacuate Seoul was more urgent and the capital city was emptier each day. Mother decided to send my second sister to Kang-Ghe ahead of us. Auntie Nak-Hae was leaving and wanted to help out by taking her favorite niece, Sang-Hie.

Sang-Hie was the perfect choice to go, because my brother, my parents' precious and only son, would have to stay with my parents and my oldest sister Sang-Soon was already learning to help fetch diapers and drinks of water for my mother. My third sister, Sang-Won, was a little too young to be separated from Mom. The rest of the family decided to stay in Seoul a little longer until my left eye was fully recovered.

"I don't want to go without you, *umma*. I want everyone to go together," Sang-Hie cried loudly, although she was excited to go on the train with Auntie Nak-Hae.

"Oh my dear Sang-Hie, we will follow you shortly," Mother reassured her. "It will be so much fun to go in the train with Auntie Nak-Hae. She will carry you on her back and buy you all kinds of milk caramel candies." Mother held my sister, Sang-Hie, wiping her tears.

"It isn't that, mommy. I don't want to leave the baby," Sang-Hie sniffled. "I want to touch her and see her. I want to see her drink the milk from you and watch you change her diapers. She is my baby, you even said."

The next day, Auntie Nak-Hae, my mother's half-sister, left to take the train to Pyung-Yang, which was the closest train station to Kang-Ghe. Sang-Hie cried with her arms outstretched toward me. My aunt held Sang-Hie tight in her arms and sped her strides away from my sobbing family.

Mother's eyes were filled with tears and her heart was broken to see her little girl screaming not to be separated from her family, especially her new baby. But mother had to remain optimistic about my left eye and stay close to the Japanese doctor at the hospital, rather than move the whole family up north away from the danger. My father agreed to stay a while longer and see how my healing progressed.

In the meantime, the *an-bang* was filling up with packed bags and the colorful wrapper blanket was always within arm's reach, ready to tie me on Mother's back. If the bombing threats moved closer to Seoul, it would take only minutes for us to take off. Often, everyone slept fully dressed.

Then one hot and humid August morning, over the crackling static of the radio, Mom heard the trembling voice of the Japanese emperor surrendering. My father hugged my mom and the streets were filled with people shouting and yelling, "*Man-Se, Man-Se, Man-Se*! Three cheers for ten thousand years of prosperity!" and "Get out! Zori-wearing barbaric Japs!" It was August 15th and I was barely six weeks old.

The bags were unpacked. The eye doctor fled to Japan along with all the other Japanese residents. Mrs. Takahashi remained with her two young daughters, Ko-Jan and Re-Jan, still wearing a Korean dress, and no one harassed them.

In the South, Seoul, the capital city, was in the chaotic turmoil of settling into an independent government as the Republic of Korea. Seung-Man Rhee became the acting president of the democratic country and North Korea was being established as a communist regime headed by the nationalist, Kim Il-Sung. The iron curtain of the 38th parallel was being drawn. *Back-e-min-jok* (the pure-white-clad people of the land of morning calm) was now separated.

Agents were popping up everywhere at the border smuggling people from North Korea through the 38th parallel to South Korea. People who dreamed of liberty streamed down continuously through the mountains and rivers, walking day and night. By the same token, young men who believed in the communist ideology snuck up to the North, leaving their wives and children.

The train from Pyung-Yang ran as far as Won-Ju which was a North Korean border town by Im-Jin River. Once across the river, refugees would be free in South Korea.

My mother waited for my aunt to come back with my sister, Sang-Hie, hoping they would find a way to get down to the South. There was no way to communicate with them and she finally had to put concerns about my eye on hold. There were no more trips to the hospital and my left eye stopped oozing.

The joy she felt for being independent from Japan was heavily clouded by the absence of my sister, Sang-Hie. She couldn't erase Sang-Hie's crying face from her mind, and her milk dried up completely.

In despair, and on my father's recommendation, mother turned to the Baptist church. My father had become a Baptist during his stay in America.

"Be joyful all the time. Pray without ceasing. Be thankful in all circumstances."

Mother recited the first thing she learned from the church absorbing each word and taking in the meaning of it while holding me in her arms. As she repeated the verse over and over, things became clear to her. She understood what being thankful in all circumstances meant. It was all about God's will. It was clearly God's will to protect her family.

If I hadn't been born, if I hadn't developed an eye problem, the whole family would have moved to North Korea. And it would have been virtually impossible for all of us, a prominent politician's family, to cross the 38th-parallel and return to Seoul.

"Thank you dear baby and thank you, Lord," she said, hugging me tight as tears welled up in her eyes and peaceful joy filled her heart.

My mother understood then that she had many reasons to celebrate the birth of the fifth miracle God had granted her. There was a reason for me to be born, destined to have a life of my own as a girl.

"You see, Sang-Eun, you were born with a purpose," Mom paused. "It will be your lifelong assignment to find out for what purpose you were born."

She put a flowery barrette in my wavy hair and hugged me tight as she finished the story.

For the first time, I realized and believed just how special I was. A girl with a beautiful smile, all the cleverness, and one perfect eye, named "Grace."

2

My father pounded lightly on the dull side of a knife, which was placed in the groove of a huge sectioned chocolate bar. My sisters and I surrounded him in anticipation of the delectable treat, salivating.

"These chocolate bars are from England," Father said as he handed a section to each one of us. The thick square piece filled my palm. I grinded the powdery edge of the semi-sweet piece with my front teeth. We watched each other, comparing speed of consumption of the delightful treat.

"That should keep you happy for a good part of the morning." Father gave us a mischievous smile and put the rest of the gigantic sheet of the chocolate back into the dark attic.

The attic was like a treasure chest. When we heard the sound of the attic door sliding open, we would drop everything and gather around the *an-bang*, where the door to the attic was. The attic had two levels; an upper level containing more delicious and rare items like chocolate bars and wafers, and the lower level with canned fruits like peaches, apricots, and pears, and of course, a large jar of honey, from which Father fed each of us first thing every morning. He would eat the first large soup spoonful of honey then with the same spoon he scooped another spoonful for my brother then my three sisters and me, in order of our age. We did this every morning, before breakfast and before any of us brushed our teeth.

"Honey is pure. It's the only organic food that will provide energy and it also keeps you from getting sick," he used to say. For all my growing years in Korea, honey was considered to be the most expensive, luxury good-for-you food item.

"Well, finish your chocolate and get dressed into clean clothes. Father is expecting an important guest today," he said.

"Again?" I said slouching and letting out a sigh.

"Yes, again." Father gave me a light pinch on my cheek.

"Dr. Chang Myun will be here this afternoon. And I need all of you to be quiet and stay away from the *sarang-bang*." He then turned to my mom and said, "I am not receiving anyone else today." Mom nodded. "If anyone else shows up at the door, I am not home." Father then changed out of his khaki pants into a silk brocade Korean suit. This signaled an important meeting with an important guest.

Dr. Chang stayed in the *sarang-bang* for a long time, and Mom served them drinks and *an-ju* herself, which was another sign father was receiving an important guest. Dr. Chang wore glasses and a western suit with a necktie. Years later, I saw the same gentle face of Dr. Chang as a candidate for vice president on posters all over the walls and fences on the way to school.

My father had visitors all the time. One morning, a distant relative sharing the "Dong" part of my father's first name, which means he was of the same generation as my father, rang the bell. When our maid opened the door, he motioned to the hired carrier to bring the crate of apples into our house.

"More apples?" I grabbed my forehead with one hand and shook my head.

"*Eiguu*! You frivolous thing! Don't mind her," Mom apologized narrowing her eyes at me. "She is the youngest and spoiled."

The servant promptly took the crate to the attic.

"Can I see older brother Dong-Je Lee?" He rubbed two hands in front of him.

"Of course, but he isn't home at the moment. It is true. You can even look in the *sarang-bang*," Mom replied. "But if you would like to come in for a while, you are welcome to."

He stayed for a couple of hours waiting for my father. I heard him telling Mom how he needed a job to make ends meet and send his kids to college. He talked about how close his father and my grandfather were. One word from my father, he said, could change his life, since my father was the head of the *Shik-Ryang-Yung-Dan*, (the food and housing bureau) for the whole country and was in charge of appointing managers of the flour mills.

Mom apologized, telling him how frustrated she was with my father because he was so inflexible and honest to a fault. He would not bend or misinterpret the rules in any way.

"It is getting to be beyond honest," Mom said. "He is losing friends, and relatives are getting upset with him because he simply will not treat them any different." But she said she would give him the message and see what she could do. She patted his back.

He sighed and took an envelope out of his inside pocket of his coat and handed it to Mom with both hands saying, "There isn't much here, but I am desperately in need of a job. I have experience in operating a mill if he would only give me chance. I won't disappoint him."

"Oh no. I can't. I won't," Mom said. "I would be in so much trouble if my husband found out that I took an envelope. My children's father just isn't like that."

"What's that, Mom? What's in the envelope?" I asked, pulling her skirt.

"Sang-Eun-ah, go and play with your sisters." Mom shushed me and motioned for me to go away.

Later, I found out from my sisters that a sealed envelope always contained cash. Mom never took the money and the relative never got to see my father.

I didn't realize how powerful a politician my father was.

"He was one honest man," my oldest sister, Sang-Soon told me one day, "He didn't have a politician's bone in his body."

I never understood what that meant, but I knew Mom often complained about living in the smallest of all the houses my parents owned.

As a politician in the freshly established, unsteady, Seung-Man Rhee government, I was told my father was rigid and stoic in every way. But I knew him otherwise. When he came home, he would lie on his back and give me airplane rides on his feet. I used to make buzzing sounds as if I was flying high. I could fly in that position for as long as he would hold my hands, balancing me.

"OK, clever girl! So what is your father's name?" He would start quizzing as I flew.

"And what's your mother's name, and your sisters' and your brother's?"

"My father's name is Lee Dong-Je and my mom is Kim Nack-Shin, my brother is Sang-In, then my sisters, Sang-Soon, Sang-Hie and Sang-Won," I would rattle off.

"Now here's a toughie! What is your address?"

"Chong-Ro-Ku, Shin-Mun-Ro 2-Ka, 7-37."

"You are just too smart." He hugged me and rubbed his cheek on mine.

For a special treat, my father used to take us individually in his chauffeur-driven Ford to a western restaurant where he would show us how to eat with a knife and a fork. My brother was treated the most because he was the only son but my father used to take me more than my sisters, perhaps because I was the youngest.

Automobiles, particularly sedans, were rare in those days.

We kept our Ford in a garage away from our house, and when the chauffeur brought the car, all the neighborhood kids gathered around the gleaming black sedan, looking into the high window, leaving smudges all over the car.

Our chauffeur, in a high-collar uniform, opened the door for my father and me and we drove away feeling the whole neighborhood's eyes on our back.

"Mr. Lee is taking his youngest baby daughter out in their automobile." Their envious voices rang in my ears.

My father taught me to eat soup, spooning away from me. The fork was to be held in the left hand packing the food in the back of the fork with the knife, which was held in the right hand.

Eating American food took skill, so he cut the steak into small pieces, so that I only had to pierce them with the fork.

"This is complicated, Dad," I said.

"You don't have to learn. Just pick it up and eat." He smiled.

"Don't they give you rice?" I whispered.

"No, they either give you rice or potatoes. Not both. Now eat. No more questions." The American food was okay, but the best part was the potatoes. I much preferred potatoes anyway.

I felt very special, and when I came home I bragged to my sisters how I learned how to use a knife and a fork and ate Western food, giving particular detail to the smooth, mashed up potatoes. "Everything is in one plate," I said. "And the soup is creamy. It is delicious."

Even though we had a staff of servants, my father used to roll up the Oriental rug from the living room himself and hang it on the block wall of our house. Then he would beat it with a heavy stick to get the dust off. He even chopped the firewood himself in the backyard.

I used to feel the callouses on his hands and smell them. His rough hands that smelled faintly of cigarettes and white mint candies always reminded me of the airplane rides he gave me and his face as I looked down at him from above.

3

For the first few years after the separation of Korea, all efforts and attentions were put into establishing two separate governing entities by both sides, and the border was not yet securely sealed. My grandfather in Kang-Khe and his family members trickled down one by one to South Korea. They traveled on the train as far as they could, then escaped on foot, dodging the armed soldiers along the border, taking a chance of getting shot.

After a year of living in Kang-Khe with my grandparents and my uncle's family in my grandfather's house, Sang-Hie was reunited with us. My second uncle Nak-Woon, Mom's half brother, carried Sang-Hie on his back to the train as my grandfather told him to. But when he ran into one of our distant aunties on the train, he shrewdly handed his responsibility of bringing Sang-Hie to my parents over to her, and she and Sang-Hie successfully crossed the Im-Jin River.

Sang-Hie, having lived away from us for nearly a year, had nightmares many of the nights for years. She woke up in the night screaming and running from one end of the *an-bang* to the other, refusing to be touched or held by anyone. My parents and my siblings watched her in terror, not sure what to do. Only my oldest sister, Sang-Soon would extend her arms asking Sang-Hie to let her hold her. Sang-Hie would shake her head and run from Sang-Soon and anyone who came close to her. Finally, mom would grab her and hold her tight. Then she calmly and softly told her over and over how beautiful she was and how everything was fine now; that she would always be with us, together, with her mom.

In 1948, for the first time in Korean history, a presidential election was held under U.N. supervision. Seung-Man Rhee became the first president of the Republic of Korea. Under the newly formed democratic government, my father continued to work directly under President Rhee. Even though both Koreas were independent from Japan, in all practical sense, the South was being superintended by the United States and the North by the Soviets.

The next couple of years were idyllic. We were a family again. Times were prosperous. My father was granted a private automobile. There was plenty of good food to eat and the house and the yard were kept by a staff of servants. We were one of a few homes that had a wooden telephone on the wall with a black mouthpiece to speak into.

In the winter, Mom conserved the firewood and only heated two rooms, the *an-bang* and the room off the kitchen where the maids slept. The heat radiated throughout *on-dol* floor (heavy oiled waxed paper over a smoothed and heated granite floor) by the heating duct that was stoked in the kitchen underneath a huge iron cauldron. The cauldron sat in the low cement counter built to fit its protruding basin.

At bedtime, we lay lined up on our individual *yo* (heavy, cotton batting filled mats) on the floor in the *an-bang* with thick fluffy *ebul* blankets over us. Every morning these mats and blankets were neatly folded and piled high in the closet until the following bedtime.

The hot *on-dol* floor kept us warm and cozy, we fell asleep in no time. However, the air stayed cold, and often I woke up in the morning with my nose feeling like ice. I once left a glass of water on the table above my head, and in the morning, the top of the glass was covered with a thin film of ice.

I slept in the front spot of the room where it was the warmest. This was one of many advantages of being the youngest. In the summer when

Mom brought home an armful of peaches and divided them equally, if there was an extra, I got it. When fish was served for dinner, mom would put the meat from the cheek of the fish into my mouth with her chopsticks, a special treat. She always said that fish cheeks had the sweetest meat.

In the summer, Sang-Won and I spent hours picking berries from the mulberry trees in the hills behind our house. Sometimes we would eat sweet acacia blossoms, one at a time, from their heavy clumps of flowers, trying not to bruise the rest. After a long rainy spell, we slid down the eroded slopes of the hills on our bottoms. We wore short dresses and our white panties turned orange from the natural clay slide. The rainy season also turned the Japanese cherries into tiny deep red delights. They were much smaller and tarter than the regular cherries, but to us they were delicious.

The hills were once covered with Japanese cherry trees, evidence that Korea had been a Japanese colony for thirty-six years. Each year, however, there were fewer, because in a vengeful effort to destroy all things Japanese, people chopped them down for firewood.

At the end of a summer day, my sister and I used to trample into the house with muddy legs and arms, our lips smudged red from the cherry juice. We ignored Mom's shouts to get back out and wash ourselves before we stepped into the house.

Little did we know that these times were not to last.

On June 25, 1950, Kim Il-Sung's army attacked South Korea in an attempt to merge into one communist country. When the North Korean army marched into Seoul to claim victory over the capitol city on June 28th, my fifth birthday, my father went into hiding because the Red Army was taking politicians hostage. Many people had left Seoul for the southern most part of South Korea to escape the invasion, but we stayed for as long as we could.

We lived in the basement of our house for days at a time to protect ourselves from bombing. When there was less threat, we slept in the *an-bang*, huddled together. It had been weeks since my father went into hiding and I wondered when we could be with him again. He snuck into our house late at night every few days bringing candles and food items like meats or dried fish. Blackouts were occurring practically every night, so we needed to keep matches and candles ready at all times. He disappeared as quickly as he came, after whispering just a few words with Mom. All of us knew not to bother Father with questions when he showed up. I didn't know why the North Koreans wanted my father, but I knew that they must never know that he had contact with us.

Every day, I feared that the front gate to the house would bang open any second like it had many times lately. Just the other day, there was banging and slamming and loud yelling at the front gate.

"Open the door right away. We came to arrest Lee Dong-Je. If you don't open up, we will break it down. Hurry, open the door!"

Too frightened to move, we all looked at our mom.

"Oh, no. Those bastards are here again," she said. Her face turned pale with fear. Then she took a deep breath and said to us, "It's OK, don't worry."

I could tell mom was scared but I believed her when she said that everything would be okay. Mom composed herself and walked through the front courtyard to open the wooden gate calmly. Several North Korean soldiers shoved Mom aside and marched into the house in their big shoes, laced up to their knees. With their guns pointing straight up, they started searching, muddying up the house and kicking the doors open as they walked through. Walking into the house in shoes was the rudest behavior and the most insulting power gesture a person could make.

All four of us, my sisters and I, stood in the corner trembling, but my brother followed them around. He even opened the doors ahead of them so they could see inside of the rooms. As far as he was concerned, the invasion by North Korea was a perfect opportunity for him to play a real live war game. He only wished he was old enough to be drafted.

"OK, bitch, you had better tell us where he is. Otherwise, we will have to take you in," one of them threatened my mom.

"Oh! My goodness. What use would you have with me?" Mom said with a nervous smile.

"I would be more useful here waiting for him. Then you will have him for sure because when he comes home, I will turn him in. You know, I am on the side of North Korea. I do so admire general Kim Il-Sung." Her act was so believable it confused me.

"Would you all like to have something to drink?" My mom went further.

"You are all working so hard for our country. I am ashamed. I wish I could do something to contribute. Look at me; all I do is take care of my children. And you are fighting for our country." Mom followed them, clucking her tongue.

"Comrade, maybe one of us should stay here and wait for him. He would have to show up sometime," we heard them say as they came out of the back bedroom.

"Children, say goodbye to these wonderful soldier-uncles," Mom said, pretending she didn't hear a word they were exchanging with each other. "These soldier-uncles are the ones who keep us safe," she continued without giving them a chance to respond.

"Don't you worry. If he comes home, you will hear from me. I do hope he comes home soon. It's been months. I just don't know where he might be hiding. Let's just hope he is not dead or injured," Mom mumbled as if she was talking to herself. Mom successfully convinced them one more time, and they left saying they would be back.

As soon as they left, Mom plopped herself on the floor and sighed. Tears streamed down her cheeks and all of us, except my brother, cried with her.

She then instructed us again and again that we must never tell them that we had seen our father.

"Mommy, why do they want him so badly? What would they do to him?" I asked.

"You don't need to know. They won't ever have him anyway," Mom assured me.

"They wouldn't kill him, would they?" I asked frightened.

"Don't ask such a stupid question!" My brother snapped at me. "Of course they want him, because he is an important government official."

I still didn't know what that meant, but I stopped asking.

A few days after that, our house was raided again. One of the Reds ordered all of us, including the two maids, to sit on our knees outside the back door on the cement floor by the well. He ordered us to sit in order of seniority, my brother first then me last, all in a row. Then he told the two maids to sit next to me. I was so frightened I started sobbing and stretching my arms toward Mom.

"She is only a baby. Please can I just hold her?" Mom begged.

"Leave her and don't touch her!" He shouted, and then he turned to me and screamed, "Shut your mouth!" He scared me so terribly, I took a big gulp and started shivering. Then another one of them pointed his gun at my brother's face.

"Ok, you tell me. Was your father here last night? I know he was. Tell me the truth!" He waved his gun as he shouted.

"Gosh, sir. I would tell you for sure if he was here. I really would. I don't even like him. He is always punishing me. I would for sure tell you the truth. But he wasn't. We don't know where he is." My brother never even blinked his eyes as he rambled on.

The man turned to my sisters, one at a time, asking the same question, threatening them. He said we would be in worse trouble if we didn't tell the truth. When he got to me, I started crying, shaking my head, no.

Mom stood next to him, begging him to put his gun away. She said that her blood pressure was rising, she was about to pass out, so please leave us.

When he got to one of the maids, he changed his tactic.

"Think, you poor soul. You are only a maid comrade. What do you have to gain from lying to me? If you tell the truth, we will reward you."

She was trembling as she said, "Yes, he was here last night."

At that, he snapped and pointed his gun at Mom.

"See, I knew it. He was here. So, where is he now? Bitch!"

Mom looked at him, unruffled, and said, "Come on now. Look at the poor girl. You scared her so much she doesn't know what she is saying. She is just saying what you want to hear. Think about it. Why would he come here knowing you are checking up on our house all the time?"

Somehow, her lies made sense to me. And once again, my mother made them believe that my father had not been home.

I shivered, and pulled the blanket down a tiny bit to expose my eyes. I peeked at my siblings and peered at the *an-bang* door to the living room waiting for my mom to finish the nightly routine. Mom was making her bedtime check to make sure the house was locked up. She made sure the maids were securely in bed as well.

Her last task was to tuck in the five of us and make sure no one was missing. My brother was fifteen years old and had a habit of sneaking out at all hours of the day or night to see the actions of the war. He thought the war was positively the most exciting thing that ever happened and was itching to be drafted. I heard mom telling a neighbor that she saw my brother standing in front of a Red soldier, and the Red stood pointing a machine gun right at his face in the middle of the street. Her heart sank as she watched him stare right back at the Red smiling and carrying on a conversation without blinking an eye. To him, it was probably the most thrilling moment.

Our living room, right outside of the *an-bang*, was set up Western-style with a sofa and armchairs on a large Oriental rug. The coffee table in the middle of the room was high like a dining table and was always covered with a white tablecloth. In the early spring, Mom would put a vase full of yellow forsythia in the middle of the table.

The table had been bare for a long time now, and the living room was always dark. No one ever sat in the sofa or the armchair anymore. All of us huddled in the *an-bang* all the time.

When we heard Mom slide open the door to the *an-bang*, we opened our eyes and looked up. When we all turned to look at her she quickly put her index finger on her mouth signaling us to be quiet. She heard a low murmur, almost like muffled chanting coming from the smallest bedroom across the living room.

She picked up the candle and headed toward the sound. We all sat up and leaned toward the door. Through the open door we could hear low voices, not clear but definitely voices.

Mom tiptoed toward the room, with her hand on her chest like she was suppressing her pounding heart. She took a deep breath and waited for a second. Then, she walked, stomping loudly, toward the room and bravely slid open the door without hesitation.

She instinctively stepped back and gasped when she saw four men sitting on the floor. They were dressed in soldier's uniforms with red patches on their shoulders and equipped with big guns tipped with bayonets. The sickening odor of their sweat and unwashed bodies made her gag.

The four men immediately stood up, reaching for their guns.

"*Omana,* thank God! It's only you. I thought I heard burglars," Mom said daringly. "You poor dears. How long have you been hiding here in this dark room?" She stepped into the room. "Why, I should have known. Well, you should have told me. Well, let me fix you a nice meal," she continued babbling. "You must be hungry and tired!"

The five of us heard everything in the *an-bang*. I was terrified, but even more than that, I was confused. My big sister, Sang-Soon, put her index finger on her lips telling us to be quiet and we all pretended to sleep. My heart pumped so fast and so loud I had to get under the blanket.

My brother whispered, "She is lying again." My big sister put her hand on his mouth and gave him an evil eye. I could hear Mom speaking again.

"You must be starving! My god!" Mom said.

"No, um, we--we are fine."

"Why don't you all come to the dining room and have something to eat?"

"No, we're not hungry," one of them said loudly with authority.

"We have an order to wait here until your husband comes home," another one added.

"Oh, my dears, you are not much older than my own son," Mom said. "I know how hungry growing boys get. Come on, you don't have to tell anyone that you ate here." My mom was persistent.

A moment or two later, they were all sitting on the dining room floor around the table.

"I tell you this is such a shame that we have to fight like this," Mom started up again. "We are the same people from the same nation, same blood. You all know we are the noble and elite race of the Orient," she said. "I agree with everything general Kim Il-Sung is advocating. I have always told my husband that he should surrender himself and support North Korea." She sighed as she dished up the rice bowl and put it on the table.

By this time, the maids were up to help with the food. My mom motioned to them to stay in the kitchen. She did not need either of them saying anything that might ruin her award-winning performance.

"I don't know if my husband will ever come home, you know, in fact, he is scared to come home. He is afraid of me. Because I keep telling him that he is too stubborn," she said grumbling. "You know, if he comes home, I will be the first one to turn him in. And he knows it, too. Anyway, enough of that! Go ahead and eat, you brave soldiers!"

She offered them hot towels so they could freshen up. She treated the smelly soldiers as if they were her own sons who had just come home from war. The men devoured the food in minutes.

"*Sa-mo-nim,* Ma'am, Comrade," one of the soldiers said slowly. "We haven't had white rice in a long time, not even mixed with barley. We've been eating straight barley bowls. This is really a treat."

Another man cut in. "As you must know, we are following orders. We are to bring Mr. Lee Dong-Je to our captain comrade. We have to follow orders, any orders and all orders."

"I know, I know, of course you do," Mom said. "Don't you worry about a thing. I will bring him to you as soon as he comes home." She turned around grumbling with disgust, "If he ever does, that stubborn man."

Her performance completely snowed them. They left that night without my father and never came back. I still wonder if I could be as wise as my mother, with five kids and a husband to protect as a war raged outside.

4

My grandfather, my mother's father, sent his second concubine to our house to help Mom care of us and deal with North Koreans' constant harassment. We called her Second Grandmother.

Second Grandmother used to put a handful of warm, roasted chestnuts in my palms when she came to visit us. Sometimes, she would put a hundred won bill in my hand and close it tight, so no one would see it. She made me think I was her favorite. She also talked to me as if I was a grown-up person. She didn't brush me off, like other adults did. Second Grandmother wasn't self-absorbed or consumed with her looks.

"She was just a poor peasant woman, without much education, but father took pity on her and hired her as a nurse," Mom said. "Then one day, he took her into his bed like he did all of his other nurses."

"She was born to a lower-class family so it was no wonder there was nothing regal about her," Mom added. "But she has a heart of gold, and that must be what Grandpa was attracted to."

For some reason, we all felt somewhat superior to her, but I liked her the way she was. She had a wholesome, homey aroma about her, like chestnuts or soybeans.

She later became the first wife, the Big Grandmother, when my mom's mother died. But even after she became the official wife of my grandfather, she often had her meals with the maids in the room next to the kitchen and slept there with them, where she was most comfortable. In his childhood pictures, her son, my uncle, Nak-Woon wore mostly dark gray or black cotton jackets. But my mom's full brother was always in silk outfits.

Architecturally, Seoul was unique, because it showed foreign influence. A large number of Japanese style homes were built or modified from traditional Korean homes during the thirty-six years of Japanese occupation.

Our big house in Choong-Jung-Ro had Western influences, as well as Japanese. "The big house," as we called it, was a government mansion and was transferred as my father's private property. But my father decided that we didn't need such an extravagant place and chose to live in the house we had always lived in, which was quite a bit smaller. Instead of leaving it vacant, my grandfather, my father's father, lived in the big house. The big house must have had at least ten bedrooms and servant's quarters outside of the main house. The house sat high up on a hill and had steps leading to a massive front gate. The large front yard was full of cherry and acacia blossoms in the spring. Downstairs, there were several Japanese style rooms with *tatami* floors and sliding *shoji* doors. The upstairs had Western style bedrooms with doors that opened in or out. The dark wooden corridor was so long, it seemed like it took me forever to get from one end to the other. The wood floor was shiny and slippery and along the hallway were the bedrooms, each bedroom with a glass doorknob.

My mother thought that the big house would be safer for us during the threat of bombing. She sent Second Grandmother and me ahead to be with my grandfather, partly so I would be out of her hair while she was preparing the rest of the family to move there, too.

The thirty-minute walk to the big house seemed to take forever. Second Grandma carried me on her back inside of a wrapper blanket. We took side streets, mostly dirt roads, until we got to the wide, streetcar railway. The rails were in the middle of the street and on the outside was a two-lane road where cars zipped along. As a child, I always imagined the street being as wide as the Han River and couldn't fathom ever crossing it all by myself.

There were no cars on the street now, only scattered dead bodies. Each time she took a big step, I sensed she was hopping over a dead body, but I was afraid to ask. I didn't want to know. I put my head down flat under the wrapper quilt and caressed my grandmother's back. I felt a great sense of security and comfort lying on her back. The wrapper quilt had two long ties and they went around my bottom and my grandmother's waist to make it snug.

When we got to the big house, my grandmother sighed with relief. She knocked on the side door softly, and then gently pushed the door open. She gasped as she realized the door was not locked. I curled my toes as I listened to her tiptoeing into the house then crunched my fists onto my chest, pressing my beating heart. I couldn't hear anything but the thumping of my heart and the slurring sound of my grandmother's rubber shoes.

"Hello? Hello? Is anyone home?" Grandmother's voice echoed through the hallway as she walked up the steps into the house from the side yard. I rounded my back, pulling my feet and arms under the body like a turtle. She carefully slid open the *shoji* doors to the largest room downstairs, my grandfather's room.

"Ugh!" She shuddered and stopped in her tracks. Her startle made me push my body up and peep over her shoulder with my hands still crunched tight to my chest. I saw the *tatami* floors were ripped. Chairs were tossed upside down and broken dishes were everywhere. There were blankets matted on the floor showing signs of someone having slept there. I pulled the blanket higher to cover my head as grandma, holding me tight with her arms, walked slowly like a cat down the hallway calling softly,

"Is anyone here? Please answer me, anyone."

"Grandma, let's go home. I wanna go home. I want my mommy." I tugged on her blouse with trembling hands.

Just then, we both heard heavy steps coming toward us. My heart was beating so fast, I knew I heard it. I hoped someone would be there, but when I heard the footsteps, I knew I no longer wanted to see anyone. I grabbed my grandmother's side so hard that, I found out later, I left deep red marks on each side of her.

"Hello? Is that you, Master?" My heart dropped and we jumped from the sound of a low, husky voice behind us. Tightening my trembling body, I peeked out to see a scrawny, ghost-like man. Terrified, I buried my face deep under the blanket again and squeezed my grandmother's chest. She gave me a couple of bouncing movements to calm me down.

"Come down to the basement. We are all hiding there," the ghost man said. "The damnedest shooting spree just ended a little while ago. It might start up again. You have to get out of here and hide with us." He nudged my back gently.

"Who is hiding? And who was shooting?" Grandma asked. "And who are you?"

"We'll talk when we get down there. Let's get out of here, quick," the man said.

We followed him down the dark corridor to the basement. I had never been in the basement of the big house until that day. It was dark, with only a thin layer of dim, foggy light filtering through the narrow window at ground level from the front yard. In the early evening light it looked like a dungeon. There must have been five or six men and women hiding there, covered up with blankets, cushions over their heads.

"Is she going to be able to keep quiet and not cry?" A woman lifted up her cover to complain to the man who brought us in.

"They are the owners of the house for God's sake. You had better get out if you don't like it," he shot back.

"Grammy, let's go home. I wanna go home," I cried.

"Shhhh! I hear something. Someone is coming into the front yard again." He put his index finger on his lips and motioned to everyone to be quiet. He and another man tiptoed to the window and peeked out to the front yard.

"I can only see their feet," one man whispered.

My heart was thumping so loudly I was afraid it would be heard.

I held my breath to stop sobbing and it gave me a terrific ache in my chest. My heart felt like it was going to burst. All of the sudden, I felt warm liquid running down my thighs.

"It's okay," Grandma turned her head and whispered. "Go right ahead."

The strange thing was that I didn't even know I was letting it go.

Pop, pop, pop. I saw everyone in the room covering their ears at the sound, so I did the same. I sobbed all through the shooting praying, "Please, God. Please, please, stop them!"

There was yelling and screaming. I heard voices shouting commands and I couldn't make out who was shooting whom. The noise seemed to last forever, and then there was silence.

Please, please. I covered my face and sobbed again. I didn't open my eyes or move until we left the house and I felt my grandma's strides slow down a bit. She was running for our lives, aware of the enormous responsibility of getting me back to my mom before the rest of my family started their journey to the big house. She ran alongside the houses on her toes to be less visible, and to reduce the slurring of her shoes. I pulled myself up trying to stay still and flat so I wouldn't be too heavy for her. I was five years old, a little too old to be carried on her back.

"Hey, you! Get over here!"

I heard a loud command as she crossed the streetcar railway. Grandma looked up quickly, and then sped faster and faster away. When she got to halfway into the railway, she started running like mad.

"Hey, I said get over here!" the soldier yelled again. I turned my head and saw him standing in the back of a truck, with his gun pointed toward us.

"Gramma, shouldn't we go over there?" My voice and body were shaking.

"No, don't say anything and put your head down," she commanded softly but firmly. I did what she ordered and that's when I heard the shooting.

A bullet whistled by the back of my head, its wind blowing my hair along.

I felt bare inside of the blanket. I felt no protection. I just wanted to run.

"Hurry, gramma, hurry!" I said. She turned the corner into the narrow dirt alley and ran all the way home, trembling and repeating over and over, "Let's get home, let's get home. Go to sleep, go to sleep. Don't cry, don't cry."

I had my head down on her back, watching the trees and the houses pass by out of the corner of my eyes and still trying to make myself as flat as I could. I grabbed my grandmother's chest tight so I wouldn't slide down while she bounced up and down with short little strides.

The streets were chilling in silence, with dead bodies scattered everywhere. All I could hear was our pounding hearts and her Korean rubber shoes as they went "tap, tap, tap, tap," echoing through the empty street.

"Open. Open, quick!" Grandma yelled as she banged on the door of our house with her fist, then shaking the double doors with both hands, "Open the door!" she screamed. I started crying. She pushed the maid who opened the door out of the way and collapsed as soon as she put one foot into the front hall of our house. I was still attached to her.

"Oh my poor dears! What's happening? Why are you here?" Mom rushed over and unraveled the blanket to pick me off her back. There was no light in our house. In the dark, I saw silhouettes of a dozen people sitting on the living room floor, all sitting in a fetal position trembling, and holding pillows over their heads. Some of them looked up but no one spoke.

"What happened?" Mom asked as she held me tight. "Why did you come back? Is everyone OK at the big house?"

"No, no, no. It's terrible. It's awful. You can't even imagine. Those bastards are killing everyone. They have no hearts." Grandmother was crying. She picked up her long skirt and wiped her face.

"Those sons of bitches! You won't believe it. They even shot at us, too." My mom glanced at the people in the living room as if she was afraid they might hear grandmother's swearing in case one of them might be an undercover spy.

"You just don't know how awful it was. You just don't know. You can't even imagine," Grandma sobbed. "Honestly, I am telling you," she said, "Sang-Eunee and I both came this close to getting killed. I don't know where I got the strength. And the baby, she was so good. She didn't make a peep and she had her head down on my back the whole time like she was sleeping. I could feel her heart racing but she didn't even cry or anything. Poor thing!" Grandma patted my back as she was wiping her forehead with the back of her hand.

"They were on a truck in the middle of the street, maybe about a hundred meters away. And the street was full of dead bodies all around the truck. Maybe they were calling me to help with the bodies, I don't know. I had no idea what they wanted from me. But I pretended I didn't hear them and ran." She took a deep breath. "And that's when they started shooting at us."

"My god!" Mom grabbed me tighter gasping.

"I am telling you, a bullet flew by the back of Sang-Eunee's head almost touching her hair, I swear." She buried her face in her hands and let out a big cry. "I just ran and ran all the way here." She extended her arms to me like she wanted to hug me, but Mom was caressing my face. Her hand felt soft and warm so I shook my head at grandmother.

"Who is at the big house now?" Mom asked.

"Well, no one right now. Your father-in-law left. The front yard had dead bodies everywhere. We had to get out of there."

"There were dead bodies?" Mom asked.

"They brought a bunch of neighborhood people over, said they were spies and shot them in the front yard," Grandma shivered. "We were hiding in the basement and kept completely quiet."

"My god, they shot people at our house?'

"Yes, the shooting wouldn't stop. Pop, pop, pop, pop! We had to cover our ears and close our eyes. Terrible! Just terrible!"

"Did you actually see them shooting?" Mom wanted to know who they were.

"Were they all men?"

"I tried to look through the small window. You know the one on the ground? But I could barely see their feet from the basement window, and we were also afraid they might see us so we stayed away from the window."

"There will be ghosts everywhere," Grandma said. "I'm telling you that house sure is haunted now, if it wasn't before."

"Oh, don't believe things like that. I am sure it is just silly nonsense."

Mom shook her head. Then she asked again. "You mean the bodies are still there?"

"Oh yeah, as soon as the shooting stopped we waited till it was quiet and got out of there."

"My god, who was hiding with you in the basement?" Mom's face looked like it had no blood.

"Half a dozen people were there from the neighborhood, since we have the biggest basement. They never found us though." Grandmother shivered again.

I held on to Mom tighter and tighter.

"What are all these people doing here?" I pointed at the people in the living room.

"When the bombing started, they came to escape," she explained. "They thought our house was a little safer since it is at the end of the block."

"If they bomb the big house, will it break?" I asked her.

"Probably, but we are safe here at this house." Mom nodded with assurance.

"But then," I asked, "what will happen to the glass doorknobs?"

"What glass doorknobs?"

"You know, the glass doorknobs upstairs in the big house?" This was the second time I'd had to remind my mom about them.

"Oh, I guess those knobs will probably get broken."

I wondered if my mom had ever looked at them. I wondered if she had ever even felt them. I remembered so clearly how magical the colors and sparkles were. Now I imagined them crushed, glass shards spread everywhere on the floor.

I felt as if I could see the sparks over the dead bodies and the dark corridor upstairs. All of it melded into a vague vision of mass confusion, fear and darkness. I closed my eyes and held onto Mom tight, feeling safer in her arms. I still felt like crying loudly, but I didn't really know why.

When I closed my eyes, I could see the dark, stained wooden doors with their glass doorknobs sparkling colorfully under the dim hall lights. I pulled on Mom's hand and placed it on my cheek. I turned her other hand and stroked the tiny canary diamond ring on her ring finger.

It almost looked as beautiful as the glass doorknob.

I fell asleep in Mom's arms, trying to touch the knobs with both hands remembering the last time I felt them, before the war, when the big house was peaceful.

* * *

I was watching my brother pack. "Can I come with you just to see the house?" I said. It didn't seem right to me that a teenage boy was moving into the big house in Choong-Jung-Ro. Mom said that he would be living with my grandfather and my uncle.

"Are you gonna live there forever?" I asked.

"Get out of my way. I'm busy," he growled. "And no, you can't come with me."

I went over to my mom and watched her as she zipped my brother's bag. "Can I go, Mom, can I? I won't get in the way. I just want to see the house. And feel the glass doorknobs," I begged.

"What glass doorknobs?" Mom said. Then she realized what I was talking about. "No, dear, you can't go. Anyway, you need to go to bed early." She brushed me away.

"But I am not even sleepy yet. I promise I won't get in the way." Mom looked at me without saying anything. Sometimes that meant, "We will see."

My brother packed everything in a rucksack and rolled up the sleeping bag. He loved that sleeping bag our uncle gave him, but to me, it just looked big and dirty. I couldn't understand why anyone would want to sleep in a bag zipped up all the way to the neck. All of our sheets were white, lightly starched and beaten until they were crisp. And, they were sewn onto the blanket so they would stay together. It didn't make any sense to sleep in a dark sack.

"Are you really gonna sleep in that thing?" I asked.

"Of course, this is the coolest thing in America," he said. "All the teenagers sleep in these."

"All of them do?" I asked with a frown on my face.

"Don't ask me so many questions. Mom, get her out of here."

Mom grabbed my shoulders and pulled me toward her.

"You know, you have to come home every day after school." Mom said to my brother still holding my shoulders to keep me away from him.

"I know, I know, I will."

"Are you sure you won't get scared?" She asked. I got the feeling Mom didn't want him to move.

"No, are you kidding me? Scared of what? You don't believe that stuff about the house being haunted, do you?" My brother snickered. "You should be glad that I want to live there. In fact, we should all move over there. Why waste a beautiful house?"

"Go on and put your coat on." Mom turned me toward the closet. "We won't stay but a minute though."

"You mean I can go? OK, I am putting my coat on." I threw on my powder blue coat with the rabbit fur collar. I loved the feel of the fur touching my chin. Quite often, I put the fur against my cheek and rubbed it up and down.

When we got to the house, the sun was setting, painting the sky with streaks of orange and red. Even though I was a little scared, I ran upstairs to one of the bedrooms.

I stood on tiptoe with both hands extended to feel the doorknob and caressed it gently. The fur of my coat was touching my cheeks. I was feeling both the soft fur and the cold and smooth glass facets at the same time. I put my eyes close to the knob, to see the inside of the cut glass.

In the reflection of cut glass I saw a mysterious combination of colors, which seemed to have a secretive power packed inside—something that would happen in a far away legendary place. It seemed so close yet so unreachable. I couldn't stay away from it.

Then, I took off my coat and hung it on the knob so the fur could touch it. I rubbed the fur from side to side. The faint light coming through the hallway window reflected off the glass knob sent out a sparkling array of colors. I stroked each facet with my fingers. It was the most beautiful thing I had ever seen. When I tried to turn it, it slipped off my hand and refused to turn.

"Mom, come and look at this glass thing. It is so beautiful," I yelled as I caressed the knob.

"Don't go in there. That's my room," my brother growled. He sure was good at ruining everything for me. I stepped away, staring at the knob.

My brother marched into the room. I hated him. I looked at my mom and said, "Why does he have to be so mean? I hope he doesn't break the doorknob."

Then, I asked softly. "Mommy, do you think this house is really haunted?" I didn't want to upset the ghosts by talking about them too loudly.

"No, dear, it's not haunted at all." Mom said. Yet, she held my hand as if she was protecting me. I knew then that it had to be haunted, or she wasn't sure herself. I turned to look at the end of the dark hallway with my back toward her. I didn't want anything surprising me from behind.

My brother unloaded all of his stuff onto the bed. The room looked pretty ordinary: two windows, a desk, a bed and a small closet, which I would never open to see what was inside. I didn't want to know. I was disappointed in how plain the room looked. It didn't seem to go with the beautiful knob at all.

I wanted to go home. Only, I wished I could take one knob home with me. I followed Mom home feeling empty. I envied my brother. He got to turn it every day.

5

Mom pulled the second pair of socks up to her knees, sitting by the stacked suitcases on the shimmering floor of the *an-bang*. The golden-brown waxed *on-dol* floor was still warm from last night's heating. A few heavy coats were piled loosely on top of the suitcases. Everyone rushed around the house gathering things and asking Mom whether or not to take them.

Since the North Koreans' attack in June, we'd waited till the end of November–one of the coldest months–to move down South. At the end of September, the allied American troops under the command of General MacArthur regained control of Seoul. Since the United Nations troops drove North Koreans back past the 38th parallel, the North Korean soldiers no longer badgered us. But the uncertainty of the on-going war between the South and the North forced my parents to make a decision to leave Seoul.

Even though we cheered when we saw an allied American B-29 fighter plane, the buzzing of them high up in the sky reminded us of the urgency of wartime. The living room was dark and dreary. The pillows and the cushions spilled onto the floor from the sofa on the Oriental rug. Since we had the largest house at the end of the block with two huge basements, Mom welcomed any neighbors who wanted to come in, run down to the basement with a pillow on their heads, and sit in a fetal position during the bombing. We did the same whenever we felt threatened.

The conversations I overheard between Mom and my aunt sounded scary, and it was becoming harder to make sense out of the bits and pieces.

"No, no, we must go to Dae-Ku. Dae-Ku will be better than Pu-San," Mom said. "At least in Dae-Ku, we could live at my father's house there." Her voice was shaky and full of tension. My grandfather was appointed as the head of the civic hospital in An-Dong and the hospital provided a residence for him in Dae-Ku, the nearest large city.

I stayed away from Mother because I had seen her mercurial when she was stressed like this. I wanted to know if we would ever see my Dad again, but I didn't dare to ask.

I put my right hand in the pocket of my long johns, touching the food Mom had packed. Early that same morning, as soon as all five of us had put on our long johns, she sewed up a large square patch of pocket on the right side and filled it with shelled walnuts, pine nuts, dried jujube fruits, and dried persimmons. On the left side was a smaller patched pocket filled with money in all denominations, and a piece of paper with our names and the names of our parents. The food was hard to access through the layers of clothing, but it was there for an emergency.

I brushed the rabbit fur collar back and forth over the gray hole before I put on my blue coat. I loved the soft collar so much that some-times I would stick out my tongue and try to feel the softness of the fur with my tongue. One day I did this while chewing gum and the white fur just sucked the sticky gum right out of my mouth. The gum quickly became twice as big in the fur. I had no choice but to cut it all out, leaving a big hole that showed the gray rabbit skin underneath. The skin felt rough, and I felt sick about it every time I wore the coat. Afraid that Mom might find out, I rubbed the fur back and forth hoping the hole would be covered.

My double-layered feet, which were shoved into my sneakers felt numb from the chill and the tightness. Through the open windows and doors, the wind knifed into my face and my nose felt like it was going to fall off at any second. I covered my mouth and nose and blew hot air into my mittened hands. I could see the hot, steamy air come out of my mouth and quickly chill again.

My brother was fourteen, my older sisters, thirteen, eleven, and eight, and then finally me, five years old. We stood in a row and listened to Mom's strict instructions.

"If anything happens, the address of my father's house is written on a piece of paper in your pockets, and there should be plenty of money to ask anyone. It's always better to pick an aged, dignified looking man to help get you there," she said. "Of course we will all stay together, but just in case something should happen, you will know what to do. And don't snack on the food unless you are really hungry. We will have plenty of food on the train and I will make sure you are fed." Mom looked down and told me that I was to hold her hand at all times. She said if her hands were occupied, then I was to hang on to her skirt, coat, or anything that was attached to her.

"But unless we get separated," she reminded me, "don't take the money out of your pockets. It is only for an extreme emergency."

"What do you mean we if get separated?" I jumped with fright.

"Oh, no, dear, nothing like that will happen," she said. "We won't be separated. But people will be running trying to get on the train, and in the crowd I want you to stay right next to me. You won't be lost if you don't get away from me."

I imagined a mob of people running while I was being buried in the crowd and could barely hang on to Mom's hand. The thought of getting lost made me want to cry.

"Can I get on your back, Mommy?"

"I might carry you on my back at times, but you will have to do some walking and running too." No matter what she said, her nervous voice scared me. But I also felt an excitement that outweighed my fear. I'd never had that much money in my pocket before, and we were taking a trip on the train.

My sisters had their heads covered with scarves tied under their chin. They each carried a suitcase in hand and my brother carried a rucksack on his back as well. I wore a red wool hat with the matching mittens mom had knitted. I wondered if my sisters were excited too, but I knew better than to ask such a question.

With all the commotion and excitement, I forgot all about our maid Jaya.

Jaya had been sent to our house from the countryside and she'd been more trouble than anything. Many nights she wet her bed and quite often she got into a fight with one of my sisters and Mom had to break them up. It seemed like she had one job, peeling potato skins. She squatted by the bowl of water and scraped them with a spoon, one after another. She then dunked them in the bowl of water to keep them from turning brown. Quite often, I squatted across the bowl from her and watched her scrape, pushing her bangs out of her face with the back of her hand. Every once in a while, Mom sent her to buy a pound of beef from the local butcher shop, reiterating, "Keep the money deep in your pocket."

I watched as my mother held Jaya's shoulders firmly.

"Now, Jaya, are you sure you don't want to go with us? I will be happy to take you along. Seoul might be taken over again, any time now." Mom looked straight into her eyes. "You will be taken away if you stay here."

"I will stay. I will be all right." She said, her voice softer than that of a mosquito. Jaya was only ten years old—like one of my sisters.

"Mother, are you really gonna leave Jaya?" My oldest sister, Sang-Soon whispered to Mom.

"I should take her--but I am really afraid to. Your father barely got the family ticket for us, and only to the cargo car of the train. Even then, it says clearly two adults and five children on the ticket. That includes your aunt. If I take Jaya, I might have to give up one of my kids. Oh, what a horrible choice it would be." Mom wiped her eyes.

"What if we take her to the train station and see what happens? The other day, Sunja's mother across the street said that ticketless people were sneaking into the train. Maybe she can sneak in with us," Sang-Soon said. Mom looked down and walked away.

I went over and held her hands. "Come. You can carry my bag for me," I said. But with her mouth stuck way out she said, "No. I don't have a ticket for the train."

Jaya stood by the front door and watched us until we turned the corner. Mom yelled, "There is plenty of rice and *kim-jang kimchee*. Take care." She didn't smile. She didn't cry. She just stood there in her layers and layers of clothing, staring at us.

By the time we got to the train station, I forgot all about her. There were lines of people in all directions, each one waving a document, perhaps their tickets. Most of them wore traditional Korean clothing. They all held bags wrapped in large scarves, and women carried heavy packages on top of their heads and there were old men with crudely made wooden carriers on their backs. None of them had suitcases like we did. I was buried in the mass of people and could only see their stomachs.

As we were gradually pushed into the door of the cargo section of the train, Mom held my hand so tightly that it felt numb. I remember thinking we had to get on board or else we would be captured. What that meant, I didn't know, but I was sure it was something awful.

After a lot of shoving, pushing, and tugging, we were able to get situated. We sat on heavy quilts laid flat on top of the luggage. We all felt relieved and somewhat safe on the train. We had made it out of Seoul.

A few men were sitting with their legs crossed drinking *jung-jong*, a mild rice wine, and chewing on dried, shredded codfish. The older ladies were lying down on their sides with their eyes closed, facing the wall. One mother was trying to figure out a way to make the floor, made up of cargo, level and smooth so that her children could sleep.

I lay on Mom's lap chewing on a piece of the dried fish a man sent over on a ceramic plate. My brother and three sisters were scattered about trying to find a corner. It was cold and dreadful sitting there, but Mom said we should be thankful that we were inside of the train.

It had been a few days since we'd left Seoul. I got used to the lumps on the quilts and the strange people sleeping next to me. I was awakened by a big jolt as the train stopped. I knew it might be more than a few hours before we took off again. Everyone got off the train to relieve themselves. The kids were sent to gather up twigs, and mothers began cooking rice on an open fire.

"Sang-Eun-ah, don't go too far," Mom instructed. "You will get lost. Stay right where I can see you." Mom motioned to my big sister, Sang-Soon and she promptly took me to the bushes, half covered with snow, so I could go potty. I squatted and watched the snow melting away under the yellow stream.

Groups of people settled on straw mats alongside the train tracks and sat around the open fire telling stories and playing cards. It might be hours before the train took off again. It stopped nearly every hour or two, but no one complained about the delay or the unsanitary conditions on the train. No one had a clear destination or anyone waiting for them, so the train was as good an escape as anywhere, even though it had no bath or warm floor.

"At least we are inside this train." The man who had been drinking *jung-jong* seemed to know a lot. "The train following us was the last train out of Seoul and I heard more people were riding on the top." He glanced at my mother and sighed. Then he asked, as he handed me a piece of dried squid, "Where do you think your husband might be now?"

"Why don't you go and find out why the train keeps stopping?" Mom brushed him off without lifting her head. I thought I heard her mumbling, "None of your business."

I held the squid's long tentacles over the fire, and turned my back to him. His drinking and constant comments were annoying.

I missed my father. The orange evening sky made me wish for morning—Christmas morning or New Year's morning, when the house was bustling with people and plenty of good food. My heart felt as if it were being rubbed with sandpaper. Sunsets in the evenings had that effect on me even before the war. I wondered if my father had made it into a train or if he'd been kidnapped and taken to North Korea. I shuddered and hung on to my mom's long skirt and reached into the stash of goodies she had packed in my pocket, grabbing a handful of nuts.

The train ride to Dae-Ku took a month. Finally, Mom said we were approaching our destination. For me, this was no reason to get excited. I didn't know what Dae-Ku had in store for me, but I knew that I needed a good scrub and a toilet. Mom kept telling me to hold it for a few more minutes because we were almost there. I nodded, though my thighs felt tingly from the terrific pressure in my bowels.

By the time we got off the train and walked for what seemed like forever, I forgot about wanting to go to the bathroom. Dae-Ku was full of dirt roads, half-frozen rice paddies, and dormant cabbage patches between houses. The roads were muddy and slippery with melted snow and rain.

As the seven of us waited, exhausted, at the door of my grandfather's house, we suddenly heard beautiful music. "Falalala...la.la.la.la.la."

"Mommy, what is that music from?"

"It's Christmas today, dear. It's from the American army barracks."

"Where are they? Are they scary?"

"No, they are here to protect us from the North Koreans. Americans are nice. They are on our side." Mom hugged me with a sad smile.

Christmas! It was Christmas today. It seemed so wrong to be standing here on Christmas day in a strange countryside. I missed my father. Last year, my father gave me a large brown chocolate bar and an English picture wordbook. It had pictures of a dog, cat, desk, pencil, and watermelon.

I wished I had brought that book. Suddenly I missed everything at home in Seoul. I missed my little desk, the bottom drawer of the sideboard in the alcove of the *an-bang*, which was assigned to me because I was the shortest. I missed the steps to the house. I wanted to cry. I wanted the music to stop.

In front of the gate of the house was a large dirt field that looked like it had been a radish or cabbage patch. The house had block walls around it, and the roofline was slanted straight, not curved up at its four corners like our house in Seoul.

A woman ushered us into a room next to the kitchen to meet everyone else who was staying in the house. There were four or five women and a few teenagers who gathered around to meet us, as well as to hear the news from Seoul about the war. No one seemed to know where my father was or what might have happened to him.

The women prepared food and set a table for us. Mom told us to wash ourselves in the kitchen before we ate. All of a sudden I had to go to the bathroom again. I had to go so badly that I could barely walk. I tugged on my mom's sleeve and the lady who had ushered us in showed me where the bathroom was. The house was Japanese–style, with the toilet situated at the end of the corridor.

I hurried to where she'd pointed and stepped down into the yard next to the corridor. There was no toilet to be seen anywhere. By then I was grabbing my bottom to keep from having an accident. I dashed back to the room where everyone was gathered and got directions to the bathroom for the second time. But by the time I finally found the toilet and started pulling down my pants, but it was too late. My legs felt like cooked noodles and my pants were already heavy with a load. I pulled my pants down and squatted over the toilet to empty it, picking up the load with a piece of newspaper from a pile that was placed neatly in the upper corner of the toilet floor.

I was surprised to see that my underpants were so soiled and even though I had been careful, my hands were covered with brown spots. After rubbing my hands and underpants with more newspaper, I pulled my pants up and decided to take a walk outside of the house before I returned to the crowded dining room. I figured this would be a good way to shake off the unpleasant odor. Kicking the thin ice off the empty field outside of the house, I walked around keeping my grossly soiled hand deep inside of my pocket.

The early pinkish sunset over the banks along the side of the house made my head tingle like cold cider. It was lonely and scary here, but it was also beautiful.

I was ashamed of my dirty hands and squatted and rubbed them in the thin ice. It cracked and melted, turning the water muddy brown.

My feet started feeling numb and my little fingers felt like they were falling off, so I walked back to the house. The moment I sat down next to my mom, she smelled me and screamed. She grabbed me by my underarms, and pulled me up. She pulled my pants down and opened my hands, holding me as far away from her as possible.

Everyone in the room scrunched their faces, held their noses and shooed themselves to the far end of the room, leaving me in the middle with my pants down to my ankles and my brown hands open.

All I could think was that I wanted to go back home to Seoul and be with my father. I stood there, my face flushed with embarrassment, and cried out loud, not even able to wipe my tears.

6

In the Dae-Bong-Dong district in Dae-Ku, where we were staying as refugees, five families lived in the same house, each occupying one room. We did not know most of these people when we arrived. I wondered if our maid, Jaya came from a place like this. Instead of my little desk and drawer, I now had one suitcase in which I kept all my belongings like books, underwear, socks, and most importantly, the Whitman Sampler box. The divine tasting box of chocolates had been a gift to us from one of my father's guests while we were still living in Seoul before the war. On the box was a design of Mr. Whitman (I assumed it was Mr. Whitman) in cross-stitch holding the same box with the most vibrant yellow background. Never had I seen such an exquisite box in my whole life. My sisters and I had sat in the middle of the *an-bang* and relished each bite, taking turns eating them. The chocolates melted in my mouth and slid down my throat.

"I get the box when we finish the chocolate," I claimed. After all, Father's guest handed it to me. My sisters told me that it was only because I was the youngest, not because it was intended for only me.

My sisters and I collected the crinkled brown paper cups that the chocolates rested in. We straightened and stacked them and saved as many as we could—except Sang-Won. She didn't see anything special about them. While we saved and treasured them, Sang-Won smelled them once and tossed them, saying, "There is nothing left to lick off the paper and they are so dark, you can't even write on it."

My Whitman Sampler box was filled with my prized items, including five small rounded river rocks I collected at the creeks to play jacks, the stacked crinkled paper cups, a bow-shaped hair barrette with tiny holes all around the edges, and a blue hair ribbon to wear on special days. Mom had ripped a strip of fabric from one of her old Korean skirts to appease my constant whining. I so badly wanted a red ribbon for my hair, but I settled for the blue silk. I constantly had to trim its fraying edges with scissors.

Our days in Dae-Ku began with the morning washing. We washed our faces in an aluminum basin in the backyard by the water pump. Three or four people stood around waiting for their turn, so that we had an audience while we went though our morning personal hygiene routine. First, we filled the basin with water, which took a few rigorous pumps with both hands on the handle of the pump. Then, using a bar of Ivory soap in an abalone shell, we scrubbed our faces, necks, underarms and feet, in that order, all in the same basinful of water. We always made sure we brought back the soap and handed it to the next person in our family.

Ivory soap was one of the items Mom bought from the black market, along with other necessities like canned meats. The meats we ate during our stay in Dae-Ku came from cans--corned beef, beef stew, and Spam. My favorite meat was Spam. The first time I tasted it, I couldn't imagine how meat out of a long square, aluminum can, could be made so soft and tender. The delicious pinkish delicacy dissolved in my mouth. It almost didn't even need chewing. Mom brought these canned meats home wrapped in a scarf from her regular trips to the mysterious place called the black market. I imagined the black market to be a dark place where everything was wrapped in black paper.

"The black market isn't dark, dear," Mom laughed as she explained. "Most of the stuff there comes from the army rations boxes. They are for American soldiers, but when they have more than they need, we get to buy it."

I thought American GIs were so lucky to eat all of the wonderful stuff. America must be an amazing place to have so many wonderful things, I decided.

Every morning, Mom cooked breakfast on an outdoor earthen stove near the water pump, and my sister Sang-Soon assisted her. Breakfast usually consisted of a soybean-paste-based soup and rice. Sometimes we ate salted fish and yellow pickled radishes as well.

Preparing rice for cooking was a lengthy process. First, Mom poured water into a bowl, and using a straw *jori,* a spoon-like utensil, she stirred the rice back and forth and skimmed the top layer of the floating rice. When the skimmed rice filled the *jori,* she emptied it into another bowl. She repeated this process until the original bowl was only left with a handful of pebbles. Then, she would wash the clean rice by rubbing it vigorously several times and rinsing it until the water ran clear. They didn't know it then, but by doing this, they were actually washing all the nutrition off the rice.

For dinner, Mom opened a can of beef stew or a can of corned beef and added vegetables like radishes, chopped cabbages, and lots of potatoes. She added soybean paste to the broth and served it with rice to our whole family.

Every so often, Mom bought nonessential items like peanut butter or a loaf of bread for a treat. Bread could never replace rice in a Korean meal, but rice was becoming scarce. We ate pure white rice bowls only on special days like our birthdays or holidays. Rice-barley bowls or rice-bean bowls became our staple. Sometimes mom picked small potatoes and cooked them with rice. On those days everyone scrunched their faces, but it was a treat for me, since I much preferred potatoes over rice any day.

My favorite meal consisted of soup made with dried cabbage and dried radish greens, called *"woo-guh-ji"* in soybean paste. Soybean paste was a must-have soup base for Koreans year-round. It never went bad and was the best way to thicken and add flavor to soup. Mom made *woo-guh-ji* soup with lots of potatoes and I always had two bowlfuls. She used to say, "You will have a bountiful life because you like potatoes and *woo-guh-ji*, the peasant foods."

Even though I loved Spam, a lunch of barley-rice dumped in clear water accompanied with salted pickled cucumber tasted delightful to me.

The American army base was located a few hundred meters from our house. Two armed GIs stood at the entrance of the base and we could see the huge Quonset huts through the open entrance. I always smelled the most peculiar stench from the huge dump mound at the right side of the entrance. It was a foreign smell. It smelled like sour tomatoes, sour milk with a hint of spoiled mint, mixed with rancid canned foods. Years later when I walked into an A&P store in Indiana for the first time, I smelled a tinge of the same pong -- the nostalgic smell I associated as foreign in my homeland.

I used to stare at the American soldiers as they walked by. They were mysteries to me. Unlike the foreign diplomats who used to come to visit my father at home, GIs talked fast and loud and they always seemed to chew gum. They walked straight and tall, ready to hand out Hershey's chocolate bars or chewing gum when the neighborhood kids and I walked near the entrance to see them go in and out.

My favorite thing to do in Dae-Ku was to go to Bang-Chun creek in the summer to cool myself. My sisters and I walked along the high banks with a fresh breeze blowing on our faces. The shallow end of the creek came to my knees. Sitting on the side of the creek, I splashed the clear water and felt the smooth gray and black rocks beneath my dangling feet. I spent hours creeping naked on the smooth rocks at the shallow end. When I found the biggest flat rock, I laid my head down on it and stared at the sky. My eyes followed the moving clouds and my body slowly drifted down the stream. Creeping back up to my rock pillow I started all over again following the clouds. When we lived in Seoul, I never realized clouds could look like slow moving animals: elephants, cows, or even dogs and cats.

All of my sisters learned to swim that summer. Sang-Won was the best. She could swim across the deep end of the creek to the other side and back in no time.

I tried walking into deeper water and holding my breath like my sisters, but I ended up breathing in the water. I felt like the water was being injected into my brain through my nose. In that split second of pain in the bridge of my nose, I imagined myself drowning, with fish and leeches grabbing my feet and legs.

After my failed attempts to swim, I resigned myself to dipping my feet in the water and watching the tiny minnows swim through the creek to the swamp.

The sky in Dae-Ku was bigger and bluer than the sky in Seoul and the sunsets were more colorful. I was told that whenever it was sunny but raining, it meant that it was the wedding day of a tiger and a fox. On these days I ran around with my mouth open, looking up at the clouds and trying to catch rainwater in my mouth. Those days made me happy because the sky was bridged with the most beautiful rainbow, followed by a swirling, dripping red sunset.

We walked home from the creek along the high banks in single file watching the orange-red evening sky. Way ahead of us, the banks touched the sky, but when we reached that point, the sky was once again above us. In the cool evening we sang our favorite song as loud as we could.

A blue breeze is blowing from the blue mountain,
Let's walk shoulder to shoulder toward the blue mountain.
Swallowing the blue breeze from the blue mountain.

With the swirling reddish sky reflecting on our faces and the sunset all around us, our voices echoed endlessly.

In those days, my sisters and the other teenagers living in the house got a kick out of telling me elaborately made up stories about how I was adopted. They had a whole list of evidence: I was different; I was the runt in the family; I was too scared to learn how to swim; and mom couldn't have had me because she was too old. Sang-Hie would usually start by telling me that I was placed under the Han River Bridge. Then the rest of my sisters and the boys would chime in with corrections and reminders of how I was rescued because I was wrapped in a five-color silk blanket and was such a beautiful baby. Then, they added, in the struggle of rescuing me, my left eye was injured.

If Mom was around, she adamantly denied the story and scolded them, but as soon as Mom left, they would start clucking their tongues again, telling me that Mom only denied it because she loved me and wanted me to be her own daughter. There were always enough stories to convince me that I was in fact adopted and ultimately, I would end up sobbing. Then one of them would console me for a few minutes before they all burst into laughter and more mocking at my expense.

I didn't understand what was so funny about making me feel lonely and rejected, but I promised myself that one day, when I had made a lot of money, I would leave the house to search for my real family. Even if I didn't really believe the story, I thought that my leaving might punish them to live in shame and guilt forever in a world where there was no more me around.

After several months in the Dae-Bong-Dong district, we moved to another house in the Sang-Suh-Dong district—a huge house owned by the wealthiest man in the area. We rented a room by the gate, which I suspected was built for the gatekeeper.

It was in this house that we celebrated our second New Year's Day as refugees. New Year's was the biggest holiday when I was growing up, full of food and family. Little children were always given a new silk *sak-dong-jugori*, a five-colored Korean costume. Mom made sure we had the usual New Year's meal, *man-du-gook*, a traditional dumpling soup, and I wore my new, stripe-sleeved Korean suit.

Mom lengthened the old skirt for me and bought fabrics in five different colors. She cut them in the same width and arranged them into a pattern. The sewing machine clattered all night putting the strips together, arranging the five colors in sequence. She said we had to make do this way until we were reunited with my father.

In the middle of the dirt yard of our new house was a large planter full of bushes and flowers. On the right side of the planter was a gym where the owner's teenage sons exercised, pulling themselves up and showing off their muscles. They sometimes let me feel their tight muscles on their arms.

Next to the gym were a small square cement pool and a faucet where the maids laid the washboards and washed clothes. At dinnertime they would scrub the rice and pick out the little pebbles. I loved to hang around them and watch everything they did. It was all so different from what I was used to in Seoul. Our maids washed the rice under the faucet in the kitchen. And they washed the clothes on the bathroom floor.

The large front yard was a perfect playground for me and their youngest son, Sung-Kon, who was only a year younger than I was. He wanted nothing to do with playing hopscotch or jacks. So we played war games and he snapped his slingshot at trees or at the gym and yelled, "Hands up! Surrender?" Then he would kick the dirt, pretending there were dead bodies on the ground.

One day he came to our gate room and slid the door open. "Sang-Eun, come on out. Let's play," he said with a smirk on his face.

"I don't want to play war anymore." I shook my head and didn't move.

"We won't. You'll see." His smirk changed into a wide-open smile and he took me into the storeroom by the servants' quarters.

We sat leaning against the large pile of rice sacks. I had only glimpsed the storeroom once before when the gardener put rattrap in it.

"What are we doing here? It's dark and scary. Let's get out." I jumped up and headed for the door.

"Wait. Come here and lay down next to me." He then lay on top of me and told me to stay still.

"What are you doing? I can't breathe. Get up." I wiggled and shoved him with both of my hands.

"Hold still. This is what the grown-ups do. They lay on top of one another and they make noises and breathe loud." He still had the silly grin on his face and his voice was loud.

I pushed him as hard as I could and ran out of the door. I feared someone might have seen us. He followed me out to the front yard chasing me, hollering at his mom by the faucet, "Mommy, Sang-Eun won't let me do 'that' to her." For a second, I thought I didn't hear him right. I really couldn't believe he actually said it loud enough for everyone to hear.

"Do what?" his mom asked.

"You know the thing grown-ups do. You know. Like, I wanted to lie on top of her."

No one, including my mother, who was sitting by the pool, said anything. I headed back to our room by the gate. I wanted to hide from embarrassment. I felt guilty. I knew there was something bad in what we were doing, but I wasn't sure what. I wondered if I might have yelled at him loud and told him he was a bad boy if he wasn't the landlord's son. I wished my father was with us.

After the scary experiences of the war in Seoul, and the constant nagging questions about whether or not I was rescued from under a bridge, I become fearful and shy. For comfort, I clung tightly to whatever treasure I could find. I kept five of my smooth rock jacks in a folded origami paper basket and two *ojami* (small bags mom had sewn up and filled with rice husks for me to juggle), in another basket. I no longer had the Whitman Sampler box. The barrettes were all missing as well, and Mom kept one barrette in her purse in fear I would lose it again.

What I wanted more than anything, more than the cross-stitch designed Whitman Sampler box was a doll I saw at the marketplace when I followed Mom one day. It was wearing a Korean five-color blouse and a knee-length cobalt blue Korean skirt showing white legs filled with rice husks. Her cloth face was as white as her legs and arms and her drawn eyelashes curled up almost to her eyebrows. Her plump red lips were drawn on but they looked real.

One day, Sang-Hie drew a Korean doll on a sheet of snow-white drawing paper she paid one won for.

"Color the doll's five-color blouse as good as you can, Sang-Eun, and pretend she is a real doll."

Sang-Hie's suggestions always seemed to hold heavy authority. Even though I knew a paper drawn doll was nothing like a real one, I colored it and put her by my side to sleep with at night. Yet, I longed to feel the rough rice husked legs and arms and touch the drawn face of the doll I had seen at the marketplace.

In March, Mom enrolled me into the first grade at a school in Dae-Ku. The makeshift Quonset hut schoolhouse was divided into many rooms and housed grades first through sixth. School desks were lined up on the dirt floor and when it rained, water came through the leaky roof and made the floor muddy. The outhouse was far away, and I usually avoided it, preferring to hold off as long as possible.

Going to school was a whole new life for me. Every morning, still in my undershirt and underpants, I stepped down from our one-room living space to the yard. At the corner of the top step, mom had set my toothbrush with a tiny dab of toothpaste and a basin full of lukewarm water with which to wash my face. When we didn't have toothpaste, Mom put a bowl of finely ground salt for us to brush our teeth with. I picked up a bar of Ivory soap and started scrubbing.

"Make sure you wash your neck, behind your ears and underarms too."

When I finished, she flung the used water to the far side of the yard and refilled the basin for the next person from a bucket of water. She repeated the same procedure for all five of us. I missed the mornings in Seoul, when our maid would grab the back of my neck with her left hand and wash my face harshly with her soapy, right hand. Even though I used to complain about this torturous morning ritual, I preferred that to this outside, refugee-style sponge bath. I was cold and sleepy in the mornings.

After washing, Mom pulled out a dress with a white round collar and slipped it over my head. Then, she spun me around to button up the back. Each Monday I started with a clean and crisply ironed dress that I wore for a whole week. If the laundry schedule was interrupted by rain on the weekend, I had to wear the same dress until the rain stopped. The same was true with our nightclothes, but the undies came off three times a week, rain or shine.

After I was dressed, she started on my hair with a fine-toothed comb, top to bottom, pulling out a handful of hair with each stroke.

"Ouch! Mommy, that hurts," I wailed.

"We have to do this in case you get head lice," Mom said. "There are lots of kids with lice at school and boy, are they contagious." She told me no one else was to touch my hair accessories for fear I would get lice from the other kids. After this, she would take a barrette and clip it neatly to the right side of my hair.

Mom had warned me about playing with other kids too closely at school for fear I would get head lice. I feared it too, ever since the day she marched over to the American GIs and uttered sharply in her beautiful English, "Please do not treat our children like bug infested animals."

They glanced at Mom and then carried on pumping DDT over the sea of black heads and tightly closed eyes, like crop dusters dusting a wheat field. That night, I heard mom sniffling from the unbearable affront to her precious children and the insult to her nation's dignity.

"Mom, that DDT smelled good," I said. "It was kind of sweet smelling." The minute I said it, I realized it was the wrong thing to say. Mom seemed to have a reason to cry and there was nothing I could do. I sat there feeling just as gloomy as her, perhaps more, because I couldn't make her feel better.

The last step of my morning routine was to slip on sneakers.

"OK, you are all set," Mom said. "Don't look away, study hard, pay careful attention and listen to your teacher," she reminded as she walked away. As soon as mom was out of sight, I would turn over my Korean rubber shoes that were leaning upside down against the lower step, drying from last night's wash. These were the shoes I changed into after school. And after dinner every night, Mom scrubbed them with lye soap.

Quickly, I took my sneakers off and slipped on the rubber shoes. I loved the feel of the rubber slipping on my feet and the noise they made when I walked. Tap tap tap. The pointy nose reminded me of witches' shoes, but I loved wearing them. They barely covered my feet all around but once I put them on they were comfortable and never slipped off. The ones for fancy holiday dresses had colorful flowers painted all over them, but the everyday rubber shoes were plain. Mom always said that they were too casual for school but I was allowed to wear them anywhere else, even with dresses.

The first time I had insisted on wearing them to school my mother's hand flew across my face and the slap stung leaving a handprint on my cheek. So I had to sneak them whenever I could.

"The sneakers hurt my feet and everyone in the class wears rubber shoes to school." I practiced excuses in my head in case I got caught, but if I snuck out fast enough, she didn't see me.

I slammed the front gate and hurried into a narrow alleyway. When I reached the big street, my heart felt heavy with fear that I might get lost and would not be able to find the school or my house on the way back. I counted the turns and alleys of each corner, but I often became distracted watching people and lost count. There was plenty to see in Dae-Ku: women carrying heavy loads balanced on their heads, men pulling horses attached to carriages so full they reminded me of a tiny ant pulling a huge dead bug. I watched a man whipping his horse as it slipped backward trying to pull a load as big as a house up the hill. As I watched, I forgot all about going to school and stood there crying for the poor horse.

But the scariest people were the lepers. I watched from afar as they begged for money or food with their faces covered. Many of them didn't have any noses or fingers. I would stand perfectly still, moving only my eyeballs to watch them. The minute a leper took a step into my direction, I ran away.

School was boring and scary. I was bored because I had to sit and listen to the teacher all day, even though I had no idea what she was talking about. I was scared because I knew I would be in some kind of trouble if I didn't pay attention. I spent most of the day just waiting for singing time. During this period, I stood in front of everyone and sang while the rest of the kids sang after me. Music made me forget my worries.

Quite often, I was picked to sing at school events. Once, at the biggest talent show for the entire school, the teachers chose me to give the opening speech. Standing on stage, the audience looked enormous.

"I would like to thank everyone for coming to our humble performance," I began. My teacher wrote the speech and I had to deliver it from memory. Mom told me that I should deliver it without making any mistakes. She emphasized that it was the least I could do since it was so amazing that the teachers would even put on a show like this at a temporary facility, it being war time and all.

On the day of the performance, my legs were trembling. I rambled on in monotone and skipped a whole sentence. There must have been a hundred people, and I had no idea what I was saying. I barely remembered to wave my arms in a circular motion like I was including everyone as I said "everyone". I knew I had disappointed Mom.

When it came time to sing, however, it was a different matter. I wasn't nervous or worried. I sang my solo with my hands linked together in front of my stomach:

When you cross a busy street, watch for the road.
Do not look away. Otherwise you will be hurt.
Red light. Stop walking and be still.
Green light. Hurry and cross to the hill.
Yellow light. Make your turn slowly up the hill.

Getting home from school was worse than getting to school because I was terrified of being stuck on the street during an air raid. The air raid siren went off every day at noon and everyone on the street stood still and waited for the siren to stop. Every day I had to go to the bathroom so badly during the raid, I ended up standing on the street corner crying and dancing up and down. The adults gave me sympathetic looks and old women whispered that it would be over in a quick second, but it felt like it would never end.

One day, in a panic that the siren was a real bombing and not a drill, I wet my pants. An old man saw me and got out of a parked Jeep and asked me, "Where do you live?"

"I live at Mr. Suh's house. We are renting a room at his house."

"You mean, Mr. Suh in Sang-Suh-Dong?"

"Yes, yes, his house. The wealthy one." I sat on the edge of the back-seat in his Jeep, afraid that my wet pants might leave a stain. The old man turned around to smile at me every few minutes while a uniformed chauffeur drove.

I looked out the window wishing I could be home with mom, or better yet, back at our house in Seoul with my father. I just wasn't getting used to the life here in Dae-Ku.

Suddenly, I realized the driver was passing the big street leading to my house. I started crying loudly. This was my ultimate nightmare coming true. These people didn't know where I lived. I jumped forward and started hitting the chauffeur.

"You just passed my house. You did. Let me off. I wanna go home!"

He ignored me and I thought I heard him telling the old man that he would take him home first and then me. Why wouldn't he speak to me? I was getting angry. Adults never seemed to tell children anything, at least not anything that mattered.

When the driver finally dropped me off in front of my house, I bowed and thanked him. Why couldn't I have been quiet and waited?

I entered through the big gate and ran to my mom who sat by the water faucet in the yard with Mrs. Suh. I hugged her and hung on to her long skirt. This felt like heaven after my ordeal, but Mom dismissed me, telling me to go into the house and change into my play clothes. I felt I had been punched in the stomach. No matter what I did, it was inappropriate. I went and did as I was told, but what I really wanted was to stay with my mom and caress her long skirt.

Later that day, I told her about my horrible experience.

"Next time, remember to count the corners and streets to turn exactly," she said casually.

"But I did. Mom. You need to take me every day and pick me up every day."

"I can't dear," she answered. "I have too much to do around the house. You'll be all right. You are such a clever girl." That was the end of it.

Mom always praised me when no one was around but if anyone else paid me a compliment, she denied it profusely.

"She is so cute and she is so clever," a neighbor commented one day.

"No, she is not that cute and she is so little. She is not as clever as her sisters," Mom said.

"Arrogance never did anyone any good for their dignity," she told me. "We must be humble. Boasting is a sign of being lighthearted. Let people find out your superiority themselves. Show it by your actions. Don't boast yourself."

This was an eternally confusing idea to me. I ended up believing if I was pretty, it must also mean that I was ugly.

Mr. Suh, our landlord, was a politician. His chauffeur waited for him every morning and took him somewhere important in his private Jeep.

Even though we were just renting a room by the gate, Mr. Suh frequently invited us to join them in the living room of the main house after dinner where they served us fruits and asked me to sing.

He told my mom that she should really pursue my music education seriously. He went as far to say he would even pay for it if she couldn't. Standing up with my hands locked together in front of my stomach, I sang for as long as he wanted. Often, he handed me a hundred won bill when I finished. More than once, it crossed my mind that maybe he was the one who had left me wrapped in a silk blanket inside a basket.

7

We moved to Pu-San when I was in second grade. Mom told us that we would finally be reunited with my father and we would live together in a rented room upstairs in a two-story house. Father found the place for us, but he was not there when we arrived. I never knew where he was and what kind of business he was doing, but Mom always told me that it was not my concern, and that he was doing well and would join us soon.

I learned that my father was able to get on the rooftop of the very last train out of Seoul on the coldest winter night. We had heard many horror stories about refugees who were unable to get train tickets and rushed and fought to dangle on the train, how they pushed and shoved to perch on the smallest spot of the rooftop and when they got a place how they huddled together under quilts to keep themselves warm and to keep each other from falling off, how they had to lay down flat when the train went through the tunnels, which were frequent.

He caught a dreadful case of pneumonia that he couldn't shake for many months. In his feeble condition, he looked for a job in Pu-San, where there were more business opportunities. When he finally secured enough income, he sent for us.

Pu-San was a slightly more modern city than Dae-Ku. The main streets were paved and there were even some two-story buildings.

We arrived at our new home late in the afternoon. I loved the idea of living in a two-story house. All of the houses I had lived in and seen so far had a courtyard inside of the front gate.

The single front door of our new house opened to the bottom of the staircase. Along the hallway of the second floor were bedrooms. Our room, the second one off the hallway, had Japanese *tatami* floors, and from the large window, we could look out to the busy street. It was a bright, pleasant room.

I skipped down the stairs and explored the neighborhood while my family was unpacking to settle into our new temporary living quarters. It was there, on the side of the street, that I met a new friend. She was straddling a backless bench looking at her textbooks. Looking over her shoulders, I said, "Those are different from my books."

"They what? Who are you anyway?" She looked up through her thick glasses.

"I said they are different from my books. I am from Seoul. My name is Sang-Eun. Do you want to be friends?" I smiled.

"Tchee-hee. What? No," She answered. "You talk weird."

"No I don't." I walked away, but she followed me upstairs and started examining our room.

"Is this the only room you have? We have a big house right across the street. My father is a gynecologist and we are rich," She proclaimed proudly pushing her glasses up. Cho-Sun was her name—my mom said later that her parents were thoughtless for giving her a common *gi-seng*'s name.

"This is your kitchen? But it is not even a kitchen," Cho-Sun said, looking at the blocked end of the hallway. It was a makeshift communal kitchen designed to be shared by all the renters upstairs. There were four rooms upstairs, occupied by refugee renters like us. The landlord's family lived downstairs in the back of their dry cleaning shop but their kids had a large room upstairs, next door to us.

The next day, Mom enrolled me at a local school and Cho-Sun and I were in the same class. When I came home from school, I heard lots of noise from our room, and I heard my mom's laughter. I ran up the stairs and slid the door open. And there he was. My father extended his arms ready to hug me. "*Abuji*!" I screamed. He was actually there in person. He was home.

"Hey, there's my baby. Are you a schoolgirl now? Wow, look at you. You grew so big!" He reached for a pile of presents and handed me a red belted jacket with matching pants.

"Red again?" I frowned.

Mom narrowed her eyes at me. "I will not have such a spoiled behavior in this house." Her voice scared me. I looked at my father and he smiled. I knew he didn't mind my grumbling. I plopped myself on his lap and he quickly lay down on his back to give me an airplane ride. "Vrrrmmm, vrrrmmm." I was a good airplane with my arms stretched out on each side.

"Will you be living with us all the time now?" I asked.

"I will, definitely," my father nodded.

To welcome him home, Mom made spicy snapper soup with aromatic vegetables for dinner that night. It was my father's favorite. Mom generally grilled inexpensive mackerel. When Sang-Soon made dinner, she would braise the mackerel in soy sauce and add sliced radishes. A piece of mackerel and a bowl of rice, accompanied by a few pieces of cabbage kimchee, was a grand dinner for me.

"You needn't make such an expensive dinner for me. I would have been happy with *woo-guh-ji* soup," my father said, but he finished every bit of his soup and licked off each bone. At dinner, Mom asked him about his horrible journey down to Pu-San on the rooftop of the train. But he didn't give us details about his horrific experiences.

"It was hard, but it is over and there is no need to dwell on it. The main thing is that we are all together now."

"It's just that I would like to know where you have been and..."

"Let's stop the useless talk in front of our kids. I am doing the best I can to support my family and it requires some traveling and I just need you to trust me," he said sternly, wiping the sweat off his forehead. The spicy soup always made him perspire. I knew my mom wasn't satisfied with his answers. She narrowed her eyes but stopped asking.

"Jobs are hard to come by and conducting a business is worse in this chaos. There is no structure in the business world and money is so scarce," my father said more softly and apologetically. Nobody, not even my brother, said a word. There was only the sniffling sound of eating the spicy fish soup.

"Well brought-up kids don't make so much noise when they eat. Try to eat quietly," Mom snapped at us.

Cho-Sun and I walked to school together every day. She loved to show me off to her friends and when I was selected to sing a solo at school event, she always told everyone that I lived across the street from her.

Quite often on summer afternoons, we would jump from our upstairs hallway window onto the rooftop of the one-story noodle factory behind us. There must have been a hundred rows of noodles hung to dry, which gave us wonderful shade. Cho-Sun and I would lie under the noodles and talk for hours. Sometimes we would grab one end of a long noodle and pull it gently off the line. We became pretty skillful in pulling a long piece without breaking it. The uncooked, salty tasting dough left an unpleasant residue in our mouths, but that didn't stop us from pulling them down and wrapping them around our fingers and putting them in our mouths, a little bit at a time. One day, Cho-sun told me that her father had given an abortion that morning.

"What's that?" I asked.

"You are so dumb. That's what you do when you don't want to keep the baby," she replied.

"But why would you get married if you don't want to have a baby anyway?" I asked. She never explained it to me, so I figured she probably didn't know either. From that day on, whenever I heard the word *pregnant* or *placenta*, it reminded me of the salty, doughy noodles. I imagined babies lying in a bed of wet noodles.

The rooftop was our secret place until my sister, Sang-Won discovered it and decided to make it her corner, too. She finished all twelve volumes of the comic version of *Jungle Book* lying under the noodles, at the opposite end of the rooftop.

When she wasn't reading, Sang-Won loved to play ball. Her right hand was always pumping up and down as she bounced an imaginary ball. She practiced swooping the imaginary ball to catch it in the back of her skirt, and pull it out with her left hand, all to the perfect rhythm of the ball-game song. One day Mom came home with a bright red ball in her hand and Sang-Won jumped with excitement. She slept with the ball and hid it when she went to school so no one would find it. By the end of the week, she'd mastered every ball game and became the most popular girl in the neighborhood.

"Hey Sang-Won, let's play ball," kids shouted as they knocked on the door every afternoon. Two or three girls teamed up and took turns bouncing the ball up and down and passed it back and forth, singing the same song day after day.

I wished I could do all the tricks Sang-Won did with a ball, but it wasn't my game. I would have given up a thousand balls for just one doll. While my sister played ball, I cut up dolls out of paper and put the paper dolls in beds with little paper blankets over them.

Though I wasn't into the ball games, I was as good at jump roping as Sang-Won was with a ball. I could skip and hop into the rope while two kids twirled the rope to a song.

Dear brother, loving brother, go and fight the war bravely.
Dear brother, loving brother, let your body bleed heroically.

I jumped in and out of the rope without making a mistake while the song was sung over and over.

One day while I was jumping rope outside, my sister Sang-Hie hollered at me. There was a long line of kids from another neighborhood who came to join in, kids I had never seen before, waiting for their turn to jump into the circle of twirling rope.

"Sang-Eun-ah, come into the house. You shouldn't be jumping rope in rubber shoes." Sang-Hie had a firm grip on my shoulders and led me into the house. "You are not supposed to play with those kids, Sang-Eun, you should know better."

"Why? Why can't I play with them? I have my sweater on."

"Some of their fathers are A-frame rack carriers," she said. "They are laborers and illiterates. You need to pick your friends more carefully."

"But Cho-Sun plays with them," I muttered under my breath. "And I like them." I followed her into the house. I didn't know friends needed to be picked but it seemed there were rules for everything. Life was quickly falling into two categories: "supposed-tos" and "not-supposed-tos."

I was supposed to wear canvas sneakers when I played jump rope and I was not supposed to talk back to older people. Asking questions was considered talking back, and most of the people were older than me. Now, I was being told to learn another supposed-to when it came to making friends.

I was still skipping my imaginary rope in the house, humming "Dear brother, loving brother," when Sang-Hie asked me, "If you could have one thing in the world, what would it be?"

"Probably a doll. A real doll with real hair and a soft body," I answered.

"You don't want a jump rope with wooden handles?"

"Nah, rope is ok," I said. "But a doll, you can sleep with, and play with." I skipped my imaginary rope. Skip. Skip. "Tons better," I said as I skipped off.

Although it didn't snow in Pu-San, December was cold. We missed the warm floor of *on-dol*. Instead, we warmed ourselves with a potbelly stove in one corner of our *tatami* room. Much of the cooking was done in the room at the stove to conserve energy. That way, heating and cooking were done at the same cost of the coal.

"I am afraid I won't have any presents for you this Christmas," Mom sighed.

"We don't care, Mom. Christmas is no big deal," Sang-Soon replied, dishing up barley bowls for us. The days of eating bowlfuls of white rice were gone. We now ate much more barley than rice, and even I knew not to expect anything for Christmas.

On Christmas morning, I woke up to a murmured conversation between Mom and Sang-Hie.

"I did, Mom." Sang-Hie said proudly. "I saved money for a whole year for them. I knew exactly what they wanted. Sang-Eun wanted a doll and Sang-Won wanted a sketchbook and watercolor palette."

And there, on Christmas morning above my pillow, sat a real doll with long black braided hair, lying on a white sheet of parchment paper. For Sang-Won, there was a thick sketch pad and a bright blue palette displaying twelve circular sections of colors with two long grooves for brushes on top.

"*Uh-ma-na.* Is this for me?" I asked. "A real doll? She's beautiful!" I grabbed the doll and hugged her tight, rocking her side to side. My very first doll! She was beautiful. She wore a Korean dress that showed her soft knees. Her pinkish cheeks were painted with dimples and long eyelashes framed her eyes. I was so overjoyed I almost felt ill. I knew my sister saved all of her money for a whole year for me (even though she and Mom said it was from Santa Claus, I knew there was no such thing). I wanted to tell her that from now on, I would always listen to her and do what she told me, no matter what. I would wash my hair twice a week like she always told me and I would make sure she approved of my choice of friends.

After Christmas, Mom convinced our landlord to knock down part of the wall of our one room and extend it out to the landlord's kids' room to make our room L- shaped. This made their kids' room only half as big. Then she very cleverly boarded up the wall and installed a wooden door to make a small extra room for my brother. Mom had decided that my brother needed his own room to study, now that he was approaching college age.

Mom put a desk and a chair in his room and it was off-limits to us. There were always lots of heavy books on the desk but I rarely saw him study. He spent lots of time in his room – mostly sleeping – even during the day. Mom said that it was because he liked to study at night when we were all asleep.

When Mom made a special meal, she always dished up the best part and saved it for my brother. She said it was because he was the only son and the oldest one and that he would carry the Lee family name. When she had some extra money she bought him the best quality red ginseng and stuffed it in a young chicken then boiled the heck out of it until it was soft and mushy. Only after he had enough of it, would we be allowed to have the leftovers.

My brother also seemed to have new shoes and new clothes all the time, unlike us. "You have to stop spoiling him. He will never learn to appreciate anything if you give in whenever he demands something," my father clucked his tongue.

"But his body is hard to fit," Mom said. "He is shorter than an average child and needs to have special uniforms made up. If you would bring home more money we wouldn't have this problem." My father said nothing for a long time and then, eventually said, "Just be quiet and stop the useless nonsense talk."

I wanted to cheer him up and say, "Good for you, Dad. Tell her again." But we all sat quietly on the floor at our low desk and did our homework, pretending we didn't hear their arguments.

A new children's monthly magazine called *Sai-Butt* (New Pal), became popular and Sang-Hie thought I should write a poem and send it to them. If selected, they would publish it. The only problem was that I had no clue what to write or how to start. I didn't even know what a poem was.

Sang-Hie and I sat next to each other at the desk on the floor in our room. It was late. My dinner sat in my stomach like a chunk of mud. I was nervous that we might wake up my brother, and also nervous about writing a poem. We sat in the dark room, only the dim flickering flames of the candle burning on the desk.

"You are very creative. You can certainly write a poem," she said. "All you do is to write exactly what you feel. Let's first talk. What shall we write about?"

"I don't know. What shall I write about?"

"Well, let's look out the window. What do you see out there?"

"Nothing," I said. "Just the moon."

"OK, then the moon it is. What does it look like?"

"Well, it's round and has some dark areas on the face."

"Great! Now, write that."

"You mean like the moon is round and has dark areas?"

"Yes, but let's look one more time. What do those dark areas look like? "

I stared out the window for a long time. "It almost looks like a face. The eyes and the mouth or something."

"OK, there you go. And whose face does it look like?"

"I don't know. It's round."

"All you do is put down exactly that. And try to make it rhyme."

Sang-Hie went through each verse with me just like that, until I came up with this poem.

Moon, Moon, the Smiley Moon
Like the face of my big sis.
A cloud glides over the moon
The moon doesn't peep or hiss
Maybe the cloud disturbs the moon
For the cloud wouldn't turn to kiss

I wrote it neatly with Sang-Hie's fountain pen on a clean sheet of parchment paper and Sang-Hie mailed it the next day. On the first day of the following month, she and I ran down to the bookstore to see the new issue. Sang-Hie flipped through the magazine swiftly and screamed, "Here it is. Here it is. Here's the poem you wrote! And it says on the top, by Lee Sang-Eun, age 7!"

For weeks, maybe months after that, I looked at my name on page sixty-four of *Sai-Butt* magazine every day.

8

My father was often gone on business trips and when he returned, an A-frame carrier accompanied him, carrying a sack of rice, a sack of barley, and sometimes boxes of candles. We were still experiencing frequent blackouts and at times we didn't have electricity for days. Wheat flour was still far less expensive and he sometimes brought a sack of flour and encouraged Mom to make noodle soup and steamed buns for us. A steamy bowl of noodle soup in anchovy broth, garnished with fish cake and green onions was a delightful lunch, but buns could never replace rice at a meal. Cooking in a communal kitchen was difficult for Mom, but having been a home economics major in college, she was innovative and gifted when it came to the culinary arts.

Since Koreans didn't cook in ovens, buns were steamed on the stovetop and baked bread was only bought from bakeries. But Mom had a brilliant idea to bake bread in Christmas cookie cans on an open fire. She kneaded and mixed the dough with baking powder to make it into a round ball and kept it warm to rise by the potbelly stove. Then, she put the puffed up dough into a cookie can. After experimenting by turning the can over a few times and timing it precisely, she soon mastered the technique of baking on an open fire.

When the mouthwatering aroma of the fresh baked bread spilled into the street outside, I visualized Mom's hands cracking open the brown, crusty bread. I would drop everything and run upstairs for the first bite of Mom's specialty.

When she'd baked a few of those round loaves, she would invite neighbors and serve the warm bread with homemade marmalade. Marmalade was the best way to use the orange peel, and butter was an extremely expensive commodity. Mom never neglected feeding us, but we were limited to essentials. Nothing was wasted and nothing was thrown away. The spongy texture of the freshly baked, warm, white bread dissolved in my mouth but my favorite part was the thick crust. She even started serving bread with marmalade and hot chocolate made with powdered milk for breakfast every morning. Soon, practically all the women in the neighborhood made trips to the black market to look for the American cookies, so they could use the cans in their new adventures in baking.

The cool ocean breeze in summer evenings enticed our neighbors outside. The front of our house became a gathering spot. Our landlord took out folding chairs from his dry cleaning store and put them on the sidewalk. People stopped by to talk about their day and exchange stories.

"Did you eat your rice?" The word, rice implied "meal" and it was a typical way of saying, "Good evening." Half a dozen people gathered around and as the sun faded, more and more people showed up holding fans in their hands. We talked until we watched the skies fill with stars and I studied the sky intensely as Mom showed me the Big Dipper and the Little Dipper every night.

"Can you see that little star off to the right side of the third one of the Big Dipper?" She was always concerned about my eyesight.

"Yes, *Umma*, I can see it fine. I have no problem seeing things at all." I would say it positively, even when I didn't know which star she was pointing at.

One evening Mom was admiring the landlord's oldest daughter who had just placed second in the Miss Pu-San beauty pageant. "You are so tall and you have such a beautiful complexion," Mom praised.

"Oh, no, I am not beautiful. I don't even know why I entered the pageant," the daughter replied. "I suppose I wanted to win some money. It was embarrassing to boast that I was beautiful, especially in a bathing suit." She reached over to caress my hair and said, "One day, Sang-Eun should enter the beauty pageant. She will win, definitely."

Just then Cho-Sun's oldest brother cut in and said, "Well, not with that eye of hers. Her left eye is crossed. A cross-eyed girl would never win the beauty pageant."

"She is not cross-eyed and don't you ever say that again! It is hardly noticeable," Mom said.

For the first time, I thought something must be really wrong with my left eye, and I finally understood why Mom was always so concerned about my eyesight. This was confirmed the next day when my brother went down to Cho-Sun's house and called her brother to come out. Even though her brother was taller, my brother punched him as hard as he could for calling me cross-eyed. Then my brother kicked him with his army boot when he fell on the ground.

"Whoever taunts my baby sister will have to deal with me first," my brother shouted.

As a seven-year-old, I still wet my bed—not every night, but enough to exasperate my mother. The cleaning up was nightmarish because the urine would soak into the tightly woven straw *tatami* floor. Mom would have to leave a soapy rag to dilute and absorb the urine, which had already seeped through. It was a long and ineffective process and made me feel shameful and guilty. Through breakfast, I kept my head down twirling my food and wishing Mom would stop cleaning the floor already.

"You were too lazy to get up to go to the bathroom," she said, narrowing her eyes at me. I tried to explain that in my dream, I relieved myself absolutely and positively in the toilet but in midstream I woke up realizing I used the entire *yo* as a toilet.

One day, she put a *qi* (a large rice winnowing basket) over my head.

"This is going on too long. This time, go next door to Yong-Han's and borrow some salt."

Koreans believed this embarrassing punishment would cure bed wetting. But my mom had rejected such an absurd mockery and never actually imposed the custom on any of us until that day.

"I won't do it. I don't care what you say. Leave me alone," I screamed at the top of my lungs. I was angry, realizing that I didn't do anything wrong. I didn't mean to wet my bed. It just happened. It was an accident. If Mom didn't trust me, she should have put a diaper on me or put a rubber mat under my bed.

What I really wanted to say was, "*Get a hold of yourself, witch woman, it's not the end of the world.*" But nothing like that came out of my mouth.

I took a heavy step toward the next door, wiping stream of tears and holding the *qi* over my head, the bottom of the *qi* dangling all the way to the back of my calves. Yong-Han's mother gave me a bowl full of sea salt and said that it would surely make me drop the shameful vice. Yong-Han stood behind his mother grinning. I wanted to take off the *qi* and smash him with it.

Yong-Han was my age and had two older sisters. It was common knowledge that the oldest sister, Ki-Soon was a half sister from her father's mistress. Mom told us that there was something not genuine about their marriage and we wouldn't be associating with them if it weren't for the war because they were nothing but low class *sang-nom* (commoners). "But Mom, he is a math teacher. He helped me with my algebra. He explains it so well. He couldn't be a commoner," Sang-Won argued.

When all the neighborhood kids played outside, Yong-Han never played. Mom had another theory about their family having some kind of secret ailment that kept them indoors, except for the oldest daughter, who was born with different genes.

One time Yong-Han came around the playground when it was my turn to jump into the twirling rope. He skittishly tried to tangle the rope, acting giddy. I got so mad I started calling him a cunning boy with no pride. He smiled and said, "I don't even know what that means." As he headed for his house, I grabbed him and pulled him into the middle of the street. Still grabbing the neck of his shirt with one hand, I shouted at him that I was inclined to think he cheats by handing in homework assignments that his sisters did for him, otherwise how can anyone who was so idiotic and malicious be such a good student, him being such a problematic son in such an abnormal family. And if he thought he was superior to me only because I had one accident in bed, he would be his father's huge disappointment. I used every sophisticated word I could think of whether it applied to him or not.

By then kids, mothers, and passersby surrounded us. Everyone's mouths dropped in amazement. I even surprised myself with some of the words that came out of my mouth.

"You should become a lawyer one day," said a woman, carrying a baby on her back who had stopped to watch.

By the following fall, we grew out of most of the clothes we had brought from Seoul and Mom was busy sewing velvet jackets for Sang-Won and me to prepare for the upcoming winter. Mom lengthened all of my pants, leaving a deep crease clearly visible.

Against my Mom's insistence that we were not a charity case, my sisters Sang-Soon and Sang-Hie dragged home a large package of "Refuge Relief Goodies" from the Baptist church. My father convinced Mom that we did need help and that if we didn't accept it, it would be an insult to the American people, who sent it to us out of the goodness of their hearts.

"When you need help, you accept it graciously. And when it is our turn to help others we will help generously," he said.

The big relief package contained mostly clothes for Sang-Won and me. There must have been a dozen sweaters all in different colors for Sang-Won and half a dozen dresses for me, as well as under-slips with eyelet lace around the hem. I never owned a slip before and I so wished to wear it out. It looked too pretty to wear under a dress. The prettiest item was a three-layered petticoat. (Mom told me that was what it was called). Each layer was fuller than the last and trimmed with different colored bias tapes and matching lace. It was made of stiff, fancy cotton and when you wore it under a dress, the dress puffed out.

Every morning, after breakfast I spent a long time deciding which dress to wear to school. The colors of the dresses were so vibrant and the collars were bordered with lace. I wondered what kind of place America was and wondered why there were so many pretty things to wear and so many delicious things to eat, like chocolate, and fun things like chewing gum with minty flavor. It just occurred to me then; What kind of people would think of something to just chew and not swallow?

"Mommy, do you think I can go to America one day when I grow up?"

"Dear, there is nothing that can't be done if you put your mind to it." Her answer surprised me.

"I really want to go one day. So I had better start putting my mind to it," I said. Mom made me believe I would go to "the Beautiful Country" one day.

One evening, a long automobile shaped like a submarine with tiny portholes drove onto our street and parked next to the noodle factory. There were a dozen holes on each side. A man in gray-stained overalls got out of the sunken front seat carrying a bell in his hand.

"Come and see American cartoon movies for only ten won," he hollered and rang the bell in between his bellows. Pretty soon the neighborhood kids came around with tightly clutched ten won bills in their grimy hands. Cho-Sun and her two younger brothers handed him two ten wons each and said that they would each like to see two moving cartoons. The man in the seedy overalls took all the crunched up bills and announced to the paid customers to get ready to watch by placing one eye on a hole, but until all the holes were taken he would not play the movie. Kids gathered around the submarine with their eyes glued to the holes like newborn puppies sucking on their mom's nipples.

I ran upstairs to Mom to ask for ten won.

"What movie is he going to show out of that shoddy machine?" Mom looked out the window and scrunched her face.

"I don't know Mom, but it's a cartoon, good fairy tales like Snow White and Pinocchio. Something good. I never saw a moving cartoon, please *Umma*."

"How do you know what he is going to show? It may be something you shouldn't see."

Mom had certain rules about supporting merchants who peddled to little kids and she let us know we must not trust them. We were not allowed to buy snacks from street pushcart vendors because they were dirty and the food might be spoiled and vendors didn't care, she said. If they had any conscience they would find a decent job instead of tricking little kids. She felt the same way about us buying comic books. She thought we should read regular books, not comic books. The only comic book she approved was Sang-Won's *Jungle Book*.

"I don't know, but every kid is watching. All the other mothers gave them money. You are the only mean mom." For the first time, I felt hateful toward my mom. I wanted to tell her that she should be nice to me if she loved me, just like she should be nice to my father.

There was one hole left, and I begged Mom a few more times, but I knew that she wouldn't change her mind. I wished my father was home. I went outside and hunched over by Cho-Sun trying to listen to the voice leaking through the porthole. I just about gave up hope when Cho-Sun's youngest brother left the hole he bought for two shows, saying it was stupid and he wouldn't waste his time on it.

"If you want to watch it, go ahead. I am done." He spat on the dirt ground and darted toward his house.

I jumped at the chance and fixed my eye onto the hole to watch the tail end of Cinderella. I saw a girl in a rag dress, pushing a broom, and a huge mouse, almost as big as her, and two other girls with the biggest noses I had ever seen. What impressed me the most was the brilliant colors—deep reds, blues, pinks and yellows—and their arms moved with such elegance, even the bad stepsisters. There was an explanation of the story in Korean in the background, but it was nearly impossible to understand. I was glad that I knew the story of Cinderella, because I understood everything just by looking at the moving pictures. I thought it was the best night of my life.

9

Seoul might as well have been a foreign country when we moved back in 1953 after the ceasefire. Nothing was as I remembered. When I first saw our Shin-Mun-Ro house, I nearly choked from a knot in my throat. I stood at the alley looking at the familiar high block wall, the stairs leading to our house, and the curved rooflines. They looked much smaller than I remembered, yet it was still the biggest residence in the neighborhood. As we approached the front door, I remembered Jaya standing there staring at us three years before. I expected her to open the door to welcome us. I wanted to tell her all about living in Dae-Ku and Pu-San, but I knew she wouldn't be there. She had probably been taken away by the North Koreans. I wanted to cry, mostly because I couldn't remember her face. Her small round face had been completely erased from my memory.

The house was dusty and desolate. The Oriental rug in the living room was gone and the sofa was torn. The doors were broken and the windows had been shattered, showing three years' worth of abandonment. It truly looked like it had been through a war.

Crickets covered the entire basement floor and invaded our bedrooms, and we could hear mice running around above the ceiling under the roof.

Mom placed two small desks, one on each side of the alcove of the *an-bang* for Sang-Won and me. She then dusted and wiped the books that we left three years before—like Andersen's *Fairytales* and Aesop's *Fables*—and she filled the cubbyholes of our desks with them. The hardcover English wordbook my father gave me for Christmas three years before was also still there. There were pictures on each page—pictures of a watermelon slice, a piano, a sparrow, a boy, and a girl, and the English words were written directly below each picture. I opened the book and stared at the watermelon slice. I moved my hand from the book to my mouth, pretending to eat, and then I pretended to spit out the seeds. I looked at each picture, taking as much time as I wanted, remembering how impatient my sisters had been with me for taking so long to turn the page when they surrounded me to share the book with them. It was still my favorite book.

The biggest difference in Seoul was the presence of curly American letters on signs everywhere on the streets. Storefronts like bakeries, camera stores, and tearooms had English writing all over the place. English lessons didn't start until junior high school, so children like me who were still in elementary school had no idea what they said.

The Western influence was evident in every aspect of our daily lives as well. Finely ground sea salt was replaced by Colgate toothpaste, and flaky Ivory detergent replaced brown lye soap. The front row of the corner store freely displayed Wrigley's chewing gum and Hershey's chocolate bars.

"Do not chew gum with your mouth open like the barbaric American GIs!" Mom still hated it when we chewed gum; popping it cost us a harsh slap on the bottom. Sang-Won was the best at popping chewing gum. She could pop nonstop, making clear, crisp sounds to the beat as she moved her lower lip in and out.

"All the Americans did was introduce the superfluous nature of materialistic things to our wholesome country," my cousin, Dai-Young, asserted one day when my mom served a basketful of Necco wafers and Hershey bars for dessert after a family dinner. He completely crushed Mom's pride in keeping up with the new trend.

The three years we spent in Dae-Ku and Pu-San quickly became a distant memory. My old friends and I were back jumping rope and playing jacks. But now, one of our favorite things to do was to find the smoothest and the least damaged tile pieces from piles of rubble at bomb sites. We walked through the half-standing walls covered with holes made by bullets and shrapnel. Undamaged tiles were hard to find, and on the rare occasions when we did find one, it would have a chunk of cement attached firmly. It would take all afternoon to grind it off against the hole-ridden wall.

Another visible change in Seoul was the high rate of postwar homelessness. Soon after we reclaimed and settled into our house in our old neighborhood, so did many homeless people. The wide stone walls behind our house, built to keep the rocks and the dirt from sliding down to the street, provided a leveled mesa where many homeless families pitched tents and makeshift dwellings. It turned into a crudely built village for homeless families, each with two or three children.

Sang-Won and I spent many afternoons lying flat on the rocks of the embankment of our house, reading comic books. From the high embankment, we could survey their living conditions and hear the noises of their daily life.

"*Eiguu*! You are a curse. Were you born to be my foe? Just to be nothing but another mouth to feed?" A mother in a dirty shift with a ripped hem hollered at her half-naked baby girl whose face and body were covered with stains. The baby cried loudly until the mother smacked her on the bottom. But then the mother quickly hugged her, wiping her tears. The neighbor at the next tent bellowed not to hit the poor child, saying she was probably hungry. The baby buried her face in her mother's breast.

At dinner time, the mothers squatted in front of a terracotta stove and cooked soybean paste soup. Sometimes the children would get a boiled sweet potato for dinner. They sat around in a circle giggling while peeling the sweet potatoes like bananas. I watched them day after day, wondering where their fathers were. Even in that terrible living condition, their giggles sounded happy.

After dinner the children used to come outside to the street and run around playing hide and seek. One day, I ran down to play with them.

"The rich family's daughter is here. Tell her to go away," one mother yelled from her tent.

"Why can't she play with our kids?" A woman from another tent holding a baby hollered back. It was the first time I noticed the baby in her arms had light brown coiled hair and grayish green eyes. She was obviously an *einoko* (mixed blooded child).

"She is so beautiful." I ran to pat her soft curly hair. "Can I hold her?"

"No, she will probably cry. She is only an *einoko*." Her mother turned around and quickly climbed back to her tent.

"But she is beautiful." I followed the mother, then I heard my mom calling me to hurry home for dinner. I could see her angry face high up over the block wall of our house.

"You never go out there to play with those beggars. What were you thinking?" Mom waved her index finger at me. She raised her eyebrows and kept shaking her head.

"They are just poor, *Umma*. Didn't you say that poverty was not a crime?"

"Their fathers are all thieves. They are the ones who try to break into our house every night. Don't talk back to me and don't go near them again."

We did have a near break-in every night. There were nights we would hear footsteps in the yard. My father would flash the light and a dark figure would dart to the embankment and jump over to the back hill. After a rainy night, we saw sneaker prints near the windows. Whoever it was, he never seemed to succeed in breaking in. But the signs of trying were evident almost every night. Mom was convinced it was the homeless beggars from down below.

I slept through most of those noises, but when I saw a window off the track one day, a sure sign of a frantic effort to get into the house, my fear of burglars became real. I would sweat before falling asleep and beg to hold my mom's hand in bed until I fell asleep. My father assured me that they meant no harm—they were just very poor and they would do anything to feed their families.

"Why don't we give them some food then?" I asked.

My father just smiled.

"Why can't we, *Abuji*?"

"Because there will be no end. And besides, they could go find work. The fathers in the tents are probably sleeping all day being lazy."

"There is this beautiful *einoko* girl. What about her father? Do you think he is a thief too?"

My brother cut in and scoffed, "She is a war orphan *einoko*. Her mother's family probably disowned them. And I am sure the GI skipped to America,"

All through dinner and in bed that night, I couldn't erase her face from my mind. She not only didn't have a father, she was cooped up in the tent all day because she was so pretty with her green eyes, curly light brown hair and the whitest skin.

I wrapped a small gift for the little *einoko* girl, the newspaper-wrapped gift pack contained one of the least damaged sky-blue tile pieces, a red comb for her light brown hair, and one section of a Hershey's chocolate bar.

In postwar Seoul, everyone was obsessed with learning English. From junior high onward, English language education was mandatory. Private English institutions were popping up all over Seoul offering additional study, especially at the high school and college level. My mom and her elite group of friends even organized a women's English study group. They met weekly and invited a private teacher who was an American missionary. They took turns meeting at each other's homes and finished the lesson with an elegant Korean lunch prepared for the teacher. This was an opportunity to practice their newly acquired linguistic skills as well as to show off their trendy domestic appliances like blenders, refrigerators, and even waffle irons.

People slipped English words like "date," "fashion," "modern," or "intelligent" into their daily conversations, often mispronouncing them. Foreign books and periodicals were pouring into Korea and Mom stressed that we needed to be competent in English if we wanted to have in-depth knowledge in any area, regardless of our career choice.

My brother started carrying a rolled up magazine like *Life* or *Time,* to show off his knowledge of English. It was a chic and trendy thing to do, but he did pick up English amazingly fast in school. He especially excelled in conversational English even though schools generally concentrated more on reading and writing. When the American Army General Van Fleet came to Korea, my brother stood next to him behind the podium at Seoul High School and gave the welcome speech. Everyone was in awe of his fluent pronunciation.

Impressed with his talent in picking up the language so fast, Mom decided to give me a head start in English. I was in third grade. After much searching, she enrolled me into a children's class at the American Language Institute and I went twice a week for an hour-long lesson to learn "the American talk."

I was the only girl in a class of a dozen boys around my age.

"Good morning, everyone." Mr. Hahn, the owner of the institute came into the classroom speaking English. No one knew what he was saying, but we figured he was probably saying "Hello."

"In this class you will only speak English. I am the only one who may speak Korean. And you can call me Mr. Hahn," he said in Korean.

"Not Mr. Hahn teacher, but Mister Hahn. You need to curl your tongue."

It seemed very strange but when he spoke English, he almost looked like an American. He moved his mouth big and wide and smiled a lot as he spoke English, but looked rather solemn and strict when he spoke Korean.

On the first day, we learned to say, "I have a nose. I have two eyes, I have a mouth, and I have two ears," while pointing at each part of our faces.

When he was teaching us to say the word *mouth,* he grabbed the tip of his tongue and showed us how the tip of the tongue had to stick out between the upper and lower teeth.

"Eww! You are touching your tongue, Mistal Hahn," said a cute boy sitting next to me. He covered his mouth and pointed at him then hit my arm with the back of his hand. By the end of the first week, we could say where we lived, what each of our parents names were, and how many brothers and sisters we had.

Eunseong Park, the boy who sat next to me, told me that our names were alike and he started saving me a seat next to him. I wished he lived in our neighborhood so we could walk home together.

10

Mom hired two new maids who were from the province of Jul-La-Do. Having lived as refugees made me realize that the maids were not much different from us. They were precious children of some parents at one time, only poor, just like we were in Dae-Ku and Pu-San. All they did was work for a strange family, who ordered them around. I wondered if they missed their families, and I wondered what kind of parents would send their daughters all the way to Seoul to become maids. My growing sympathy toward them made me watch them closely.

Laundry seemed to be their biggest chore of each day. Every day the two maids washed everything from underwear to school uniforms in a gigantic aluminum vat with a washboard propped against the side. They squatted by the vat and rubbed the laundry with their prune-like hands. After rubbing the soiled collars of my sisters' summer uniforms, socks and other dark colored items were washed in the same vat until the water became dark gray. Then all of the clothes were rinsed twice in another vat in that same order, from light to dark.

Next, they starched. Starching was a huge process. First, cooked rice was boiled until it was completely pulverized. Then it went into a white cheesecloth bag that they rubbed all over the blouse on the washboard in a smaller tub half-full of lukewarm water.

Every so often, all the white laundry, including the white sheets, was boiled in the iron cauldron with lye. The lye looked like rock candy. It turned them whiter than snow. Then they all went on the clothesline to dry, sometimes for days. When they were hung to dry, they were so white you could almost see a tinge of blue. On rainy days, everything was hung in the bathroom over the two large, round tubs.

The washed and dried sheets underwent yet another procedure. First, they were folded and beaten on a rectangular limestone. This stone was specially designed to unwrinkle large linens. It had four round feet and a polished top. The two maids sat at the stone facing each other and beat the folded sheets and pillowcases with smooth wooden clubs as if they were drumming a kettledrum. I watched them beating the sheets in an alternating rhythm, and never missing a beat. It occurred to me as I watched their perfect rhythm why we always had two maids.

Our maids also prepared dinner every day. Preparations for dinner began early in the afternoon with a trip to the market. Most families, including ours, didn't have refrigeration at home, so we had to buy and prepare our meats on the same day.

One of our maids would make the daily trip to the market. The market was a good fifteen-minute walk and the maids considered it an important outing.

When Mom bought them clothing, she would often say, "This is to keep you warm when you go to the market." Or, "Try not to wear these sneakers around the house. Save them for going to the market." Our maids got decked out in their good shoes and carried a purse to keep the daily allowance for the biggest task of each day--dinner.

By definition, *ban-chan* in Korean means side dishes. Korean dinners consist of many small plates of *ban-chan*, sometimes as many as twenty, that accompany the main staple, rice. The number of *ban-chan* at a meal was a benchmark of affluence. A decent dinner included at least seven or eight *ban-chan* and at least two of them were meats. Meats might be a bowlful of tiny anchovies fried in soy sauce, sugar, and garlic, or boiled beef in soy sauce with spicy peppers and garlic (*jang-jo-rim*). A small bowlful of *jang-jo-rim* was stripped into small slivers to stretch its quantity for the whole family. (Years later, my kids named it "string beef" when my mom made it for them because it was shredded into narrow pieces like string cheese.) Garlic spiced up virtually every dish. A pound of beef or pork could be cubed and put in with vegetables and potatoes to make a pot of stew-like *ji-ghe*, with lots of garlic. Every family used their own unique recipes for this delicious brew.

Our after-school snacks were seasonal vegetables like boiled potatoes, boiled sweet potatoes, or corn on the cob. When it was time for the maids' yearly chore of making soybean paste, our after-school snack was a bowlful of boiled soybeans. In the winter, the snacks were mostly dried food; dried squids or if we were lucky, expensive dried persimmon.

My father was no longer in politics, I assumed, because we were not receiving guests like we used to. But he went to work every day and managed to provide a good life for us.

Seoul was becoming more Western every day, and while the people embraced new appliances and clamored to learn English, they did not discard their traditions. While memories of antiquated lifestyle quickly faded, some of the traditional Korean customs were practiced even more elaborately.

Holidays like New Year's Day and *Chu-Suk* were celebrated with bigger feasts, as if to make up the wartime poverty. On those days, all the relatives came to our house, "the big father's house," to celebrate with my grandfather who had moved in with us. My grandfather lived on his own in Pu-San through the war in an effort not to impose himself on any of his sons. But as soon as we were settled in our house in Seoul, my father invited him to live with us to fulfill the oldest son's duty.

Chu-Suk, the Korean Thanksgiving, was August 15th by the lunar calendar, which fell around late September or early October. By the time *Chu-Suk* came around, our house was freshly painted, wallpapered, and the floors shined to gleaming golden brown again in all five bedrooms.

Chu-Suk was celebrated with, among other things, *song-pyun*, pine-scented rice dumplings filled with sweetened beans and sesame seeds. Mom, my oldest sister, Sang-Soon and our two maids all gathered around the evening before the holiday to shape the half moon shape dumplings. They made hundreds of them, then covered them with pine needles and steamed them in a big iron pot.

We were home for the holidays. We were home in peace again.

When I tried on the brand-new five-color Korean costume Mom bought me for *Chu-Suk,* I put it on the day before and weaved in and out of the circle of ladies all evening, who were busy preparing for the following day's feast.

There was something so homey and warm about *Chu-Suk.* Perhaps because it seemed like it was the beginning of the busy activities that went on for the rest of the year.

When the *Chu-Suk* celebration was over, it was time to get ready to make the *kimjang kimchee* (winter *kimchee*).

Mounds of salted cabbages were stacked up neatly in a huge, round, tin washtub in the middle of the dining room. Ladies squatted around the tub; each attending to her specific chore in the assembly line for the yearly ritual of making *kimjang kimchee.*

Mom would make her trip to the marketplace at five in the morning on a mid-October day in order to pick out the best-quality Napa cabbage. She usually bought between 150 and 200 heads of cabbage. The supply needed to last all winter long, and it had to be buried in earthen barrels in the backyard to keep it from freezing. If that happened, the pickled *kimchee* would taste bitter, the texture of the cabbage would become mushy, and it would be ruined.

Even though Mom wasn't usually involved in the daily cooking of meals, she was the commander of this project. There were two maids, my oldest sister, an aunt or two, and a couple of neighbors who offered their helping hands in hopes that the favor would be returned when it was time for them to make a huge batch of their own family recipe of *kimjang kimchee.*

Napa *kimchee* was the first of the three different kinds they made for the upcoming winter; it was also the most involved in both preparations and quantity.

The first two ladies in the assembly line sliced daikon radishes, the main ingredient of the stuffing. Between them was a tub, which they filled with evenly julienned radishes. They pounded their knives on the chopping board as their whole bodies moved in synchronized rhythm. Then, they swiftly picked up the chopping board, dumped the sliced radish pieces into the tub, and put another long daikon radish on the board almost as fast as my eyes could follow. A couple of ladies next to them would peel and mince garlic and ginger. Another chopped green onions.

Next in line was a woman who mixed the stuffing. With both of her arms elbow-deep into the tub, she mixed the radish concoction until it became fiery red and lustrous with juice. Occasionally, she would pick up two fingers full of the radish mixture and put it in her mouth, then added more cayenne pepper, salt, or cured sardines. Some families added minced shrimp, shrimp sauce, walnuts, or pine nuts.

When she decided the mixture was ready, she tore off a small piece of the salted cabbage leaf from the big tub and wrapped it around the mixture, transforming the round leaf into a bite-sized package. The cabbage leaves had been cut in half lengthwise and were already limp from sitting all night, sprinkled with salt. Only then would it be offered to my mom for her final approval. Mom would chew and roll the *kimchee* pouch around in her mouth, staring at the gigantic tub and concentrating on her inspection of the sample piece. Finally, she would nod her head granting ninety-percent approval. Then she would ask my oldest sister to taste for the remaining ten-percent approval.

"I think it's good. What do you think, Sang-Soon? Why don't you wrap one up and have a taste to see if anything is missing."

"I am sure it is fine, Mother. It is too spicy for me," my sister would say, shaking her head.

Kimchee is simply defined as "pickled vegetable." The unfermented stuffing is much hotter. After a month-long fermentation, the stuffed *kimchee* matures to its full flavor and is no longer stinging hot.

But the women stuffing cabbages made a meal out of tasting the samples one after the other, blowing and sucking in their breath to ease their burning tongues.

I would bring stacks of sitting mats, so the ladies could relieve their legs, which were numb from squatting for so long. For being helpful, I too would get a taste or two of the delicious sample, with only a tiny bit of the stuffing.

By the time each layer was filled, the stuffed cabbages became twice as fat as their normal size and pinkish from the juice running all over. Now it was ready to be packed in the giant earthen jars. These jars were as tall as me and wide enough to hold a few of us.

It took nearly all day for a roomful of ladies to make the cabbage *kimchee*. The cucumber *kimchee* and the soup *kimchee* were done the next day. Cucumbers went through the same procedure, but the middle sections were cut lengthwise on all four sides to make room for the radish mixture stuffing.

After fermentation, *kimchee* was sour in taste and crispy in texture; it accompanied every meal, even breakfast. People loved to boast about their family recipe of the *kimjang kimchee*, and it was often served on a platter sliced diagonally to show the layers of stuffing.

My father's favorite was *dong-chee-mee*, soup *kimchee*, which was a mild pinkish juice with a few floating radishes and chopped green onions. Of course, *kimchee* would not be *kimchee* if it didn't have plenty of garlic and ginger. I remember my father would drink a cupful of the *dong-chee-mee* and say, "Yum...better than any kind of cold cider you can find!"

The jars were tightly sealed with closely woven linen and the heavy lids were placed on top before being buried halfway into the ground. They reminded me of dwarfish men sitting with big hats on. But Mom didn't like the way the maids had to bend down and fish out the stuffed cabbage and ladle the juice every day. She also worried about rain getting into the jar. So, one summer, Mom hired half a dozen workers to build cement, outdoor basement to store *kimchee* jars and firewood. Even though I was too scared to walk down the steps into the dark sunken room, the flat top of the basement gave me a wonderful place to play hopscotch.

The next big holiday was New Year's. The several different kinds of *kimchee* that were made and stored away were perfectly fermented for the big holiday feast. As the oldest daughter-in-law, my mom would present my grandfather with a brand-new silk Korean costume especially ordered for January 1st. This was probably the only time my father would dress himself in the traditional costume as well. However, he refused to have a new one made for him every year. He wore the same old bluish-gray silk brocade suit that had been stored away in the drawer with naphthalene. He would take it out of the drawer and hang it on the clothesline for a day or two. Then he would shake it vigorously to air out the repugnant smell of naphthalene. All throughout the delightful day we would smell him, but no one ever complained. My parents got dressed up but my sisters no longer had to wear Korean costume now that they were a little older. Instead they received new outfits. I wore the Korean costume, as I was still considered young enough to dress up. Everyone got dressed in their new outfits early in the morning, waiting for the relatives to arrive.

The biggest ritual was the showing of respect to each of the older relatives by presenting *se-bae,* a deep formal bow until our heads hit the ground.

My grandfather waited in his room for us to come and bow in our new outfits. My sisters and I used to line up at his door taking turns going into his room to give him a deep bow and receive the money he paid us. As he handed out money -- usually a hundred won -- he spoke a few words of advice. Something he had been thinking about or something that might apply to our New Year's resolution. To me he usually said, "Hurry and grow so you can be a help to your parents," or, "Study hard so your parents will be proud of you."

Se-bae, done right, took a little bit of skill, especially for girls; we were supposed to keep our hands on our sides and go down slowly while keeping our body still until our bottoms touched the floor first. Then we were to bow our heads down without losing balance. None of us ever learned to do it correctly.

It was easier in a Korean dress as we could hide under the long dress and stick out our feet or spread our legs slightly apart to keep balance but in our winter pants we ended up laughing, and my grandfather would cluck his tongue and say, "*Tzu tzu*, this is a disgrace. You girls are too modern for the Lee family," followed by, "This year, learn some manners."

My mom treated herself to a new Korean outfit and *durumagi*, a matching overcoat, also in silk, that she changed into right before the guests arrived.

Mom had been preparing *man-du-gook* (dumpling soup), *kal-bi* beef, and assorted vegetables. Food played a main role in all of the Korean holidays, but especially on New Year's, because whatever we did on this day was considered an example of things to come in the New Year. So, it was important to have abundant feast so the whole year would be bountiful. We were also told to be diligent and kind and generous to each other all day long, so we would be diligent and kind the rest of the year.

By the time I bowed to every one of the aunts and uncles, little mothers and little fathers, and all the other relatives who sat around the room, I had racked up quite a large sum of money and I was blissful and content.

Then I had my own ritual. I would run down to the fruit market row in Kwang-Wha-Moon in my new outfit and rummage through the pile of rare fruit looking for a perfectly round orange with the brightest color and no blemishes. After the ten-minute run back home, I would peel the thick skin and carefully take the sections apart. The millions of tiny pieces of pulp all stuck together, forming a plump and juicy slice. As I peeled off the white membrane, my mouth salivated like a water fountain. I savored the sweet delicious juice as I popped each wondrous piece into my mouth. I still don't know why I didn't buy two or three at a time. Perhaps it was because they were outrageously expensive. They cost a hundred won apiece. A school snack was ten won and with thirty won, we could buy a bowl of noodles on the way home. I suppose even in the bliss of affluence, in my right mind, I couldn't bring myself to indulge by giving away two precious hundred won bills at a time, however delectable the oranges might have been. But as soon as I swallowed the last piece, I would run down to the fruit market again and again for anther exorbitant treat, a privilege I enjoyed once a year on New Year's Day.

11

For the following month, my pocket was still filled with hundred won bills—almost two thousand won. One day, my sister Sang-Hie approached me, waving her savings account passbook.

"Wouldn't you want to have one of these?" she asked.

"What for? Aren't those for grown-ups?"

"No, anyone can have one if you want your money to grow."

"Why would I wanna do that?"

"Don't you want to have lots of money of your very own? Start with what you have right now and every time you have some, put it in the bank and one day you will have more than you ever thought you would."

"But what if I want to spend it?"

"Well, you save what you don't want to spend. You spent a lot to buy oranges. Now you want to save the rest."

Sang-Hie's talk made sense and it even excited me, but I was reluctant to give away my pocketful of wealth to some bank indefinitely. However, I let her hold my hand and lead me down to the bank. Sang-Hie filled out and stamped my never-before-used personal seal on different forms and then handed me a brand new passbook. I stared at the neatly printed numbers, 1600 won in my own bankbook. It was a strange thing. As I held it, I felt, for the first time in my life, not only wealthy, but also secure and protected, a feeling that I never wanted to do without again. I wished I hadn't wasted so much money on oranges. It would have been wonderful to look at 2000 won in the bankbook, had I bought fewer oranges. From that day on, I began to have a firm conviction that a person should always save money, no matter how little.

Sang-Hie's love and wisdom continuously influenced my life as a child and I was soon conditioned to believe she knew everything and that she was always right. Soon after we moved back to Seoul, my parents made a sizable purchase—a used Yamaha upright piano. In Pu-San, my sisters and I used to walk to my piano teacher's house every day to practice and take weekly lessons from her.

One day when I came home from school, I saw my old piano teacher at our house. She and her family also moved back to Seoul shortly after we did. Mrs. Kim Shin Duck was finishing up a visit with my mother.

"So, think about it. All your kids are very talented; they would really benefit from having a piano in the house." She was describing a piano with ivory keyboards in a lustrous black cabinet.

She bowed to my mom and smiled at me, revealing her profound under bite and protruding lower lip, before she left. She and her three children's lower jaws stuck out an inch more than their upper jaw. To me, it was positively the neatest look. I thought I might come to have an under bite like them if I let my lower jaw protrude long enough. I used to walk around with my lower lip stuck out until I couldn't stand it any longer.

In those days, all pianos were imported, and owning a piano was a sign of affluence. Coordinating two hands at the piano was difficult and had made me lose interest in learning, but the idea of having a piano at home excited me.

To get ready for the ostentatious ebony piano, Mom installed a new kind of flooring called linoleum in one of the largest bedrooms. A piano shouldn't be placed on a warm floor, so mom made the room Western style by placing a table and chairs in the middle of the room and the piano against a wall opposite the door. The room was heated by a potbelly stove. With the curtains on the double-paned window, the piano room looked elegant and up-to-date. Even my grandfather would peer into the room occasionally with an approving look.

Of all of us, Sang-Hie continued taking piano lessons diligently and excelled the most. Our piano room became a music room for my mom to show off her daughter's talent in front of company. It was also a room where Sang-Hie and Sang-Soon entertained their friends. Sang-Won and I were not allowed inside, unless our hands were washed. My brother would go in anytime and play, at times for hours. He played songs he knew with his own version of harmonization.

"Look how talented I am! I can play any song with a synchronized harmony. Who needs piano lessons?" Every time he bragged we all turned our noses up at him and rolled our eyes.

By the time she was in high school, Sang-Hie started teaching piano to neighborhood children and they came to our house to practice every day, but everyone had to wash their hands before they could open the piano. Sang-Hie not only possessed a talent for teaching, but she also took pleasure in seeing accomplishments in her students.

"Music needs to breathe just like people. At the end of the slurred phrase, take time for the music to breathe."

"Practice slowly and repeatedly. Then practice with feelings. Think how the piece you are playing makes you feel. Let it happen. Let the piano sing." She had a unique way of explaining, even to a young student. She also motivated her students to drill "Hanon" exercises for firm basics.

"Sang-Eun, would you like to take piano lessons from me if I paid you?" Sang-Hie made every effort to inspire me to play the piano.

"What do you mean, you would pay me? How does it work?"

"Well, I will give you a lesson a week and give you assignments. You know, a few pieces to practice for the following lesson. And I will pay you ten won per piece you can play without making a mistake at the lesson."

"Wait, you are gonna pay me?"

"I will."

"Wow! I would like that. What a deal. You mean, if I could play ten pieces well you will pay me one hundred won?"

"That's right. But here is the condition. When I pay you, you must put that money into the bank, into your account. You can't just go out and buy candies with it."

I didn't know how and why Sang-Hie always had the best ideas. But she did. I practiced every day and leaned the whole book of *Beyer* in no time, and more and more numbers were added to the balance of my bankbook.

For her first high school sewing project, Sang-Hie made me a dress, one with a bias binding around the cap sleeves and a matching bolero jacket. All the other kids in the class made their own dresses. When the piece was finished and graded, she was so anxious to put it on me, she waited on the street corner for me to get home from school. Her face lit up from the satisfaction of the perfect fit as well as the print selection of the dress. When she had some money saved up, she dragged my mom to East Gate marketplace for new fabrics—polyester and nylon—spending her hard-earned piano-teaching money only to make more dresses for me in all different colors and designs. I even got to wear a belted dress, which made me feel like a grown-up high school girl for the first time.

One day, a woman across the street with a daughter two years younger than me borrowed the dress Sang-Hie made for me. The following week her daughter showed up wearing the identical dress. This made Sang-Hie mad, but Mom told her she should be proud to be so admired that a neighbor would copy her idea.

Mom combed my hair every morning and put a barrette in it. On holidays, Sang-Hie curled my hair with a red-hot curling iron. She constantly corrected my slouched posture and nagged incessantly about my nervous habit of eye blinking. "Be elite. Learn to be a sophisticated young girl," she used to say.

During our month-long summer vacation from school, our standard assignments were to keep a daily journal and collect insects. For one reason or another—never intentional–I always waited until the very last day to come up with all thirty days' worth of journal entries. My mother was amazed that I never repeated a sentence and filled the notebook with a freshly made-up diary for thirty days all on the last night of summer vacation.

But I didn't put off insect collecting. I went almost every day to the back hill with an insect net in my hand and spent half a day running, picking berries, and climbing acacia trees looking for insects. My knees were always skinned and scabbed, and I wore out two pairs of rubber shoes in a month.

One day, Sang-Hie interrupted my zealous effort of running and waving the insect net in a swarm of dragonflies.

"Hey, Sang-Eun, I need to take you somewhere important. Go on and change your dress and put your sneakers on." I loved going places with my sisters because on the way home, we would usually stop at the bakery and have sweet buns.

"Where are we going?" I asked, rushing home ahead of her.

"They are holding an audition for the children's choir today. If you make it, you will be working under teacher, Byung-Won Ahn all summer long. The choir will be performing on the radio during the children's hour. Wouldn't it be wonderful? I know you will make it. You have such a beautiful voice."

The audition was held in the auditorium of the YWCA in Myung-Dong. There must have been fifty girls all dressed up in pretty nylon dresses hanging tightly onto their mother's hands. Dresses made with nylon, the new see-through synthetic fabric, had become a chic must-have clothing item. They came in all different colors and the convenience of never needing to be ironed made them even more desirable. I was the only one with a high-school-aged older sister instead of a mom and the only one in a freshly pressed cotton dress and no bow on my hair. All the mothers wore their Korean nylon dresses of short blouses with long ties that hung down to the middle of their long flowing skirts.

Sang-Hie knew I was intimidated. "Teacher Ahn used to teach at my school. I know him very well," she whispered into my ear. "You needn't worry at all."

After we were seated, Teacher Ahn taught us a German children's song in Korean about the splendid morning dew. Then one by one we went on the stage and sang what we had just learned. He taught us by singing each line as he conducted and nodded his head back and forth to the pianist.

Some girls had their hands linked together in front of their stomachs and others had them hanging at their sides when they sang. Most of them covered their scrunched faces when they finished singing as they came off the stage. My sister leaned over and whispered to me, "Don't make faces like them. Be confident whether you did good or bad. And smile when you finish."

I quietly nodded. When my name was called, I walked up to the stage smiling. The pianist started playing the prelude and I linked my hands together. I only remember pressing on the floor with the bottom of my feet to keep them from shaking. I didn't care whether I made it or not, all I cared was that it would be over.

I was one of thirty selected. Sang-Hie paid fifteen hundred won for the program out of her own pocket for two weeks of choir practice.

"It's like throwing away one hundred won if you skip a day. You must never skip it. And you need to keep yourself clean and neat. Make sure to wash your hair at least twice a week." On the way home Sang-Hie talked with such conviction, I nearly thought we would stop at the bathhouse. When we got home, Sang-Hie made red, pink, and blue bows for my hair with silk fabric from Mom's armoire.

Walking to the YWCA was long on hot summer days, but I never complained. I couldn't waste a hundred won. For the most part, I enjoyed singing in the group, though I didn't always have a solo part. We were given a few sheets of music each day and learned all the songs we were given. I learned to harmonize with the alto part even though I was always in the soprano section.

On the following Monday, the first day of the second week, I was so tired from the daily walk to the YWCA all the way at the edge of Myung-Dong, I had the hardest time getting up in the morning. I was so groggy I could barely open my eyes.

"What happened to your face? It looks horrible," the younger maid screamed when I approached the faucet for my morning wash.

I ran back into the *an-bang* and stood in front of the mirror and saw my blown-up face and swollen eyes. There were blotchy spots all over my face, on my cheeks, my nose, and even my upper lip.

"*Omana*. Look at me. What happened to me?" Horrified, I shrieked and ran to Mom.

"Oh, it's OK. These things happen to children sometimes. It will go away." Mom calmly got some ointment and dabbed it all over my face.

"I won't go to the choir practice today. I can't show my face to anyone looking like this." I refused to get dressed or go outside, much less go to choir.

"You do not quit your commitment for little spots like that. There are things you must do when you don't feel like it," said Sang-Hie. To Sang-Hie, it was out of the question to skip choir, even when I looked like a leper.

What I had was the most severe case of impetigo, and my scabs lasted through the second week up to the day of the recital.

"Hey, Sang-Eun, you lucky girl, guess what? I am going to use mom's makeup on your face today to cover the scabs. They are barely visible, but it will be fully covered with the makeup." Sang-Hie uncovered my blanket with a big smile. I had been lying under the blanket refusing to go to the recital.

"You are just saying that. It won't cover up. I look horrible. I am not going. I have gone for two weeks and have not wasted the money. So let me stay home today."

"You are so silly. And you can't be that selfish. Don't you know that the choir won't sound nearly as good without you? Every time I go and listen, all I hear is your voice. You carry a perfect tune. And your voice always stands out. You have to think of others. Just because you have slight scabs, are you going to let them down?"

Grudgingly, I got dressed and Sang-Hie covered my face with Mom's Coty face makeup and powder. I stood there staring at the pictures of powder puffs on the lid, and as she rubbed the makeup on my cheek,

I wished I was dead. With my face hung low, I was dragged to the recital.

I still looked horrible, but I liked smelling like Mom. I felt grown-up and hoped someone would notice the smell the whole time I was singing in the back row.

At the dress rehearsal, Teacher Ahn motioned me to come to the front row to sing a solo part. I had been hiding in the back row covering my face with both hands. When he cued me to sing, I started singing but realized my voice shriveled almost to a whisper. It was like trying to scream but no voice was coming out, like I was in a dream.

"What's the matter with you? Sing loud, sing out, let it out," Teacher Ahn screamed.

"But, but, I can't. I don't know what happened."

I covered my face, wiping my tears and let out a heaving whimper. I stared at Sang-Hie, pleading for help. I lost my first and last chance to sing a solo part. Sang-Hie looked like she was in pain and at the same time, angry. I saw the same expression on her face years later, when she did not make the May Queen at Kyung-Ki girls' high school.

Sang-Hie taught me how to walk confidently in my coveted Kellybrook penny loafers that she bought for me at the black market with her own money. She believed it would correct my sagging walk in my cheap un-proud sneakers. When I started my period, Sang-Hie also showed me how to fold the sanitary napkins and how to wash them with lye soap.

Growing up, every word of advice Sang-Hie gave me became a word to live by. Almost a decade passed, and it wasn't until she left for America that I realized just how much Sang-Hie did for me.

12

"Mom, can I have one hundred won for an offering?" I yelled, slipping my feet into the rubber shoes the maid had scrubbed squeaky clean and drained overnight.

"I don't have any change right now," Mom answered. "It's OK not to give any money today. God doesn't always want your money."

"But everyone pays money," I insisted. "Even the poor kids."

Mom opened the clasp of her alligator bag and tossed me a 50-won coin.

"I can't give a coin, Mom. Give me a paper bill." I argued some more, but left with a coin in my hand. I liked going to church and it was important to me that I paid at least one hundred won when they came around with the pouch that looked like a velvet insect net.

Sang-Won started going to the junior high school services at Jung-Dong Methodist church in her proud Kyung-Ki uniform. She suggested that I join the children's Sunday school next door. Sang-Won and I walked to the church every Sunday together until the church changed the junior high group's meeting time to an earlier time.

In Sunday school, there were kids from other nearby schools like Suh-Dae-Moon Elementary and even as far as Chong-Ro, which gave us a chance to compare the recess activities and games played at other schools. For some reason, kids liked to talk to me. I was often the center of a big circle of kids whispering and giggling before the service. If there was gossip, they came to me first. If someone was too poor and had only ten won for an offering, I heard it first. If someone got a whipping the day before for not doing her homework, or got sixty percent in her math class, I heard it first.

I walked along the tall wall to the end of the street to Jung-Dong Methodist Church all by myself. Children's Sunday school was held upstairs (we used to call it the Upper Room) in the flimsy two-story wooden structure on the left side of the church property. The main sanctuary on the right was a brick building and the pastor's residence was slightly set back in between the two structures. In the summer, zinnias and dahlias bloomed in the middle of his garden and the front of the garden was covered with colorful portulakas. Behind the flowers, they grew zucchinis, tall sunflowers and huge leafy castor bean plants. When I entered the gate of the church, the wide, freshly swept courtyard felt perfectly balanced surrounded by these three structures.

I ran upstairs and walked into the service that was already in progress.

"So, seeing her mom so sick and their hut being so deep in the mountain…"

Teacher See-Young Lee, a college student, was telling a story. The entire roomful of about thirty kids sat on the built-in bleachers and sighed. I sat quietly in the back row and listened.

"The little girl bravely ran down the pitch-black mountain road toward the doctor's house. It was a matter of life and death. She had to get her mom's medicine." I opened my eyes wide and ran along with her in my imagination. I wanted to spur her on to the doctor's quickly. "It was rainy and the mountain road was slick. She stumbled and fell. Her dress was soaked. But she only had one thing in her mind—to get her mom's medicine. Nothing would scare her or stop her from running all the way down the hill." Teacher Lee swallowed to catch his breath. "'Doctor! Doctor! Please! My mom needs the medicine, quick.' Her voice echoed off the dark mountain. She banged on the doctor's door and woke up the medicine man. He promptly handed her the magic powdery medicine to cure her mom and free her from her dreadful pain. She bowed and thanked him and headed back to her little hut. As the doctor got back into his bed, he had a nagging, unsettling feeling. He kicked off his blanket and went to the medicine cabinet. He searched through the bottles and labels like a madman." Teacher Lee stiffened his body and widened his eyes.

"'Oh my God!' he shouted as he realized he'd given her the wrong medicine. He had been half asleep when she banged on the door and, by mistake, had given her the arsenic that was positioned at approximately the same location of the cabinet, only on a different shelf. And now, it was too late. She would have given it to her mom by now and it must have dissolved in her stomach already. He didn't know what to do. There was no phone at the girl's house. He couldn't even see straight. Then he remembered that the only person he could turn to—as well as the only person who could perform miracles—was God himself. With rising panic, he began praying. 'Dear Lord, I have made a dreadful mistake. Help me. I don't know where to turn or what to do. The little girl will have given the arsenic to her mom and her mom will be convulsing and soon will die. Do something and do something quick to save her. Otherwise the mother will be dead, I will be sent to jail, and the girl will become an orphan.' He repeated the prayer over and over. Then he cried. He felt helpless and scared. All he could do was pray to God. But his extreme anxiety got worse and worse. He continued to pray. In a deep despair he got down on his knees. 'I promise I will live the rest of my life serving you, if you would only save her mom by undoing my careless mistake.'"

"The streams of his tears blurred his vision and he was becoming weaker. He paced as he prayed and sobbed. He stood by the window and looked up to the black sky through the pouring rain, holding his hands together in prayer. Just then, through the window, he saw a small figure flit by his direction. Without thinking, his eyes followed the black figure. Just then there was a loud knock on his door. 'Oh dear Jesus, I hear the police at the door now,' he thought. 'They have come to arrest me for murder.' He prayed again. 'I will even go to jail gladly if you will just keep her from dying.' Then he heard the shrill cry of the young child."

"'Please open the door. Please! Doctor!' a screaming from outside continued. 'I'm so sorry. I ran so fast to give my mom the medicine and just as I got to the door, I tripped and fell and spilled all the medicine. Doctor, doctor. Could you please make me another batch of the medicine please?'"

My Sunday school teacher See-Young Lee mimicked the little girl banging the door with his eyes closed. I was completely spellbound by the story, my mouth dried and my eyes wide open. Everyone in the entire room sobbed and cheered as the story ended with the doctor hugging her and giving her the good medicine.

Teacher See-Young Lee taught me a valuable lesson in the power of prayer. His emotional story taught me to have faith in God. I learned to pray to God when I felt sad, lost, or worried, because I knew God wanted me to come to Him and talk to Him as my own father. He was the Lord. He was the almighty God. And he loved me so much that he sacrificed His only son for me.

Kids at Sunday school put on a pageant for the Christmas Day service at Jung-Dong church displaying Mary and Joseph and the Magi bowing to the baby Jesus in the barn. Teachers See-Young Lee, Ki-Bock Lee and Sung-Hwal Park directed the show and Kyung-Yul Lee conducted the choir. I was in both parts of the Christmas pageant. I didn't know what virgin meant, but I believed everything the teachers said about Mary giving birth to Jesus by miracle. I wanted to hear more and more stories about Jesus. I invited neighborhood kids to church, bragging about the stories our teachers told us.

I took a friend from my neighborhood to a service one year at Christmastime. Her family was Buddhist and her mom would have been furious if she ever found out. I told her that Jesus loved everyone, and He would make sure that her mom wouldn't punish her. We sat at the end of the pew in the big sanctuary and I showed her to bow her head down for a few seconds of silence. It was the first thing we were instructed to do by our Sunday school teachers.

"Close your eyes and try to feel God's presence," I said to her.

"What do you mean, feel God's presence? Do I have to?"

"Yes, you do. That's what you do in church."

"It's called *mook-do*. You don't have to hold your palms together like you are praying. Just be silent. That's all."

Obediently, she did exactly that and made sure she didn't open her eyes before I did, all in an anticipation of hearing stories I had built up to her. But there was no storytelling that day. Instead, the teachers handed out boxes of gifts that had come from America.

Teacher Kyung-Yul Lee placed a cigar box on my lap and another that resembled a shoebox on my friend's lap. In my box, there was chewing gum, barrettes, bobby pins and the tiniest gold safety pins all linked together. The best was a mechanical pencil and a small wire bound notepad, so the pad could flip all the way around.

I closed the lid quickly and sighed. I didn't want anyone to see them. I felt so rich. It was unimaginable to have so many wonderful items in one box. I wanted to keep my newly attained treasure tight in the box.

"What did you get?" my friend asked me.

"Oh not much of anything," I answered. "What did you get?"

"I can't believe what I have. Do I get to keep it all, really?" She covered her mouth and could hardly breath.

In her box, there were pencils and a yellow box of crayons (the kind you can only get at the black market), a whole row of barrettes clipped on a piece of stiff paper, small notebooks like mine except she had more than one. And even a small handheld game of numbers. I wished she would share something I didn't have in my box with me, since I was the one who brought her to the church. "Wow. Of course, you get to keep all of them," I said, but couldn't smile. I wanted to cry. It was much better than my cigar box.

There were no stories that day. Our teachers told us to go home and enjoy our presents. My friend and I walked back home on the sidewalk, along the tall wall, and she examined the contents of her box over and over.

That was the end of her church experience. I thought of her every time I passed by her house on my way to church, but I never stopped again to see if she might be interested in going. Her mom died of stomach cancer the following month, and her father said that she was never to show her face at a Christian church again.

Teachers at the Sunday school took turns telling us stories. I learned the importance of keeping a Bible close to you from the teacher Ki-Bock Lee. Mr. Ki-Bock Lee was the best at mimicking voices and putting emotions into his storytelling.

"It was during the American Civil War," he began, with his roaring voice, attempting to set the scene of a war. "Soldiers lined up and marched and fired to the command of the captain. One by one, each row fell to the ground and pretty soon there was nothing but dead bodies and blood all over the field." Ki-Bock Lee aimed an imaginary gun and closed one eye to focus toward a target.

"James, a young soldier lay passed out on top of another body. When he came to, he looked around and found out there was not a living person in sight. He was covered with blood and his legs were underneath a dead soldier. He pushed the heavy body off his legs and checked himself, amazed that he was not injured. He was covered with blood, but it wasn't his blood. He felt his head and his hair. It was all there. 'But how am I alive?' When he reached for his heart to make sure he was breathing, he felt something hard. He pulled a small leather-bound New Testament out of his pocket. It was ripped and a bullet had burst the pages, but the back cover was intact. James then realized the Bible had protected his heart. He took a deep breath. That small Bible was the last gift he'd received from his mother. He had carried it in his pocket and read a scripture a day. There were days when he didn't have time to read but by keeping God's word close to his heart, he felt comforted knowing that God was with him."

The room was silent and Mr. Ki-Bock Lee finished the story with a prayer in which he asked God to open our young hearts to receive Him, and that He would help us make a habit of reading a Bible verse every day.

Mr. Ki-Bock Lee was a gentle person, but he scared me one day. The kids were gathered in the Upper Room looking for a seat on the bleachers, talking, giggling, laughing, and ignoring the teachers' repeated attempts to calm us down.

"Please find a seat and sit silently to get ready for the worship service," the teachers repeated. But the room became more chaotic. Now the boys were standing on the bleachers throwing paper airplanes.

"Stop it."

All at once, we heard a loud smack of a yardstick against the front bleacher. I turned to see Mr. Lee in extreme anger. He rolled up his pant leg, turned his back to us, and placed his foot on the bleacher, and whipped his own calf like a madman.

"It is my responsibility to lead these young hearts into God's presence. I deserve to be punished. Lord, punish me for allowing this unruly and disorderly conduct in your house. Let the children realize you love them and allow them to understand your desire to fill their hearts with the Holy Spirit." He sobbed and muttered as he kept whipping. His leg started bleeding.

I felt sad, guilty, and sympathetic toward him. At the same time, I was confused. Was what we did so sinful that he had to beat himself so severely? I sobbed with him. I wanted to say we were sorry but I was too scared to say a word.

These Sunday school teachers were young college students who devoted their lives to teaching our young tender minds and preparing them to receive God's love. Their stories planted the seed of faith and trust in my heart; a seed as small as a mustard seed, waiting to sprout. I didn't know it then, but one day I would learn of God's love for me and of the power of prayer through my own experiences.

13

The evening was perfect for staying inside as the summer torrential rains showed no signs of letting up. Mom brought the round dining table to the middle of the *an-bang* to enable all of us to sit around it and do our homework. When we finished our homework, we were to read ahead to prepare for the next lesson. Mom sat between us, using Father's Swiss army knife to make a stack of freshly sharpened pencils. Rain pounded on our roof, ran down the window, and splashed in puddles all around the house. The intermittent thunder made us flinch and move closer to each other.

"*An-maaa! An-maa!*" (Massage! Massage!) We all stiffened at the sound of the slow, deliberate murmur of a blind masseur. It resonated eerily between the pouring and pounding. Rainy nights like this brought out aches and pains in many people and they wanted massages. Blind people made the best masseurs because they had such a perceptive sense of touch. My parents never used them, but I heard from the kids at school that their parents regularly employed them. To me, there was something very creepy about it, and hearing them on rainy nights made it doubly spine chilling.

We worked in silence until we heard a soft knock at the front wooden gate and a very soft voice, barely audible. "*Yu-bo-se-yo*, Would you open the door please?"

"Someone at the door?" We all looked around at each other quizzically.

"Did you call a blind masseur, Ma?" My brother asked.

"No, I have no idea who it is." Mom got up to open the door and we all followed her.

"Who is it?" Mom hollered standing in the hallway.

"Uhh..It's... I am...Please help me." Mom scurried to open the door at a woman's soft pleading voice.

In the dark, standing closely to the door underneath the overhang above the gate, was a woman. She had both of her hands behind her supporting a bundle.

"Who are you? What's the matter?" Mom asked, leading her through the courtyard into the entry hall. They continued a soft conversation at the entryway. Mom then brought a young woman of about Sang-Soon's age into the living room and untied her baby from the wet wrapper blanket. Mom asked if she had eaten.

"It's OK. Thank you," the woman said. She stared at the floor while she spoke to my Mom, repeatedly stealing looks at us.

"My husband and I... lived in the countryside with my in-laws but he... died a few months ago, two months after my baby was born, from an illness... no one could figure out. And his family had rejected me and my daughter. They blamed me... for his death. They said that I.. brought bad luck to their family. I have been wandering looking for a place to stay and... someone told me that I must go to Seoul to be a maid. At least then I will have a place to sleep and eat. I know I have a baby but I can do all the work carrying her on my back."

"Where are your own parents?" Mom asked.

"They never made it out of North Korea. I lived with a distant relative until I was arranged to marry my husband. The family I lived with told me not to come back once I married into my husband's family, on account that a girl is a 'foreigner in her own home once married.' I was not welcome back."

Her hair was combed back into a bun, the sign of a married woman.

It showed off her clean blemish-free complexion. She bounced the crying baby a couple of times and the baby calmed.

Mom invited them to stay at our house in the maids' room until she could find an appropriate home for her, since we already had two maids. Jung-Hee, the baby, quickly became the center of our attention. My sister, Sang-Soon loved to cuddle her and often fed her at the table with us. Normally, the maids ate their meals in the kitchen. I so wished she was my little sister. Every day, I came straight home from school, excited to see Jung-Hee.

Jung-Hee crawled as fast as she could on her chubby legs and arms when her mother would take her off her back. But every time Jung-Hee crawled away, her mom quickly smacked her bottom and picked her up.

"Don't get away from me. This is not your house. You need to be still and don't bother anyone here."

"Does she miss her *abuji*?" I asked, watching her grab Jung-Hee.

"No, she doesn't. I don't either." She waited a second and continued. "I despise him. Why did he have to die and leave us helpless?"

"But he was sick, wasn't he? He didn't mean to die. It's his family who was mean."

"Well, actually, I don't blame them. Even the fortune teller told them that I was a bad omen to them." She sighed. "Your mother was so kind to take us in. I will never forget her kindness."

"Do you think you might get married again? So Jung-Hee would have a father?" She looked up in shock at my question, then let out a small sigh and smiled.

"Oh, I will never get married again. No one will take me, a bad omen with a bastard child."

"But she is not a bastard child. She had a father. He couldn't help it if he got sick. Maybe Mom would adopt Jung-Hee so you can get married."

"Oh no. She is my life. I won't ever give her up. I would rather die than lose her."

Later that night I told Mom about the conversation June-Hee's mom and I had.

"You have to stop meddling. Be a child and stay away from adult business."

"But Mom, she thinks she is a bad omen. There is no such thing."

Mom said nothing, but I knew that no one as sweet and gentle as her could bring about disasters.

Jung-Hee's mom was clever at sewing and embroidering. During the time she lived with us in the maid's room, she mended all of our lost buttons, sewed up ripped hems, and lengthened pants and skirts we grew out of. Every morning, she would have all of my sisters' and brother's uniforms ready, neatly ironed.

After a few months, Mom sent both Jung-Hee and her mom to her friend's family who needed a maid and a wet nurse. It turned out Jung-Hee's mother had plenty of milk and she was able to work as a wet nurse as well as housekeeper. We were sorry to see them go. For weeks after they were gone, we talked about Jung-Hee at dinner, and I no longer looked forward to coming home from school.

I saw Jung-Hee again almost five years later when I was in junior high school. Mom took me with her on her visit to their rented room. Jung-Hee's mom still possessed the same soft dispositions except she now smiled when she spoke. In the golden *on-dol* floor, Jung-Hee sat next to the terracotta fire brazier crunching on something in her mouth.

Her mother stopped knitting and welcomed us. She had been knitting sweaters and even coats in all designs to order. Her customers increased by the day and she couldn't make them fast enough. She no longer had to work as a maid. In addition to the knitted items, she made embroidered tablecloths, piano covers, and stereo covers.

Mom admired and praised her work and Jung-Hee's mother insisted that we stay for dinner. I could see that life was good and she and Jung-Hee were content.

"If it hadn't been for you, I would have still been wandering on the street. Who knows what might have happened to me? I owe it all to you,

Mother." She called my mother "Mother." "And who knows what might have happened to Jung-Hee?"

Their room was clean and tidy but sparsely furnished with only a few items on the floor. Every item on the floor had white embroidered linen covers, even the bedding stacked in the corner. A black leather-bound Bible rested on the table over the beautifully embroidered table cover.

While they were visiting, Mom told me to take Jung-Hee out to the yard to play. Jung-Hee stopped crunching and got out her jump rope.

"Do you want to go outside and jump rope?" she asked.

"Sure, I will. Will you show me how?" I took the five-year-old's hand.

Then as if it had just occurred to her, Mom asked, "Jung-Hee *umma-yah*, what was she eating by the fire brazier?"

"Oh, she loves to eat burned charcoal. She would stir around the ashes when it is cooled with the long chopsticks and picks the smallest ash-colored ones and eats it. I can't stop her. I figure her body must need it. At times, she crunches it so deliciously, she makes me want to try it." She laughed brightly.

"Seriously? She eats charcoal?" Mom was awestruck.

"I know. It's strange, isn't it?" Jung-Hee's mother answered casually.

"Did you ask a doctor?"

"Well, I suppose I should."

When we left their house, Jung-Hee's mother gave Mom a gold-colored knit sweater and told me to bring all my embroidery assignments for my school project. She told me that she would finish it up for me in no time. Jung-Hee followed us and clutched on my arm and said, "*Unni*, will you come back and play jump rope with me again?" I felt a sudden surge of overwhelming longing to be her older sister. All my life I wanted to have a little sister to love and to carry on my back. And to share my most precious possessions, like the ones I used to keep in my Whitman Sampler box.

Suddenly it made sense to me that Sang-Hie didn't want to leave me to go to Kang-Ghe with Auntie when I was born. In some ways, I wished Jung-Hee's mother was not so skillful. A little part of me was wishing that they still depended on us like the rainy night they knocked on our door. Even though I knew deep down that I could never be her older sister, I was elated to be called "*unni*," older sister, for the first time in my life and hoped she would call me *unni* the next time I would see her again.

But the next time never happened.

About a year later, Jung- Hee's Mom showed up at our door knocking softly, just as soft as the first time on that rainy night. Her eyes were swollen and her face looked pallid like the first night, but without a baby on her back. She bowed to my mother deeply and said lifelessly, "Jung-Hee died from an illness nobody could figure out. Just like her father."

For the first time, I knew what a breaking heart felt like. Realizing that I would never see her innocent face again and never hear her call me *unni* again, my heart felt like it was exploding to pieces.

Why does God take a little girl like her? What had her Mom done to deserve two unexplainable deaths of two people she loved more than her own life?

With friends from Seoul Yego, on Ewha campus after school
Sang-Eun is standing right of Mr. Cho.(middle)
Mr. Park is on the right

Sang-Eun in junior high school
I am not wearing the school badge.

On Ewha campus under cosmos
Sang-Eun, right, with Jin-Hee.

With Young-Hae, right

From left, Sang-In, Mom, grandfather, Second grandmother

Debut concert with KBS Symphony Orchestra, 1961

Reception after the debut concert
Front from left, Mom, Mr. Lim Won-Sick, Sang-Eun, Mr. Kim
Back, Sang-In, his date, two friends, cousin, Sang-Hie, Sang-Soon

My friends came to see me off on September 14, 1965.
Kimpo Airport
From left, Kyung-Hee, Ko-Sook, Sang-Eun, Min Kim.

Sang-Eun and Mr. Kim, her cello teacher in Korea
September 14, 1965, Kimpo Airport.

14

My grandfather had a steady *gi-seng* named Cho-Sun who visited him regularly. I always knew when she was coming because right after breakfast my grandfather would dress up in his brocade silk jacket and pace the front yard with his hands locked behind his back and a smirk on his face.

My mother rushed around getting ready for her English class or her monthly ladies *ghe* (investment club). She always made sure she had some kind of appointment when Grandfather had his *badook,* checker party.

"Don't go near Grandfather's room. He is expecting lots of company today and he doesn't need to have you bothering him or his friends. And Cho-Sun will be here today to pour him drinks, too," Mom warned me before she left.

"And go change into a clean dress and put a flowery barrette in your hair," she said. "You don't want to look grubby to his guests."

I didn't understand why I had to look presentable if I was to stay away from them. I always got the impression my mom didn't appreciate my grandfather taking over the *sarang-bang* when my father invited him to live with us.

"Don't bother the maids either. They will be busy making *anju* for Grandfather," she added, rolling her eyes and making a face. *Why is she so short with me?* I wondered. I never bothered the maids anyway. I also didn't understand why she disapproved of my grandfather having a checker party when she wasn't even home on those days.

My grandfather had his best suit on. His sleeves were half-moon shape, tight at the wrist and wide at the elbow, forming big pockets when he put his hands together across his stomach. He kept his money in those pockets and sometimes a wad of perforated toilet paper for tissue. The V-neck was lined with a narrow white collar, freshly starched, and his silk jacket had two huge genuine amber buttons. I loved to touch the dangling amber buttons and feel their smoothness. Sometimes I would look through them or swing them back and forth until he would growl at me to get away from him.

As a ten-year-old, I had enormous curiosity about Cho-Sun. I'd never actually seen her since she usually came around while I was in school. I wondered where she lived, if she had a mom, or if she was a mom. Has she ever been married? If so, why did she come to our house? Does she sing and play the *ka-ya-keum*, the traditional Korean instrument *gi-seng* play? Where did she meet my grandfather? Did my grandfather used to go to where she worked so she could pour a drink for him and maybe sleep with her? And most of all, would she sleep with him now? But none of these questions would be answered today. I had already been told to remain unseen in my clean dress.

The house smelled like bitter bark from the black herbal medicine Mom had been brewing all morning. It was a long and laborious process to brew, but my father insisted that my mom brew the precious *han-yak* (Chinese herbal medicine) herself for my grandfather.

My father would go to the Chinese herbal clinic where the herbalist would pick the best combination of ginseng, shaved deer antlers, and half a dozen kinds of different herbs. If there was enough money, he would even include a tiny piece of a bear belly button or bear gallbladder.

At home, Mom would begin to brew this very expensive pouch full of mystery in a small earthen pot with a handle over an earthen charcoal stove. It needed to simmer constantly, but not boil over, so she ordered the maid to watch it and never leave the pot. The good-quality black herbal medicine was rare and it was a special treat for him. It was supposed to keep him young and healthy for another ten years at least. We were expected to put up with the gagging smell of it.

Today, at his checker party, he was getting the medicine and Cho-Sun. It must have been a really special day.

Once Mom had the medicine brewing, she put the maid in charge of fanning the fire and Mom checked on her periodically.

"Keep the lid closed so it won't evaporate and make sure it doesn't boil over," she said. "And for God's sake! Stop fanning so much!" She narrowed her eyes toward my grandfather's room, showing her discontent about having to go through this ordeal.

When Mom finally took the mystery pouch out of the pot, she hung it on two sticks and twisted the sticks until she squeezed out every last drop. After boiling for a few hours, the heavy cotton burlap bag looked dark and even more mysterious. She poured the concoction into a light blue, glazed ceramic bowl on a saucer, and it was ready for him to drink. She then opened the dark-brownish, grayish pouch and distributed its contents to the rest of the family. She said the magical potion was all consumed in the concoction and the contents probably didn't have any nutritional value left, but since it was so expensive, it wouldn't hurt to chew it up well and swallow the darn thing.

I never dreamed of eating the gross stuff but always was the first in line to get the sweet sugar plant, *gam-cho,* which was used to curtail the acrid taste of the medicine. I chewed and chewed and the sweet taste never seemed to disappear. Eventually I would spit it out, because my jaws were tired and aching from chewing.

Mom placed two sugar cubes on the ceramic saucer for the final touch. Then she ordered the maid to serve the magic potion to my grandfather.

"Mom, can I take it to him on a tray? Please, please. I won't spill. I promise." I was desperate to see Cho-Sun.

"Are you crazy?" she said. "You can't bring it to him. You will tip the whole thing over and spill it all. And it's burning hot. You will even burn yourself."

I decided I would just have to wait till Cho-Sun came out of the room to go to the outhouse, or to ask for a drink of water.

After sitting on the top step of the front hall for a while, I went out to the courtyard where I could hear what was going on in Grandfather's room. I heard noise from the clinking of checker chips but the old men were pretty quiet.

I pictured the room full of old men around the small checker table. In my imagination they all looked grungy and smelled of old people. A few of them probably had long pipes hanging out of their clenched mouths. One of my grandfather's cousins, who always arrived first and stayed the longest, had skin that reminded me of Mom's alligator purse. My grandfather said he became that way from smoking a lot of opium when he was younger, and I always wondered if his pipe still had opium in it.

And what was Cho-Sun doing? I knew women didn't play this game. It was a man's game and an old man's game, at that.

I stepped back to the front hall. Mom was all dressed up in her Korean silk suit, carrying her alligator purse with the big jaw clasp.

"Are you going out to Yang-Ji tea room, Mom?" I asked as she got her shoes out of the shoe closet.

"Shhhh, don't talk so loud!" she said.

"Why not, Mom?" I whispered.

"Because those men don't think housewives should go to a tea room," she said, glancing at the closed doorway of my grandfather's room. "They think tea rooms are only for widows or modern women."

"But you are modern, Mom, what's wrong with that?" I wanted her to go out even though I knew my father wouldn't have approved of her going to a tearoom either. I also knew she did anyway, many times.

"Tea rooms are generally full of young and single people," she said. "And they think good, old-fashioned wives belong at home sewing, embroidering, or cooking, not roaming around smoke-filled tea rooms and listening to American love songs."

"You mean, like your favorite song, 'Love is a Many-Splendored Thing?'"

She just smiled as she fixed the barrette that had slid down to the bottom of my hair almost to my shoulder.

After Mom left, my secret wish was granted when the older maid asked me to bring a tray of snacks to Grandfather. Dried shrimp, dried squid, peanuts, and sweet black sesame seed sticks filled the three-legged tray. I picked it up and walked slowly while the maid was watching, but as soon as I turned the corner, I took short quick strides. I slid the door open and carried the tray into Grandfather's room. The combined odor of the gang of old men and the dried fish I was carrying nearly made me throw up.

"You are bringing the *an-ju*?" Grandfather asked.

"Yeah, Grandpa. *Ajuma* said I could." I picked up the tray to bring it close to Grandfather, and took the opportunity to glance at Cho-Sun. Then I took a second look, with my mouth open. I looked back and forth from my grandfather to her.

She was not pretty or glamorous. She even looked old. Her lips were not red and she wore a casual skirt and a blouse. I had imagined a lady in a purple-colored Korean dress with a long green jade stick holding her tightly combed bun at the back of her neck. She didn't smile or acknowledge me.

I suddenly wanted out of the room. I didn't want to look at my grandfather sitting cross-legged on the satin mat and Cho-Sun, next to him with her legs stacked together to one side, with no notable expression on her face. I wished my sisters were home so I could tell them about the disappointment of Cho-Sun, but I was alone.

I plopped myself down onto the top step of the kitchen and stared at the busy maids as I chewed on a piece of a dried squid. I knew my morning was wasted, as were the dried shrimp. I wasn't allowed to have any of the expensive dried shrimp. There was only enough for my grandfather and his very ordinary lady.

15

The snow was piled up along the Shin-Mun-Ro sidewalk. Our maid held my hand to keep me from sliding. I sped up to keep myself warm, my breath forming clouds in front of me. I pulled my muffler up over my face. The wind knifed through my jacket, sweater and long johns into my little body. My wool socks and the sneakers weren't enough to protect my numb feet from the icy sidewalk.

In her other hand, our maid carried my book bag. I could feel her cold bare hand through my glove. I freed my hand from her grip and shoved hers into the pocket of the skirt that she wore over her pants.

"*Ajuma*, I'm ok, I won't fall. Keep your hand in the pocket," I said, looking up at her pink cheeks. Her neck was exposed between her scarf and her sweater. She put my arm in hers and kept her hand in the pocket. I smiled and pulled it away.

"Really, I am ok." I said.

"If you fall, I will be in trouble," she insisted.

I was afraid the kids on the street might notice me walking hand in hand with a maid. Or worse yet, they might think she was my sister or a relative. She must have been wearing three layers of sweaters, each one shorter than the one underneath, green, gray and beige. Her Korean rubber shoes barely covered her socks.

I felt sorry for her because she had to leave her own parents in the countryside and live with us. I didn't know where her parents were and I didn't know why she was working for us, but some of these questions were supposed to be left unanswered. Everyone in my family, especially my brother, didn't think twice about ordering her around.

"Bring me a cup of coffee and hurry," my brother would say. Sometimes he'd even wake her up to fix him dinner when he came home late at night. My mom was not any more considerate than him. When there was a knock at the door, Mom thought nothing of telling her to get it, even if she was in the middle of doing the laundry or cleaning up the house.

All the other kids carried their own school bags, but Mom said now that I was a fifth grader, my book bag was too heavy for me to carry, especially on a cold day like this. Fifth and sixth grades were the most important. I was supposed to spend both years doing nothing but studying for the junior high entrance exam.

At the gate of my school, our maid handed me my bag and headed home. I thought that she must enjoy this morning walk even on a cold day, because it meant she was out of the house and away from my brother.

Walking to the school was the best part of fifth grade for me as well.

A cauldron and a broomstick would have been more appropriate for my fifth grade teacher than a desk and a chalkboard. Her cheeks were covered with pimples and when she got angry, which seemed to happen almost all the time, they turned an even brighter shade of red. Her shoulder-length, permed hair was parted and neatly combed, and there was never a single hair out of place.

Her black hair was tied back tightly today and her lips were painted red. She stood behind the podium in the classroom as we went through our morning ritual of singing the national anthem. There was nothing warm or sweet about her looks, and she never smiled. She never showed any emotion.

"Sit up tall and straight, and do not talk!" she shrieked. Her sharp commands echoed through the classroom and I felt stabbing pains all over my skin like a chilly wind.

"Now close your eyes and concentrate," she said. I never understood what she wanted us to concentrate on. This was one of the things we were just supposed to know. I closed my eyes and thought of my cats at home and thought how lucky they were to be curled into a ball on the warm floor. I thought about all seven cats at home, the black and white mother cat, the five black and white kittens and the calico big sister cat. They were well fed and their fur was silky from our constant petting. The thought of the soft fluffy black and white fur made me smile.

"Sang-Eun Lee, what are you smiling about?" my teacher yelled.

My heart pounded fast.

"I told you to concentrate." The witch woman approached my desk, waving a switch in her hand.

"I am not smiling, Teacher. I was just concentrating."

"Why can't you be smart like your sister? You are less than the dirt between your sister's toes." She poked my chin with the end of the switch. "When you were born, I bet you were a shock to your family in the worst way." She spat out with disgust.

The witch had been Sang-Hie's fifth grade teacher, and in her eyes, Sang-Hie was a gift from heaven. She was a model student who did everything well and made her look good.

This time her words angered me enough that I looked straight at her and blurted out, "Well, my sister is Sang-Hie and I am Sang-Eun. We are two different people!" I burst into tears. "You can't expect us to be exactly the same. Can you now?"

Before I even finished my sentence, her right hand flew across my face. For a fleeting second, I couldn't see straight. My cheek felt as though a thousand bees had stung me. Then I felt another blow and a few more that seemed to go on forever.

Did she actually slap me on my face? I clenched my teeth and tightened my fists. How dare she! Wait until I tell my dad. He will not let her get away with it. In a rage, I sobbed. I despised her.

Weeks went by but I never told anyone about the slapping incident.

I realized I couldn't tell anyone, because I would only be blamed for talking back to a teacher. Each day that went by, I became more fearful of further abuse, all for being less of a student than Sang-Hie. Every day I prayed that God would help me get away from this witch woman.

One day, mid-semester, my prayer was answered miraculously. The witch left our school for some unknown reason. There was a rumor she was either getting married or having a baby. Her replacement was a new teacher from the southern province of Kyung-Sang-Do. He had a strong accent, and as city kids, we were not afraid to mimic him. There was an unspoken understanding that anyone from anywhere other than Seoul was not as elite and polished as we were.

He wore a dark gray suit and nervously introduced himself. "I graduated from college in the province of Kyung-Sang-Do, therefore I do have a southern accent. I am trying to lose it, but it is very hard. Therefore, you will have to forgive me when I speak. Most of the words are the same, but every once in a while I might use a different expression, therefore it might sound funny to you." He went on and on using "therefore" at least a dozen times, making excuses in detail about his speech. I felt sorry for him. He so wanted to be accepted.

Every year, my mother treated my teacher out to a fancy drink and dinner. So this event would have occurred inevitably, but I decided to prompt her.

"Mom, he doesn't know too many people at our school and he needs to be entertained," I said. "Plus, you haven't treated my teachers in a long time." I insisted that she do her annual duty before he had time to form a bad impression of me. But mostly, I wanted to thank him for saving my life by replacing the witch.

Sometimes Mom sent my teachers wrapped gifts like a set of silver spoons and cocktail forks, silk fabric, or sometimes money in an envelope. It was her way of thanking them for taking care of her kids. But in spite of the dinners and gifts Mom sent them, they simply couldn't make me into as good of a student as my siblings.

The new teacher, however, didn't seem to think that I was such a terrible student. At least he didn't know any of my sisters to compare me to. The rest of the year went by without an incident and he actually smiled at me every time our eyes met.

I looked forward to summer vacation. The month of sleeping in and no homework made me forget the endless agony of school. During my fifth-grade summer vacation, I climbed In-Wang Mountain with the neighborhood kids for an insect hunt. Each of us held an insect net in one hand and lunch pail and water bottle in the other. Our back hill would have been good enough to catch a few different kinds of butter-flies or a dragonfly, but we were on a mission to catch rare varieties, and those would only be on the deep untouched mountain—or so we thought.

We walked in our sneakers for almost an hour before we reached the bottom of the mountain. I started getting tired and hungry. "I think we should eat before we start climbing." I was always the first to whine.

"How high do you think we should climb to find insects? I heard butterflies don't fly in the deep mountain. Maybe we should start looking right here," I said.

Since I was the smallest, what I said didn't matter much. We started climbing and I took up the rear. The steep path was slippery and I took each step carefully. There were tiny unknown wildflowers on the way up and lots of white clovers. We all stopped and picked the white flowers and split the soft stem in two. Then we tied them around our middle fingers like we were wearing a huge ring. Everyone had a white puffy flower ring on their fingers and I put a few in my hair with a bobby pin.

When we got up to the top, huffing and puffing, we could see the Ma-Po River on one side, far away. We put our hands to our mouths like a megaphone and yelled, "Hellooooow." Our voices echoed all over the mountain. "Hellow, helloow, hellow."

Standing on top, we could see the rocky side of the mountain covered with moss. A stream seeped through the moss and formed a pool of water at the base of the mountain. There, several women sat pounding their laundry on a flat rock. From where we were standing, they looked like giant ants.

I was in awe of the beauty of the whole mountain. I felt so close to the sky, it made me want to dance and sing. Just then, I saw the most beautiful butterfly. It was flying effortlessly like a rose petal floating in air. I stretched the net and stepped forward to catch the pale yellow flying mystery. I don't know how it happened, but my foot slipped and I started rolling down the mountain, my body and head bumping and hitting rocks, trees, and dirt. I rolled all the way down to where the women were washing clothes.

I thought I had died. When I came to, my head was pounding and I couldn't open my eyes. My clothes were bloody and my nose was stuffed with something. I had a hard time breathing. I saw one of the women ripping her blouse and making a strip to tie on my bleeding forehead. The sky was blocked by the neighborhood kids and women who had gathered around to look down at me. I closed my eyes and felt my head throbbing. I didn't know how long I lay there.

When we finally headed back home, the kids took turns carrying me on their backs. After a few turns from all four of them, I insisted on walking on my own, but they supported my arms and held my hands.

I was ever so disappointed to find no one at home except the two maids. They gave me ABC, the headache medicine, and cleaned me up and told me to lie down in the *an-bang*. The older maid put Mercurochrome all over my arms and legs. She brought a mirror and when I looked into it, I was horrified. My eyes were swollen shut, one cheek was three times bigger than the other and my mouth was ripped and covered with bloodstains. It looked like my mouth was moved to one side. I wailed and sobbed for a while and fell asleep.

My father was usually gone most of the day and evening. Mom said that he had to work long hours in the evening to get the new business going. But when I woke up, my father was sitting next to me with his hand on my forehead. He was the last person I expected to see home, but the one I was most happy to see.

"Daddy, look at me. I slipped on the mountain. I hit the rocks and I bled a lot."

"Shh. I know, I know, dear. You will be all right. Are you hungry? Let's have some soup."

He sat me up halfway and fed me soybean sprout soup in beef broth one spoonful at a time. All evening, he sat next to me and read the newspaper. He told my sisters to be quiet so I could sleep. I felt so important and loved, it almost made me glad that I was hurt.

16

Gasping, I ran into the dark and dreary train station. I pushed through the crowd of people and went to the sign, "TO IN-CHUN." I knew the routine from the many trips Mom and I had made to my grandfather's (her father's) house. Only this time, I had to figure out how to sneak on the train without a ticket. By now, I was too big to pass as a four-year-old to get on free. I was small for an eleven-year-old and I might have passed as eight, but not as four.

I looked around just to make sure no one was following me, but they wouldn't have anyway, because no one knew where I went. I felt a strange mixture of fear and relief but most of all I felt free—free from books, tutors, and from my brother and sisters' ridiculing remarks.

All I wanted was to get away. I didn't care where, as long as I didn't have to face the unbearable anguish of memorizing numbers, years, and names, and away from the stress everyone was putting on me.

I left my book bag and lunchbox in my desk. I even left my coat hanging on the back of my chair. After lunch/play period, when everyone was going back to the class, I casually headed in the opposite direction toward the school gate near the row of toilets. I decided that I would simply say I was going to use the toilet one more time before we went back to the class if anyone saw me. When I came near the gate, I looked back quickly and snuck out of the gate as swiftly as I could. Once outside, I ran all the way to the train station.

They had to know that I was missing by now. My teacher might have called my house, but there wouldn't be anyone there but the maids, and neither of them would have any idea where I might be. I was a little scared, but at the same time I felt triumphant like I had showed them all.

People were lining up to get on the trains. I looked around and examined each person. There was a young woman standing with a train case and high heels. She could have been a runaway like me. Most runaways didn't know where they were going, but I was headed to my grandfather's place in In-Chun, a definite destination. I knew I would be treated well once I got there. My grandfather was a well-known doctor and the head of the state hospital in In-Chun.

A young man got in the line to In-Chun and two old men got behind him. The young man motioned to them to go ahead of him. I thought I had seen him when I first got to the station. He was reading a book, leaning against a post. He looked like he could be someone's favorite uncle. I took a deep breath and swallowed before I approached him.

"Can I ask you something, sir?" I asked hesitantly. "I am going to my grandfather's in In-Chun and I lost all my money. If you will buy me a ticket, I will pay you back as soon as we get there. My grandfather is the head of the In-Chun state hospital. His name is Seung-Soo Kim. You might even know him. He is very well known."

The man looked at me with a little frown on his face, baffled. The two upper pockets on the chest of his navy-blue uniform jacket told me that he was a college student—he might even have been a medical student.

"How old are you and where is your mom?" His eyes were wide open. "Why are you going to your grandfather's all alone?"

I wasn't prepared to answer these questions. "Well, my mom said it was OK to go alone and she gave me the money to buy the ticket but I lost it." I amazed myself. Lies were rolling out of my mouth like I had been practicing. He looked at me as if he was still confused. He waited a second and said, "Do you know how to get to your grandfather's from the train station in In-Chun?"

"Oh yes, I do. But I will just go to his hospital. Everyone knows where the state hospital is. It is the biggest one in the city," I said.

"Just stand here in front of me and don't say anything. I will be right behind you. Just follow everyone and walk through the gate." The kind college man put his hand on my shoulder like I was his little sister. He handed his ticket to the man who was wearing gray gloves that were probably white at one time and he punched a hole on his ticket. The gray-gloved man never even looked at me. Inside the gate, we ran down the staircase to the awaiting trains. There were no designated seats so he said we had to hurry to get a seat.

How could one man be so kind and my own brother so mean? I bit my lips to keep my eyes from tearing as I thought about that morning.

"Mother, what are we gonna do with her? She is so stupid. She had to have been adopted. No one in this family is that stupid," my brother went on and on at the breakfast table. Tears ran down my cheeks and I couldn't say a word.

I knew I was a terrible student because I never got above 90 points in anything—not Korean, math, science, geography, or history. Out of the 80 students in the class, I was anywhere from 30th to 50th in rank. This order changed each week according to the test scores and we were seated in order of our test scores. The first row was from number one to ten. And the second row was from eleven to twenty. I always sat in the third or fourth row. It didn't matter that I was fine with it. I was told over and over by everyone in my family that it was humiliating to sit anywhere but the first row. But no matter how hard I tried, I simply couldn't bring up my scores. Even on the days I thought I had done well, the test results were always lower than I expected.

The worst part was the ragging, mocking, and jeering I had to put up with when I brought the scores home. All three of my sisters and my brother would tell me how immature I was and what a common run-of-the-mill kid I was. Even Sang-Hie, who was usually protective of me, would say things like, "You need to shape up, if nothing else, then for Mother's sake," or, "Do you know that Mom is aging because of you?"

This morning my brother said, "Even the relatives call her 'the-not-so-smart-Lee-girl.' What are we gonna do with her?" He then finished with the most humiliating remark. "No one in this family has failed the entrance exam to the best rated junior high school. Just watch her now. She will ruin the reputation of the Lee family. She won't ever get into Kyung-Ki junior high school."

If I didn't care, why was it so important to everyone else that I went to Kyung-Ki? But talking back to any of them would only result in worse scolding. I had to endure every insult and mockery, all for the crime of not being a good student. I sat there shoveling food into my mouth and getting more and more furious. I wanted to yell, "Leave me alone. I am doing the best I can. And I am not the worst student. There are lots of kids behind me." Instead, I got up and walked out of the room. My brother's scornful remarks were still ringing in my ears.

"Just watch her leave when I am talking. How dare she."

"Oh, go to hell," I mumbled under my breath.

I walked to school, ignoring my mother's caution to look both ways before crossing the street. I wanted to plunge myself right in front of a streetcar. Or better yet, I wanted to wait for the traffic to get real busy so I wouldn't have to pick which car to throw myself in front of. I wondered if my brother would have any remorse if I died.

On the way to school, my head started pounding. I often got migraine headaches and stomach aches that made me throw up all over the desk and the floor. Sometimes my teacher sent me to the nurse's room to rest for the next period and sometimes he sent me home. I never made a big deal out of vomiting–I didn't think I deserved to be pampered.

Immediately after I got to school, the teacher passed out a stack of tests. My head pounded back and forth like I was in a moving boat. Just as I picked up my pencil and read the first question of the daily tests, I started heaving and got violently sick all over the desk. It came out so fast that I didn't even have time to cover my mouth. My teacher was annoyed and sent me to the nurse's office and told me to stay an hour while the other kids cleaned up the mess I had made. The nurse gave me two pills and told me to go to sleep, and that she would wake me up in an hour for the next period. Amazingly my headache was gone when she shook me and I went back to class for third period.

Tired and weak from throwing up and groggy from the morning nap in the nurse's office, I almost wished I was sick again so the teacher would send me home. Back in the class, listening to the noise of pencils scratching at every desk, I wished desperately I could just disappear—go somewhere. That's it, I thought. If I could just run away somewhere, then I would never take another test. The thought kept coming back into my head. Run. Run away from this miserable life. I had to leave to go somewhere. But where? Then I thought, go to In-Chun, to my grandparents. I knew my grandfather would welcome me. He might even tell me not to worry about anything.

I asked Kil-Ja, my best friend, if I could borrow thirty won for bus fare to Seoul Station. When she said that she didn't have it, I decided to run to the train station.

I sat on the train next to the nice college man I wished was my brother. I took a deep breath. I wondered if I caused my mother and father to fight again. My father wanted me to apply to Jin-Myung junior high school like my teacher recommended. As far as he was concerned, Jin-Myung junior high school was an excellent school because they were famous for teaching girls good Korean traditional manners. I wondered if I got my teacher in trouble by the school principal. I decided not to worry about them anymore. What was done was done and I was on the train to see my grandfather.

I thought about what I would say to my grandfather. I will worry about it when I see him, I thought. My heart beat faster with excitement and anticipation of seeing my grandparents.

The college man was talking with an elderly woman he had greeted earlier. I had an impression that they knew each other well. After they exchanged their initial greetings, he told her about me. The woman looked me over from my hair to my shoes and smiled. Then she unwrapped her scarf package and pulled out a sesame-seed-covered taffy stick.

"Would you like one?"

"No, it's OK." It was my favorite kind of taffy but I was always told to decline any offer from anyone, especially any food item. It was not supposed to be polite to accept things so quickly.

"Oh, here, have one. I just bought them in Seoul." I bowed and accepted one and said, "Thank you very much."

She and the college man talked for a while softly and I saw her nodding repeatedly. I thought he asked her to help me. All of a sudden my helper was not my choice any more. I picked him because he looked so gentle. I started to examine her. *She might be OK*, I thought. After all, she gave me taffy. Her beige Korean costume was clean and well pressed. She started fiddling with her package, untying and tying her floral scarf a few times over so the square box of the taffy was securely centered in the scarf. She wrapped a few small bags of ginger on top of the taffy box she bought from a wholesale store in Seoul.

After the hour train ride, we arrived in In-Chun. There must have been six or seven stops on the way and the college man got off at Sosa. Sosa was a community of Elder Park's followers and the village was called Shin-Ang Chon (Zion village). They were a completely self-contained community with their own farms, factories, and stock of animals. But there was something non-Christian about them. I wished he wasn't Elder Park's follower.

"Well, good luck finding your grandfather. This grandmother will help you. I have to get off here." He held my hands with both of his hands and I felt a jolt of pressure on my nose. I wished he could take me to my grandfather's hospital.

The elderly woman told me that she would take me to her house first, then a high school girl would take me to my grandfather's hospital. This high school girl she kept referring to might have been her daughter, although she looked a little too old to have a high-school-aged daughter. I knew it would be impolite to ask. Adults didn't seem to like kids asking questions. "It's none of your business. Stop interrogating," I was told many times when I was simply curious.

She picked up her long skirt and reached into a pocket on her bloomers. She then took out a piece of paper and wanted me to write my grandfather's name.

"Is it OK if I write it in Korean?" I asked squeamishly. I was ashamed that I didn't know how to write my grandfather's name in Han-Moon, Chinese characters. Han-Moon was another subject in school that gave me a headache.

Their house was a small Korean-style home. Right inside the front door was a tiny dirt courtyard and in the courtyard was a well with a wooden roof over it. A dried gourd ladle was hanging on one of the posts holding up the roof. The dirt courtyard was immaculately swept and showed broom prints.

She asked me to come into the house as she led the way, bending under the cloth line.

"I think I can find the hospital from here," I said politely.

"No, just wait, she will be here in any minute."

I didn't want to go in or wait for her. I felt uncomfortable receiving hospitality from this family who seemed so much less affluent then my family. I felt somewhat superior to them and going in there and waiting for her might be stooping to their level. But little girls weren't supposed to argue with adults. I went into the house bowing and said, "Thank you very much."

We were supposed to bow for everything. We bowed when we saw anyone older than us. We bowed when we said, "Thank you." We bowed when we said, "You are welcome." We bowed when we said, "How are you?" We bowed when we said "Goodbye."

Bowing itself didn't bother me at all. And it was easy to do. But I was supposed to bow my head down if an older person said anything in an advising manner. I was supposed to know what not to ask and what not to mention. This made me utterly confused. So I preferred to keep my mouth shut rather than get into trouble.

I must have sat in their small room on the *on-dol* floor for fifteen minutes before the high school girl came home. The girl called the older woman "Mom" and the women told her that she needed to take me to the state hospital to meet my grandfather. She then left to deliver her ginger and taffy. The high school girl looked at me with a big smile. *These people are all so very nice*, I thought.

"Well, all right then. I will take you. Just give me a second to change. I gotta get out of this school uniform." She talked and moved like a tomboy. She must have been born in the year of the horse, like my sister, Sang-Won. In fact, she even looked a little like my sister. She changed right in front of me and I turned around to give her a little privacy. She took off her navy-blue skirt and put on a pair of jeans. Blue jeans were expensive and hard to acquire since they were only sold at the black market. I looked at her jeans and made a mental note to tell my sisters about her blue jeans with the red plaid cuffs.

"Are you hungry?" she asked. "Right around the corner, there is a wonderful noodle soup place. We will stop there first so you can eat something."

"No, I am not hungry at all. And I probably should go quickly before my grandfather goes home from the hospital."

"But it won't take but a minute. You shouldn't go hungry. Anyway, you gotta taste their noodle soup. It is yummy." She made a gesture like she was eating with her chopsticks and drinking the soup.

We left their house and headed for the hospital. I was glad because I didn't know how to get there. I had intended to ask anyone on the street and walk to the hospital no matter how far it was.

"Is it very far from here?" I asked.

"No, not at all. We will walk. We won't need to take the bus."

She held my hand. Now I really felt like a runaway. I hoped that she would notice that I was well dressed in knit pants and a matching sweater. I felt a terrible urge to talk about my sisters and boast how they went to Kyung-Ki and Ewha girls' high schools. And how they were all on the honor roll and how they were so talented. But I didn't, feeling her strong grip on my hand.

When we stopped at the small one-man noodle shop, he very cheerfully said, "Come in, come in. You brought a little friend today?" He
then started ladling the soup in a bowl for the noodles. The shop had
two long picnic tables and as I sat at one, my feet dangled from the
bench. I stared down at the dirt floor of the shop. Even though I was a
little hungry, what he was making didn't look very appetizing. He was
ready to add the cooked vegetables.

"Oh, wait. I am sorry, I didn't bring any money. I just changed into
these jeans and forgot all my money was in my uniform pocket." She
waved her hands. For some reason, being in the noodle shop and being
in the care of the strange high school girl and the cheerful shop owner
made me feel lonely. Everything seemed so foreign to me and I wasn't
sure if I wanted to be a part of it.

As we left the noodle shop, the sun was going down and I began to
feel chilly. The streets looked unfamiliar and I felt like crying. I hoped
Grandpa would be happy to see me and Grandma would make it all
better for me. He was a gentle, loving man who loved children. In a
society where being physically affectionate was unnatural, he always
expressed his fondness by hugging or kissing us on top of our heads.

When we turned into a wide street behind the exhaust of a bus, the
high school girl said goodbye to me and pointed to the hospital.

"Aren't you going to come in with me?" I wanted my grandfather
to thank her.

"No, I gotta go. I got loads of homework. You are sure this is the
hospital, right?"

"I am sure. I've been here lots of times before." I bowed to her and
thanked twice. I ran up the second floor where my grandfather's office
was and ran into the room without knocking on the door.

"Grandpa, I am here."

"Oh my, my baby is here, come and give Grandpa a hug." I knew he
would be happy to see me.

"Where is your mom?" He asked, looking at the door behind me.

"She is not here. I came alone."

"What? You didn't come all the way here alone, did you? Your mom wouldn't let you come all the way here all by yourself." He walked out the door looking for my mom. This time his face was a little stern.

"What happened? What are you doing here?"

"I—I—uh—just came. I left school at lunchtime and came."

"You what?" The fear and shock on his face scared me and I quickly said, "Grandpa, let's go to your house. I want to see Grandma and take a bath next door."

Every time we were there grandma wanted us to jump in the hot tub at the bathhouse next door. Most homes didn't have hot water out of the faucet and being able to take a hot bath anytime was a treat.

Grandpa picked up the phone and called Grandma and she soon showed up to take me home to their house. By then, they had already called the college where my Mom was teaching and Grandpa had stopped smiling.

When I got to their house and got in the bathtub, Grandma came in and sat by the tub fully dressed.

"Tell me, baby, what happened? Did your brother hit you?"

"No, he didn't."

"Well then what happened? Tell Grandma."

I loved this grandma of all the grandmas. She was the one who carried me on her back during the war from the big house in Choong-Jung-Ro.

"Nothing, Grandma. I just had to come here. I didn't want to study. I am tired and I don't want to go to junior high school. It's too hard."

"Humm. Yeah, it's hard," she said. Thankfully, she didn't ask me any more questions.

Unlike our house with a courtyard between the front gate and the entry, their house had a huge window facing the street in the front. In the past when we visited him, my grandfather would open the windows to let the fresh air in while they folded up their bedding in the morning. As soon as the windows were open, the neighborhood children would run over to him and plop themselves on his lap. Grandfather would check their tonsils or ears, telling them to clean behind their ears or wash their hair more often. They lingered until their moms came and grabbed them apologetically.

While I waited for dinner to be served, I went upstairs to the patients' overnight rooms. The first room off the stairs was the biggest, and it was the room my mom had stayed in when she came for her surgery. She brought me along, probably because she couldn't leave me at home. The maids' jobs were mainly to cook and clean but not to take care of the kids.

The room was set up exactly the same as when Mom stayed after her hemorrhoid surgery. I remembered so clearly how my heart ached as I watched Mom moaning in pain. I stayed up all night standing at the foot of her bed waiting for her to request for water or for the bedpan. The nurses were sleeping next door, but I was afraid they might not hear Mom's soft voice so I stayed up all night.

I was fearful she might never recover. At one point, Mom made an agonizing sound and asked me to wake up the nurses. She was dying to urinate but was not able to go. I banged on the next door and one of the nurses quickly brought a bedpan.

"She couldn't go in it. What will happen to her?" I panicked.

The nurse went downstairs to wake up my grandpa. Grandpa rubbed his eyes and said it was normal. He then put what looked like a long, clear, thin rubber hose into her.

"Sang-Eun-ah, go downstairs and sleep with grandma. You don't need to be here." His matter-of-fact way scared me even more. Grown-ups always told children to go away when things got serious or interesting. I stood by the door and watched the kidney shaped aluminum pan fill with yellow liquid.

I stared at the bed where she was lying; remembering her face, pale in pain. "I am sorry Mom. I am not so clever as you think," I mumbled.

"What the heck are you doing here? Don't tell me your Mom let you come here alone. You ran away, didn't you?" A loud voice startled me and I jumped like I had been caught stealing. My cousin Dae-Sung was standing behind me at the doorway in a tank top showing his muscles.

He was holding dumbbells like he was working out. He had been living with my grandparents since his father, my mother's younger brother who was a boys' high school principal, kicked him out of his house. He failed the entrance exam to a junior high school and spent all of his time hanging out at the karate studio befriending all the wannabe gangsters. I had made up my mind that for an educator, my uncle made a very poor decision because living with my grandparents was more of a treat than a punishment.

I was stunned how quickly he figured out that I ran away. I didn't want to answer his scoffing but I did feel an unexplainable camaraderie because he was sent here for the same reason I was here—he didn't want to study.

"At least I came here on my own, I wasn't kicked out like you were," I said sharply.

"Well, I tell you what! You will never make it into Kyung-Ki. Your mom is dreaming. You are stupid. And you even have one bad eye."

At that, I darted to his chest and pounded him with both fists with all my might.

As far as I was concerned, he was as mean and bad as they came—he might even be worse than my brother.

"And this is my house. Grandpa is my grandpa. You are only a girl from his daughter. Do you think Grandpa really cares about you and your siblings?" he added.

All of a sudden, I felt sick and wanted to throw up. His words penetrated my heart like a knife.

Unlike other typical Korean daughters-in-law, my mother refused to give her soul and body to her in-laws. And she came and went as she pleased to her father's house without her father-in-law's permission. Still, I always knew that Dae-Sung and his siblings considered my grandparents' house as their own and we knew that all of my grandparents' inheritance would go to them. They were the ones who would carry the Kim name. This made me feel a step removed, and I couldn't claim my grandparents as close as I would have liked, since we were only their maternal grandchildren.

All throughout dinner I gave my cousin the evil eye and waited for my grandfather to ask what happened, so I would have a chance to get him in trouble without having to snitch on him voluntarily. He sat with his back slightly rounded and never said a word, shoveling the food into his mouth with only his undershirt on, holding his chopsticks midway like a peasant. He reminded me of hired help.

Just when I finally took my eyes off of him in disgust my grandfather said, "Dae-Sung-ah, next time you need to put something decent on at the dinner table. Don't show up to eat in your undershirt again."

He didn't answer my grandfather. He only got up to go to his room, which was one of the patient's rooms upstairs, leaving the empty rice bowl with his chopsticks balanced on top.

That night at bedtime, Grandmother started spreading the *yo* in the front room. The upstairs rooms were still too cold to sleep in, and fuel was too expensive. Two rooms downstairs had heated floors.

Grandmother spread the matching colorful dragon-patterned silk quilts for Grandfather and herself. Then she made a cozy bed for me next to her. Dae-Sung's bed was to the left side of me.

The thought of sleeping next to him made me sick, but I was in no position to complain about the sleeping arrangement. By the time Dae-Sung came downstairs, he was in a good mood, smiling.

"The chamber pot is right outside of the room in the hallway." Grandmother pointed to the hallway and I wondered if she knew I wet my bed not too long ago.

I lay with the quilt tight around my neck facing my grandma. I thought about what might have gone on in my class this afternoon after lunch. I pictured my teacher's angry face questioning my best friend, Kil-Ja, for any clue as to where I might have gone.

I woke up from a deep sleep when I felt something touching my lower body and felt a slight draft. Still hazy from a deep sleep, I wasn't sure what was happening. I then realized Dae-Sung had already brazenly unbuttoned my long underwear and was ready to push his penis toward me over my underpants. I wanted to scream and wake up my grandparents. Instead, I abruptly turned around toward Grandma. I was upset and humiliated but was afraid my grandparents might get mad that I did something wrong by not waking up immediately or for sleeping next to him.

Realizing I woke up, Dae-Sung grabbed my upper arm and tried to turn me around toward him. I lay stiff and pretended to sleep with my eyes tightly closed. As he tried to turn me forcefully, I turned my shoulder away from him briskly toward Grandma. My upper body hit Grandma and she patted my back a few times in her sleep.

I was quiet the next morning at the breakfast table. I wondered if my grandma knew anything and when I saw Dae-Sung he pretended nothing happened. I wondered if it was all a dream.

I felt ashamed, confused, and guilty. I ran away and imposed rudely on total strangers who were poor, against everything my parents taught me. The shame compounded with anxiety for making my mother worry and age. And now, the bad behavior of this evil cousin was weighing heavily in my heart. I missed Mom, and though I didn't want to go home to Seoul, I didn't want to stay here either.

When Grandpa got dressed in his gray Western suit to leave for the hospital, he took out his wallet. I didn't expect him to give me a daily allowance.

"Is this about what your mom gives you in the morning?" Before I answered, he took out a hundred won with his soft wrinkly hands and handed it to me. As he did, he smiled and gave me a light squeeze on my cheek. Aside from his dark, bushy eyebrows, he reminded me of my mother. Standing up with his feet apart and his toes slightly outward, their postures were alike, too. All at once I missed my mom. I was sorry I ran away. I wished I could undo yesterday's escapade. However, at the moment, I didn't have to study and for that matter, I was glad.

A hundred won could buy a lot of things. A bag of candies was ten won. In the summer, a Popsicle from a street vendor was ten won. Ice cream was only thirty won. He certainly didn't expect me to go buy a notebook or a pencil, I didn't think. It was all to buy snacks and buy comic books, neither of which was allowed by my parents.

Midmorning after my grandpa went to work I followed Grandma to Grandpa's hospital. He wanted to examine my throat because I was always getting sick.

"Grandma, does my mom know that I am here?" On the way, I finally unloaded my dreadful curiosity.

"Tee hee. Do you really want to know?"

"Yes, I do. I just think Mom needs to know I am not as smart as she thinks I am."

"Well, then why didn't you tell her that?"

"I tried. But she always says that I am not trying hard enough. I try so hard. Do you know that I sleep only six hours a day? And my school has a real high standard? I would be the smartest at any other school."

"Hmm." Grandma gave another moan and never told me if my mother knew that I was at their house safely.

When we walked into Grandpa's office, he was talking to my mom on the phone.

"Tell her teacher she needs to have a tonsillectomy. Yeah? Tell him whatever you want. I don't know what? She can even go to junior high school here in In-Chun. Yeah? What's the difference?" Grandpa never raised his voice on the phone, but he convinced Mom that I needed to sleep more and study less.

When we came home, I asked to sleep upstairs. I knew my grandparents would send Dae-Sung before they let me sleep alone upstairs. That night at dinner, as if she knew something, my grandma asked Dae-Sung, "Why don't you sleep upstairs in your room, now that it's not so cold at night anymore. It is a little crowded for all of us to sleep in one room."

I spent the next glorious month doing "rest and do-nothing" in In-Chun. Grandpa insisted that I simply needed to have a month away from books and pencils. Every afternoon neighborhood kids, most of them younger than me, came over and we jumped rope and played jacks.

I found out my grandparents were investors in the bathhouse, so when we were all dirty, I let the kids take baths for free. They ran home and came back with a bar of soup and clean underwear and I policed the giggling girls to make sure they scrubbed their body before they went into the hot tub. I never missed going to school or worried about falling behind in schoolwork.

17

My grandfather wasn't the only person who told my mother to ease up on me about schoolwork. My father often snapped at Mom for making me study too much. In the grand scheme of things, he thought it didn't matter which school I attended as long as I remained happy and kept a clever spirit.

"Let the poor girl be a child and send her to any school her teacher recommends," my father said.

Some of my classmates' mothers devoted their whole lives to full fill their ambition of sending their kids to the best-rated high school. They made daily visits to the classroom in their flailing Korean skirts, to observe and to bring hot lunches to their children, but mostly, to earn the teacher's favor. They competed by bringing hot lunches to the teacher—each one trying to outdo the lunch that was brought the day before. It was tricky to figure out what his favorite lunch was, since asking him was considered uncouth.

Every day, a few minutes before the bell rang, a delivery person would place a hot lunch on his desk, at the request of an anonymous mother. Sometimes it was Chinese *ja-jang-myun,* or a rice omelet with ketchup. Sometimes, a mother would splurge and have *bul-go-gi,* thinly sliced marinated beef, delivered. My teacher would say, "Oh dear! But

I brought lunch. Who is this from?" And without fail, some kid would yell, "It's from such-and-such's mother."

After a month of being away from school, it wasn't easy to go back to reality. I still had to face the dreaded junior high school entrance exam. A month was a large chunk of time to miss when every day was loaded with more memorizing and more math problems to solve. I couldn't run away again. After coming back to Seoul, I only had to study more to make up the lost days. Being absent for a month compounded the problems and re-entering the classroom was embarrassing.

"Teacher Kim, Sang-Eun is here. She's back." A few kids alerted my teacher when he didn't acknowledge me on the first day back. Then, after the first period, he took me to an empty office to give me a long lecture. I don't remember what he said except that he used words like "losing face," "dignity," and "shame."

By the beginning of the second semester of sixth grade, my now doubly miserable life began every morning at six a.m. From morning to night, my days as a sixth grader were drenched with fear—fear of failing the entrance exam to Kyung-Ki junior high school.

I couldn't share my terrible frustrations with anyone – not even with my best friend, Kil-Ja. Kil-Ja was seated in the second block of twenty Ewha-bound kids and her parents were very proud of her. The first twenty were candidates to Kyung-Ki and the second twenty were Ewha-bound. However, some parents preferred Ewha for their daughters. Ewha, a private school, was a bit freer in spirit. The students at Ewha were allowed to grow their hair longer than shoulder-length and they could even braid it. They were allowed to wear brown or red leather penny loafers. Kyung-Ki kids had to wear navy sneakers and no overcoats were allowed to cover their uniforms, even on the coldest winter days.

I never saw the blue sky or the orange sunset. I never even heard the chirping of a bird. Every morning I brushed my teeth, washed my face, and ate breakfast like a zombie robot. I was tired from being up until midnight each prior night, studying. Walking to school and walking home were the only small joys in my life. By then, I was healthy and I had to carry my own book bag and I alone was responsible for getting to school on time.

I carried my heavy, red plaid book bag, switching hands back and forth from time to time. I passed by streets full of people going to school, work, or just standing in front of their doors watching passersby. And for a few moments on my way to school, I hummed a song, kicked a stone on the street, skipped in and out of imaginary hopscotch, or mimicked our maid's provincial accent.

My head continued to throb in class. I would close my eyes and press my temples to stop the pain, but it still made me throw up. The vomiting was happening more and more frequently and I learned to recognize when it was about to happen. As soon as I started heaving, I would run to the bathroom or to the trash can at the back of the class. Even then, my teacher got annoyed at the disruption.

The daily test results determined the probability of acceptance to various junior high schools and our teacher drilled us in the memorization of all the facts and numbers. Mothers organized tutorial programs and invited the teacher to spend a few hours with their children for an extra study period. One mother insisted that her child move in with the teacher's family at any cost so he could monitor her study habits. These mothers came to school daily in their long Korean skirts. Years later, the government banned this "wind of the flailing skirt" group from coming to school every day. They said that the bribery of teachers had become out of control.

My mother was always a step behind in this practice. But Mom did start making biweekly visits to the school and tried to learn through trial and error what it would take to shove me into a school I clearly didn't qualify for.

Mom enrolled me in a tutorial program. By the time she found out about it and enrolled me, it had already been in progress for a few weeks. The kids in the program were mostly Kyung-Ki and Ewha-bound kids. My classroom teacher, Tae-Hyu Kim conducted it at one of the kids' houses.

Every day after school I grabbed a quick snack around the corner from the campus, then went off to the nightly tutorial session until nine o'clock. A dozen of us sat around a long oval table and memorized and repeated facts and figures. We took tests and corrected each other's papers. The idea was to master all the questions so that when we actually took the entrance exam, we would know every question and answer forward and backward. But no matter how hard I studied, it only got more confusing to me. Each day, the questions seemed newer and got more difficult.

In addition to headaches and nausea, at the end of the day after staring at books all day and all evening, my eyes got bright red and I started seeing double.

"Isn't this the most horrible life? Studying like this?" I asked my best friend, Kil-Ja, one day. Kil-Ja softly answered, "My uncle told my mother that if I make it into Ewha, he will take care of me all the way. My parents don't ever need to worry about me. I have to study."

"What does that mean?" I asked.

"Well, I'm not sure, but I think he is going to pay my tuition."

The only good thing about going to the after-school tutorial program was that Mom gave me money to buy a snack every day. During the fifteen-minute break, we carefully picked a candy bar from the corner store or steamed dumplings filled with meat and vegetables from an old Chinese man's four-table-restaurant down the alley, or a bag full of twisted, deep-fried dough sprinkled with sugar. Sometimes I bought a newspaper bag of freshly deep-fried squid. I liked buying a bag of tiny steamed sea snails. I would bite the tip off the pointy tail and suck out the juicy, salty, slimy piece into my mouth.

A month before the day of the big entrance exam, knowing that my test scores were not escalating, Mom panicked and hired a live-in tutor. By then, the tutorial program was over and we were to drill the same study materials on our own. School went on each day until five o'clock. Sometimes my teacher would continue torturing us until five-thirty or even six o'clock, giving us a one-hour lunch break. I walked home tired and gloomy, quite often with a headache and red blotchy eyes, seeing double.

Once, I got a ninety-one in math, my most hated subject, and I couldn't wait to get home to tell everyone. I wanted to carry the test paper face-up for the whole world to see.

"What marks did you get today?" Mom asked at dinner and the tutor stared in despair.

"I got ninety-one today in math."

"No way! She couldn't have gotten over ninety. She simply isn't that smart, Mom. She has developed mutational phenomena in her brains." My brother made it sound as if I scored well by a fluke.

"You might as well prepare yourself to spend a lot of money, Mom. I hope we won't have to sell the house, now that father's business is failing." My heart was heavy, knowing that I added more problems to Mom's nightly agitations with my father on his newest business venture, a stupid one, according to Mom.

"Sang-In-ah, stop treating her like she is dumb, I know she is bright and her IQ is exceptionally high. She is just a little immature."

Even though Mom defended me, I saw a glimpse of wistfulness on Mom's face as my brother rambled on relentlessly.

There was only one thing that would enable me to go to Kyung-Ki high school if I failed the entrance exam. My parents would have to donate a substantial chunk of money to the school. Then I would be admitted, and when I showed up at the school I would be labeled as *bo-kyul-sang,* meaning, "back-door-entrance-by-money." The kids scoffed at *bo-kyul-sang,* and these students were not able to hold their heads up all throughout their years in school.

After dinner, I dragged myself to the study room where my tutor was waiting for the rest of the night. By midnight, I memorized the names of every king in the *Yi* dynasty, capital cities of each country in the whole world, and was able to locate each country on the blank world atlas. I even knew that the U.N. ambassador's name was Hammarskjöld. And that a flute was a woodwind instrument like the clarinet, even though the flute was not made of wood.

Only then was I allowed to go to the bedroom where Mom was already sound asleep. I was tired and sleepy but had no relief. All I could think was, *I may fail the entrance exam. And what would I do if I fail?* I knew life would no longer be worth living. The newspaper had once reported on a child that committed suicide after failing the entrance exam. The rumor was that every year, there were more suicide attempts the paper was not reporting.

Worried, I fell asleep next to my mom, wishing that she would stretch her hand out of her blanket to touch me. She hated to have her neck cold and hated to have me come into her blanket. But I so yearned to feel Mom's skin against mine every night, hoping tonight might be different.

The exam days were approaching. We each had to submit the application form to our first-choice school, and another one to the second choice in case we failed with the first one.

My teacher had no say in the matter but to oblige my mom's request and allow me to submit an application form to Kyung-Ki girls' junior high school. Parents bought their children new winter outfits for the exam, mostly colorful knitted sweaters and corduroy pants and overcoats. Exams were done in January and the new school semester started in the spring.

Taking a bath on the day before the exam was absolutely forbidden, in fear that it would wash off the knowledge we had packed into our brains and bodies. The first two days of the exams at Kyung-Ki high school were grueling academics. We stayed in the same room, and each hour different teachers came in with test papers on different subjects. We got a ten-minute bathroom break between the hours.

The classroom was so quiet that you could hear the person beside you breathing. I heard the sound of shuffling test papers. I wanted to grab my head with both hands to stop it from spinning. I looked around and saw stony faces, eyes closed tightly, mouthing history facts so as not to forget them before they were able to put them down. Some faces were flushed red. I prayed only for my head to stop spinning.

While we were in the test room, parents and older siblings waited on the school grounds, biting their nails and holding their breath. At the end of each test, we handed in the answer sheets but kept the question sheets. On the way home after the second day, mom took my sisters and me out for ice cream to celebrate the ending of the most stressful part of the entrance exams.

The third day was art and music oral exams. We were taken one at a time into a room and had to name the music instruments as the teachers pointed at them randomly. When a male teacher in dark glasses pointed to a black instrument, I couldn't remember the word clarinet—the name I had repeated a hundred times while looking at the picture. Next, I was told to read music written in the treble clef; do, mi, sol, fa, mi, re, do, and so on. Then I had to identify whether different sheet music was written in 4/4 or 3/4. This part was easy for me. Then he asked me in what time a waltz was typically written.

For the art section of the exam, we were expected to identify different artists, from impressionist to modern. The whole test-taking ordeal ended with an interview by a group of intimidating figures like the principal, vice principal, and a few other important people at Kyung-Ki. After the routine questions like my father's occupation and my address, they asked me why I would like to go to Kyung-Ki girls' high school.

"I don't know. I guess my mom wants me to go here. Maybe because my two sisters go here." I squirmed and they burst out laughing.

Once the exams were over, I thought I had died and gone to heaven. For four weeks, I slept, played and never opened a book. Finally, the day of the announcement of acceptance arrived. Our numbers were to be posted on the front wall of the school building. My three sisters and my brother and Mom and I all walked to the campus.

The playground was full of kids, parents, uncles, and aunts wearing scarves and overcoats waiting for the posters to go up. Each student held her hands together in front of her chest as if she were praying.

Some parents showed up at seven in the morning even though the results wouldn't be posted until nine o'clock. The kids who had been accepted to Ewha or Sook-Myung junior high school got their results the day before, so they showed up to share their joy and find out who failed at Kyung-Ki girls' high school.

Standing there with them, I could already see myself in one of those prestigious uniforms. I had to have been accepted. Why wouldn't they accept me? Why should I be any different than my sisters? I had studied so much, and I even had a live-in tutor. I convinced myself that there was no way I hadn't passed the exam. My tutor had even gone over the exam papers with me after I brought them home. He had said confidently, "I am sure you passed. You knew all of the answers."

I stood holding my sisters' hands, skipping like I was playing hopscotch.

"Aren't you worried, Sang-Eun? How can you skip?" Mom gave me a disgusted glance. I immediately stopped skipping but giggled nervously.

Like most of the mothers, she wore a *durumagi* (a silk brocade topcoat) with the Korean costume underneath and Korean rubber shoes. She was taking small steps and alternating her feet to keep them from getting cold. The wait was long, but people were afraid to leave for breakfast in the fear that they might post the results.

Finally, two male teachers brought a long scroll of white paper. They unrolled it along the front wall of the main building horizontally, way above my head, and everyone gathered around. I pushed into the front row of people, praying to see my number, 588. It had to be there. I scanned the 500 columns, squinting to read the numbers. 568, 574, 586, 587, 589, 590. I looked again, but 588 wasn't there. I had failed. I looked again and again, but it didn't change.

My legs suddenly felt weak. The faces on the playground zoomed in and out of focus. I felt like everyone was looking at me shouting, "You failed, you failed."

I fell to the ground and started wailing hysterically, thrashing my arms and legs. I had finally cracked.

I imagined a black mark of shame on my forehead, and knew that my life would never amount to anything. My sisters, in their proud uniforms, carried their stupid little sister out the gate. I felt everyone's stare on our backs. I was sure they were saying how stupid I was and what a disgrace I was to my family.

For two straight years I had stayed up late at night memorizing world history and solving math problems. I knew how to convert Fahrenheit temperature to centigrade. I could name every country in South America. I could name every one of the Great Lakes and the national parks in America. I knew what a bassoon looked like, even though I didn't know which end to blow into. Years of labor and effort were dissolved into nothing overnight. But it was worse than nothing. With nothing, you can start fresh. I now had to face the future. I believed that there was no hope and there would be no joy in my life ever again, for everyone would know me as failure.

I cried so much, I didn't know I had so much tears. My heart ached when I looked at my mom's disappointed face. Failing took every last bit of self-confidence I had, and something else, too. I knew that my clever spirit would never be the same.

18

Junior high school started and I went to the ill-reputed and shameful Duck-Sung school. Looking back, it shouldn't have been such a traumatic experience. Some kids voluntarily chose to go there. But because I was told all my life that I would be a failure unless I went to a certain school, the thought was firmly embedded in me and I began to truly believe that I was a failure.

Every morning I walked all the way to school with one hand over my left chest covering the school badge. At school, I stayed away from most of the kids. I wanted everyone at school to know that I was not one of them.

I wished my parents had donated a lot of money so I could be a *bo-kyul-sang*, and wear Kyung-Ki's badge. But I knew it was out of the question. My father had just lost all of his investments in an attempt to start a brokerage firm—or so I gathered from the bits and pieces of harsh conversations Mom and Dad often exchanged.

Mom's unhappiness over my father's failing business made me stay away from her and I wasn't the only one. My father stayed mostly in the *sarang-bang*, even for dinner. Almost a year earlier, my uncle, who was a pediatrician, decided to share the son's responsibilities and graciously invited my grandfather to move in with his family. Since then, my father reclaimed the *sarang-bang* as his quarter.

The maid set the small dinner table for one and carried it to the *sarang-bang* for Father. Every time my parents faced each other, they seemed to fight, and the mood in our house became more ominous each day. Whenever my mom got mad at my father, I knew she was wrong, but I never voiced my opinion or showed sympathy to him. I felt sorry for him and I wanted to tell my mother that she was not treating him right, that he was a smart man and he did have a good business sense.

Even though the house was gloomy, walking into the house after school still gave me a little relief because I got to take off the disgraceful uniform.

"Look at her in that appalling uniform," my brother said on the first day of school.

His voice made me cringe. "No one will ever want to marry you with a diploma from that school," he said. I never said anything to defend myself. There was nothing to defend. I had put a scar on the whole family's reputation.

The night before the first day of junior high school, my father had promised to have me transferred to Kyung-Ki or Ewha by the end of April.

"Close your eyes and ears and stick it out for a month. Just till the end of April. We will figure out something by then," he said.

"*Abuji*, are you sure? Do you promise?"

"You are the smartest and the cutest kid in my book. They don't know who they are missing. The principal of Kyung-Ki high school is a friend of your mom's. I will tell you what I promise. I promise you are and will always be my precious and clever daughter. I don't want you ever to forget that. My *mak-doong-e*." My father often called me *mak-doong-e*, meaning youngest child. He picked me up, and then he lay flat on his back and raised his feet so my stomach would rest on the bottom of his feet.

"Put me down, Dad, I am too big for an airplane ride," I screamed, but I was afraid he might really put me down. The loving attention was so undeserved. I was not smart or pretty and I besmirched my family's honor—or so I was told over and over. It would be presumptuous to take a rare moment of affection for granted. Secretly, I took pleasure in every second as he humored me and tried to make me smile.

"I would rather take a year off and study with a tutor at home and take the exam again to go to a good school next year, Dad. Please don't make me attend Duck-Sung junior high school." I begged some more. I didn't dare ask Mom. It would only add to her aging. I was ready to go through another year of agony—anything was better than having to wear the disgraceful uniform and the badge.

I didn't know what was in my father's plan, but I believed his promise and counted the days. I had heard that Ewha had accepted the other girl in my class who failed Kyung-Ki in exchange for donating an upright piano to the school. It was possible that my father was planning something similar to influence my admission. His words comforted me, and I clung to this promise, and it helped me get through each day.

On the 29th of April, as the teacher-appointed class president, I was told to go visit my homeroom teacher who was in the hospital. After the visit, I walked home in the dark, anticipating exciting news. Just two days before, my father had delivery men fill our outside basement with a cord of wood, and bought three sets of porcelain china for his two brothers' families and our family, which made me wonder if his business was doing well enough to buy an upright piano for a junior high school. In any case, tomorrow was the last day of April. I took big strides to get home quickly for the good news.

I turned onto the hilly cobblestone street from the busy intersection and stepped across two to three stones at a time in almost complete darkness. I hopped over thin slices of light that were coming through the cracks of doors in the neighborhood.

As I was approaching the alley where my house was, three taxis roared and screeched to a stop next to me. I jumped onto the first step in the alley.

"You almost ran me over!" I turned around and screamed. "Oh," I gasped. I saw my three sisters get out of one car and my mom out of the second car. For a split second, I fumed with jealousy. They must have gone out to dinner or out to a bakery for after-dinner snacks or desserts.

As I ran to hug Mom, I took a step back. A chill whipped through my body. Something was wrong. In the headlights of the taxi, I could see her eyes were bloodshot. Mom had been crying, and all of my sisters had red eyes as well. I took a step back and Sang-Hie pulled me over and whispered, "Father passed away of a brain hemorrhage. It just happened at the little father's house." (We called our father's younger brothers "little fathers.") She barely got it out of her mouth with a sniffle.

"At the little father's house? Why? What happened? When? Why there?" It couldn't be. He couldn't die. He was my father. I didn't believe her. She must have meant that he was sick like he could have almost died. I never thought my father was invincible, but losing him so soon was unimaginable. I didn't even get to see him. He had to say goodbye to me if he was going to die. This couldn't be happening. I felt like I was sinking into the ground.

I plopped myself down on the second step of the narrow alley and watched two men carrying my father's body up the steps. As they made the last turn into the gate, I howled uncontrollably, making a noise only an animal would make. I couldn't breathe, but I kept howling, the pressure building up in my chest.

They placed Father in the *sarang-bang*. Staring at his face, Mom caressed his cheeks with both hands. I stood in the doorway and watched her. It was a terribly confusing sight. Did she love him?

Mom straightened his face and stared some more. I was choking on a convulsing whimper. I wanted to talk to him and tell him all the things I couldn't tell him before because I was supposed to be an obedient little girl. They fought more and more. Mom would cry and Dad would take off, sometimes for days. I never knew what they fought about, but I never told him that I was on his side.

One day, I saw him sitting alone in the *sarang-bang*, his eyes welling up with tears. I knew that Mom no longer shared a bedroom with him. I should have gone to his room more often and talked with him. I should have let him know that I understood his pain, if only I'd have known that he would die soon.

During my mom and dad's happy days, my father quite often went out to a dinner business meeting or a work-related party. When he came home, he joined us for a nightly snack and laughed and talked with us. Then he slept in the *an-bang* with Mom.

I don't remember when my father started sleeping in the *sarang-bang*. It must have been shortly after my grandfather moved in with my uncle. There was an unspoken dimness in everyone's heart after this, but we all went on as if it was normal. The separate sleeping arrangement also removed us from my father little by little. We started spending more time with Mom in the evening and the room would fill with giggles and laughter. When Mom would open a can of cling peaches or a box of wafers for an evening snack, we would often neglect to serve my father.

I cried and cried until I lost my voice and my face swelled up. Now that I would never see him again, I wished that I could tell him how I always felt badly that we were not including him, and how I thought Mom was wrong to exclude him. My heart was now filled with confusion and guilt.

By ten o'clock, the house was filled with workers, cooking what seemed to be enough food to feed a thousand. One of the bedrooms became a makeshift sewing room. Aunties we hadn't seen for years showed up to help make the mourning garb for the immediate family. The two cats were kept on a leash in the basement for fear that they might influence the departed with their evil spirits. Although it was customary to keep cats away, I was told by one of our maids that cats would lift up the casket by jumping over it on account of the strong demonic spirit they possess at the time of human death.

All night, visitors arrived, and Mom told us that we needed to take turns keeping Father company until he was buried. The late visitors were welcomed to stay overnight since they would not make it back to their homes before the midnight curfew. Close friends and relatives were expected to pay a visit as soon as they heard the sad news. It wasn't respectful to wait until morning. With each new visitor, Mom cried all over again and looked genuinely sad. At least she seemed like it. Then why was she so unhappy with him?

I stayed in my school uniform all night because *sang-je,* the children of the dead, were supposed to be present to receive the visitors. The front double gates were wide open and the living room was brightly lit. Father was still in the *sarang-bang,* except he was now laid at the end of the room behind the silk accordion picture screen. The screen was placed backwards to expose the plain sides. A small, low table was placed as an altar in front of the screen, and on the table was incense, which was to burn constantly as part of the sacrificial rites. Above the incense bowl was my father's picture draped with black ribbons.

Everyone, including those planning on staying the night, waited for the "calling the spirit of the dead" ceremony, the most important rite on the first night.

I was having a hard time staying awake, tired from a long day and exhausted from crying. Mom told me to try to stay awake to watch the ceremony. The ceremony commenced at midnight on the night of death while the spirit was still fresh.

"Is it scary, Mom?" I asked.

"No, it shouldn't be. The funeral director will be chanting. That's all. But all *sang-je* should be present." I didn't know what to expect. It seemed a little scary, curious, but mostly primitive.

"But, isn't it superstitious and un-Christian?" I whispered to mom.

"We need to follow the ritual. It has nothing to do with being Christian. As Koreans, we need to follow the traditional pre-funeral ceremonies. We are Koreans before anything." Mom shoved me away.

The next morning I realized I had fallen asleep and missed the whole thing. My grandfather came over to stay with his dead oldest son for the remaining days until the funeral. He was full of disgrace for allowing his son to die before him. He squatted down on the edge of the entry hall and said, "With any luck, I might fall off this ledge and die. Wouldn't it be wonderful?" he said in a monotone, and let out a long sigh.

His feeble body looked weak, and he felt more and more uncomfortable being at our house. Parents were not supposed to come to the funeral of their children because it was their responsibility to keep them safe and it was considered a humiliation and disrespect to show your face at the funeral of your own child.

"Grandpa, Dad died of a brain hemorrhage. No one could have prevented him from dying. He was under a lot of stress. It was no more your fault than it was mine. Actually, I probably killed him since I was supposed to die the day before yesterday," I held my grandfather's hands. "It is true. It was all my fault. Just two days ago, my school went on a class picnic on the bus and on the way, the bus rolled into the rice paddy and a lot of kids were injured. I came out without a scratch. My homeroom teacher was badly injured, which was why I had to visit her yesterday," I implored.

That day, my father had shouted with joy. He had said that he had gained another daughter since I received a second life by surviving the bus accident. My father was the only one who made a fuss over me. I tried to console my grandfather, but in my deepest heart, I truly believed it was me who should have died.

A few weeks prior, my mom and a few of her friends went to a psychic on a whim. Even though Mom didn't make a habit of visiting a psychic, the Buddhist monk scared Mom enough to consider the alternatives.

"You will lose your husband before the month is up," the psychic declared with authority.

"You are joking, right?" My mom didn't want to believe him.

"Well, there are a few things you can do to prevent it." He made it sound hopeful, and after a few more thousand won bills were placed on his money plate, he gave her the obscure solution.

"Someone needs to leave the house first, I don't mean necessarily by death. But just leave the house, even temporarily. You just have to transform this period full of negative forces into positives."

"Like what?" Mom wanted him to be specific. But that was the end of the visit. She was supposed to figure it out.

My brother had always wanted to enlist in the army before graduating from college. But my mom's answer was always no. A college degree for all her children was her utmost goal. My big sister Sang-Soon had wanted to move into the college dormitory even though we didn't live very far from Ewha University. Mom thought either was a possibility, and she debated, but never made any decisions or took any action because she didn't really believe the money-hungry psychic. But his voice nagged her unpleasantly and she wished she hadn't gone to see the darn monk.

Knowing this, I knew it was my fault. If I had died two days before, thus leaving the house, father would still be alive. My heart ached like it was under a heavy rock. Why didn't I die? I was only a disgrace to the family. Father was the provider of the family. My life was not even one-tenth the worth of my father's. I cried and cried but was afraid to tell anyone that it was me who actually killed him.

I was also afraid to tell anyone that I no longer had any hope of going to another school. He died a day before he was to make good on his promise. But I also knew my hopelessness was no one's concern.

For the next few days, visitors came to pay respect to my father by lighting incense and bowing to the picture. Some people gave three bows and cried for a long time. Some people stared at my father's picture and then held our hands one at a time. Some gave a deep bow to my mom. This was happening all day and night before the official funeral.

We took turns, two at a time, keeping my father company by being in the same room with his body. He was never to be left alone. I could understand this part of the tradition, but the whole incense thing seemed supernatural. However, I obeyed and lit the incense daily. I thought the rites and funeral preparations were disturbing, but mostly interesting, though it seemed wrong to admit it was interesting. The reality of my father's death did not hit me for a long time. The mood in the house was dissonant. In the midst of all the sadness, there was also gaiety. Groups of men were playing *wha-to,* a Korean card game, drinking *jung-jong,* and exchanging stories about father. Others were laughing and crying at any insignificant gestures or comments, all in the name of guarding and keeping the dead body in the company of friends and family for his final days at home.

On the day of the funeral, I put on the beige, raw cotton Korean funeral attire. I looked hideous. The blouse was too big and long and the skirt was too stiff. My father's coffin was moved to the entry hall behind the altar. I sat next to the altar by my father's coffin with my siblings all day receiving guests in the funeral garb. We were excused only for meals and to go to the bathroom. My brother had the eldest *sang-je* outfit, which was a cover-all with a few split panels made of stiff light brown raw linen. And he wore a hat made of the same material that stood straight up like a chef's hat. It made him look weak and ridiculous.

Outside, the block walls of our house were completely draped with black and white fabric from one end to the other. It went around the corner all the way to the hill.

Several straw mats were laid out in the front yard to set tables, full of food. Every beggar in town was to come to feast on this occasion, for they were fed until they were full and could still ask for more. We were supposed to treat them and feed them graciously. Maids were busy turning the tables as fast as they could, making sure there were only disposable chopsticks on the table. Guests were served in the house with sterling silver spoons and chopsticks.

For the funeral, my father's altar with the picture and the incense pot were placed in the entry hall. The entry hall had three steps into the living room, so the visitors could stand on the lower level of the steps and bow without having to take their shoes off.

Some people cried loudly and some quietly. Most of the men didn't cry but acknowledged us and some of them held my brother's hands. The ambiance was much more solemn and formal on the day of the funeral.

Lots of women came to me and said that a little person like me shouldn't ever have to wear the *sang-je* outfit. I thought they meant that

I should have worn some other outfit. I didn't realize that they felt sorry for me for losing my father at such young age.

Lines of well wishers went down the narrow alley onto the cobblestone street. We must have had hundreds of visitors all morning. Mom told us later that we had received some eight hundred visitors. My legs were numb from sitting down on my knees and my eyes were swollen shut from crying all day.

After we received the last visitor, it was time to leave for the burial ground.

The altar was taken down and my father was moved back to the *sarang-bang* and

the funeral director asked all of us to stand and witness the ceremony of closure, also known as "entering the casket ceremony." I nearly gagged from the funeral director's sour medicinal smell combined with cigarettes. He opened the casket in front of us so we could spend a few last intimate minutes with our father. At first, I turned my face, not wanting to see him. As he opened the casket, the level of wailing from the immediate family rose and filled the room and leaked out to the entire neighborhood.

In a quick glance, I could see my father's face was covered in a white cotton cloth. The funeral director then wrapped the body tightly in a long strip of white cotton fabric. For the life of me, I couldn't understand what possessed him to do this. Why restrict him like this? Why not make him comfortable? Just as I was about to jump in to stop him, he started hammering nails into the flimsy pine casket.

"Stop that nonsense! How do you expect for his spirit to get out? What is the point of nailing it shut so tightly?" I grabbed his right arm and twisted it as hard as I could.

"What is the matter with you, Sang-Eun?" Mom shot me a horrified look. She then physically removed me from the director and I threw him a last punch with my fist, howling. My sister Sang-Soon gave me a quick nod with her wet and swollen face, approving my startling behavior.

The beady-eyed funeral director, now drenched with perspiration, went right on with his business, never showing any emotions at all.

What an indignant way to send my father to an unknown world. He could have at least shown up in a suit and a tie to pay his last respects.

My brother, my mom, one of my uncles, and I rode in the hearse through the winding, bumpy road to the top of *Mang-wooh-ri* Mountain where my father's plot was. As the head of the funeral procession, the hearse was barely moving, heavy and somber. For much of the ride in the confined vehicle, I stared at the casket, feeling my father's presence, and silently prayed.

"Heavenly Father in the sky, please bless my father and welcome him to heaven. I know he will be going to heaven because he has been a good man. And forgive Mom for not being the best wife to him."

I opened my eyes and peeked out of the window between the curtains. As we rode up higher and higher, we came to a full view of the mountainside with mounds of graves everywhere, each sitting like an upside down rice bowl covered in green Korean grass. In front of each mound was a heavy lime stone table next to a tall head stone.

Some tables on the mountain were set with scrumptious food for the spirits of passed ancestors. Facing the table, generations of well dressed sons and daughters bowed their heads down all the way to the ground.

It was a mountain of grief and loneliness. The thought of leaving my father there deep under the ground made me shudder.

Just then, all of a sudden, Mom, my uncle and I stiffened in shock. Out of nowhere, my brother, banged on the partition between us and the driver with the staff he was carrying (part of his ridiculous funeral garb). I jumped with fright because it was such a loud bang.

"Can't you go any faster, you stupid idiot?" he screamed.

"Just stop it. You terrible kid! Just stop it," my uncle screamed.

Then Mom added her screaming. "Swear in front of your father that you will stop this kind of behavior. Right now." My heart was pounding from fear that some other horrible thing might occur. I looked straight ahead, and clenched my teeth and narrowed my eyes, cursing my brother. I wished it was he who died instead of my father. The driver stopped the hearse and opened the back door to confront us about the banging.

"I can't stand this long drawn out ride. Can't you go any faster?" My brother was still extremely agitated. I wondered why God would take my father and not my brother. I clutched on my mother's arm and cried some more.

"The hearse leading the funeral procession is supposed to move slow and solemn," the driver replied politely but firmly.

"We know. It's just that my son is so upset he took it out on you. I am so sorry. I am so sorry," Mom apologized profusely. Without a reply, the driver shut the back door and got back in the driver seat.

The pallbearers' job was tough, having to carry the heavy casket to the top of the mountain. A colleague of my father's who owed a lot of money to my father spent two nights on the mountain looking for the best plot, combing the peaks and the valleys of every inch of the mountain. A plot on the top of the mountain plateau looking out on open view and particularly the view of a running stream far ahead was an ideal one. My father's grave had all of the open feelings so that if he ever got tired of laying down six feet under he would have a great view.

With our funeral attire, we wore slippery white Korean rubber shoes, and we all had a stick to support us from sliding down the mountain. I held Mom's hand and we followed behind the eight men carrying the casket. I was afraid the lopsided casket might hurt my father and he might be rattled inside. I kept my eyes on the men and the casket and prayed that they were strong enough so they wouldn't drop my father.

All of a sudden I noticed a long green caterpillar crawling on one of the men on the left side of the casket. It was the furry green kind that live on pine trees and are known for their sharp stinger. I shook Mom's arm with both of my hands.

"Mom, Mom. Look! There's a *song-chung-ee* on his neck. He is going to get stung."

"We do not disrupt the funeral procession," she whispered to me. She said that there was nothing she or anyone could do about it.

How sad! I was sure my father would understand if we asked everyone to stop for a second. My neck was hurting as if I was the one being stung, and this time I cried for the man. None of these nonsense customs made any sense to me.

When we reached to the top of the mountain, the whole mountain looked like it was covered with black and white from all the mourners' outfits. A rectangular hole was already dug and all of us stood around the casket as it was lowered into the ground. Our relatives and friends surrounded us and filled up the mountain with echoes of loud weeping.

When the fresh mound was packed down to a perfect half dome, it was time to allow the dead spirit to depart with a feast. Since the limestone table was not installed yet, Mom placed a small, red-lacquered table in front of the mound. She and my aunts arranged rows of small dishes, a full course Korean meal for the spirit. They placed rice and soup in the front row, *san-juk*, marinated and pan fried beef, *kal-bi* beef, chicken simmered in soy sauce and various kind of vegetables cooked and marinated in spices. Finally, Mom poured *jung-jong* into a tiny cup to be drunk in one gulp, and put it by the rice bowl. It was all for Father's spirit to drink and eat before he departed for good.

"Do they really think Father is going to drink and eat the food?" I whispered to Sang-Hie.

"Don't be disrespectful. He might. At any rate, they believe he does." Sang-Hie narrowed her eyes at my scoffing and continued in her low voice, "I heard that the food table weighs much lighter when the ceremony is over."

I wanted to believe Sang-Hie. But I wanted to say, "maybe the soup evaporated and the food dried up." But I decided to go along with the pagan ritual.

On the way down from the mountain, Sang-Soon held my hand tight and whimpered to me, "Just think. We will never be able to call '*abuji*,' ever again. We will be father-less children forever."

To me, it was much more than that. He was the only one who accepted me and my life as they were. "Let her be a child and keep her clever spirits alive," he said to Mom many times. I would miss that acceptance by him. Only my father could give me that unconditional acceptance that gave me complete security. I fit his mold of a perfect *mak-doong-e*. With his departing, a large part of my identity departed as well.

19

"*Oh-mo-na*! Oh my! This is the ultimate Christmas gift," Mom exclaimed, watching Sang-Hie carefully pull a brown canvas case out of a wooden box.

"Is it really my cello? Is it really?" I asked.

"Yes, it is. I can't believe it arrived today, the day before Christmas all the way from England," Sang-Hie said.

I watched as Sang-Hie unzipped the canvas case. She held the neck of the instrument to steady it and grabbed the zipper so it wouldn't scratch the body of the cello. My mother stretched both of her hands out like she was ready to catch it if the glistening hourglass shaped body slipped out of my sister's hands. She said repeatedly, "Careful, careful."

It was the shape of a violin, only it was red and the size of a small child. It reminded me of a dainty little lady. It had ornate F holes in the front on each side of its thin waist.

"Oh what a beautiful color. I never knew a cello came in bright red. Can I hold it?" I waited for Sang-Hie's approval before I hugged the finger board, my very own cello in my very own size.

I plucked one string lightly, afraid it might pop. Then I tightened the hair on the bow—I learned this from watching Sang-Hie's friend Duck-Ja when she and Sang-Hie were rehearsing for a recital—and drew the bow against the middle of a string above the bridge, as if I already knew how to play.

"Be careful! You might break the hair of the bow. And I suggest you don't even touch it until you have the first lesson. After all, it is the only half-size cello in Korea," Sang-Hie said.

I wiped the entire surface very gently with a piece of flannel Mom handed me before I gave it back to Sang-Hie to put it in its case for safe keeping. This was a brand new experience for our entire family. No one knew how to play the cello. No one even knew how to take it in and out of the case, or what to do with it once it was out. And it was all mine. Anyone in my family could go into Sang-Hie's room and tinker "Chopsticks" on the piano, but I didn't have to share this with anyone. I hugged and carried the canvas bundle into my room and laid it on the floor.

That night in bed, I softly sang the Breval Sonata in C major. Sang-Hie and Duck-Ja rehearsed many nights at our house and I could sing the entire first movement from beginning to end from listening to it all those nights. I thought if I sang it enough times I just might be able to play it on the cello right away. I drew the imaginary bow under the quilt and quivered my left hand, mimicking the vibrato as I sang along under my breath.

It was a strange feeling to be given a beautiful, expensive, one-of-a-kind cello that belonged to me and me only. I felt important. It gave me a strange confidence. I now had something to look forward to—a vague hope and purpose.

Sang-Hie's love for me was instinctual from the day I was born. She was the one who convinced Mom to buy me a cello when I failed the entrance exam to Kyung-Ki junior high school.

"Too many kids are playing the piano or the violin. The competition is too severe," she said. Her logic made sense to my mom.

"Cello is just being introduced here. And one can be the best if they only have the desire. And Sang-Eun sure has the talent."

"What a brilliant idea!" Mom agreed. "Then she can go to the prestigious Yego, Music and Art high school, and save her face once and for all."

Once Sang-Hie and Mom decided that the cello was my music career choice, they contacted Mr. Kim, Duck-Ja's teacher. From Mr. Kim, we found out that I was too small even for a three-quarter-size cello and that there was not a single half-size cello in all of Korea. We would have to order it from abroad.

Ordering anything from a foreign country was nearly impossible in those days. Only diplomats had free access to order foreign merchandise. My brother, at the time, with his ability in English, had befriended the Vietnamese attaché and the two of them frequented beer halls and tearooms. My brother often took him to the Student's Cultural Club meetings where they only spoke English. The foreign diplomat liked going places with my brother because it gave him an outlet for his social life in an unfamiliar surrounding. It seemed odd that they communicated in English, which wasn't either of their native languages.

The Vietnamese attaché gave my brother practically free right of entry to the embassy. In turn, my brother would often bring him to our house unannounced for Korean dinner, but Mom never complained about entertaining him.

When Mom asked my brother about the possibility of ordering a cello for me through the Vietnamese embassy, my brother frivolously bragged, "Are you kidding me? Of course! He would do anything for me and my baby sister."

I was shocked to hear my brother say that. He had always mocked me and I never thought that he might have the slightest love for me. Then I remembered the night he carried me on his back all the way to my pediatrician uncle's house when I had a fever of 104 and tonsillitis. My parents were at an event and it was after ten o'clock, so there was no public transportation. In my delirious state on his back, I felt awestruck. I felt the same way now. A little part of me wishfully thought that he must actually have loved me a little.

The diplomat made the choice to order it from England, and all we could do was pay any expenses and wait. The anticipation of this kid-sized cello, for nearly eight months, percolated in my heart with a dream of being a notable cellist one day. Each day of waiting, I convinced myself that it was more than a dream, it was a promise from above. It was my destiny. I only needed the instrument.

Mr. Jai-Hong Kim came to my house for my first cello lesson the next morning on Christmas Day.

"We only wanted to tell you that we finally have the cello," Mom said. "We didn't mean for you to come over right away, especially on Christmas Day."

"Christmas is not a big deal. I was just as excited as all of you to see the cello and have Sang-Eun get started. When it comes to music, there are no holidays." He beamed with excitement, his big smile showing off his profound double eye lids.

Mr. Kim took his gray pinstriped suit jacket off and started tuning the cello. In his heavily starched and pressed, snow-white dress shirt, he hovered over the tiny red hourglass figure. His cuffed pants had creases as sharp as a knife's edge and were high enough to show his matching gray argyle socks over the skinniest ankles. His hair was smoothed out with pomade and perfectly combed. Everything about him was in place.

He tuned the cello by twisting the pegs as he drew the bow against two strings at a time. The way he was tuning the cello with his left hand on the peg reminded me of the movie, "Love in the Afternoon," where Audrey Hepburn sat turning her cello in the orchestra. I imagined myself playing in an orchestra in an exotic place one day.

"First I would like to show you how to take care of the instrument. Your cello is like your body. You shouldn't let it get too cold or too hot. And when you take it outside, it needs to wear a coat. Keep it away from direct sun. And I will show you how to keep it clean. It only gets dry baths. You never let it get wet, not even a drop of water." He then showed me how to sit with the cello in front of me. He had me draw the bow against the middle string. My left hand rested on the shoulder of the cello. I was not yet to touch a string on the fingerboard. I wanted to ask him how long before I could play the Breval Sonata but I decided to be quiet. I didn't want to get in trouble on our first meeting.

During my first lesson I learned the names of the strings A, D, G, and C. I learned to screw the bow tight. I learned to draw the bow back and forth on a string counting to four as steadily as possible without lifting the bow from the string.

The first sound I made was on the D string, then a long and continuous G.

I was fascinated with the sound. The gentle, deep sound of the G string vibrated through my stomach.

The higher-pitched A was charming, but I quickly went back to the mellow D. When I curved the bow to play the C string, my thighs felt like they were vibrating as well.

It was fun to practice and experiment by putting my left fingers on the fingerboard and bowing the strings with my right hand, but that soon ended when my sister, Sang-Hie grabbed my shoulders.

"You are very talented in music. I know because I taught you piano. You can be the best if you really want to be. But no matter how talented you are, if you don't practice the basics you will never be good. Let's make up our minds to practice three hours every day. It will be boring and tedious and you will get blisters on your fingers. But it will all be worth it one day. We just have to make up our minds and do it with our teeth clenched." She emphasized the word "we." Her powerful voice persuaded me and her promise of making it a joint effort encouraged me.

As I listened to her, my desire to become the best cellist rushed adrenaline through my body. I couldn't wait to draw the bow some more.

For the next week or so, I sat every morning and every afternoon practicing by drawing the bow back and forth, up and down, slow and steady, over and over for three hours, concentrating on making the bow parallel to the bridge on the strings.

Mr. Kim was amazed how quickly I was copying him and how I drew the bow straight and steady. My mom and my teacher agreed that

I would need a practice tutor, a music student who would come to my house every day for an hour to monitor my practice.

Jung-Sook Shin, a senior at Seoul National University, monitored my practicing every day for a year. She loved to see the progress I was making. "Don't get so good too fast. I won't be able to teach you then," she said.

I started playing pretty melodies each week and kept up the etudes. I began to imagine being the most wonderful performer, winning all the competitions and performing as a soloist with a symphony orchestra. Then maybe I could redeem a little bit of my disgrace.

My teacher Mr. Kim was fastidious in everything he did. His wife told my mom one day that he insisted on her ironing his dress shirts herself because he didn't trust the cleaners and if she ever ironed one less than perfectly, he would dunk the ironed shirt into a bucket full of water so she would have to start all over. He made her nervous and edgy and she would never gain weight for as long as she lived with him. He almost always wore suits and when he sat in a taxicab, he first wiped the seat with his white handkerchief.

His meticulousness carried into his teaching. Every note I played had to be in perfect intonation. If I had a hard time learning a piece, he had me play only the notes, ignoring the rhythm. This always baffled me. I needed to get into the melodic line with the rhythm to feel the music. But I followed his direction and learned each piece systematically.

After a year, Jung-Sook Shin no longer came as my practice coach. I saw Mr. Kim twice a week and was given a mountain of etudes to practice and master. Most of Mr. Kim's other students were older than I was, yet my biweekly assignments almost doubled theirs. I learned all the pieces with ease.

Teacher Kim was pleased with the way I followed his directions. But he didn't hesitate to reveal his frustrations when I didn't meet his expectations. When he gave me Boellman's Symphonic Fantasy to learn, which I thought was way above my skill level at the time, he screamed at me for not playing well.

"I don't know what I'm doing wasting my time teaching her," he mumbled to himself. After the lesson, I cried all the way home thinking I would never become a decent cellist and maybe I should quit the darn thing right then.

However, I continued practicing and showed steady advancement. He started feeling confident in me as a prospective performer. But his goals for me weren't limited in my cello playing. He also wanted me to learn how to present myself gracefully at all times, especially on the stage.

"Sit up straight when you play the cello and don't slouch when you walk." He constantly corrected my posture.

I never wore the school uniform to my lessons but wore "made in USA" labeled jeans with plaid cuffs and bright-colored jackets. In those days, Mom was quite generous with me, out of pity for having to attend the disgraceful school. Sang-Hie and Mom used to make frequent trips to the black market in East Gate to acquire hard-to-find, made in USA garments for me. Living in class-conscious Seoul, where social class was defined largely by materialism, I was happy that she did. Mom continued to teach Home Economics at a university and I assumed we must have had some assets my father left. Either way, Mom managed to provide continuously for my lessons and made sure I was dressed well.

Mr. Kim never said anything about my clothes, but I knew that he approved of the way I dressed by the way he looked me over each time I had a new outfit. To him, it took more than just mastering the cello to be a first rate cellist. It took knowing how to dress tastefully and carry myself like a well-bred young lady.

My left eye with the poor vision drifted and settled into a comfortable position that surrendered to the moves of my healthy right eye, giving me a cross-eyed look even in the morning after a good night's rest. Doctors called it "lazy eye." It never bothered me when I was younger, but as I got older, I became more insecure about it. On days when I read a lot, my left eye became bloodshot and extremely tired. By the end of the day it didn't want to stay open. Strangely enough, reading music three feet away on the music stand when I practiced the cello didn't seem to tire my eyes. But reading a book in a close proximity was only comfortably done a few pages at a time.

One day after my cello lesson, Mom took Mr. Kim and me to a Western restaurant at a brand new Dong-Myung building where all the waiters wore white shirts and white gloves and the tables had white cloth napkins. Unlike Korean restaurants where people came in and sat themselves as they pleased, a waiter seated us.

At these fancy luncheons, adults usually talked to each other and I sat quietly pretending to understand everything. The truth was that it was the most boring time for me, but I put up with it gladly because I got to use a knife and fork and dine with a napkin on my lap.

After a fashionable lunch of "hamburger steak" (we always called it hamburger steak, but later I found out it was meatloaf), Mom ordered coffee for herself and Mr. Kim and ice cream for me. Mr. Kim took a sip and then blurted out "Do you think you will ever let Sang-Eun have corrective eye surgery?"

"Her left eye drifts, doesn't it?" Mom put her cup down.

"Well, I think you should. It might take some time away from her cello practice, but I think it will be good."

I didn't know what he meant by good. Would I see good or would I look good? I wondered if he knew how weak the vision was in my left eye.

The following week, Mom took me to the renowned Dr. Chang-Soo Choi at the Severance Hospital. He had just returned to Korea after studying ophthalmology in America. Sitting in a dark swivel chair in his white coat, Dr. Choi pulled my left eye open with his fingers.

"Well, I am afraid to say once a child reaches a certain age, these corrective surgeries no long work." Then he put my chin over a monstrous machine and put his face on the other side of the machine. Our faces were so close I thought he was going to touch my nose with his.

"Well, we will give it a go. It will correct some but there is always a chance that it might drift again. The vision is so weak it can't function on its own so it just follows the good eye, and when the nerves get tired, it will drift away."

"Tell me something, doctor. Will this surgery be strictly for looks? Or is there anything you can do to improve her vision with surgery? What about contact lenses? Is it possible?" Mom asked, hoping she had finally found someone who might give her a hopeful answer.

"You might let her watch TV with her right eye covered. The stimulation might trigger and regenerate the damaged nerves. Who knows?"

"I will do that, Mom. Let's buy a TV," I jumped in excitedly. They both gave me a quick glance and went back to their discussion of my eyes.

He politely explained to Mom that my vision was not likely to get better because as long as my right eye was functioning well, my left eye would not have the motivation to work at it.

"Then why did you tell me to watch TV with the right eye only?" I asked.

"Well, nerves are mysteries," he said to Mom, again ignoring me. It was confirmed that nothing would help the vision in my left eye. It was "clinically dead."

When we left the doctor's office, Mom said squeezing my hand, "What a good doctor he is. He will take good care of you."

"I don't know, Mom. Didn't he say that it couldn't be corrected a hundred percent? What if it hurts? What if it bleeds a lot? I am scared, Mom."

"Oh, it won't hurt. You will be under anesthesia. You won't even know it."

Four metal beds lay on each side of the spacious hospital room. Seven of them were occupied by moaning old ladies. Mom and Sang-Soon unpacked my over night bag and helped me settle in the bed by the window. The moaner directly across from my bed, who had a large growth under her chin, sat up and started asking me questions. Her scratchy voice made me envision charcoal in her throat. She wanted to know what I was in for, how long I would be in, and if my mom would stay with me since I didn't look old enough to stay alone at a hospital, and if she should ask for a rollaway bed for Mom.

"I am having an eye surgery and I don't know how long I will be staying. It depends, and no, my mom won't be staying with me," I answered all in one shot, zipping and unzipping my overnight bag. I couldn't keep my eyes off her growth though I thought it would be impolite to stare at it. Just the same, it would be hard to sleep across the bed from her.

I asked the head nurse in a whisper if I could be moved to another room, possibly with younger female patients. She shook her head and I thought her white cap might fall off. Her cap stuck out horizontally by catching on the neatly braided and twisted bun at the back of her head. I was fascinated with how it could stay up there all day.

Mom and Sang-Soon stayed through my evening meal, which consisted of a few different kinds of broths. I wished at least one of them would stay longer, until I fell asleep, or at least until a nurse gave me the enema.

They nodded goodbye to everyone in the room and told me to sleep well. I gave a slight wave and hoped for some physical contact from Mom, but she quickly turned the corner. Even though Mom often hugged me and kissed me on the cheek, Koreans have never been known for being demonstrative with their emotions in public. I pulled the cover over my head, afraid I might cry or worse yet, that the charcoal woman might start talking to me.

I grew more and more sullen about having to undergo a surgery for something even a doctor couldn't guarantee. He only guaranteed a small improvement, and there was nothing he could do about my vision. If the doctor wasn't sure of anything, could my eyes possibly get worse?

I woke up to a gentle shake from the head nurse. "Wake up dear, it's time to see the doctor," she whispered. "You won't need anything. Just follow me."

The brightly lit surgery room reeked of rubbing alcohol. The room looked huge and the nurses laid me down on the cold, stainless steel bed in the middle of the room with a large lighted round mirror above it. A few nurses cling-clanged the metal instruments and lined them up on the tray by the bed.

"This will only take a second and it won't hurt at all," a nurse said as she pricked a needle on my upper arm. Every noise bounced off the cement floor and echoed off the white plaster walls, then quickly disappeared.

The next thing I remembered was waking up in the night to the sound of my mother's voice.

"Mom, what are you doing here at night?" I sat up. "Turn the light on. I can't see anything."

"Oh, my poor youngest child. They had to wrap both of your eyes tight to keep the eyeballs immobile." Mom hugged me and I felt her hand caressing my hair.

"What? But why the good eye?" I scrunched my face, groping the blindfold.

"If one eye moves, the other will automatically follow it. The doctors don't want any movement in your operated eye. It will just be for a few days, then they will open the good eye," Sang-Hie said.

All of a sudden, I had a horrifying fear that this darkness might never go away. I knew it wasn't a logical fear, but the pitch darkness was suffocating me with anxiety that I might never see again. I wanted to claw off the bandage.

"Why did he change his mind? He told me that he would only have to cover the operated eye. This is just not fair," I cried, pounding the bed with both hands.

"Dear, you must not cry. Tears could delay the healing process. It may even hurt it."

Hearing mom's plea, I quieted down, scared. I wanted it to heal quickly, but I felt betrayed. Dr. Choi told me that he would patch only the operated left eye for a week. I wondered what else he had told me that wasn't true.

"Did you sleep well, sweet child?" I heard Dr. Choi's voice. It also sounded like a group of people surrounded my bed. Dr. Choi was making a round with a group of interns. "When can you rip this off?" I asked.

"Sang-Eun-ah, where did you learn such impudent behavior?" Mom screamed before he could say anything. "I am sorry, forgive her. She is a spoiled youngest child."

"But—but Mom, he said he wouldn't—" I stammered. I wanted to make my point.

"Just be quiet," Mom said again, and I clenched my mouth.

I heard the doctor telling Mom that he would most likely take off the patch on the right eye in three days.

Dr. Choi then undid the patches to make sure there was no bleeding or excessive swelling. He told me to keep my eyes closed the entire time he examined them. I imagined a dozen white-gowned doctors surrounding my bed and discussing my eyes as if I were a monkey at a zoo. They may have looked me over and talked about my deepest insecurity without my permission but I couldn't even see who they were or what expressions they might have made.

For the next three days, I stayed in bed and Mom and Sang-Soon took turns spoon-feeding me each meal. After three days, Dr. Choi undid my right eye as he promised. The left eye was to be covered for a while, he said. I didn't question how long. I was only thankful I could see. I was relieved and regretted getting mad at the doctor.

I was not allowed to read or do anything that might strain my eyes for the remaining week at the hospital. I made a nurse's cap out of a white sheet of broad paper and wore it on my hair using a bobby pin. The seven moaning ladies all laughed and thought I was clever.

On the morning of my discharge, the doctor removed the patch on the left eye and let me look in the mirror. Even though I didn't see much difference, I nodded my head when the doctor asked me if I liked the results. Mom said that my left eye looked perfect.

I was discharged with a patch on my left eye and was told to wear it for the next few months, which I did, though it felt like an eternity. I also made weekly visits to the eye clinic at the hospital and each time, they put ointment in my eye and held a heat lamp over it for 20 minutes.

By the first lesson after my eye surgery, my teacher Mr. Kim decided I was big enough to move up to a three-quarters size cello. He found a new larger cello for me and sold my half-size cello to one of his younger students. He arranged all the transactions in a matter of a week and Mom trusted his every decision.

At the first lesson on a larger cello, he taught me how to vibrate. He had me move my second finger up and down slowly, then faster and faster, all the while my finger pivoted solidly in one spot on the fingerboard. This was a big step that I had waited eagerly to learn, because with vibrato, the sound of the cello became smooth, rich and melodious. I felt like a bird that had been creeping along the windowsill until it suddenly found a pair of wings for the first time.

20

After my father died, my brother's behavior drastically changed. Quite often, he stayed out all night, saying he was at a friend's house, and on the nights he came home, we wished he had stayed out all night because he came home drunk.

"A son of the *yang-ban* should be taught to drink correctly with good manners so they will know how to conduct themselves appropriately," Mom said. "Your father didn't believe such a thing should be taught. So your brother only knows one way to drink—to get drunk." She justified his drunkenness by blaming my father.

Every night the siren went off at 11:30 to forewarn the midnight curfew. When my brother staggered home past midnight, he walked through the back alleys to avoid the police. Mom would greet him at the door, grateful he made it home instead of spending a night at the police station. When he came home in the morning after staying out all night, Mom was still grateful that he came home safely.

I was unfortunate enough to open the door for him one Sunday morning. I was enjoying my morning cello practice in the quiet house.

"*Eiguu*, Sang-In-ah! What am I gonna do with you? When will you mature and act like an oldest son?" Mom muttered and sighed, looking at his grubby face. She then went to get soup and rice for his breakfast.

Mom always fed him vegetable soup for his hangover. I followed her into the kitchen.

"Why can't you ever tell him to shape up or get out of the house? He needs a strong hand, Mother. You are treating him like he came home from working all night. Father would have never approved of his conduct." I shook my head.

"Just let me handle him. It's your father's fault. He should have trained him better."

"Come on, what are you all doing? Lay out my bedding. I didn't sleep all night. I don't want any food right now," my brother growled at no one particular. I couldn't stand it anymore and went back to my practicing.

"Sang-Eun-ah. Stop scratching the cello. I need to sleep."

"I need to practice more than you need to sleep, you son-of-a-bitch!" I muttered under my breath and put away my cello.

When he stayed out, he would usually come home mid-morning the next day and demand that the maid lay out his bedding so he could sleep. He would wake up in the late afternoon and have the maid bring the basin of water so he could wash himself right in the *an-bang* where he had slept all day. Instead of his own room, he always slept in the *an-bang* where Mom and I sometimes slept.

When he finally got up, he would get dressed and stand on his tippy-toes to check himself out in the mirror. He desperately wanted to be taller, but no matter how he tiptoed, he was still five-foot-four.

If Mother was not around, he would ask the older maid to lend him some money out of her stash from the monthly salary.

"All I have is a hundred won for emergencies. Your mother signed me up in a *ghe* so my stash will grow. You can have my hundred won if you wish."

A son of the *yang-ban* (nobility) or not, I shunned his revolting behavior. When my friends happened to see him, unshaven, with a cigarette dangling out of his mouth and wearing pajamas in the late afternoon, I lied and told them that he was sick with a deadly disease and couldn't get up early.

My sisters and I steered clear of him until he went out again for his next drinking binge that evening. He stopped having dinner with us, which we were glad about.

In spite of Mom's efforts to make him finish law school at Seoul National University, my brother enlisted in the army and was sent to Non-San for lock-in training for three months. It was the initial mandatory training camp where enlisted young men were put through brutal physical endurance tests. Since Mom's efforts to keep him in school didn't work, Mom hoped the training would make him somewhat responsible.

My sisters and I were ecstatic to get rid of him for a whole three months. This meant a happy home with no violence, and I believed Mom was relieved, too.

During his absence, Mom freshened up our house by re-wallpapering and re-flooring the *an-bang* and the *sarang-bang*. Then she knocked down the wall between the *an-bang's* alcove and the front hall, and enclosed a small room for me. This rectangular room was just wide enough for me to play my cello freely without touching the sides of the room. Two sides of the room had double-frosted glass walls to keep the sound in. When I sat in the room to practice, I felt like I was playing in a glass sunroom.

At one end of the room, I placed a small desk. I did a lot of letter writing there, but very little studying. I liked writing letters. I wrote to friends — and some imaginary teachers and imaginary boyfriends. I also kept a journal that I addressed "dear diary."

When I practiced the cello, I sat in the middle of the room on a chair with a pink ruffled cushion Sang-Soon *unni* made for me.

On the opposite end of the room, I placed a lacquered table and displayed my collection of pretty things. In the middle of the table was an empty burgundy vase with etched cherry blossoms, and around it were a small lacquered wooden jewelry box, a clear plastic box full of tiny seashells, and glass animals in all colors. I could spend hours in my little transparent room, practicing the cello and rearranging the inside of my desk or my collection.

Sometimes I went into my room for privacy, but I also liked the idea of feeling like a flower in a glass hothouse, especially on a rainy night when I could hear the pitter-patter of the rain on the roof. The rain could pour for days, or even weeks in the summer. At times, I didn't want the rain to stop because I loved the cozy feeling of rainy nights.

On one of those pouring nights, my sisters, my mom, and I stayed up late talking and giggling. Just after we went to bed, a loud rap on the front door awakened all of us.

"Wake up. Open the door!" At the second rap, everyone came out of their rooms to the living room. It sounded like my brother. My heart dropped. It was so peaceful without him. What was he doing home? He was supposed to be at a lock-in training for three months.

"What are you doing home?" Mom dashed to open the door. "Did they send you home? Did you flunk out?"

"No, I begged and begged and the lieutenant let me off for three days." He smiled triumphantly for beating the system.

"But no one leaves Non-San. I have never heard of anything like it," Mom said, wide eyed in disbelief. "Are you sure? They really gave you three days off?"

"Yup. They did, Mom. I can sway anyone if I turn on my charm. How can they say no to this face?" He lifted his chin with one finger and laughed. None of my sisters found it amusing.

Three days of hell began, though he didn't drink as much this time. He spent every evening sharing his clever scheme with his friends and praising himself for his cleverness. Mom said that two months of training at Non-San was already worth it—he was shaping up, but I didn't believe her.

After the three-month training in Non-San, my brother was stationed in Jin-Hae as a lieutenant. His duty was translating documents on military operations and strategies and he then briefed it to American officers. He had long abandoned the idea of finishing law school. As an army officer, he had the luxury of being saluted by plenty of lower-ranked soldiers. He also had the financial means to make frequent trips to fancy bars, as well as privileges at the officer's clubs. His life of bliss was just right for us as well, as long as he lived in Jin-Hae. Jin-Hae was a southern city by Dae-Ku; it took a few hours to get there by train.

I was in junior high school then, and old enough to know that he was leading a double life, living in sin with some runaway in Jin-Hae. When he came home for the weekend, he and Mom would whisper privately and all I heard was Mom clucking her tongue. Sometimes, I would hear a few words here and there like "pregnant" or "her parents." But Mom never berated him for fear that he would drink and become violent.

Her name was Sook-Ja and when he showed us her picture on one of his frequent trips home, I was astounded at how beautiful she was. Having Sook-Ja waiting for him in Jin-Hae made his trips home short. I felt indebted to her for taking my brother off our hands and I started liking her not just for her beauty but also for preserving our happy home. But the peace was short-lived.

Everything changed when he was transferred to Seoul to work at the Eighth Army. He moved back home then, but made weekly trips to Jin-Hae to be with Sook-Ja, who was waitressing at a tearoom.

One Sunday night when he came back from Jin-Hae, he brought her with him and demanded that my mother let her move in with us until she found a job at a tearoom in Seoul. Seeing her once a week was not satisfactory to him. This was appalling behavior, even for my brother. After a long argument, Mom said that she could stay, but she would have to sleep with the maids and not with my brother.

Our maids liked having Sook-Ja live with us, because she was helpful. I liked having her too; whenever I came home from school she always greeted me with a bright smile and a warm snack, asking me how my day went. My brother's drinking sprees diminished and he was home more. Since Mom didn't allow Sook-Ja to eat with us (she ate with the maids), my brother often ate alone, and she sat across the table from him, talking and watching him eat. There was no doubt in my mind that they were in love.

Mom's biggest concern was that if word got out, my brother's marriage proposal inquiries would be in jeopardy. Having a relationship with a low-class tearoom waitress would definitely eliminate offers from *yang-ban* families. To neighbors and visitors, Mom wanted the situation to appear as if we had a third maid.

One evening, I was practicing the cello when through the glass I saw a woman in our entryway. She was dressed in a silk Korean dress and had a stern look on her face. Mom led the woman into the *an-bang*, then came into my room and told me to stop practicing because she needed absolute quiet. My room was too close to the *an-bang*, where they were about to discuss a serious matter.

"Who is she, Mom?" I asked.

"Never mind. It doesn't concern you. Children don't need to know."

"But Mom, you are telling me to stop playing the cello, but you won't tell me what for?" Mom looked like she was ready to erupt fire. If the woman wasn't in the next room, Mom might have slapped me on the face. I stopped playing and went to my sister's room.

Mom and the woman stayed in the *an-bang* whispering for a long time. Then they summoned Sook-Ja from the maid's room. That's when I found out from my sisters that she was Sook-Ja's mother. The three of them talked for a while and we could hear Sook-Ja's raised voice and her loud sobbing. She didn't seem scared to yell at her mother. Soon after Sook-Ja stopped crying, the woman threw up her arms and stormed out of our house.

It turned out that Sook-Ja was a high school graduate from Dae-Ku. To our surprise, she was born to dignified upper-class parents. She was arranged by a matchmaker to marry a wealthy man in a neighboring town, but she refused. When her father ordered her to go through with it, Sook-Ja ran away.

Sook-Ja's mother was attempting to take her back home. When Sook-Ja refused, her mother insisted to my mother that my brother must marry Sook-Ja, since her body was now used and damaged. Mom made it clear to her that the only son of the oldest son of the highly regarded

Lee family could not possibly marry a common tearoom lady. It simply wasn't going to happen.

But Mom talked to Sook-Ja that evening. She had promised Sook-Ja's mother that she would try to talk some sense into her head and convince her to go back home and marry someone in her hometown while she was still young, before she became an "afternoon-fish."

My brother, for the first time, obeyed Mom and agreed to have her move out. I knew it was the right thing, but I couldn't help but feel sorry for her and wished she could live with us. I watched her smooth white hands gently pack all of her meager possessions in a large scarf. Every once in a while she stopped and wiped her tears with the back of her hands. I felt a surge of pity toward her, and it seemed like she felt my compassion as she looked at me with those heavily double-folded eyes that all Korean girls envied. She gave me a quick smile, showing her deep dimples, and said, "I will be all right. Can you blame your mom for kicking me out?"

I hadn't thought about how unfair life could be until that moment.

She was probably the most beautiful woman I had ever seen. What had she done to deserve such a life? To me, she deserved better than my brother. If only my brother was firm about marrying her, he might have earned a small amount of respect from me. But he picked this time to be submissive. But I also understood Mom not allowing her to marry my brother. What would I tell my friends about her if she was my sister-in-law? That my brother married a tearoom lady? The irrational social classification was already embedded in me, too. I walked back to my room feeling very much like a hypocrite. I shook my head and picked up my cello to practice.

After Sook-Ja moved out, my brother's drinking reached a new level and his temper was more unbearable. Fear skimmed our thoughts every evening as we laughed and giggled in the *an-bang*. If we heard the front gate rattling or any noise resembling the doorbell, we were ready to split off into our own rooms, leaving my mom alone in the *an-bang*.

One evening, all five of us were sitting around after dinner like we usually did, sharing fun stories. Sang-Hie stood up to imitate one of her teachers. "Would you believe some of the teachers only come in to have refreshments and leave as soon as they stuff themselves?" Sang-Hie said. "Mr. Moon was one of them. And I will be damned if I let him out of the class before the victory celebration was over. We wanted them to stay and party with us. Since I was assigned as the doorkeeper, I stopped him from leaving the room." She got up on her feet as she covered her mouth to keep from bursting out laughing.

"He pointed at his penis with both index fingers, and said loudly, 'I need to u-u- urinate. I will be back. I-I promise.' Mom, honestly, the whole class couldn't stop laughing for at least ten minutes. What an idiot!" She shook her head. "Just then, one girl passed a coal bucket by the heating stove in the middle of the class and said, 'Here, tell him he can use this. But he can't leave.' So then we laughed for another ten minutes. I swear the party was a disaster," Sang-Hie went on excitedly.

"Oh, the poor guy. You should have let him go quietly, Sang-Hie. Such an indignity for a teacher." Mom covered her mouth to try to keep from laughing as she picked up another piece of the apple peel to massage her face with the wet side. She always said this was the trick to keeping her skin looking young.

"Well, he deserves to be embarrassed, Mom. Who would point at his thing like that for god's sake? The damnedest thing was that we all know he is in love with the geography teacher, Miss Hundo."

Ignoring Mom, Sang-Hie went on: "Who would name a girl Hundo? In any case, just think if they ever dated—he is gonna call her 'Hundo Si,' Mom, just imagine that." Looking at my puzzled expression, she added, "Hundo Si? Miss Hundo? It means jock-strap in Japanese." This time, Mom nearly stopped breathing from laughing so hard, apple peels dripping off her face.

Evenings like this were the fondest memories of my childhood. Sang-Hie usually dominated the conversation, and we were a captive audience, laughing the entire evening. Even Mom didn't rush us to do our homework. She always said laughing was the best thing to keep us healthy.

"Wait, wait. I hear someone at the door," Sang-Soon hushed us.

In a split second, we were all situated in our own rooms and I slid into Sang-Hie and Sang-Soon's room. My room was by the front entrance and since two sides of the room were glass, I didn't want to be seen by my brother. Sang-Hie sat on the piano bench and Sang-Soon and I sat on the floor with our feet tucked under the *yo* in the warmest part of the room to keep the heat in. Sang-Soon grabbed a book and pretended to read.

Sang-Won was already heavily into her books in her room; she was studying to be an engineering major. Mom converted the hot tub room into a study room for Sang-Won to provide a quiet environment for her to study. She spent most of her time in there making volumes of her own condensed engineering notes.

Through the *chang-ho-ji* (rice paper doors), we could hear my brother breathing heavily, struggling to untie his army boots.

"Ma, I am home. Where is everyone?" I could hear my brother's raspy voice with his curled tongue. He was drunk again. I heard him kick his boots off at the entry hall and his heavy footsteps toward the *an-bang*.

"Shh, he is drunk again," Sang-Soon whispered.

My heart started pounding as I heard his steps and the sound of the sliding door slamming shut. We stared at each other.

The murmurs from the *an-bang* could turn into screams at any moment, summoning any one of us or the poor maids. Not knowing what might happen was giving me a sour stomach and a headache. As the seconds passed, I became more and more nervous. Maybe for once he was in a good mood, I hoped.

"Sang-Soon-ah, where are you? Come in here," he yelled through the closed door. Mom came quickly and slid open the door. Our three sets of eyes fixed on her face in despair.

"Sang-Soon-ah, did you not see your brother at Yang-Ji tearoom today? Did you mean to ignore him?" Mom, in a pleading voice timidly attempted to prepare her for the interrogation.

"What tearoom? What's he talking about?"

"Just apologize and tell him that you never saw him. Please."

"I didn't do anything. Why does he always accuse me of ignoring him outside of our house?" She didn't budge.

"Sang-Soon-ah, just tell him you are sorry, please."

"But Mom, I did nothing wrong. Why should I? You need to stand up to him, too." Her red face was already trembling in readiness to defend herself.

"I can hear you. What are you two yakking about? Get over here." My brother slid open the *an-bang* door and hollered with increased madness.

Sang-Hie started pounding on the piano as if she wanted nothing to do with the argument going back and forth. Sitting behind the piano, I realized I had been holding in my whimpering for so long that I finally burst into an uncontrollable sob, and was near convulsing.

"What's the matter, Sang-Eun? Don't cry. He is just talking. Nothing will happen." Sang-Hie stopped playing the piano and held my hands.

"Something will. It does almost every night. I miss Dad. I wish he was alive so he could beat the heck out of him. I hate him. I wish he was dead."

"I know. I do, too," Sang-Hie let out a big, long sigh.

I looked at her face and tried to read her mind. I wondered if she really hated him as much as I did. I felt mildly guilty for wanting him dead. I held her hand for a long time enjoying sisterly warmth, hoping she felt the same way as I did.

"Sang-Hie-yah! Get over here." This time his voice was angrier.

"Just a minute, I gotta go to the bathroom."

I thought she was brave for trying to buy time.

Eventually he called all three of my sisters and asked each one of them if Sang-Soon had seen him at the tearoom. He wanted to know if she talked about it when she came home.

"Everyone in this house is ashamed of me. None of you appreciate me. You all look down on me and pretend you don't even know me if you see me on the street."

"That's just not true, dear. I tell you all the time how smart you are.

And the girls are really proud of you," Mom stammered pathetically, trying to calm him down, gently holding his arms.

"That's so ludicrous. How do we know if she did or not," Sang-Won said bravely from the doorway. "Anyway, what difference does it make if she did ignore you? I don't even know why I am here. I have tons of studying to do."

Sang-Won had wide shoulders from working out in the swimming pool all the time. She swam freestyle in the Asian Olympics, and I so hoped that she could take on our little older brother. But before she even finished her sentence, he slapped her across the face and knocked her down. She fell flat on the floor. Mom grabbed her and tried to help her up, but Sang-Won pushed her hands away. I ran to my brother and tried to grab both of his hands. I didn't know what I was going to do, but I had to do something. He pushed me away and I fell backwards into the living room.

"You are a terrible person! What did I say for you to hit me like that? Huh? What did I do? I won't stand it anymore," Sang-Won stood up and held up two fists in front of her face like a boxer.

"You think you are going to fight me? Are you kidding me?" my brother growled.

I was so proud of Sang-Won. I wanted her to go on and hit him back. *Hit him. Kick him. Come on. Use your shoulders.* I was silently cheering her on. But Mom quickly pushed her out the door and took her to her room. She put her black velvet coat on her quickly and pushed her out the front door.

"Go on, go to uncle Chang-Whan's house. Stay there until I come to get you. He will kill you tonight if you stay here. Why did you have to go on and talk back to him like that? Just go. Uncle will protect you."

Mom came back into the *an-bang* and said quietly, "Sang-In-ah, we all need to go to bed. Why don't you sleep it out and forget what happened tonight? Just forgive them all and go to sleep." At this, Sang-Soon gave Mom a piercing look.

"Forgive what, Mom? What did we do?" she snapped.

At that point, my brother grabbed a handful of her hair and pulled it as hard as he could. He held her long, permed hair and dragged her along the gleaming floor.

"What are you doing? You horrible person." She screamed and yelped from the pain.

"Stop it! stop it!" Mom and Sang-Hie twisted his hands to release her hair. Once he let go of her hair, he slapped Sang-Hie's face.

"Did it ever even occur to you that we went to father's cemetery yesterday?" I didn't know what made me think of that, but I grabbed his hand and waved my finger at his face. Just then I felt a terrible sting on my face and I fell to the floor.

I heard a crashing noise, and screaming and crying. The room looked like a hurricane had hit it. A low table rolled sideways and the lamp flew to the other end of the room. The two maids stood shaking at the doorway.

"Get out of here, you two bitches. Sluts. I don't ever want to see you again. Ma, bring Sang-Won back here. I will get to the bottom of this. Where is she?" His eyes glared and his short body was shuddering with anger.

"I don't know where she went. She got scared so she took off. Come on. Forget it now. She might have gone to her friend's house. Go to sleep now. Just forgive her now," Mom pleaded, pulling his arm.

"Go to sleep? Do you think I could sleep now? Huh! Go find her, Ma. Right now," he demanded.

I shivered looking at his red face. I imagined that was what the devil's face must look like. It was blotchy with red and blue and his eyes were bulging with fire. His breath was nauseating with the smell of alcohol.

He ran to each room and slammed the doors as he hunted for Sang-Won. He looked under desks, behind the piano, inside of the closet, and even inside the armoire. Finally, when he couldn't find her, he ran down to the kitchen to the opening of the heating duct. He demanded that my mom bring all of her belongings, from her school uniforms to books, notes, and everything in her desk.

"What's the point of educating her? What's the use, huh, Ma? I will burn everything," he said. I honestly thought I was looking at a crazy, starved animal. My clever sister, Sang-Hie quickly went into Sang-Won's study room and stuck volumes of her engineering notes under her skirt. She swiftly entered her room and opened the upright piano and placed the notes gently over the rows of piano hammers.

"What if he opens the piano?" I asked in fear.

"Are you kidding me? He is not that smart. He would never open the piano. He doesn't even know it opens. Stupid jerk!"

He started burning all of her belongings one by one by putting them into the duct, and we all watched him in terrified horror, completely and utterly helpless. The maids brought each item as ordered and handed them to him with their heads bowed. He ripped her books and threw them into the flame. He threw her blouse, her pants, anything he could get his hands on. Mom hung onto his arms and legs and pleaded and begged. "Please, Sang-In-ah, please. Can we just give them away to some needy child? We just got the new uniforms for her. It's brand new. And the books—oh please, you don't burn books. Somebody can use them. Oh please, Sang-In-ah."

I hated watching my mom pathetically begging her own son. What had possessed this intelligent woman to be so weak?

I don't know how late it got. I was still sniffling in bed wiping my eyes and blowing my nose quietly. Thinking about what had just happened and how anyone could be that evil made me angrier and angrier. I knew then that I would never forgive him and never consider him as my brother again. Never.

I wondered why God would take my father instead of him. And I wondered how someone that horrible could have been born to my parents. I cried more out of confusion. I no longer felt guilty for hating him. I would never soften again -- no matter how much he apologized. I wanted him dead. I knew that only then would there be peace in my family and in my heart.

I wanted to get up and play the cello, but I couldn't. I needed to get away from it all. I closed my eyes. I could still see him crazy wild. I could see his face. I shook my head and closed my eyes tight.

Through the frosted glass of my room, I could see the silhouette of my brother holding my mom's hands. He must be begging for forgiveness again. Pathetic little creep.

"Mom, I am so, so, sorry," he was sobbing so hard he could barely talk. "I will never do it again. I don't know what happens to me when I drink. I promise I will never get drunk again. I mean it this time, Mom. Please, forgive me, Mom." His nasal voice made me even angrier. I shivered. This was his routine behavior. Mom was holding his hands and reassuring him with the long "You can do it and we will all help you" speech.

They were both pathetic and miserable. I couldn't help but lose all my respect for my mom for being deceived again and again, and allowing him to repeat this awful behavior.

I couldn't stand the sight of them any longer. I kicked the blanket and headed for my sister's room.

"Can I sleep here?" I groped in the dark.

"Of course, Sang-Eun. Come and lay down here." Sang-Hie moved over and made room for me between her and Sang-Soon.

"Sang-Hi-yah," Sang-Soon whispered. "I wonder if we should go over to our uncle's house to see if Sang-Won ever got there. I am worried."

"I was thinking the same thing." Sang-Hie turned the light on, put on her coat and said, "I will go."

Sang-Soon looked at me and said, "take her. I don't want you to go alone. I will stay here. I don't think we should all go. It will be too visible to the police." Sang-Soon put a muffler around my neck and said, "Take side streets and alleys. It's past the curfew. The last thing we need is for you two to get caught and spend a night in jail."

For the first ten minutes or so, Sang-Hie and I knew we shared the same thoughts even though we were silent. We knew Mom was weak, and we both missed our father. We both hated our brother and wished he was dead.

Going to my uncle's house was easily done by side streets. Once we crossed the main streetcar railroad and ducked into another alley, Sang-Hie let out a convulsing sob that she had been holding in for a long time. Squeezing her hand, I sobbed with her.

"I just don't know what the answer is," Sang-Hie mumbled.

"There is no answer. I saw him crying to Mom again. But I know he will do it again. Tonight was the worst so far. Why do you think God took Father instead of him?" I didn't want to come right out and say I wished God had taken him instead. I was waiting for her to say it.

"I truly wish he was dead," Sang-Hie said, emphasizing *truly* and *dead*.

"Me too. Do you think it's wrong to wish that?"

"I don't know. But God understands, I think."

"Do you think there is a God?"

"I don't know. At times like this, it is really hard to believe that. Why does he let him do this to us if there is a God? There is no proof about God. I just don't know."

I was confused. Of all of my sisters, I believed and listened to Sang-Hie the most. And here she said she didn't know. I wondered if I should still continue to pray. I should have asked my Sunday school teacher one day, but I had stopped going to church ever since I had to study so much. I decided I would pray anyway since it wouldn't hurt. I repeated over and over quietly, "Dear Lord, change brother. Make him a nice person." This made me remember that I hadn't prayed for a long time.

When we reached my uncle's, the whole family was still awake. Their four kids were all staring at my sister with sleepy eyes and the oldest daughter, who was my age, kept telling them to go to bed. But there was no way any of them would fall asleep now that we were there, too. Sang-Won's eyes were bloodshot and she was looking down at the rice cakes in front of her, pushing them around the plate with chopsticks.

My uncle never got the whole story from Sang-Won. He didn't push her to tell him what had happened. And of course Sang-Hie and I didn't tell her what happened to all her books and belongings, not even that Sang-Hie had saved her precious notebooks, dozens of them.

My uncle said that she arrived at his house in her slippers and the coat over her pajamas. She had cried loudly in his arms and wouldn't say a word.

"What happened?" My uncle turned to Sang-Hie and me. Just then Sang-Won came out with a screaming plea, "I never want to go home. I want to live here with you and Auntie. I hate him and I think Mom is stupid to let him get away with it. She simply can't handle him. She doesn't even love me anyway." She wouldn't stop crying.

"What are you talking about, Sang-Won?" That's just not true. Your mom loves you. Don't ever say that." My uncle patted her back.

"It's true. You know, she pays all that money for Sang-Eun's cello lessons and she always takes her out shopping and stuff. And she just bought Sang-Hie a new piano. She wouldn't do anything for me."

"Then why are you the only one in your family to learn fencing and why are you the only one who has riding boots?" Sang-Won didn't have a response for that. My uncle had a fencing studio and he was Sang-Won's teacher.

My uncle looked at us, "Let her stay here tonight and I will bring her to your house tomorrow." My uncle hugged Sang-Won.

But Sang-Won didn't give up. "Mom needs to be strong. She can't be that weak with him. He needs someone strong to discipline him. We can't go on like this. Can I live with you? Please?" She pleaded, looking around at my aunt and their four kids. The two boys smiled and the two girls nodded their heads excitedly. My aunt caressed her hair and silently handed her a tissue. The warmth and attention were enough to make me want to be one of their children, too.

21

On the evening after the Seoul Yego entrance audition, Mr. Lim called my house to congratulate my mom and me. He told Mom how pleased he was to have such a talented cello student as a freshman.

I never thought a musical giant like him would welcome me personally into the creative environment I longed for. It probably was the happiest day of my life, and would begin a series of happiest days for the next three years. I felt I would ignite with joy wearing the badge of Seoul Yego. I was finally a winner in the world of competition.

Seoul Yego was an offshoot of Ewha girls' high school, founded just eight years prior to my acceptance. Mr. Won-Sick Lim, a well-known conductor, wanted to create a setting for young artists to concentrate on their talents and he recognized that to do so, they needed to be encouraged in a freer environment.

When Mr. Lim brought the idea to Mr. Bong-Jo Shin, who was the principal of Ewha girls' high school, Mr. Shin supported the idea enthusiastically and Seoul Yego nestled into the fourth floor of Ewha's main building. Mr. Shin was the principal at both schools for the first years, until he handed Yego over to Mr. Lim, saying, "How will a baby grow if the mother doesn't nurse him? I only helped the mother deliver the baby."

We were privileged to have Mr. Lim as our principal because he was considered a leader in the music community. Mr. Lim invited well-known musicians, mostly college professors, as associated staff members to Yego so they could give us private lessons. Among the cello associates were my teacher Mr. Kim, Mr. Chun, Seoul National University's professor, and Mr. Yang, the principal cellist of KBS Symphony Orchestra. These musicians obliged gladly to be on staff at this elite school and gave lessons to us at a fraction of their normal fee.

These musicians were the jurors at our entrance audition. Auditions for the piano students were held separately but simultaneously in front of all the piano teachers. Kyung-Sook Lee accompanied me on the piano. Kyung-Sook was exempt for the entrance audition because she had already won a few music competitions and was Mr. Lim's pride and joy. Kyung-Sook was there to accompany anyone who showed up without a pianist, as she was the best sight-reader as well. Mr. Kim had arranged for her to come to our house a few times so we could practice together. Walking into a roomful of jurors with Kyung-Sook and seeing my teacher Mr. Kim smile at me allowed me to play with ease. I only played halfway into the first movement of the Romberg Sonata when Mr. Lim tapped on the table and nodded at Mr. Kim.

Ewha girls' high school was founded by American Methodist missionaries at the end of the 19th century and the campus benefited from their early industriousness. Lush vegetation covered the grounds—grass and flower gardens and wisteria that arched over walking paths. Other high schools in Seoul were stark in comparison, with only a square gray building standing alone in the middle of a dirt playground. The same group of missionaries had also founded Ewha Women's University, where I planned to apply for college.

Three mornings a week, thousands of Ewha girls and our small group of about two hundred Yego kids filled the amphitheater in the center of the campus for morning service. These morning assemblies consisted of prayers, hymns and a sermon from the school chaplain, Mr. Mah, or a short pep talk from Mr. Shin. One morning, Principal Shin told us that we should realize how smart and special we were—that we were the cream of the crop of the whole country of Korea. He began by telling us that the Jews were the smartest race in the universe. "Look how many famous scientists, artists and musicians came from Jewish heritage," he said. Having acknowledged this, he then said that Koreans were just a little smarter than the Jews. Another morning, he said that we would all be mothers one day, and that we would each have a few children who would eventually become the future leaders of our country. Educating us properly and truthfully would conceivably change the history of Korea. Korea's future would depend on how we raised our children.

Then he picked up the Bible. "All truth is in the Bible," he said. "Make it a priority to read the Bible and follow God's teaching. Show your children the priority of life. Show them what's essential and what matters in life."

This was the first time I looked at the Bible as being filled with truth, and also the first time I began to think of it as the "Holy Book".

Even though I was joyful every time I walked onto Ewha's campus, a tiny part of me still felt a little uncertain and inadequate. Acceptance to Seoul Yego was determined primarily by audition. Candidates performed for the jurors and submitted a transcript. That was all that was required. In a competitive and class-conscious society I had come to believe that if a person wasn't a good student, they probably wouldn't be any good at anything else. Deep down in my heart, I knew I wasn't as smart as the Ewha kids, and this kept me from feeling thoroughly elite. But I didn't let the nagging feelings interfere with my happy daily routine.

For all three years of high school, our morning curriculum included Bible study twice a week, taught by Mr. Mah. Bible study in high school delved much deeper into God's word than my early Sunday school story hours. We even had to memorize difficult and insignificant names like Maher-Shalal-Hash-Baz. However, Mr. Mah told us the one thing we must always remember was John 3:16: *"For God so loved the world, that he gave his only begotten Son, that whosoever believeth in him should not perish, but have everlasting life."*

"That says it all right there," he said.

Ewha teachers also taught us morning academics. Morning classes didn't inspire me. Molecular formulas in chemistry, integral equations, and calculus gave me a headache. Civics was boring and German was a confusing language. During morning classes, my mind drifted to cello playing. I would examine the blistering callous on my thumb and position it on the back of my right forearm—my imaginary fingerboard—and exercise landing my fourth finger, which was the weakest.

Quite often, I saw piano majors doing the same thing. They would put their hands on the desk and drill trills or practice strengthening their fourth finger during morning classes, especially on days before finals and midterms when we were required to perform before jurors.

Sometimes, I would take my cello bow to school and hold it under the desk while trying to relax my right arm. Drawing the bow with a stiff or tight arm produced a shallow sound, but a relaxed arm created a deeper, mellow tone.

Bowing techniques like spiccato couldn't be achieved with a tight right hand either. During class, I mimicked the motion of bouncing the bow up and down and side to side with a relaxed right hand and arm. When I came home, I would try to allow my relaxed bowing arm to fall on the strings and transfer the weight of my arm into a difficult bowing technique that I had thought of during those boring morning classes.

As sixteen-year-olds and passionate aspiring music students, we only knew extremes of sentiment. Nothing was ordinary. The sky was not blue, it was electric blue and a red rose was passion incarnate. Everything around us was too precious to leave to go home for dinner. After school, my classmates and I would rather have sat under the tall flowering cosmos, absorbing the beauty of what God had laid out for us.

We expressed these embellished sentiments in the music we played. We played music in minor keys sadder than perhaps the composer intended. We tried to feel the insanity when we played the Hungarian Rhapsody. Bach and Vivaldi taught us a higher level of sacred virtuosity with unbounded interpretation and freedom.

In music appreciation class we listened to Arthur Rubinstein and Rudolf Serkin playing a piano concerto and compared each note and the styles of each player. We shed tears over Mimi's death in the romantic tale of La Boheme.

Not until Seoul Yego, did I enjoy my school life. The world I lived in then was truly special. I was surrounded by other young artists who felt, ate, and breathed music like I did. Between our weekly lessons, we practiced and discussed techniques.

My teacher Mr. Jai-Hong Kim taught me to treat each note I played on the cello with equal importance. "There are no insignificant notes. Every note has its own place of importance," he said. "Even grace notes. Especially the grace notes. Grace notes are ornamental, but they heighten the characteristics of the music and complete the piece. Without them, the music wouldn't have soul," he said, putting his index finger on his lip. "It is much like putting on an expensive suit but a terrible looking tie. They are the necklaces, the scarves and the purses for women to accessorize and make the outfit complete. A woman needs to have style to dress well and know how to put it together. But the style comes from the heart. The same way, to play the grace notes well, you have to feel the music from the heart. When you feel and breathe the music, you will automatically know how to play each grace note. Let it flow in your heart. By the same token, when you know how to play grace notes, then you will feel the music."

As he tried very hard to make me understand the significance of grace notes, and as I listened intensely, something happened. I saw the significance of grace notes as the soul of the music, and at the same time I learned an essential life lesson. Just as there were grace notes in music, there were grace notes in life. I wasn't sure what they were, but I was convinced that they were the very heart that completed a person. They were the characteristics, the intangible energy that gave a person purpose and made them note-worthy. They seemed to come humbly as of secondary importance, but determined the character of a person. I realized that a life without grace notes would be wearisome, uninspiring and purposeless.

With this new but vague awareness, I started putting my whole self passionately into whatever was laid out for me and found joy in the search of my grace notes. I felt an inherent need to find that energy, something that would charge my music and my life, because without it, whatever "it" was, my blissful life in music still felt incomplete. What I didn't realize then, and wouldn't until I became a grandmother, was that God was at work.

For practical purposes, I kept track of the works I studied. In a ledger, I listed the names of the music I had learned on the cello, including etudes, sonatas, concertos, and all other incidental pieces. I also listed all the pieces I was planning to learn in the near future. I wanted to have my ledger filled with many repertoires. I made goals to master a new piece by a certain date. I even made schedules for learning and mastering various techniques and skills.

It never occurred to me that I started allowing my goal-targeted competitiveness to take over the divine-natured grace notes. Rather than allowing my passion to come from the heart, I allowed my competitive desire to take over.

Even though Seoul Yego was a co-ed school, more than ninety percent of the students were female. In our class, three scrawny music major boys sat in the back row. Not having anyone at which to direct our hormones or our romantic sentiments, many of the girls put their dreamy pursuit on the blameless and improbable male teachers. Every young male teacher was subject to silent admirers. We justified and took pride in ourselves for appreciating the mature qualities of older men. Of course, we all knew it was not a viable situation. It was much like falling in love with a movie star we would never meet—just as we fell wildly for American actors.

Girls paid good money for pictures and posters of foreign movie stars and pasted the walls of their rooms with them. After the movie "Splendor in the Grass" came out, many girls fell in love with Warren Beatty's dreamy, pensive character. However, Gregory Peck was always my pin-up guy after "Guns of Navarrone." I never thought any human could be as handsome as Gregory Peck. I must have seen the movie half a dozen times.

We hoped for opportunities to meet guys from the boys' high schools, and high school social clubs were popping up for this very reason. I decided to join a club that was geared toward music appreciation. The club was organized between the girls from our school and boys from Kyung-Ki boy's high school, which made it all the more attractive.

The first time I saw Young-Soo, who was the self-appointed president of the club, I thought I was going to throw up from the butterflies in my stomach. I blushed from feelings I never knew existed in me before—my pounding heart and my turning stomach mingled with a wonderfully warm sensation that almost made me teary. When I turned away from him, I felt his gaze on my back.

"Can we get together one day for the calendar planning?" he asked me after the second meeting. I thought I would positively die, but I answered immediately with a smile, "Sure, you could come over to my house on Sunday."

He accepted with delight, saying, "Maybe you will play the cello for me."

I shocked myself by boldly inviting him. Since dating in high school was unheard of, there was simply no place for high school students to meet. We were not allowed to date. If anyone did, they would have to slink out wearing something other than their uniform and try to sneak into a movie because anyone could spot us as a high school student because of our straight hair. High school girls were not allowed to curl their hair. I got in trouble many times by Ewha's disciplinary counsel and accused of curling my hair. They didn't believe me when I said repeatedly that I had natural wavy hair.

The following Sunday Young-Soo came to my house and Sang-Hie served us fruits and joined us in our conversation in the living room. Sang-Hie's joining us made our visit a little less awkward and when she left us alone, we talked a little bit about the club meetings and decided that the meetings should include music appreciation opportunities and occasional recitals by the club members.

His visits occurred regularly. I gloated at the opportunity to become equal to my sisters. I had always envied my sisters' visitors in elite uniforms and Mom welcoming them by serving Coca Cola and rice cakes. Now I had my own guy, who was tall, came to see me in his Kyung-Ki uniform.

We talked on the phone frequently and I received letters from him in the mail. I replied in crinkled pink stationary and thought of him constantly. The tone of our letters became more and more amorous and personal.

For his birthday, I gave him the tiniest and prettiest seashell collection in a clear plastic box, and for Christmas I gave him three monogrammed handkerchiefs I found at the black market.

I was no longer intimidated facing friends who went to better junior high schools and I hoped that they would know that Young-Soo thought I was pretty terrific. I smiled brightly when my sisters smirked at me when he came over. He became my treasure to show off to everyone.

My life was consumed by two thoughts: cello and Young-Soo. I thought about him when I played cello. I thought about him on the way to school in the morning and all day until I went to bed.

My teacher, Mr. Kim devoted his life to being a cello teacher. He had the ability to make a star out of raw material and I considered myself his raw material. Insecurities seeded inside of me made me doubt him when he said I had tremendous talent, but he believed in me and this led him to put forth a determined effort to make me a stage performer.

He said there was no such thing as a natural-born prodigy. He said inborn talent and potential couldn't materialize without correct coaching and cultivating. He wanted to entice my mother to develop an uncontracted partnership with him in order to rear me into a polished performer. Mother's share was to provide financial means for a better cello and for more frequent lessons if needed.

He talked about Myung-Wha, his pride and joy who was two years older than me. "If I teach one thing, she will figure out three," he used to say. "And she has a mom who would sell her soul and move to the moon if it's necessary to make her famous." Myung-Wha and her family moved to America as soon as she graduated from my high school so she and her sister, who was a violinist, could attend Juilliard and Curtis.

After Myung-Wha left, Mr. Kim started planning my life as a would-be famous performer. He also put high hopes in Yun-Ja, who was one year ahead of me at Kyung-Ki girls' high school. He'd often assigned both of us the same piece to work on, clearly comparing us.

However, soon after I met Young-Soo, my practicing dwindled. I practiced vigorously only when there was a reason, like a music competition or playing for a jury for a final. Yun-Ja practiced diligently all the time. While I was not a great sight-reader, I learned a new piece quickly. Sometimes I would skip days of practicing since it only took me a couple of days to learn a piece for the following week's lesson.

During my sophomore year in high school, Mr. Kim planned my debut concert as a soloist with KBS symphony orchestra. Mr. Kim reserved the Boellman's Symphonic Fantasy for Yun-Ja and he decided I should play the Boccherini Concerto. When I expressed desire to play the Saint-Saens concerto, he said that I was not emotionally mature enough for it. He then added that Myung-Wha *unni* had played Boccherini for her debut and if it was good enough for her it should be good enough for me, too.

Mom and Sang-Hie started making a detailed list of the things to do for my debut concert. Sang-Hie made the guest list for complimentary tickets. Mom scheduled an ornate dinner party for the conductor to give him a chance to hear my playing before we started rehearsing at the concert hall. To get ready for the dinner, Mom hired a handyman and repaired the torn rice papers between the decorative dividers on the sliding doors throughout our house. Our cats loved scratching the heavy rice papers on the doors to make holes to jump through.

Mom took me to her friend Madame Choi, to make my concert dress. Both Myung-Wha and Yun-Ja went to the well-known designer Nora Noh for their dresses, but mom said that Madame Choi was a quality designer and would only charge a fraction of what the snooty Nora Noh would. It was evident that my hopes of meeting and wearing a Nora Noh were not going to happen. I would probably never have a chance to meet the tall, chic trendsetter I often saw in the newspaper. Nora Noh was a household name in elegant dressing and anyone preparing for a special occasion knocked on her door in Myung-Dong, ready to spend a fortune.

On the way, I whined one more time, "Couldn't we go to Nora Noh's salon like all the others?"

Sang-Hie promptly scolded me. "Don't be so immature. Just because you will be performing in Shi-Kong-Khwan, do you think Mom should go into debt? Mom's been spending half of her salary to pay for your lessons every month. You should be grateful that you get to wear a dress instead of your school uniform."

Madame Choi's shop was off the main street of Myung-Dong. The line of storefronts displayed mannequins of all kinds in the windows. Some wore evening gowns with beaded evening purses, some wore school uniforms or business suits, but none of them were half-naked or showed cleavage like we saw in many of the American fashion magazines.

We walked up the dark cement stairs into a bright and sunny Western-style room. Two sofas casually faced each other, and behind one of the sofas was a large desk. A telephone, a few magazines, and a couple of carelessly thrown on tape measures covered the ornately inlaid desktop. A long clothing rack full of dresses in all lengths, colors, and fabrics blocked the opposite wall from end to end.

Madame Choi manipulated her skinny, wrinkled hands with blue-painted nails to draw a beautiful dress with dropped short sleeves. "What do you think of something like this?" she asked with a forced smile, her hand at the waist of her tight gray skirt.

"I will wear anything you recommend." I decided to drop my immature and brash attitude after Sang-Hie's intimidating reprimand.

Sang-Hie reminded me over and over that all these preparations weren't justified unless I performed perfectly. Memorizing a piece came easily to me, and my fingers were flexible enough to be able to play without warm-up exercises. The rehearsals went well and the guest conductor, Nam-Soo Lee assured me that it would be a successful performance. However, the dress rehearsal was an unforgettably embarrassing experience. I made so many mistakes, I even stopped at one point and the conductor had to start from the top. I cried and wanted to back out of performing the following night, but Sang-Hie grabbed my arms unsympathetically and said, "It's the best thing to make mistakes at the dress rehearsal. It is like an antibiotic. You will have full immunity from all mistakes for tomorrow night's performance. Imagine if you didn't make any mistakes today. That would be awful. Those mistakes would have to show up sooner or later."

The awaited evening came and I wore a mauve, ankle-length silk dress with dropped sleeves and Sang-Hie curled my hair. Backstage, as I waited for my turn, Mr. Kim told me to go over the whole piece. Just as I started tuning my cello, I became so nervous I started shaking. "Teacher, I have to go to the bathroom first." I got up and laid my cello on the floor. I headed for the bathroom watching Mr. Kim picking up my cello.

When I turned the corner, I rammed into a man in a dark gray suit. When I looked up, I saw that it was Mr. Won-Sick Lim, the principal of my school, who was also the music director and principal conductor of the orchestra.

"I was just coming to see you," he said, "Are you all right?"

"No, Teacher Lim, I feel so nervous I can't stop shaking. I feel dizzy and I think I am getting sick." Before I could turn around, he very confidently placed both of his hands on my shoulders.

"Performance is playing the music you have practiced and perfected, just as you did at home. The only difference is you are sharing your music with an audience. You present it to the audience by showing the best you can. In order to do the best you can, you need to play with only one thing in mind. Concentrate and get into the music you know and play with your heart. Let your heart sing. Don't think about who might be out there watching you play, whether it is your best friend, boyfriend or some one who might criticize you or praise you – not even your parents, for that matter. You are not playing to impress anyone or to prove anything to anyone. Play from your heart, feeling the music you

know from practicing over and over. Only then, the audience will feel it
with you. To do that, sing along inside as you play. Your mind should be
on nothing else but singing the melody."

It was the most powerful talk anyone gave me throughout all my
performances. His grave, dignified voice rang in my ears even as I walked
up the stage, and I did not think of anything else but each note I was
playing, singing along inside.

After the concert, my teacher Mr. Kim said that I had proved him
wrong.

He had believed that a performance was considered successful if only
seventy percent of the best practice was presented. But I had performed
a hundred plus percent on the stage, he said. I didn't know exactly what
he meant by that, but I knew that I was his favorite student and he was
passionate about grooming me into a polished performer.

When my family and relatives surrounded me backstage praising
me, my brother, in his officer's uniform, smiled proudly and handed
me a bottle of cold Coca-Cola with a straw sticking out. For a fleeting
second, I felt a punch of tenderness toward him. But just as quickly, I
realized how nice it would be when he was finally gone for good. He had
been getting ready to leave for America to study business or economics.
Now that he had completed his military duty, he was able to obtain a
passport.

In those days, I stayed up late at night writing letters to no one in
particular, and going through the desk drawers arranging and rearranging
all my treasures like my seashell or postcard collections. My favorite
postcard was one with a small house built in the hollow of the trunk
of a giant redwood tree somewhere in Northern California. I collected
anything pretty and beautiful I could find. I collected notebooks made
in Japan because they always seemed to have colorful covers. The manu-
script music notebooks had bright red covers. In the top drawer I also
kept a catalog from the Curtis Institute of Music in Philadelphia. I
would periodically open it and look through it from cover to cover then

slide it back into the drawer after smoothing it out to make sure there weren't any creases.

What I treasured most were the letters from Young-Soo and the articles he wrote in his school magazine. I practically memorized every word he wrote to me in his block penmanship. I would read them over and over again, pausing at words like "love" or "adorable" or "missing."

I also spent a lot of time at the desk arranging dried yellow and red fall leaves. When Young-Soo wanted to borrow a poetry book, I gave it to him with two bright red miniature maple leaves stuck inside. And when he returned it to me, he exchanged them with yellow gingko leaves.

One day in English class, I drifted away daydreaming like all the other days, staring blankly at the chalkboard. I was not aware when the teacher, Mr. Cho, called on me. He came toward my seat and tapped my head with the third call. "What are you thinking about, kid?" His gentle voice didn't lift me out of the lulled state of my mind. But with the word 'kid,' his gray suit sleeve brushed my cheek, leaving a faint scent of sweet cologne. Just then with his soft-spoken admonishment, I felt the most peculiar feeling. It was a feeling I had not experienced before, but it was pleasurable and I wanted to hear his voice again. It felt as if something was pressing my heart and I wondered if a heart attack might feel like this.

Unlike other English teachers, he spoke slowly and gently. Most of them seemed to be vibrant and fast-talking as they rolled their tongues pronouncing all the 'R's and 'L's with exaggerated and expressive intonations. This new feeling was what made me wait for English class every day, and I made sure my uniform was pressed and bleached white for him. If I ran into him in the school corridor, I blushed, and my friends started teasing me. It was a different feeling than I had for Young-Soo. I didn't want to hold his hand. I just wanted to listen to him, quietly.

Quite often on Sundays I went to school to practice cello. It was not unusual for kids to come to school to practice, as each classroom had a piano and the school building was quiet. My friend, Young-Hae also came to school every Sunday after church service to practice.

On this particular Sunday, I settled in the teacher's lounge because my classroom was on the fourth floor. I propped the music against a large vase of spring flowers on a round table with a white tablecloth in the middle of the room. Through the open windows, the slight breeze carried a delightful fragrance.

I ran through the scales and arpeggios briefly but decided to skip the etude. The spring air, the flowers, and the fresh greenery through the windows were all too perfect to waste on drills and exercises. I started playing all the pretty melodic pieces. I played the Swan. I played the Boellman's Symphonic Fantasy. I played Kol Nidrei. The slow vibrato of my left hand was completely in sync as I swiftly maneuvered all five fingers following the music faster and slower never allowing the bow to leave the strings. I was in my own world where no one could possibly enter or even understand as I strung out the beautiful melody, note after note, like precious beads of pearls. I held a note in the high register with retardando and came down to a lower register with a satisfactory sigh. I took a breath. Tears were running down my cheeks. This must be what heaven was like, so wonderfully satisfying and beautiful.

It was when I started to play the second movement of the Lalo Concerto that I was aware of some movement behind me. When I stopped playing and turned around, I couldn't believe my eyes. Intoxicated in my world of music, I thought I was dreaming. Mr. Cho was leaning against the window behind me, painting me playing the cello. I started shaking and my heart started pounding. I didn't know where to go or what to do.

Unconsciously, I bowed lightly to him, which was what we did whenever we saw a teacher anywhere. I felt my face hot from blushing and my legs felt like cooked noodles. I needed to sit down. But first I had to disappear. Before I could say anything, he walked over to me with his sketchbook. I stared at the painting of me, my black head above the white loose blouse, my body clutching the hourglass-shaped instrument, the scroll of the cello and a couple of pegs peeking out from my black disheveled hair. My arms were moving. It was alive. It was a beautiful piece of art. It showed the intricate beauty of the cello in the background of the black squiggly notes on the five lines of the sheet music. And it interweaved with the pastel spring mixture of flowers. The contrast of black hair bouncing from left to right as if it was moving with trembling vibrato and the delicate body of the cello peeping from the sides of my loose blouse as I moved. I was seeing myself in a fusion and balance amid total chaos.

As I was staring at it, I had a daring thought as I realized what would have made the painting perfect. The thought shocked and embarrassed me, and I never wanted anyone to know what I had imagined. But to make the painting perfect, I should have been naked. My loose waisted blouse was what made it chaotic. It didn't belong in the painting. Instead, my smooth and soft off-white skin should have followed the firm curve of the cello. Only then could I hear the deep resonating melody in the painting. I felt lightheaded.

"I am sorry but I have to go." I left the room, my body trembling, the breeze cooling my face.

Standing at the window of my classroom upstairs, I stared out at the lavender wisteria blossoms. I don't know how long I stood there when I heard, "Sang-Eun-ah, what are you doing standing there?" I quickly turned around and saw Young-Hae with an armful of Beethoven Sonatas.

"Oh, Young-Hae, the most wonderful thing just happened." I ran over to her. "Mr. Cho, our English teacher just watercolored me. You know, while I was practicing the cello, downstairs in the Yego teacher's lounge."

"He what? Why? Did he ask you if he could?"

"He just did. I didn't even know until I got up to take a break. He was standing behind me with a brush in his hand."

"Are you serious?" She took a moment and then said, "That's not nice of him."

"What do you mean, it's not nice?"

"Think about it. Just a quick thoughtless glance from him would make you lose sleep at night. And here he was painting you, staring at you while you are practicing your music, your way of expressing your emotions," She shook her head.

"If that wasn't leading you on, I don't know what is. When all along he showed no interest in you which was the most decent thing he has done, him being married and all."

"Oh," I nodded at her wisdom. I felt like a cat watching a bird fly out of his paws.

22

Shortly after my debut performance, my brother left for America and my mom received weekly letters from him in which he said how lonely and miserable he was. He managed to enroll at Pepperdine College in downtown Los Angeles and even worked part-time at Coast Federal Savings and Loan. My brother's absence only compounded my exciting life.

In October of 1961, as a sophomore in high school I participated in the music competition sponsored by Yon-Sei University. This competition was not my first choice. Every major university held one, and I wanted to compete in Ewha Women's University's, where my teacher was a professor, and it was one of the top two prestigious music contests. The other was Seoul National University's.

"Teacher, I would really like to compete in Ewha University's competition. I will learn all the required pieces and will practice to perfect them, I will," I said.

"Kid, you need to leave an opportunity for older sister to win. I refuse to have two of my students compete with each other. What if you would win? What would it do to your older sister's morale and ego? You will have your chance to win next year at Ewha. This year you may play in Yon-Sei's competiton." He had many older students and he called them all my "older sisters."

"But there will always be an older sister, next year also. It doesn't seem right to stay away just because someone older wants to participate," I mumbled barely under my breath. I wasn't supposed to question a teacher's judgment no matter how unreasonable it seemed.

A week later, I talked my best friend Jin-Hee, into participating in Yon-Sei's competition with me. Her mom was a piano professor in Dae-Ku and had arranged for her to live with her aunt and uncle in Seoul.

"I will write to my mom and see what she says." Jin-Hee seemed reluctant and wanted to ask her mom first.

"Don't be silly. Why don't you just go ahead and win it and surprise her. You will win for sure, I know," I insisted. Plunging into a competition with a friend gave me a certain moral support. And because Jin-Hee was a pianist, we wouldn't be competing with each other.

I played the Bach unaccompanied Suite No. 3 for the Yon-Sei competition and placed first. Jin-Hee played Chopin's etude, "Black Key" and also placed first. My school announced our awards through the microphone in the amphitheater at the morning assembly. After the assembly, a crowd of Ewha kids who were heading for their classes gathered around to congratulate us—the kids I had known from fifth and sixth grades. I sheepishly acknowledged the attention but inside, I was floating with glee.

I accepted my teacher's decisions and executed the tasks whether it was a concert or a music competition. On the stage I performed flawlessly. I prepared for each event by submerging myself into practice for hours and hours, sometimes skipping school and skipping meals.

By the time I was a senior, I felt comfortable enough to appear on TV and perform on a day's notice at various occasions from a large repertoire I had built up. Big organizations called our school, requesting a few music students to perform at their functions for their distinguished guests. The school almost always sent me with a pianist or a violinist. I performed at the "Korea House" (a traditional Korean-style house built to show off to foreign guests), in a Korean costume, in front of a few dozen diplomats from all over the world. I performed at the

Hyun-Dai Corporation Chairman Chung's birthday party. I performed at the American embassy at a Friday night event.

In my senior year, I asked Mr. Kim to prepare me for Ewha Univerisity's contest.

"Let's think about it. You still have an older sister to relinquish your chance to win. You might just skip the high school years and partake in the Dong-A competition in your freshman year in college." Mr. Kim struck a match and lit a cigarette as if he didn't want to discuss it any more. "That's what I think," he said.

"What if I participate in Seoul National University's competition and let older sisters enter Ewha's?"

"How can you say that when I teach at Ewha? Seoul is a rival university and all of Mr. Chun's students submit their entries to compete at Seoul. And you want to be a part of that? What a slap in my face."

"But, but, this is my last chance as a high school student. I would like to do another competition this year."

"Kid, I don't want to talk about it. Case closed. Do what you want."

Adults always gave me their final word when I simply expressed a reasonable desire, and if I questioned further, they would start yelling and call me an impudent child. My grandfather was that way, and so was my mother. My father was the only one around whom I had never felt that threat. Instead, he had calmly explained things to me when he thought I was being unreasonable.

That night, I came home and composed a letter.

Dear Teacher Kim,

I am writing to you because you told me that you didn't want to further discuss my desire to participate in the music competition. I understand your reasoning for older sisters to have a chance to win. And I should perhaps stay behind and wait for my turn to win. You are the teacher and each of your students is important to you. And I appreciate that. However,

*here is the truth. The competitions are open to all high school students, and
I have just as much right as anyone regardless of age.*

*I respect you and I can't imagine how much you have taught me. But this
situation leaves me no choice but to look for an alternate preparation. I
need to find a teacher who will honor my wishes. However I will eternally
be grateful for all the efforts you have put into grooming me into a desired
cellist."*

I did not mail the letter until I made a visit to Mr. Yang, a cello
teacher who didn't have an association with any colleges.

"Would you please teach me and help me get ready for Seoul
University's competition?" Mr. Yang was one of the staff members of
Yego. He was a juror at our midterms and finals. He had heard me play
many times and always gave me an A.

"Of course I would love to be your teacher. Don't concern yourself
about anything. I am a teacher. I teach as best as I can and support whatever the students want to do, unless of course there is an excellent reason
not to. Nowadays, students get wrapped up in the battles of teachers."
He shrugged his shoulders, "I don't get into such a scuffle with other
teachers." He laughed, showing his white teeth. His laugh lingered
to the next sentence. "Life is too short. If you are not happy, make a
change, that's my motto." His plump, short body stood solid against the
floor. "Take me, for an instance. I don't have a degree so I probably will
never be able to teach at a university. But I am happy doing my thing,
teaching and being a principal cellist in the KBS Symphony Orchestra,"
he continued, again shrugging his shoulders. "Music should be enjoyed.
Rivalry shouldn't be a part of music."

I didn't realize how brave I was at the time. Changing music teachers
was a cardinal sin and the ultimate betrayal, but I didn't think much
about it except that I was tired of someone else making decisions for me.
I had no intention of betraying Mr. Kim and going to any other university but Ewha. If I had an intention to go to Seoul National University,
I would have gone to Mr. Chun, who was teaching at Seoul.

For the following few weeks, kids at school whispered about my disloyalty to Mr. Kim. Sang-Hie even thought I was extremely audacious, though she supported my decision. She, too, had wanted me to enter another music competition.

During the subsequent midterm performance, Mr. Kim did not look at me once. He kept his eyes fixed on the music he was holding the entire time I was performing. It not only made me feel like a rat, it also made me feel timid and nervous.

Mr. Yang's personality couldn't have been farther from Mr. Kim's. His teaching methods were just as different. With a piece of music, he emphasized understanding the style of the particular period and intention of the composer rather than concentrating on playing to dazzle the audience. After studying with Mr. Yang for six months, I played the Boccherini Sonata No. 6 at Seoul University's competition.

When I was on the stage of the university's auditorium and saw the row of jurors in the third row, I couldn't stop shaking. I looked at Sang-Hie who accompanied me on the piano. She smiled and nodded. Her smile gave me such assurance and comfort, I quickly settled on my chair and took a deep breath. Then I started singing inside to transform the nervous adrenaline into a succession of notes.

I didn't think I performed nearly as well as I did at all my rehearsals with Sang-Hie, but I won first place and was also honored with the chancellor's award. Switching to Mr. Yang was bad enough, but it was even more of a slap in the face to Mr Kim when I won the most prestigious high school competition and presented all the glory to Mr. Yang, whom I had only studied with for six months.

Sang-Hie was the most influential figure in my becoming a cellist, but by now, my whole family supported me. They praised me when I won competitions and spoke proudly when I appeared on TV. I went from the Lee family's "youngest daughter who was not so smart" to "one who redeemed herself by finding her true talent." I went from a disgrace to the topic of conversation.

My mom and my oldest sister Sang-Soon made sure I was nourished when I practiced. Sang-Soon would make me fried rice omelets and bring them to me quietly, tip-toeing in fear that she might interrupt my practicing.

Mom would leave a plateful of my favorite, *sam-kyub-sal* (boiled and sliced pork) on my desk with shrimp sauce and *kimchee*, just in case I took a break and had a few minutes to eat.

But my third sister, Sang-Won was different. She buried herself in books. She thought the rest of the family didn't understand the true meaning of life, and thought we only cared about superficial worldly desires. She made a face at me when I said I wanted to wear a Nora Noh. She wore a jacket with holes at the elbow when she climbed a mountain, while we always wore custom-made jackets or imported sweaters. But she didn't hesitate to ask mom for a pair of expensive riding boots and new fencing gear. When Mom wouldn't get her new riding boots, Sang-Won told Mom that her priorities were mixed up because she would support Sang-Hie and me so we could wallow in an opulent lifestyle. Sang-Won thought that musicians were nothing but show-offs who only recognized fame in shallow luxuries.

Since my father's death five years earlier, my mother had managed to buy me a decent cello—although for concerts I almost always borrowed one from either a music store or another student of Mr. Kim's who owned a better instrument. Mom also managed to upgrade Sang-Hie's old German-made piano to a Yamaha in her junior year of college so she could prepare for her recital. But the house we lived in required constant maintenance and updating, so when I was a senior in high school, Mom made the decision to sell our Shin-Mun-Ro house with seven bedrooms and move to a two-room apartment beyond Young-Chun marketplace.

"I have always wanted to live simply in a Western style apartment and have a flushing toilet," she said as if a weight was lifted off her shoulders. We accepted Mom's decision quietly, and Sang-Soon and Sang-Hie accompanied Mom when she looked for a new place for us. When they graduated from college, Mom depended more and more on them. They worked and helped Mom with the rent, and the three of them made the financial plans and monthly budget.

In Seoul, most people still lived in a residence with a yard, and they thought apartment living was mainly for diplomats and missionaries who resided in Korea temporarily. No matter how much the government and the builders promoted apartment living, I could count the number of apartment buildings in all of Seoul in one hand.

In the apartment, I no longer had my own room and had no privacy, but my life as an active high school girl didn't change much. With Mom and her four girls, our house was more like a girls' dormitory than anything else.

Sang-Won, who now was an English major at the Foreign Language University—her desire to become an engineer was long gone—got used to studying with me practicing next to her. Mom stopped hiring a maid and decided we should take turns cooking and cleaning.

Mom, Sang-Soon, and Sang-Hie did most of the cooking and Sang-Won and I did the dishes. To make our lives easier, Mom bought a new manually agitated washing machine. It had a hose attachment to fill it up with water and soap. We had to crank the handle and check the cleanliness of the laundry at regular intervals. Then the same procedure was repeated for rinsing. Once it was rinsed twice, we had to hang the clothes on the line to dry in the patio. I thought it was more trouble than washing a few pairs of underwear by hand and hanging them in the bathroom, but Mom loved the rocket-ship-looking laundry machine.

The washing machine was just one of many household gadgets Mom collected. We had a waffle iron, room heater, two different types of toasters, and two coffee percolators, some new and some used, all purchased at the surplus store or at the black market.

In that same year, the Ministry of Education declared a new procedure for admission to college. Everyone, regardless of their choice of major or school, had to pass the state mandated exam, designed to eliminate all non-college-bound seniors. Although the exam covered only the very minimum required level of high school proficiency, to me it was another potentially devastating failure, where I might not only lose face but also the fame and reputation I had built up.

Once we passed the state mandated exam, we were to submit transcripts and applications to the respective colleges, and then take another daylong exam on every subject. The degree of difficulty of these exams varied in line with the exclusiveness of colleges. With Ewha University, being my choice, I needed to concentrate intensely on academics. I regretted neglecting schoolwork for the two-and-a-half years I had been at Yego. I wished I could turn back the clock or freeze time. The more I thought about it, the more it brought up bitter and painful memories.

Desperate, I asked if there was a chance of us immigrating to America.

"Don't be ridiculous and start studying," Mom snapped.

"What about me just going to America to a music prep school? Kyung-Sook Lee went in 10th grade. She went to Juilliard prep school."

Mom rolled her eyes and I realized I had no choice but to start studying.

I reshuffled my daily schedule and stayed late at school to study. In calculus, the class that scared everyone the most, we asked the teacher to brush us up on the basics of the equation. Some people thought trigonometry was easier but I resented it with a passion. I didn't understand why in the world I would need to figure out the rationales of triangles to play the cello.

However, I began cramming fact after fact of history and geography until my brain hurt. I asked Young-Soo to come over to help me with German, and he obliged willingly. As a pre-med major seeking to get into Seoul National University, he devoted the whole senior year to nothing but studying. Helping me with German enabled us to see each other and be constructive.

I looked for an English tutor to make me a perfect speller. Sang-Hie hired a chemistry and physics tutor for me, a female brainy physics major from Seoul National University. The room turned into a scholar's den, with books stacked up in every corner and my cello put away in its canvas case. As a music major, I also had to be prepared to audition in front of the music faculty of the respective colleges. Even though the audition weighed heaviest in all combined scores, I knew I didn't need to worry about cello playing.

By the time the winter wind knifed through my navy uniform, going to school lost all fun. I knew my life was about to be knifed as well. I wondered if God had teased me with a glimmer of success only to take me back to my true self, a born failure.

As a busy high school girl aspiring to be a concert cellist, I had not put a lot into God and my spiritual dedication did not extend much beyond the biweekly Bible class taught by Reverend Mah. I called myself a Christian, but my daily life didn't reflect it. It had been years since I attended Sunday church service, but I didn't feel like I was missing anything

As a last resort I decided to pray to the Almighty God, "Please, allow me to go to a college of my choice. I don't know how, but let me pass all the written exams, please, please. You are the only one who can make miracles happen. And I believe this will take a miracle."

I prayed every morning on the way to school and every night before I went to bed. Then one winter morning, my homeroom teacher, Mr. Woo-Keun Lee came into the class holding Dong-A Daily.

"Great news! This morning, the Ministry of Education announced new modified guidelines for prospective music majors only. Those of you who proved your expertise by winning first place in any of the high school level or open music competitions may apply to any college of your choice and you will be accepted, provided you receive your high school diploma. No entrance exam of any kind is required."

For a split second, I thought the cold weather froze my ears. I simply didn't believe what I heard. I was convinced there was a God, and He knew and cared about Sang-Eun Lee.

That day, I spent all afternoon turning our apartment back into a cello studio. My cello was uncovered and rested against a chair. I filled a vase with flowers on my table and replaced the stack of books with my framed debut picture. I wiped my empty desktop until it gleamed and I repeated, "Thank you, thank you, thank you, Lord."

23

I applied and was accepted to Ewha University where my teacher Mr. Kim was a professor. He was extremely pleased with my coming back to him. Mr. Chun, Seoul University's cello professor, thought I entered their competition because I wanted to go there. When he found out that I applied to Ewha, he summoned me to convince me that I should be loyal to the school that gave me an honor. "What about my teacher Mr. Kim? My loyalty still lies with Mr. Kim. He was my teacher from the beginning. He was the one who got me started," I replied. "I never intended to turn my back against Mr. Kim."

In Korea, the start of a college was marked by an induction ceremony just as graduation was honored by a commencement ceremony. Going to the induction ceremony was an occasion to celebrate. It meant that we had achieved the uppermost level of education at an elite university, and it was a big affair for anyone who was beginning a new college life. Everyone showed up in new, colorful two-piece suits and matching pumps and nylons.

The new semester started in the spring, so during the month of February and March, between the time of announcement of acceptance and the beginning of the new college semester, designer shops in Myung-Dong displayed colorful and elaborately designed suits luring young girls who were about to launch a new phase of their lives. No more navy and white uniforms, no more sneakers or flat penny loafers. We were free to dress in whatever we wanted, free to go to movies, free to date, and best of all, free to curl our hair and even get permanents.

All of my friends got their suits made in a solid color. I had my jacket made in salmon with a brown tweed collar and matching skirt. But the quintessential accessory that symbolized our status as college girls were the nylons. We paid exorbitant amounts of money for nude, delicately woven threads that weighed next to nothing. When I put them on my lotioned legs, I wore thin white gloves so that my calloused fingers wouldn't snag them.

"The Shining Star," a thirty-minute TV program that spotlighted young talents, asked me to appear on the day of the induction ceremony. I didn't want to do it. I knew that there would be many other opportunities to be on TV, but there was only one induction ceremony in my whole life. Sang-Hie tried to convince me otherwise, telling me that they reserved half an hour just for me, and would end with a five-minute interview. If I turned it down they would ask someone else, a violinist or a pianist, and might never ask me again.

"It's also shown at the primetime when everyone stays home relaxing and watching TV after celebrating the big day, the start of their new lives," she said. And I would need all day to get ready for it by keeping myself calm and getting my fingers limber, which meant I needed to stay away from the excitement of tasting college life. I hated not to be a part of the kickoff event, but I agreed.

By then I had a closet full of concert dresses, all made by Madam Choi. Sang-Hie and I picked a royal blue knee-length dress; I was always told to wear a dark colored dress on TV. Sang-Hie made a matching bow for my hair.

With Sang-Hie's accompaniment on the piano, I started with the Bruch's *Kol Nidrei* then the Beethoven's *Twelve Variations* and ended with the Saint Saens's *Swan*. As soon as I played the last note, a female announcer approached me and interviewed me while I remained seated holding my cello.

When she asked me if I would go abroad to further my study in music, I answered without hesitation, "If that's what God intends for me, it will happen. And I will happily abide by His will."

College was full of new experiences; even the fifteen-minute city bus ride to school gave me a thrill. Previously, I had always walked to school. On occasion, I had ridden on the bus but never when it was so crowded before. The seats on the bus ran all along the windows, leaving plenty of space in the middle for passengers to stand. The standing passengers held handles dangling from the ceiling of the bus, and when the bus was full, two or three people shared the same handle. I could barely reach the ring on my tippy-toes with my arm fully extended. I quickly learned not to stretch my arm to hang on, especially in the summer when I wore a sleeveless dress. In those days, girls didn't shave their underarms, so we kept our arms close to our body all day long when wearing a sleeveless dress. To make matters worse, we dressed up to go to school. I took an hour to put nylons on, curl my hair, and get dressed in a suit to get in the grimy taxicab or on crowded bus where I would inevitably snag my brand-new nylons. But we did it day after day.

Before long, the bus ride lost its excitement. Having sweaty bodies close to me on the bus wasn't my favorite way of traveling, so I often went in a ride-sharing automobile, which had four rows of seats. On the days I needed to take my cello to school for orchestra rehearsal or a cello lesson, I took a taxi. By then, I gave cello lessons to younger students and was able to afford these small luxuries. But however luxurious taxicabs were compared to the bus, they were no limousines. Most taxies were square jeeps (*shi-bal* taxi) or tiny four-door sedans called *sae-na-ra*.

since it was considered nerdy to carry a book bag in college, I carried my cello effortlessly in my right hand and an armful of music and books in my left hand.

Because Ewha was a Christian university, students were required to attend chapel three times a week. In addition, Christian Literature class was required twice a week. Reverend Mah from my high school was promoted to Ewha University the same year I started college. Though the Reverend led most of the chapel services, this responsibility was also

shared with other Christian professors from various departments. When
it was a music professor's turn, they would often ask me to play a cello
piece to fill some of the time so their sermon could be short. I usually
played an excerpt from Kol Nidrei, Jesu, Joy of God, or variations of
hymns.

Sometimes, as I sat with thousands of other students in the auditorium, I wondered how so many girls from Buddhist families and
non-believer families sat through the services day after day. Even though
he was a wonderful teacher of the Bible, Reverend Mah's sermons became
monotonous and repetitive, and three times a week quickly became too
much for me. I started passing notes during the services or writing letters
to Young-Soo.

One day, when I was still enjoying the novelty of college life, Mr.
Kim called me into Mr. Chung's office during their regular teatime. Mr.
Kim had lunch with Mr. Hee-Suck Chung every day. Mr. Chung was the
violin professor and the conductor of the school orchestra. Their offices
were right next to each other. My teacher's room was stark, with a piano
and a desk, although Yun-Ja, who was a sophomore cello student, made
sure he had a vaseful of flowers on his desk at all times. In contrast, Mr.
Chung's room was fully furnished with a sofa and two armchairs. The
top of the upright piano was decoratively enveloped with an embroidered cover. He always had a tea set on a tray on the coffee table and the
two of them shared Japanese tea between lessons and classes.

Mr. Chung was quite a bit shorter than my teacher, but they both
looked like they had just stepped out of *GQ* magazine, Mr. Chung in
his gold-rimmed glasses and a bow tie, and Mr. Kim in his tight-fitting
Italian suit.

Mr. Kim gave me the sheet music for all three required pieces for the
music competition sponsored by Dong-A Daily. "Let's start working on
all three pieces right away. The dates of the competition will be posted
in the paper today. The preliminaries will start in August and the final is
at the end of October. We have just about five months to master all three
pieces," Mr. Kim said, his eyes fixed on mine.

"Unlike all the high school music competitions, Dong-A's competition is the highest level and the most prominent music competition, open to all age groups—college students, college graduates, everyone. You need to put your social life on hold. No more going to tearooms, no more going to the movies. You need to focus on practicing," he said, "There will be plenty of time to meet boys. Right now, nothing is more important than practicing the cello."

Mr. Chung chimed in teasingly, "By the way, your mom allows you a life in the lap of luxury. Look at you in another new outfit. You look like you are going out on a date." For some reason, I seemed to inspire Mr. Chung's sense of humor every time he saw me. He mimicked me playing the thumb position in the high register on the cello, stretching his arms, nearly standing up as if his arms were hugging and climbing a huge cello. "I guess a short person understands another short person's problem," I shot back at him, giggling.

Mr. Kim laughed at the exchange of banter, then reiterated, "No dating, your social life can stand still for a while. Don't even go to the Meeting."

"But I'm not going to miss the Meeting," I protested.

The Meeting was an appropriately named event. Since Ewha was a women's university, each department provided an opportunity to meet college guys from another university. Our music department's choice was the engineering school of Seoul National University. The committees contacted each other and agreed on a place and time to meet. It was like a giant group blind date. Even though I was dating Young-Soo, I had looked forward to going to the Meeting ever since school started. I wasn't about to skip this party for anything.

Our first Meeting was at a tearoom on a Saturday night. The tearoom was closed to the public for the event. Since the highest test scores were required to enter the engineering school, all of my friends were excited to meet potentially the smartest and most perfect men.

We were given a seat number in advance and when we entered the room, we were to find the respective seats where the guy with our matching number would be waiting. It was an uncomfortable setting, but there was something consoling about being in a group and doing as we were told.

Most of the guys sat awkwardly when their dates found their seats.

When I found my seat, my guy got up and introduced himself to me in an accent from the province of Kyung-Sang-Do. He told me later that he was from Dae-Ku.

"I am Sang-Eun Lee. Nice to meet you," I said, giggling. I was somewhat disappointed at his ordinary build and not especially good-looking appearance. I didn't know what I anticipated, but I spent the evening wishing I was with Young-Soo.

The next Monday, I told Mr. Kim that I wouldn't go to the next Meeting, and I started practicing for the Dong-A competition.

Sang-Hie excelled in whatever she pursued, and the dean of my college, Young-Ee Kim adored her. Upon her graduation as a piano major, the dean of the Ewha University's music school recommended her as the music producer when the KBS-TV station requested the dean's recommendation.

After working at the TV station for a little over a year, just after I started college, Sang-Hie left for America to go to graduate school at UCLA on a scholarship. Mom sold our Yamaha to buy her a one-way plane ticket to America, the land of no return.

To my mom, Sang-Hie's leaving meant losing another one of her children and she knew very well that she might never see her again. When my brother Sang-In had left for America two years earlier, Mom cried, not because she might never see him again but because she knew God gave him another chance to shape up and become somebody she could be proud of. She had heard that in America, in the land of opportunity, all the foreign students studied hard and learned to be responsible. America straightens out uncontrollable, ungrateful, and spoiled people, even juvenile delinquents.

To her, America was the cure-all, get-rich-quick and get-mature magical place. For that magic, getting lonely and homesick was a small price to pay. By the same token, she recognized, despondently, that she might never see them again.

When my brother left, my sisters and I celebrated, because it meant the end of living in fear. But Sang-Hie's departure was entirely different to all of us, especially to Mom. In those days, outstanding achievers all seemed to have the goal of moving to America, to this mysterious place where the precious children of Korea disappeared one by one—a place with clean flushing toilets and houses surrounded by lawns instead of block walls.

Mom knew that each of her offspring would eventually leave her and she knew it would happen quickly once it started. But she also knew that she should support our dreams and be grateful. After all, the selected ones had the privilege of a chance to study in the "Beautiful Country" (America literally translated), and people envied them.

The night before Sang-Hie left, Mom rubbed her bloodshot eyes, twisted her handkerchief, and held Sang-Hie's hand. She said, "I know you will do well and know that you will study hard. I won't worry about you. There are two things you need to put first when you are in California. Take care of your brother, make sure that he straightens out and studies hard and secondly, you need to see to it that Sang-Eun gets over to America to further her talent."

I sobbed, staring at them. Sang-Hie had been by my side for every big and small event I went through. I was only a freshman at Ewha University. Would I be able to function without her? Would I know how to dress for a concert? Would I know how to compete? Who would give me a pep talk and boost my self-confidence?

Sang-Hie never cried. The next day, Sang-Hie walked up to the plane with poise and waved at us as she carried the orphan baby she was responsible for delivering to adoptive parents waiting in America—a job offered to students for a hundred dollars each.

Coming home from the airport, the streets of Seoul felt empty, as did my heart. That evening, my boyfriend Young-Soo, by then a pre-med student at Seoul National University, wanted to cheer me up and took me to Renaissance, a tearoom where they played classical music requests. As college students, we were allowed to date openly and go to Renaissance. Sitting next to each other, we listened to the Bach's unaccompanied cello suites, which made my heart seem even emptier.

At one point, Young-Soo said, "You know, one day you will go to America and see your sister. Then you will miss your mother and remaining sisters and perhaps even me. But that's what life is all about. You meet, separate, miss, and grow. I think this is a turning point of your life. In the grand scheme of your entire life, losing Sang-Hie is a small part of your life experience. It's that small click that will make you grow to another level. I believe whenever you are emotionally stressed, whether it is from a deep hurt or from life's game of conflict and competition, we need to use it as a catalyst and learn from it." He peered at me and moved one side of his mouth like he wanted to smile.

"Where did you learn to talk like that—that dog-shit philosophy?" I smirked, pleased at his wisdom.

"Yeah, it is nonsense philosophy. But I can assure you, the line between sober and drunk is only one sip of alcohol. Happiness and unhappiness are only as far apart as a sheet of paper. It's the small things that matter. We can either benefit from them or brood on them."

Silently, I extended my open hand and he placed his into mine.

24

I sat on the closed toilet seat and went over the entire concerto, fingering on the back of my right forearm as if I was playing the cello. I closed my eyes and sang as my hand vibrated on the pretend fingerboard. Living in a tiny, two-room apartment, the bathroom was often a quiet escape, especially today.

My stomach felt like a twisted rope. I rubbed my stomach to ease the nervous cramps. I wished Sang-Hie were here. She would think of something to say to calm me.

"You have such a gift. You know how to put your feelings into your music. You can really sing on the cello," she would say.

"When you perform, the audience can tell you are completely into the music you are making. You get into it and everyone knows that you are in your own world." Her words always made me feel confident and forget how nervous I was. What's more, I started believing everything she said.

Before she left for America, Sang-Hie always played the piano accompaniment for me when I performed. Having her on the stage with me gave me great comfort and security.

Today, for the final performance of Dong-A Daily's competition, my accompanist knew when to accelerate, she knew when to slow down, and how to make contrasting dynamics, all by my slightest nods. She felt the music I played by the way I moved the bow. And from our countless days of practice, she and I could play the whole piece by heart. But she didn't have the ability to accompany my heart like Sang-Hie did.

Today was the end of an agonizing three-month-long selection process. Hundreds of musicians of all categories entered every year. We had to play two preliminaries onstage in the recital hall behind a curtain so that the jurors would not favor their own students.

The required cello piece for the first preliminary was the Breval Sonata in G major. I was ready but scared, like a bull facing a bullfighter. The jurors dropped a dozen contestants that day, but I passed with ease. The compulsory piece a month later for the second preliminary, also by memory, was the Golterman concerto No. 1. We performed on the stage of Seoul National University's auditorium. This piece was full of thumb positions and double stops. Even though I practiced tough passages slowly and repeatedly to the point where I could play with precision, I was unusually nervous and before the performance, I couldn't stop shaking.

On stage behind the curtain, my fingers managed to climb the cello in consecutive thirds up to the highest notes and then slid down in octaves to the romantic melody. At one point, the chilling exhilarating sensation of the music pierced my heart and made me cry and I nearly forgot I was on stage being judged.

Suddenly, every note felt strangely foreign to me. I felt lost and helpless as if I was being chased by the notes. I had to think what came next. I was so conscious of every note I was playing. In my severe nervousness I skipped fourteen measures in the second movement where the main theme recaptured. I still don't know what happened. If my pianist hadn't caught my mistake and quickly maneuvered the detour with a perfectly smooth transition, I would have been one of the dozen who were dropped from the competition with a "See you next year."

My teacher, Mr. Kim was the first to come out of the auditorium. He didn't have to say a word. I knew he was furious.

"You won't ever learn to concentrate, will you?" he screamed. "I don't know how you could make such a horrible mistake! Are you insane?" He threw up his hands, "How you made it, I will never know," he said, and walked away.

Today, the remaining six cellists were to perform the third and final performance in front of a live audience at the national theater that housed an audience of two thousands. I had practiced day and night for months. The callouses on my fingers, especially on my thumb, had softened and become blisters and calloused again, over and over. Many nights while I practiced, I would feel the fingerboard wet from popped blisters on my numb left thumb. I went through packs of Johnson and Johnson's Band-Aids for my blisters. Sang-Hie always said that callouses were like badges of honor. Some nights I would see the light of dawn and realize that I had practiced all night.

"Do you know what you are gonna wear?" Mom rudely interrupted by hollering through the bathroom door, bringing me back to reality. I stopped playing in the middle of the cadenza of the first movement on my right arm. I ignored her.

I came out of the bathroom and dusted powdery rosin around the bridge of my cello. Then I dusted off the bow and packed it very carefully. Mom followed me with a plate, shoveling an omelet into my mouth. I shook my head, signaling I was full. I had no appetite. "Let me get dressed."

I knew all the other contestants had prepared their wardrobe months ago. I opened the closet where I had half a dozen dresses that ranged from long to mid-calf. But this time I was not interested in making a fashion statement. The thought of putting on a glamorous dress was not appealing. I wanted to be comfortable and focus on the music. I decided God would approve of me for looking modest and not showy.

I took a bath the night before, so I didn't have to wash my hair that morning. Washing hair or clipping fingernails were unthinkable on the day of a competition. Everyone knew not to take a chance of washing off the techniques and skills that we had practiced and polished for months and months.

I pulled out a navy and brown vertical-striped boat neck knit top and navy pleated skirt. I held it up against the mirror and gave myself a satisfied nod, "This will do. This way, I don't even have to tuck in the top." Then I put on my navy sneakers. There was no dress code and I was going to get full mileage out of "comfort first." I knew Mom might tell me that I should dress better, so I had to be prepared to defend myself against her nagging.

Mom fussed around in the cab on the way to the final competition.

"Would you like the window open?"

"Can I hold the cello or are you OK?"

"Driver, can you go any faster?"

Mom's mannerisms bothered me more than ever today. I ignored her, realizing that she was probably more nervous than me. As annoying as she was to me, I needed her today. I made up my mind to be cordial to her all day. *Do not snap at her,* I thought to myself, but her next comment put me over the edge.

"We still have time to go back home so you can put the long blue dress on, you know."

I couldn't be civil any longer. "Mother, I want to be comfortable and I want my two feet flat on the floor. Wearing heels would make me nervous. So leave me alone."

Mom's mouth quivered a little and I felt sorry immediately. But I couldn't worry about her. I would apologize to her later.

There were cello contestants already waiting backstage for their turn to play. The violin contestants had performed earlier and the scattered chairs and dim lights gave me a sense of eerie envy. Mine would be over by the end of the afternoon. I started getting painful pressure in my stomach again. If I happened to miss a note I might as well pack up and move to Manchuria or Alaska where no one would ask me what happened.

I looked at everyone's wardrobe, from the long evening gowns to short cocktail dresses to school uniforms; no one had sneakers on. I settled in one corner and started tuning my cello. Each contestant had an entourage. I was there with only my mom. My pianist would be meeting me shortly and my two sisters would be there to watch.

Since the thirty-some judges would have to sit through the performances all afternoon, some of the contestants were saying that the best time to perform would be earlier on, when they were wide awake. Others said that it was better to go last when they were so tired they wouldn't be as critical. I closed my eyes and silently prayed.

"Dear Lord, please let me just play without making any mistakes. Please keep me from having a memory lapse. And please let me win first place, if you think I deserve it."

Finally, it was my turn to perform. I raised my head and looked at the audience. The jurors were supposed to be in the middle of the second level, but it was dark. I couldn't see anyone; I knew there were thousands of people, waiting for me to perform.

I felt lightheaded. It was such a scary feeling, like I could burst into hysterical crying or just collapse. I would take either one, if only I didn't have to go through with it.

I closed my eyes as I was tuning.

Don't look and don't think. They are not here. This is just another rehearsal, I repeated to myself.

I gave a brief nod to the pianist to start the prelude. I heard it a thousand times, I knew every note of her part on the piano by heart. As I was listening to her play I could feel myself getting deeper and deeper into the music I was ready to play. It was the original version of the Boccherini Concerto in B flat major.

I was amazed at the beautiful sound I was making. The first movement had many fast passages and I played with no difficulty—as good as ever. I started getting excited to play the cadenza where I could really express and show off my skills.

The second movement was slow and melodic. I put my left ear close to the fingerboard as though my cello and I were one. As I felt my tears running down, I realized only vaguely that I was on the stage. I played from my heart. I was no longer nervous. Nothing was bothering me now. I had practiced enough to know every note forward and backward.

The third movement was light and technical. This movement always made me happy. In the cadenza, I was hitting the high notes that resembled violin-like techniques. I gave a better-than-satisfactory performance. As I bowed deeply and left the stage, I heard the applause go on and on and on. I did it, and I didn't make any mistakes.

The next day, Dong-A Daily showed a large picture of me with a detailed article about my first place performance. They also reported that I was the only nominee who was considered for the Grand Prize, which was the highest honor among all the first place winners across all categories. Once nominated, two-thirds of the jurors' votes were required to win it. I was short by one vote.

My mom blamed it on the way I dressed.

25

In the few weeks following the Dong-A competition, the freshman mailbox at Ewha University's music department was full of fan letters addressed to me, mostly from young college guys, some from lonely military men, and a few college girls from another town wanting to be pen pals with me. I cherished all the letters because they made me re-live the flawless performance I had given in front of a live audience.

One day, as I was leaving the campus, a medical student from Yon-Sei University, which was adjacent to my school, appeared with two tickets to a movie. He waited for me at the bridge to the gate to Ewha University.

"*An-nyung-hase-yo*? Perfect afternoon for 'Gone with the Wind,' isn't it?" Bowing slightly, he was all smiles, waving two movie tickets.

"I am not allowed to go to a movie with a stranger." I sped up. One of my high heels caught the groove in the pavement and I nearly fell. I envisioned my books scattering and me flat on the cement with holes in my nylons and mud on my raw silk suit.

"Oh, but I am not a stranger. I sent you a letter asking you to perform at the Invitational Concert at our school. I also talked to you on the phone a couple of times. I am the one who called. I would like an opportunity to talk about it over dinner after the movie." He ignored my blushing face and followed me to the bus stop. He even got on the bus with me.

"How do you know I will play at your concert? By the way, where did you get my phone number? I don't even know who you are," I said, recalling the phone call.

"You might as well agree because I will skip classes and wait for you every day until you go with me. You wouldn't want me to flunk medical school, would you?" I felt a slight gravitation toward his persistence. The fact that he was a medical student didn't hurt either. There were plenty of pretty girls who had guys following them every day on the way to and from school, but this never happened to me before.

On the bus, he leaned toward me as he hung onto the round ring for balance.

"What time is the show?" I asked, and his mischievous smile turned into delight.

When I came home, Mom wasn't too happy about the late hour.

"I went to see 'Gone with the Wind.' I did nothing wrong, Mother," I said.

"Your head is getting way too big. I can only imagine what your attitude would have been if you actually did win the Grand Prize." Mom narrowed her eyes and shook her head.

I went into the bathroom and slammed the door. My head was not getting big. Winning the competition, receiving fan letters, and having guys follow me was only beginning to shake the long lived-in feeling of worthlessness. I was relishing my newly earned fame, and I wanted to enjoy the privilege of being able to snub some people.

As I performed more and became more known, there was a noticeable change in my life. Suddenly, phone calls came from old friends who wanted to be reacquainted. I received more invitations to birthday parties and there were groups of friends wanting to include me at their intimate gatherings. Distant relatives and family friends wanted me to give their children cello lessons. Girls who had wanted nothing to do with me now smiled when I ran into them, and people stopped me on campus to acknowledge my appearance on TV.

But this newly acquired popularity didn't lift the heaviness of my heart. That year, for the first time in my life, I learned what a true broken heart felt like. I had been dissatisfied with Young-Soo's rigidness. With him, there were always priorities and plans. Nothing was done on impulse. On the other hand, I only knew how to approach all things in life one-way: fervently with zeal. With the intention of intensifying Young-Soo's tepid passion, I sent him a letter giving him an ultimatum.

"… If you think of me as one of your many anatomy books, something you need to learn and memorize to make you a better medical student, I am not the one for you. If you consider me as one component that will complete you as a well-rounded, classical-music-loving medical student who even has a girlfriend who appears on TV often and attends a prestigious college, I am not the one for you…. I don't fit into the mold of your ideal girlfriend to enrich the person you are. In short, I am not the one for you…'

When I met him at a tearoom on his request, his response hit me miserably.

"You are right. You may not be the one for me. And I may not be for you. In any case, I need to concentrate on my studies right now. I can't be as devoted to you as you would like me to." He was not only rational, his tone was cold and unnerving.

"You mean, this is it?"

"I think so. That's what you wanted, isn't it?"

I had not expected him to react this way. My hopes of having him crawl to me and tell me that I meant the world to him were shattered and I became a blubbering idiot.

For the next few weeks and months, I didn't think I could survive. My heart truly felt broken. I walked around like a zombie. I cried at everything. I cried at a horse drawn carriage, because I felt sorry for the horse, having to pull the heavy load. I cried for an old beggar, wondering where his family was. I cried when one of my kittens died.

Young-Soo's image was constantly in my head. To get rid of his image, I burned all of his letters in an aluminum bucket and destroyed the picture frame he made for me for my birthday by stepping on it.

Drinking beer was considered chic, but now I had a real reason to drink. On one of those frequent visits to a beer hall with girl friends, I ran into Eunseong, whom I had met years prior in my children's English class as a third grader. He was the boy who told me our names were similar. By then, he was a violin major at Seoul National University.

This was the second time I had run into him. About a month before that, I had seen him at a combined university fundraiser concert where I performed a solo representing Ewha. Seoul National University's orchestra performed as well. After the concert, he recognized me backstage and said hello. I was happy to see him again.

"Would you allow me the honor and let me buy you a beer?" he asked, smiling shyly.

"Sure, join us please." He joined a group of my friends and after a few more drinks, we started to talk about music. We discussed famous symphonies and concertos. I marveled at his vast knowledge and loved to hear what he had to say about the pieces I was working on—something I could not share with Young-Soo.

"Can I call you sometime and continue this conversation?" Eunseong asked me as he got up to leave.

"Of course, my phone number is 3-4451. I would love to talk to you." There was something encouraging and heartening about Eunseong. I too wanted to talk to him more. I was drawn to his innocent frankness. There was nothing pretentious about him.

Winning the Dong-A competition gave me opportunities to become more active in chamber music as well. The phone rang one day and it was Min Kim. Min was a violinist three years my senior. While attending Yego, he and Myung-Wha Chung and the pianist, Mi-Jae Yoon formed a piano trio. I remember, as new students at Yego, my friends and I had marveled at their awesome performances of the Beethoven and the Mendelssohn trios.

Min Kim also had a small library of sheet music that he had collected. In high school when I had a chance to play simple Haydn or Mozart trios or string quartets, I used to run to his house and ask to borrow the precious sheet music.

"By all means, you can borrow any one I have," he said, "If I don't have it, I can tell you which teacher to ask."

He encouraged us and was excited about younger students' enthusiasm for chamber music. By the time we were in college, he had developed a reputation as the leader in the ensemble. I was surprised and happy to hear from him after so long.

"Sang-Eun, I was wondering if you would like to play piano trio with me and Mi-Jae Yoon." For the first few seconds, I didn't believe my ears.

"Oh, of course. Thank you for asking me. I would love it." It was not only easy to agree right away but it was an honor to be asked by him and Mi-Jae. When she was attending Yego, Mi-Jae was considered the best in both piano and academics. At the award ceremony, her name was always called a dozen times.

For the first rehearsal at Ewha University, Min picked me up at my house in a taxi cab. He showed up at my door wearing a khaki jacket, clearly made in the U.S.A., with the sleeves rolled up. He stuck his violin case backward under his arm.

"Well, I thought we would play some Beethoven today." He smiled big, brushing his hair off his face.

The first piece we played was the *Archduke Trio,* by Beethoven. Mi-Jae introduced the lyrical theme on the piano and Min and I entered melodically in duet, giving the cello an equal time. The piece showed a peaceful control emotionally and harmonically, then built up to dramatic and majestic concord.

We continued to rehearse twice a week at Ewha University. Since Mi-Jae lived in the dorm on Ewha campus, Min and I often went to dinner after rehearsal, and after dinner we went to drink beer. We sometimes went to drink *mak-gulle,* a trendy Korean barley drink, which had the consistency of milk. Unlike beer, it was served at hole-in-the-wall pubs. And instead of peanuts, *mak-gulle* was almost always accompanied by myung-bean pancakes. Myung-bean pancakes were full of sliced pork and vegetables and had the texture of potato pancakes, which meant we could skip dinner and get straight to drinking.

More and more, I began to feel safe and comfortable talking to Min about things I normally wouldn't share with a guy. One night, I drank lots of the sour-tasting *mak-gulle* and started singing and banging my chopsticks against the table. "Wise men say, only fools rush in. But I can't help falling in love with you. Shall I stay, would it be, would it be a sin…" I told Min how I was dumped, only because I was playing games. I blubbered to the guy at the next table how stupid I was and how I wouldn't ever be happy again. When he asked why, I whimpered and said, "Why else? My cat died."

The next day, I told Min that I never wanted to talk about Young-Soo again. That he was out of my mind and I would start dating Eunseong. Eunseong and I had spent time together as friends, but my heart had still been with Young-Soo. After my idiotic behavior that night, I knew that it was time to let go.

Because Min, Mi-Jae, and I had all won in the Dong-A music competition, we were asked to play in the "Winner's Concert." Rather than playing solos, we decided to play the Tchaikovsky Piano Trio in A-minor together. By then, we had developed such camaraderie, musically and personally, we were excited to experience this musical endeavor.

One day, during our rehearsal, Min said, "What do you say we perform this piece by memory without the music?"

Mi-Jae and I looked at each other. Our mouths dropped. This was unheard of. Chamber music had always been played with music.

"You mean, we won't have the music stands on the stage? Won't even take the music to the stage? We just play by heart?"

"That's right. And I will stand up, won't even use a chair to sit on."

I looked at Mi-Jae skeptically. "Well, I suppose we could."

"Sure why not. We can do it." Mi-Jae nodded.

On the night of the Winners' Concert at the National Theatre, I walked onto the stage first and Mi-Jae and Min followed me. The applause stopped when Mi-Jae sat on the piano bench and I sat on my chair. Min remained standing. We practiced plenty of times to memorize each note, and even more times to play perfectly together.

My long red dress had gold threads embroidered in it, and when I sat, my skirt spread into a full circle. My cello was buried in the skirt and my white arms looked like slivers coming out of the puffy short-sleeves. Min wore a black tuxedo with a white bow tie. Mi-Jae wore a long blue dress with cap sleeves.

Once we all settled in our positions, Mi-Jae nodded her curly head confidently and played a couple of measures, then I opened with a lovely cello solo. The three of us played as one, completely emerged in a world of ensemble by heart. We were young, and nothing scared us then.

Looking back, I don't know if we could have done it if we had known how scary it was. One misplayed note by any one of us would have caused a catastrophe—a total failure of a performance.

The next day, the front page of the morning newspaper reported in large print, "Tchaikovsky Piano Trio Performed in the Absence of Sheet Music Brought Tchaikovsky Back Profoundly Alive."

In the winter of 1964, my sophomore year, Sang-Hie took the audio reel of my Dong-A Daily performance to the dean of the music department at Valparaiso University in Indiana, nearby where she was living. Without difficulty, I was admitted and offered a full scholarship.

Admission to an American university was an essential part of the bureaucratic rules and prerequisites for obtaining a passport. In those days, having a passport was a privilege. It gave a person a glimmer of eliteness. It somehow signified intelligence as well as affluence. Students who were going abroad had to excel and pass the difficult English and Korean history exams. Unless there was a world conference, or a business meeting, average people didn't have opportunities to go abroad. I had known a few people who had been to Hong Kong or Tokyo as tourists, but going to America or Europe for pleasure was unheard of.

The thought of holding a passport in my hand made me feel excited and privileged. Going abroad to study Western music was the dream of every music student. As the thought of leaving Korea before I graduated from college began to materialize as a reality, I started neglecting the required classes at school. I often skipped classes like the Bible study or German, and I spent more and more time with Eunseong.

As we spent more time together, my feelings for Eunseong became stronger and stronger. I began to recognize his genuinely caring personality. I appreciated and loved the purity of his heart. There was no pretence in him. He only possessed honesty and decency. And the thought of leaving him to go to America started haunting me like the most sorrowful and saddest nightmare.

26

Prospective travelers crowded the front desk at the American embassy. They handed their papers to the receptionist, pleading for a favorable answer. They all wanted to go to the United States. The receptionist's only response was a monotone, "You are just going to have to wait for your turn to be interviewed by her."

He shuffled stacks of papers briskly, without making eye contact with anyone, sending the message that he couldn't be bothered with the same questions over and over. He placed the rearranged pile of papers next to the inkwell on his desk and stuffed the end of his necktie between two buttons of his wrinkled white dress shirt. As far as I was concerned, his necktie and his feeble influential tie to the Consul General could take a plunge into the inkwell.

The weather was unbearably hot and humid, even for August. The receptionist distributed papers as he called out names. Several people were leaning against the back wall fanning themselves with their folders. I felt humiliated for the whole Korean race. Some of these people had waited all morning because the appointments were made at random, sometimes booked three at a time. Our time was not valued.

I stood by the window with my arms crossed and stared at the receptionist, waiting for him to call my name. My brother-in-law, Sang-Soon's husband, who had earned his doctoral degree in England, accompanied

me in case I needed an interpreter on my third and the last chance to
beg for a visa. The blue, vinyl, straight-back chairs in the waiting room
were all occupied. So were the four rows of matching benches. I turned
around to look out the window. The streets were filled with taxis, street-
cars, and buses that emitted a gray fume. Pedestrians bumped each other
on the sidewalk with no apologetic body language.

This was how Seoul existed. No one ever said, "Excuse me." No one
ever said, "I can't stand this hot and humid weather. Someone had better
do something to make this place more livable." They just accepted the
city the way it was, always bustling, dusty, and most of all, crowded, like
the waiting room. No one complained about having to wait two hours
for a five-minute interview with the American Consul General.

All of us were waiting to get her approval to go abroad to the US to
study, to be medical doctors, to conduct a business, or simply to immi-
grate. One woman had the sole authority to issue a visa that would allow
us to leave Korea and enter America.

The American Consul was a middle-aged woman, whose plainness
surprised me both times I saw her. She wore cotton flowery dresses that
hung on her lanky body and thick black-rimmed glasses. When Korean
men came to be interviewed, they wore their business suits, and ladies
wore custom-made suits and high heels, looking a few times savvier than
the consul herself in her hickish cotton dress.

Doctors who finished medical school in Korea received their visas
with no problem. American hospitals welcomed Korean doctors, but it
was harder for students. It took me a month to make the first appointment and another three months for the second appointment. To schedule
an interview, we had to go through a receptionist and then an evaluator
who made sure we had all of our documents and passports in order,
before she could give us her valuable five minutes.

She turned me down both times. After the second rejection, the
consulate ordered me to take the TOEFL exam. Only when I passed it,
she said, would she issue the visa. Then she added, looking especially
hard at me through her black-framed glasses, "I don't understand why so
many young Korean girls want to go to America. It's not easy to study in

another language, you know. I will allow it only if you pass the English exam."

"Miss Sang-Eun Lee," the receptionist called my name as he pointed at me with a folder. My brother-in-law and I weaved through the room of people. I threw my shoulders back. I was determined to convince her that if the university gave me a full scholarship and invited me to come to study and give a concert, she had no business getting in my way.

I showed her the letter written to her from Dr. Hoelty-Nickel, the dean of the music school at Valparaiso, Indiana. The letter was eloquently written and to the point.

It stated that the Dean had studied music in Germany without knowing the German language. He also told her that she should send me as soon as possible because my concert date was already scheduled and coming up shortly and the fall semester was ready to begin.

"Will you be coming back after the concert? If so, I can give you a visitor's visa," she said.

"No, she will need the student visa. She is invited to study there for a year," my brother-in-law cut in.

"But that's just the whole point. How is she going to study in America not knowing the language?" She looked back and forth from me to my brother-in-law like she was interrogating us.

It was obvious to me that she did not want Korean students in America. I was fuming. I had failed the English exam, and I knew this was my third and last chance to interview with her. I was desperate.

"Music, international language, you don't know?" I blurted out sharply in my broken English. "I don't have to know English too much like I am scholar."

"Of course, you couldn't communicate with music," she responded emphatically shaking her blond hair.

"Music is communicative art." I curtly got up and stormed out of the exit door. My brother-in-law followed me out, chuckling quietly.

That was the end of the final interview. I walked out of her office, leaving my destiny in her hands.

The receptionist told me to wait in the waiting room once again to retrieve my passport. I was scared to look at my brother-in-law. I knew I blew my last chance, a chance at being a world-famous cellist, a chance at going to the Juilliard School of Music, a chance at going to the Curtis Institute of Music, a chance to become somebody.

I stared out the window. A beggar was sitting on a filthy straw mat with his back against the building, his arms outstretched toward the pedestrians. A group of young men looked away as they walked by him. A few giggly girls scurried around him as if they were afraid of being contaminated. Biting my lip to keep myself from tearing up, I opened my purse and took out a five hundred won note, getting ready to put it in the beggar's opened hands. It felt like the whole world was coming to an end.

"I should have begged. I shouldn't have walked out. What was I thinking?" I said to my brother-in-law.

"Miss Lee," the Korean receptionist called my name.

When I approached his desk, he handed me my passport.

"When will you be leaving for America?" He asked with a smirk in his face. "There is a chartered plane leaving on the fourteenth of September. I was told to inform everyone leaving that seats are still available. I will make reservations for you if you think you can be ready by then."

I stared at the visa stamped in the passport and nodded. I would be ready.

I suddenly felt like I might suffocate. My excitement swelled inside of me. I was actually leaving Korea, maybe for good. I would buy a one-way ticket. Coming home was not a part of my plan.

I walked alone down the narrow isle of the open market of Young-Chun, recalling what just happened that morning at the American Embassy. I had humiliated myself and acquired the awaited visa like a charitable gift, much like the five hundred won I dropped in the beggar's hands. My emotions whipped into frenzy wildly as I took in the different sights of the neighborhood that I would soon be leaving.

Flies were swarming over the vegetables and the dried fish in the market. Near the cashier's stand, a merchant's wife was sitting on an uncomfortable apple crate, nursing her child. The next stand had scrumptious fruits like oranges, apples, grapes, plums, and some bruised bananas. In the middle of the store, a couple of flypapers were hanging from the ceiling of the tarp that was pitched on poles over the dirt floor. People touched the fruits as they haggled.

The nursing child had stains on her legs, like she had played in the dirt and dripped fruit juice on her body. She was squeezing and caressing her mother's swollen breasts. Way too old for nursing, I thought. I clutched my purse and keeping my arms close to my body so as not to touch any sweaty, smelly bodies. I was equally careful not to step on anything that might get on my off-white high heels.

I turned onto the next street. Both sides of the muddy unpaved streets were lined by small businesses. There was a hair salon with two stepping rocks to the front door. The dry cleaner's sliding glass front door was covered with sale prices and a list of services that looked like disarrayed graffiti. A mannequin was wearing a striped shirtdress holding a straw purse at a dress shop window, and a public telephone booth stood next to the dress shop.

I may never walk on these dirt alleys again. Things I had once disdained suddenly became precious to me. I felt wistful walking through the smutty alleys of the marketplace I had avoided. What had I done to myself?

"I will miss all of this, I am going to take this way home every day until I go to America." I looked at the blue sky above and sighed. I felt tightness on the bridge of my nose. "I don't want to leave this place." My eyes welled up.

Prompted by a terrible urge, I turned around and headed toward my high school. I had to see my high school teachers and say goodbye to them.

27

The three-hour delay at the airport gave me a few more moments with the family and friends who came to see me off.

"Don't look so gloomy, Sang-Eun," my best friend, Jin-Hee whispered to me. "You are finally going to America. This was your dream, remember? You know it's everyone's dream and yours actually came true. Think how lucky you are. You know we all envy you."

"I don't feel lucky at all. I can't go, Jin-Hee. What was I thinking?" I squeezed her hands tightly and gazed at her, trying to remember everything about her face. I hugged her and put my cheek against her freckled cheek.

I stared at the fine wrinkles around my mother's eyes and quietly wiped my tears. She stood erect and confident. She had earned every one of those wrinkles. And now, her youngest was about to leave her. It must have given her some relief knowing that she no longer had to worry about my tuition or my winter overcoat, but she didn't look relieved. Her face looked as if she hadn't eaten in a week; small and dark, it reminded me of dried soybean, left to shrivel in a lunch pail.

I wanted to hold her hand, the same hand she had extended out of her quilt the night before as she moved to lie beside me and said, "Let's fall asleep holding hands."

"Mom, what will happen to me? Will I be able to handle the strange place with strange people, in a strange environment? What will I do if I go crazy from missing home so much?" I whimpered, sobbing.

"You will be all right. You have always had the most realistic attitude about everything. A contemporary person holds such perspectives. Do you know what that means? It means you not only adapt to all of the current viewpoints but also to the current situations and adjust your thought process accordingly. For an old timer, I feel I too have always been modern. I yearned to live in Western conveniences. Moving into an apartment was not hard for me at all. Sure, I missed the space we had at our old house. I missed having the yard but you do what you have to do to be innovative and eventually to survive in the most successful way you can, given the situations you are in. And I always felt you, of all my kids had that ability. The most important thing is to accept the life that is provided for you gratefully. Only then will you adapt and truly enjoy your life in a new environment. I know you will. I am not saying it will be easy, but soon you will love that strange place. I guarantee it." Mom let out a sigh as she finished her long speech and held my hand tight. "My *mak-doong-e* will leave me tomorrow."

As I tried not to cry, the throbbing tingled in my nose and shot up to the top of my head. "And when you get desperate, remember to be thankful. Remember you are privileged, privileged to have opportunities to go abroad, to further your talent, your God-given talent. And most of all, remember to pray," Mom said.

The airport was crowded and noisy with people crying and laughing amid the click and flash of camera shutters. Crying brothers, sisters, husbands, and wives stared at the ground, not able to face each other. Almost everyone who went abroad made a routine stop at the Peninsula hotel terminal for the final check-in before they headed for the airport. This filtered out half of the well-wishers, but the closest friends and families followed us all the way to the airport to see us off. In addition to the cabs and privately owned automobiles, airport buses accommodated everyone who wished to be at the airport.

I stood surrounded by my family, friends, and relatives, each holding

SANG-EUN LEE BUKATY

armfuls of flowers. We posed for photos from every angle, collectively and individually. They all wanted me in the middle.

I recognized a few people who were getting on the same plane from the numerous trips we all made to the American Embassy to get visas. The travelers were easy to tell apart from the well-wishers. The men wore gray or navy suits, and ladies wore colorful suits and carried large leather or canvas bags with the prominent letters TWA or PAN- AM. And every one of us held a large brown Manila envelope containing our chest X-rays—these were for the health department checkpoint, to prove that our lungs were free of tuberculosis.

Looking at Mom's fine wrinkles, I wiped my eyes with the back of my hand. *I will come back one day and give a wonderful concert and make her proud,* I thought. *I will come back only when I make it. Only when I become a famous cellist, no matter how long it took to become a "dragon from a small stream."* I let out a big sob and covered my mouth to hide my uncontrollable bawling.

A gentleman who looked about thirty years old introduced himself to me and said that he got the seat next to me so he could help me with my cello. He was my cousin's friend and a medical doctor leaving for Boston.

Eunseong followed me around as I moved from person to person to say good-bye. I couldn't bear to look at his swollen eyes and crooked mouth. Sang-Soon was busy handing me fresh tissues as I wiped my tears and blew my nose. I held each of their hands as I said goodbye and thanked them for coming to see me off.

"I will study hard and won't disappoint you," I said to my uncles and aunts.

"I promise I will write to you every week," I said to my friends, Jin-Hee, Sookie, and Kyung-Hee. Then I turned to Min Kim.

"Let's play Tchaikovsky piano trio at Carnegie Hall one day. Try to come to America soon. And we will play it by memory without the music again. I will miss having beer with you."

Lastly, I held Eunseong's hands and whispered, "Do come to America as soon as possible. I will miss you so much." I had a terrible urge to hug him and kiss him but I knew I couldn't do that in front of everyone. I held his warm hands and whispered, "I will wait for you no matter how long it might be." He caressed my cheek with the back of his hand and I leaned into it, both of us aware of all the eyes upon us.

Even though no one said it, there was an understanding that this farewell might be forever. In our culture, we were raised to be constructive and studious. Whether we played a musical instrument or became a baseball player, doing the best we could and accomplishing our goal was drilled into our heads for as long as I remembered. Going to America was a high mark of accomplishment. Only the most talented and brilliant young ones got to go to America. But just going to America was not the end goal. We all went with one thing on our mind, and that was to be somebody important and famous.

I had heard of people who left in years past and never came home. A few did return, but not for decades. They were brothers or sisters or fathers of someone we knew, someone we only had heard of, a ghost of a person who once existed in a family. I had no idea when I might see my mom, sisters, friends, and especially Eunseong again.

I straightened my pale pink skirt as I walked slowly down the tarmac toward Northwest Airlines, my heels clicking loudly with each step. At the top of the tarmac, I saw my mom wiping her eyes. I felt tightness in my chest and was having hard time breathing.

When the door of the plane slammed shut, I could not control the stream of tears. A mere steel door was separating me from the only life and home I had ever known. In a split second, I was alone. However fearful or unprepared I was, emotionally or financially, my life as a twenty-year-old foreign student was about to start, thousands of miles from home, in a strange country, where I spoke only a few words of their language. In all the years I dreamed of going to America to study and become a world famous cellist, it never occurred to me that I would start off in such misery. All this naïve, immature young girl could do was to cry her eyes out until they were bloodshot. I didn't know why I was crying and I didn't know what I wanted. I just stood there inside the plane and sobbed and sobbed.

A Chinese steward calmly guided me toward my seat and gave me a smile.

I started crying loudly and grabbed the steward's arm.

"Please, I changed my mind. I don't want to go. Let me off." I felt desperate as if I was in a dark hole and suffocating. "Please, I need to breathe," I screamed. The steward again smiled and led me with a gentle push to my seat.

"Help her. I will bring her some orange juice," he said to the man sitting next to me.

I was stuck in the middle seat between two men. The one on my left was my cousin's friend who had already asked a stewardess to put my cello in the closet. The one on my right had slicked back hair and smelled strongly of Old Spice. The smell of the jet fuel fumes and his cologne was making me sick.

"Please, I need a bag…." The little white paper bag was filled before I could even finish my sentence. The steward strapped me down in spite of my protesting that I needed to clean myself up. I felt lightheaded and knew I was only dreaming. This was not really happening. I felt sleepy and wanted to vomit some more.

A pretty Chinese flight attendant brought me a glass of orange juice and nearly forced me to drink it. "This will make you feel better," she said. The smell of her perfume made me even more nauseated. I unbuckled the seat belt, grabbed another bag out of the seat pocket, and buried my face into it. In the next few seconds, what little breakfast I had, plus the orange juice was all in the bag.

My tears dried out, and with a blank look, I stared at the "Fasten your seat belt" sign. I had no more energy to snap the seat belt. The seat was tight and upright and my legs were tired from waiting around so long. My suit was already wrinkled and the narrow high heels were cutting into my swollen feet.

Finally the seatbelt light went off and I got up to brush my teeth and freshen up a little. When I settled back in my seat, the man on my right wanted to see my passport. Apparently he had been home to Korea to get married after living in Bloomington, Indiana and attending graduate school at Indiana University. His new bride was to come to meet him next month. He had to rush back to make it to the new semester. We talked for a while and he soon found out that I was twenty years old and that I was a music major, starting in the fall semester at Valparaiso University in Indiana as well.

When we arrived in Haneda airport in Japan, it was late afternoon and the streets were glossy from rain. We had ten hours to kill before our Pan American Airlines flight would leave for Los Angeles, California. Taking my cousin's friend's suggestion, we got in a cab with two other people and went exploring Ginza in Tokyo, the busiest shopping district.

The department store was clean and spacious. Every store was cleaner and nicer than Seoul. There were lots of beautifully made sweaters and dresses. They were the ones I used to see in the Japanese magazines. There was a white blouse that looked exactly like the one my sister Sang-Hie sent me from Tokyo on her way to America two years before; the lace was edged diagonally forming diamonds all over the front. Inside of each lace-bordered diamond was an embroidered flower.

No one bought anything in Ginza. We all shared a mild jealousy over Japan's vastly advanced market. Deep in my wallet, I guarded my one hundred and ten dollars. The Korean government only allowed each student to bring fifty dollars. But by flying in a chartered plane, I was refunded sixty dollars, which I was allowed to bring with me.

By midnight we were on Pan American airlines headed for Los Angeles.

I covered my legs with the blanket and looked out the window. As the giant bird ascended above the busy streets of Tokyo, I silently prayed for the blessings of God's wisdom to guide me through the next indefinite number of years in America. Then I covered my mouth to swallow another eruption of sobs.

28

America, the land of my dreams, the land of unlimited possibilities. I stumbled down the tarmac into the blinding California sun in my white strappy sandals. I turned back to see the prominent letters "Pan American" on the gigantic iron bird that was the bridge from my old life to a new life I was about to begin. I watched them shut the steel door tight, closing the last link to the precious days of my girlhood. They now seemed like ghostly memories.

From the time I was five, when I first buttoned my blue coat with the rabbit fur collar that said "Made in U.S.A.," I became aware of this faraway land called America, where everything was made better. I was aware of it when Mom bought me yellow No. 2 pencils and smooth notebooks with snow-white lined pages, as opposed to the thin off-white pulpy sheets of Korean make. I was aware of it when I got my first pair of red penny loafers in high school. America was always in the back of our minds.

It was odd to take the first step into the world I had only fantasized about. I stopped for a second to take in the clean and spacious Los Angeles airport. Standing in the middle of it, my heart thumped. As I exited at the gate, a faint, yet familiar smell filled the air, a combination of milk and canned consommé, faint but the same smell near the Eighth Army barracks in Dae-Ku. It was so distinctly foreign. A fear came over me and I wondered if I could fit into this modern world. It certainly seemed big enough to hold all of the immigrants' hopes and dreams, and certainly bright enough for their futures. I looked up at the gleaming buildings covered with huge glass windows. The buildings were transparent, not a single murky cement wall anywhere.

I hoisted my cello in one arm and tucked the envelope with my chest X-ray under the other arm. I brushed my skirt, smoothing out the wrinkles and brushed my hair with my fingers trying to make my disheveled and exhausted body a little more presentable. My eyes were welling up again.

Reflections on the large aqua windows made it hard to see the arrival gate. I thought I saw my brother standing in the very front. His five-foot-four body looked even shorter among the tall American people, as if he was squatting. He ran toward me, his round face lit up with a huge smile and his tie flew back, covering his face. I hugged him, wrapping both of my arms around his neck. A few years of being apart made me forget how much I hated him.

"You are a lady. Are you in college now? I expected to see a young girl in a school uniform," he said, speaking in Korean. He grinned looking me over from head to toe.

"Greet Mr. Rogers," he said, pointing at a gentleman who was standing behind him. "Mr. Rogers, meet my baby sister, Sang-Eun." At my brother's introduction in English, I automatically smiled and bowed deeply to Bob Rogers. As I bent down to bow, I was astounded at his incredibly large and round shoes. They could have been small boats. I had never seen such big shoes in my entire twenty years of life. He stepped toward me and held my hands. "So glad to meet you, Song-Uun." One side of his mouth slightly curled downward when he smiled. His voice was low and buttery. For some reason, his gently slurred speech and his askew mouth made me feel comfortable.

"Thank you. Me too," I answered looking over at my brother, pleading for him to save me from having to speak in English. Bob Rogers then quickly grabbed my carry-on and my cello. As he asked something about the baggage, his green cufflinks caught my eye. They looked like shimmering river rocks cased in gold, which seemed appropriate for a handsome American middle-aged man of substantial size.

"What is he saying?" I asked my brother. I pulled the cello from Bob Rogers and gripped it under my right arm by the neck effortlessly and hung my carry bag on back on my shoulder.

"He wants your claim tickets. Be polite and let him carry your cello. He just wants to help," my brother said in Korean.

"But, but, it has everything in it. Passport, plane tickets and money. And...." My brother laughed and Bob Rogers laughed too.

Bob walked ahead of us. He didn't pick up his round black feet when he walked. Half of his feet never left the ground.

Then I noticed about a dozen Asian men who kept staring at us.

"Who are those Asian men? Why are there so many Asian men in America?"

I asked my brother. As I glanced at them, one of them, dressed casually in a shirt and slacks, approached us and asked my brother in Korean, "Your sister?"

"Yes, she is. But guys, she is just a baby and will be going to Indiana to study," my brother answered abruptly. The Asian man nodded slightly to my brother and walked away.

"Crazy guys! Better not waste time away from books," my brother mumbled in Korean loud enough for them to hear. The rest of the men trudged along, still peering at me.

As we walked down to the baggage claim area, I asked my brother, "Why did you tell him I was a baby? I am not a baby. And who are they?"

"Oh, they are all Korean students living in Los Angeles. They heard that a chartered plane was arriving today from Korea. They were hoping to meet young Korean female students, potential wives," my brother rolled his eyes and explained in English so Bob would understand as well.

"Korean students are all very homesick. Most of them are dying to be married, to Korean girls, of course." He shrugged his shoulders as if it was not his problem. I decided he must not be as desperate to be married. I hoped Mom was right. She always said that America changes everyone for the best. In order to succeed among big-nosed people, they had to get up earlier and go to bed later. And study even on the weekends instead of going to bars. And they had to be thriftier and survive on a bare minimum and save. "This experience will make them responsible and appreciate what they had in Korea before they left," she used to say.

As I stood in front of the luggage chute, I remembered what I was supposed to say the minute I saw Mr. Rogers, the line I practiced a dozen times. Bob Rogers had been generous enough to volunteer to be my sponsor in America. This was in accordance with the government regulations with regard to the foreign exchange student program.

"Mr. Rogers, it is so nice to meet you," I said abruptly.

"It is my pleasure to meet you, finally," Bob said, and patted my back, smiling at my rehearsed protocol.

"With all the excitement, she forgot to acknowledge you," my brother said in his beautiful English, clapping and tilting his head back laughing.

The clean, wide halled, multi-story airport had the most modern equipment, from the round luggage chute to the mechanical walkway. Along the walkway the walls were covered with designs made of small pastel tiles. So far, I could characterize America in two words: "clean" and "bigger." There were more gates at the airport, people were bigger, they smiled more, and they talked more and faster. And it was immaculate.

I saw a man and a woman kissing, not letting each other go. I automatically turned my head, afraid that they might be embarrassed. Ladies were walking freely, swinging their arms, and laughing out loud. When they laughed, they showed off their white teeth without covering their mouths. In fact, there wasn't anything that was not exaggerated.

The freeways were another incredible sight. Four lanes on each side were filled with huge luxurious cars gliding ever so fast. In the early evening dusk I marveled at the wide organized lanes. There were street signs in white and green which appeared at fixed intervals in clear and easy to read letters.

"So this is America. What happens next?" I muttered under my breath.

Somewhere here would be my future and my dream. Would all those sentences that had started with "When you go to America…" be here waiting for me? The most wonderful music schools and conservatories? Opportunities to study with world famous musicians? Would the teenagers drive cars and high school girls wear beautiful dresses to school, instead of uniforms? Would they curl their hair and smoke anytime they wanted? Would the expensive Helena Rubinstein frosty lipsticks I used to buy at the black market be a dime a dozen?

The streets were dark and looked wet as if it had rained. I was crying again and I dabbed tears off of my pink eyelet skirt with my handkerchief. I felt void and hollow.

We arrived at the Rogers' house in hilly Brentwood. Frances greeted me at the door by stretching out one hand awkwardly to shake my hand. I shook her hand and bowed at the same time as I said "Hello," smiling.

Frances Rogers was tall, almost as tall as Bob. Her hips were uneven. In the middle of her wrinkled face, under short gray hair, were a long hooked nose and beady, piercing eyes. Her flabby upper arms stuck out of the short sleeves of a flowery cotton dress in muted green. If I didn't know any better, she could have been Bob's mother.

My brother carried my suitcase into the guest room and I quickly freshened myself up and changed my underwear before I sat down at the dinner table. Frances's table was formally set with white linen and sterling on an unpretentious rectangular table. She served a salad of fresh Boston lettuce and lots of watercress, both of which were new to me. Her dressing was homemade, made specially using only a third of the oil so that Bob could keep his weight down. As she brought out salmon steaks with mashed potatoes, Frances quickly apologized for using only a tiny bit of butter on the mashed potatoes. Apparently, Bob was on a strict diet. She said something about doctors and dying young and something called cholesterol.

"Oh, but that's just perfect for my sister and me, because butter is not in the Korean diet," my brother responded with a diplomatic, perfunctory laugh. He sat up straight with his forearms resting on the table. You wouldn't think he was short. And I understood his English enough to see through him. Did he forget we slathered butter on toast and even rice sometimes?

In a few short years, he had managed to learn to disguise himself in a new rehearsed and polished image. He acted and talked like dignified Oriental nobility who possessed only elitist characteristics. He even declined the second glass of wine Bob offered. After spending only an hour with him, I remembered why I hated him so much.

"Sang-Eun-ah! It's bad manners to put your elbows on the table," he admonished me in Korean when I put my elbows on the table to cup my face. His voice was not unkind, but his smiling reproach became universally clear to both Bob and Frances because I removed my elbows in one hurried motion.

"Well, what do you know? In addition to tuition, her scholarship covers three meals a day plus the room," Bob said, chuckling proudly as he looked over the letter I received from school.

"I hope they serve decent food with some nutritional value. Instead of stuff like hot dogs." Frances scrunched her face as she looked at me.

"What's that? Dog?" I looked at my brother.

My brother clapped and looked up laughing gregariously and said, "It's not that kind of dog, you silly." And all three of them laughed.

"Would you like some?" Bob picked up a small bowl of brownish-pink vegetable and passed it to me.

I bowed and took the bowl. "What is this thing?" I asked my brother in Korean.

"*Kimchee.* Cabbage *kimchee*," Bob answered proudly.

"*Kimchee*? Look funny." I realized right away that I was impolite. After all, it was imported from Hawaii and they got it especially for me from an Asian store.

By the time we finished dinner and my brother left, I was hazy and disoriented. I hadn't slept for over twenty-four hours and my head felt swollen from so much crying. I took a shower in lukewarm water trying to clear my head, shaking it to get rid of the fogginess. I washed my underwear with bath soap and hung it to dry on the towel rack, but put my nylons back into my suitcase. I knew how much they dripped when they were wet, and I didn't want to make a puddle on the bathroom floor since I realized there was no drainage on the floor. All the while, I kept thinking how strange, how very strange Bob and Frances were.

My first night in America was sleepless. I started sobbing again as soon as my wet head sank into the large down pillow. There was no more familiar smell of soy bean paste through the screen window, or the discord of haggling from Young-Chun market place before closing, or the honking of impatient taxi drivers—all of which used to put me to sleep like dissonant lullabies. That had been my home just until yesterday.

No matter how hard I tried I couldn't control my sobbing. I lifted my head off the pillow trying to catch my breath. I knew I was suffocating. It seemed all the air in Los Angeles was not enough for me to breathe. I wept until I got a migraine, then I crawled out of the bed and sat up at the desk and put my hands together and prayed in desperation.

"Dear Jesus, give me strength. Make me strong." I then opened the Bible Eunseong had given me as a parting gift.

"Just open any page and read. You will find it comforting. The Bible has amazing power to give you peace, because it is the living word of Jesus," he had said.

I opened and read in Ephesians 2:10, *"For we are God's workmanship created in Christ Jesus to do good works, which God prepared in advance for us to do."*

"God has prepared me in advance in Him to do good works. I am His perfect workmanship. He has plans for me," I repeated over and over, not completely comprehending what it meant. Through the cracked drapery at the window, dawn was breaking through.

29

When I got up the next morning, the house smelled like bacon and toast, but there was no sign of life anywhere. I tiptoed through the unfamiliar house. Bright sunlight poured through the open draperies into the long, rectangular living room. An uncomfortable looking straight back armless couch sat along the wall opposite the window. Two matching burgundy high back armchairs sat facing each other, each with a lamp beside them.

As I walked by the lamp table, I inadvertently brushed and dropped an opened folder, which contained a pile of magazine and newspaper clippings. When I bent down to gather them up, I saw a name, JAQUELINE DU PRE, in large print above a picture of a young girl in a pleated skirt with her hands resting confidently below her waist. Had they been reading up on cellists around the world in anticipation of my coming here? Suddenly, I felt honored.

At the far end of the living room near the kitchen was the dining room where Bob had served the odd-looking *kimchee* the night before. I walked into the kitchen. The window above the sink framed the wide-open hillside with no tall trees, only random clumps of bushes between brown rolling hills that looked like a painting.

Next to the kitchen was another sitting room. I peeked in and saw an upright piano and a built-in bookcase. The middle shelf of the bookcase displayed a variety of rocks in different colors and sizes. Some looked smooth, gleaming like jade, while others looked coarse and dull. I picked up a heavy round rock that looked like a block of sandwich meat. There were specks of white fat within the reddish meat. I turned it to examine all sides of it. The white fat was spread evenly throughout the rock; it looked exactly like salami.

A square cabinet that looked like an LP record player sat against the only remaining wall by the glass door. I picked up a record jacket that was loosely placed on top. My heart pounded when I recognized Pablo Casals on the cover. He had his index finger on his lip smiling playfully at a younger gentleman who was obviously his student. I once read a long article in *Life* magazine (I had to look up every other word in the dictionary), about his love of the Bach unaccompanied Suites, and how he played all six of them first thing in the morning. Ever since the article, I had a new reverence for and desire to understand Bach in depth.

My heart thumped faster as I looked at the long play record jacket of the original version of the Boccherini Cello Concerto in B flat major— the piece I played to win the Dong-A competition. It was the piece that brought me to fame. I didn't know such a record even existed. I had listened to the Gruzmacher-revised version of the concerto performed by various cellists. I didn't know anyone had performed the original version. My mouth dropped in awe and the impulse to play the record immediately made my heart pound.

"Good morning. Did you have a good rest?" Frances's whiny voice startled me.

"Yes," I nodded and bowed.

"Bob made us breakfast, I'm sure," Frances said. "Would you like some coffee?" She noticed the record in my hand. "Did you find the record? Bob brought it home when we learned of the piece only by listening to the tape of your performance. You know the one you sent us."

She continued on, saying something about Bob making drip coffee every morning before he went to work. And today in my honor, he even made bacon which meant Frances could have fried eggs because she would only use bacon grease to fry eggs.

After the clinging and clanging of pans and dishes, Frances served me a breakfast that consisted of fried eggs, bacon, toast, coffee, and fresh squeezed orange juice. I missed my hot cocoa but drank coffee with heavy cream instead. Frances used her whole arm to stir the coffee, jiggling the loose skin under her upper arm.

"Song-Uun, I know you miss your family and friends. But I hope it will be helpful for you to know that you have a busy year ahead of you and that there are many universities who would love to have you on a scholarship." She spoke slowly and loudly, enunciating every word as if I were deaf. I sat across the table from Frances feeling like a little girl in the principal's office. Her deafening voice sounded as if she was admonishing me rather than admiring me. Later I found out that she was hard of hearing.

She also told me that she had taken my tape of the Boccherini Concerto to Mr. Rejto and he had said, "Very good. Excellent," after listening to it.

"Mr. Rejto teaches at USC. And when I called to tell him about you, he was very much interested in meeting you in person. You will have a chance to meet him in the next couple of days. I will call him today to make an arrangement. Make sure you take your cello. He would probably like to hear you play," Frances said.

"Does Sang-Hie know him?" I asked.

"No, I have never even met him," Frances shook her head and continued.

Frances and Sang-Hie met at UCLA when Frances was teaching a course in "Foreign Students' English." They visited while they were both waiting in the foreign student office and she gave Sang-Hie a ride when they were finished with their appointments. On the way, Frances invited Sang-Hie for a cup of tea.

"By the time I finished my second cup of tea, I fell in love with your sister." Frances told me. She invited Sang-Hie to come and stay with them in their Brentwood home. Sang-Hie lived with them until she met Kil-Sup at a Christmas party and moved to Gary, Indiana to get married. During the few months she lived with the Rogers, Frances drove Sang-Hie to the bus stop on Sunset Boulevard every morning and picked her up at the bus station at the end of the day from UCLA.

By mid-morning, I was tired and weary of her nonstop talking and I knew we were expecting guests later.

"May I, uh, excuse?" I asked, ineptly covering my mouth as I yawned.

"Of course you may. When Mrs. Ryang comes, I will knock on your door." Frances smiled.

My view from the desk chair of their guest bedroom was a curved driveway bordered by manicured bushes – the very image of the typical American home I had seen in picture books. I was sitting at the desk, dozing, when Susan and her mother Mrs. Ryang drove into the Rogers' driveway. Mrs. Ryang was Sang-Hie's sister-in-law. Frances had arranged lunch with Mrs. Ryang and Susan during my short stay in Los Angeles before I departed for Indiana to begin the fall semester.

Mrs. Ryang wore a gray and burgundy round-necked dress with cap sleeves. She stood tall in her dark gray pumps and looked perky in her short, neatly teased hair. She held her hands together in front of her chest the whole time she talked to Frances.

Susan stuck her right hand out to Frances and said,

"Mrs. Rogers, my name is Susan. So pleased to meet you."

"Dear, the pleasure is mine. I would like you to meet Song-Uun. This is Sang-Hie's younger sister."

It wasn't Susan's poised manner that fascinated me. I couldn't keep my eyes off of her dark eyes and long eyelashes. When she shook my hand, I giggled and tilted my head, unable to take my eyes off her makeup. Each time she blinked, I could see the dark eyeliner drawn halfway up to the eyebrow. The wide eyeliner disappeared into her eyelids when she opened her eyes, making her eyes big and round.

"Do you know how to speak Korean?" I asked her.

"*Cho-keum*," she answered in one word in Korean that resembled a three-year-old child talking.

Mrs, Ryang suggested that we go to a Chinese restaurant in Hollywood, owned by her neighbor in Baldwin Hills. At lunch, Frances and Mrs. Ryang talked to each other the whole time, most of which I was oblivious to, and Susan smiled kindly every time our eyes met. She passed a plate of shrimp to me and when I didn't know what to do with it, she quickly served me a few pieces. In Korea, it was rude to ask to pass a plate, rather we reached to serve ourselves.

I found out Susan was the same age as me. Comparing my powder blue cotton knit skirt and matching blouse to Susan's red suit, it occurred to me we were as far apart as the Pacific Ocean between Korea and America. Her Korean was about as bad as my English. She ate and talked freely, never covering her mouth, while I sat quietly staring at her eyes. And yet, we must have had the same childhood background twelve years earlier, jumping rope in an alley in rubber shoes and walking to school carrying our book bags.

I wouldn't realize until years later that my third day in Los Angeles would become the deciding point of my life, when Frances took me to meet Mr. Rejto, a cello professor at USC.

"Come in, come in," the Hungarian-born cellist greeted me with both of his arms open, kissing me on the cheek. Frances reiterated the same story about me to Mr. Rejto, just as she had told it to Mrs. Ryang the day before. I heard words like Valparaiso, full scholarship and award-winning.

I played the Lalo Concerto when he asked me to play. Before I finished the first movement, he stopped me, "Excellent! Very, very good. Such a little girl has such strong fingers. Any sonatas?" He said and I played the Boccherini Sonata No. 6. Then he asked me if I studied the Bach unaccompanied Suites.

"Yes, but didn't play all. Didn't finish. Stopped."

"Stopped?" He laughed, broadening his meaty cheeks. "That's OK.

Play some Bach. Any one." I played the Allemande of number three by memory.

"Good, good." Mr. Rejto's praise somehow didn't seem like he was impressed with my Bach playing. But I must have been wrong, because he invited me to come and spend the following summer at the Music Academy of the West in Santa Barbara to study with him on a scholarship. I wanted to pinch myself in disbelief.

When I was in Korea, I had heard that Heifetz and Piatigorsky gave master classes at the Music Academy. I felt the blood rushing through my body with excitement. There was so much to ask and to talk about. How long was the summer camp? Would I be playing in the orchestra? How many students would there be and where would they all come from? But he rushed us out the door, still laughing, telling us that he had an appointment.

At dinner that night, Frances spent a good half hour talking about her foot surgery, which cost her thousands of dollars. She said that it was caused by wearing narrow high heels as a young career woman.

"In this country, people dress comfortably when they travel and wear flat supportive shoes." She put her elbows on the table, linking her hands together to support her chin. "I was a young girl and only cared how I looked, you know? But ever since the surgery, I can only wear flat shoes." I realized the only reason she brought up the subject of her surgery was so I wouldn't wear my narrow high heels the next morning on the plane going to Indiana.

Bob Rogers rested his elbow on the table, propped his cheek on the back of his hand, and stared at his bread plate the whole time she spoke. As if trying to stop her explication, he blurted, "Valparaiso, Indiana, Watch out! Here comes Song-Uun, an accomplished cellist!" With a wide smirk in his face, he raised his water glass and said, "We need to celebrate."

The next day, both of them took me to the airport to see me off. I wore a white blouse and a white pleated skirt and carried a yellow spring coat, and wore white flats on my feet.

The plane to Chicago was half full. Sitting with my arms crossed, I looked down from the window at the orderly planned city of Los Angeles. Freeways carrying speeding cars separated rows of houses with front lawns, parks, and baseball diamonds and freeways crossing one another, jumbled with buildings both tall and short. Of all those cars, buildings, and dwellings, there wasn't a single thing I was connected to.

"Where are you off to?" A gentleman next to me asked.

"Off to? I am sorry. Don't know? It means?"

"Where are you going?"

"Oh, Chicago. Because I arrive to Valparaiso, Indiana." I answered smiling apologetically as I did each time I spoke English.

"Oh, the Lutheran school. It's a great little town, beautiful campus."

I nodded nervously hoping he wouldn't ask me any more questions. With my limited knowledge of English, after a short introduction of my name, where I came from, and where I was going, which would take five minutes at the most, I could no longer carry on a conversation.

A few hours later, through the evening fog, I saw the tall buildings of Chicago bordering Lake Michigan. In the twilight, Chicago looked exactly like what I had seen on picture postcards. Somewhere there, Sang-Hie would be waiting for me. The thought of her made me smile.

30

Sang-Hie and I stayed up most of the night talking. When we saw the light sky of dawn breaking, we forced ourselves to stop talking and sleep for a few hours. We finally got up mid-morning, long after Kil-Sup had gone to work. Sang-Hie and I took the 40-minute bus ride to Valparaiso to meet Dr. Hoelty-Nickel, the dean of the music school.

"Oh, you are finally here, Miss Lee?" he said, laughing jovially and biting his cigar with his front teeth, as he grabbed both of my hands. I thought he looked and sounded like the French actor Maurice Chevalier.

"Now, how do you pronounce your name?"

"Sang-Eun," I enunciated slowly.

"Oh, I see." He looked me up and down and turned to Sang-Hie and said, laughing, "A tiny little thing, isn't she? But she sure can play the big fiddle."

He then talked to Sang-Hie and I sat and pushed my hair behind my ears every time they looked at me. The new semester had begun the week before, so he wanted me to register that day. He handed me the class schedule, and then showed us the cafeteria where I would be eating all my meals, and then he showed us Memorial Hall, where I would live for the next nine months. At Memorial Hall, we met a tall, heavily built woman in a sleeveless, cotton dress and blond hair that looked so

unnatural, it had to be a wig. She introduced herself as the housemother
and extended her hand. I clumsily shook it and bowed.

"My name is Sang-Eun," I said.

"Oh, I see," she replied looking away.

She took us to a room in the middle of the first floor, which was
small but tidy and well organized. There were two built-in dresser
drawers. A freestanding dresser was tucked in the corner by the window
as an afterthought, as if the room was build originally to house two girls.
And there was a third bed, also like an afterthought, next to the bunk
bed. The housemother told us that my roommates were Helen Haas and
Marilyn Kern and that I would meet them when they returned from
their classes later that evening.

Sang-Hie and I decided to have lunch on campus. While we were
standing in line in the cafeteria, Sang-Hie suggested that I give myself
an American name.

"How about Sandra, it's close to Sang."

"Sandra Lee? It's too much like Sandra Dee. I don't think I like
that."

At the moment, I couldn't think of adding one more change to
my life. Shaking hands, addressing everyone by their last names each
time I spoke – Dr. Hoelty-Nickel, Mrs. Wood, Miss Lee – in addition
to saying "thank you" and "please" was already too much to remember.
And quite honestly, I didn't understand why people hugged so often for
no reason, or even kissed on the cheek – sometimes even on the lips.
With all this other confusion, I knew that if I changed my name, I might
not remember what the heck I was to be called.

That evening after a *kal-bi* and rice dinner that Sang-Hie made in
my honor, the three of us and my large suitcase piled in Kil-Sup's car and
went back to Valparaiso to move me into the dorm.

Marilyn and Helen were just about to sit down to supper at Marilyn's
desk when the housemother knocked on the door and introduced me as
their new roommate.

"Oh, excuse us. We will come back when you finish dinner," Sang-Hie said, and politely smiled.

"Oh, no. Please come in. We eat in our room every night. Please. Can we help her unpack?" Marilyn walked toward me and grabbed my suitcase. But Sang-Hie and Kil-Sup left, insisting that they finish their supper and telling them that I was fully capable of unpacking on my own.

I walked back and forth, silently filling the dresser drawers and then made my bed the way Frances showed me while I was in Los Angeles. I bit my lower lip and smiled at both of them whenever our eyes met. By my dresser, I noticed a large box full of cans of vegetables like peas and carrots.

So much had happened in last three days. I had met the Rogers at their affluent Brentwood home in the hills of Los Angeles. Meeting Mr. Rejto and casually playing for him had turned out to be an audition for entrance to USC if I wanted it, and an invitation to study on a scholarship at the Music Academy of the West the following summer. Now I was about to spend a year in a town where I did not know a soul, in a room with two strange people, communicating in a language that I barely knew.

I wished I could call Korea and talk to Mom and Eunseong. But I knew it was a silly thing to wish because calling Korea cost approximately twenty-five dollars for the first three minutes. Even if I had the money, I didn't know how to call. International calls were not direct then. A person called the operator to order the call, then hung up and waited until she made the connection and informed you that the connection was successful.

"We will show you around tomorrow morning. I don't have a class until ten in the morning and Helen will be home in the afternoon to show you around," Marilyn spoke covering her chewing. I smiled and nodded.

"I am from Minnesota and Marilyn is from Providence, Rhode Island. Neither of us has ever been out of America. We would love to hear about your country," Helen said.

I glanced at their supper. Their dinner consisted of beans, corn, and tuna out of a can. Later I learned that Helen's grandfather was a farmer who owned Green Giant, a large canned produce company in Minnesota. Helen and Marilyn cooked all of their meals in a coffee percolator.

"How do you say your name again?" Marilyn asked standing at the sink next to the door, drying a coffee percolator.

"Sang…Eun…" I emphasized Eun which seemed to be the most difficult part of my name.

"Son Gwen?"

"No, Sang-Eun."

"Oh, I see." Marilyn smiled.

Marilyn tossed her long curly hair and patted my back as she pointed to Kinsey Hall. "Have a good class. And remember your name is June now." As she turned around toward her class in another building, her long blond hair swayed against the back of her lanky body.

The night before, Marilyn and Helen had decided that "June" was the best American name for me, since my birthday was in June. So June was born in a small dormitory room with three beds, in Memorial Hall at Valparaiso University.

Each day had presented me with a myriad of foreignness, and becoming June was the strangest and the most outrageous thing of all. Since my name was nearly impossible for any American to pronounce, I agreed with both of them, refuting Sang-Hie's idea of taking the name "Sandra," and became June.

A few leaves fell from the apple trees on the way to Kinsey Hall. The campus was already beginning to show fall colors. My heart felt like it was pressing against my back and I had to take a deep breath to relieve the pain.

The music theory class was small, with only about ten students total. I wondered if all the classes were this small. Mrs. Anderson had her left ankle wrapped up with an ace bandage under her light brown, heavy support hose and she huffed and puffed, introducing me to the class in her very soft voice. Her large bosom was almost popping out of her navy blue suit. She put out the strangest warmth that made me want to hug her rather than shake her hand when she introduced herself to me.

She announced that I had come to Valparaiso University as a "special student" and that I would be performing with the University-Civic orchestra as their soloist. And for the next whole year, I would be studying at the university on a full scholarship.

As I stood sheepishly in front of everyone while Mrs, Anderson introduced me, I dropped my Walter Piston's music theory book. When I bent down to pick up the book, a guy sitting in the first row quickly moved toward the floor to pick it up for me. As our hands collided, I inadvertently knocked his glasses with my hand and they dangled precariously on his pointy nose. For some reason this jolted me and made me smile and I said, "Hi everyone, I came from Korea and my name is Sang-Eun Lee, but my birthday is June, so my new American name is June. So please call me June."

Everyone laughed and each one said something kind.

"Welcome to the class, June"

"Welcome to our country, June."

"I hear you are a remarkable cellist, June. Welcome to Valparaiso."

I sat next to Dana, who said "hello" as I sat. Her hair was cottony blond and it was teased up high and then down to a perfectly even length at her neck and slightly curled under. Her nose was high and her skin was smooth and blemish-free.

"May I execuse? Please?" I ran out of the class. I didn't know why I was crying. I just knew that I couldn't breathe. I felt like I was trapped in an airless space.

"Are you OK?" Dana followed me out the hallway and patted my back. "I am from Pennsylvania, myself. I know what it's like being away from home." Strangely, her kind words only made me distance myself further from everything around me. *She has no idea what she is talking about,* I thought to myself.

On the following Sunday, Marilyn dressed up in a light green suit and alligator stamped shoes with a matching clutch purse. Helen dressed up in a pink jumper she had ordered from the Sears catalogue, and I wore a blue suit. We went to the service at the university chapel. There was something holy and solemn about the Lutheran services, even though I could hardly understand a word. Throughout the whole service, I prayed. I prayed that God would make me strong, that He would motivate me to practice hard and give me skills to play the cello well and that He would guide me to fulfill my dreams. And most of all, I prayed that He would let me be reunited with Eunseong soon. If that was God's will, I added. And then I added again, let it be God's will.

While I never ate the Green Giant vegetables cooked in the percolator, the cafeteria food was becoming harder and harder to swallow each day. I yearned for seaweed soup, some delicious *kal-bi* meat, and succulent white rice with a swig of *kimchee* juice to wash it all down.

One day, while waiting in line in the cafeteria, I saw plain white rice piled on a serving dish. I got excited looking at it. It was white rice – not Uncle Ben's, not brown rice, but plain white rice. The server poured some kind of brown sauce over the rice for each person. Waiting for my turn, I swallowed, nearly tasting the soy-sauce-based meat sauce. But then I saw raisins and pineapples floating in the sauce, and when I took a bite, the sweet taste nearly made me gag. What I wouldn't do for kimchee juice over plain rice, sitting across the table from Mom.

Sang-Hie commuted from Gary to the American Conservatory in Chicago by train to finish up her master's program, and Kil-Sup taught math at River Forest High School. Talking to Sang-Hie on the phone was costly, so we communicated by mail.

Dear Sang-Eun,

Kil-Sup and I heard the most horrifying news today about a young Korean student in Chicago. This girl came from Korea a year ago and was planning to attend the University of Illinois. Her family was poor and couldn't send her the tuition. She worked for a year and saved enough money for tuition, but she still had to hold down a night shift to pay for her room and board. She was tired, homesick, and lonely. Evidently, after only a few months into the semester, work at school with her limited English was getting unbearably difficult and she felt she couldn't go on anymore.

On top of being lonely and poor and scared, she now learned that she was failing her major class. Yesterday, she threw herself from a tall building and killed herself. I didn't know her personally but I knew of her.

When my girlfriend from Chicago called me with the horrible news, I was so scared, my stomach started churning and I got a severe headache. How well I could relate to her. It could have been any one of us in her shoes. We all know how tough it is to be in this country trying to make it on our own.

I thought about you immediately. I know you have me to talk to and consult with but all of a sudden I realized how lonely you must be in the dorm, not even being able to converse freely.

Let's try to study English really hard so you won't have problems studying and I will help you with all your subjects while you are here in Indiana close to me.....

I dropped the letter and sat vacantly for a while. *Why am I here?* I thought. All at once it became obvious to me that I was not anywhere I was supposed to be. Yes, I would be performing with the University-Civic orchestra as their soloist as was planned. Yes, I was in America as I dreamed. But Valparaiso was far from the school I yearned to attend.

With the image of America and the image of me living in America, I somehow conceived a notion of myself being taller and speaking perfect English with no accent, and I envisioned myself playing the cello better than ever. I imagined myself dressed impeccably, living happily and satisfied, just because I was in this country. But my latent expectations of being in a dreamland, living the perfect life, couldn't have been farther away from the reality. It was all tainted by an unbearable homesickness.

It was like looking through the lustrous glass doorknob with mysterious sparkles when I was five years old and being disappointed when I saw the ordinary room behind it. All my expectations were crushed. Right now, I was in a giant open prison called America. I certainly did not belong here.

I missed the dirty alleys of the marketplace in Korea, I missed all of my giggling girlfriends, and I missed the piano trio practice sessions with Kim, Min, and Yoon, Mi-Jae. I missed Eunseong so much that my heart ached.

In December, when every building on campus was decorated with Christmas trees and the air was filled with Christmas carols, I finished the concert – the main reason I was invited-- and started panicking about what I would do when my year at Valparaiso would end. I had so many decisions to make, I was worried about how I was going to pay for room and board, and the reality of loneliness along with my disappointment in school were hitting me all at once. Unconsciously, I was building a wall around me away from the blue and green round-eyed people. More and more each day, their curled tongues and the dramatic intonations of their fast talk made me realize I was truly in a foreign country. I was an alien. I was among the aliens. All the dreamy aspects of America were slowly being crushed and it was becoming a living nightmare.

In Korea, I had been told that in America, you could eat all the chocolates and oranges you ever wanted. In America, bobby pins and barrettes were so beautiful and smooth, they never poked your head. In America, you used disposable Kotex. You would never have to wash white strips of cloth and boil them in lye soap. In America, everything was tall and everyone was good looking with pointy noses and long eyelashes and they ate a pound of beef in one sitting. In America, people were so polite they would say, "excuse me" when they slightly brushed your arm on the street. In America, everyone, even teenagers, drove their own automobiles. And if you lived in America, you would learn English so quickly that you would be fluent in no time. But no one never, ever, told me how horribly sad and lonely a place America could be. No one ever told me how to recover from the painfully agonizing loneliness that would freeze and block all of my emotions.

While I was struggling in Valparaiso, two of the Korean single men from Bloomington, graduates of Indiana University, wrote to me expressing the desire to meet. The letters were addressed to Sang-Eun

Lee at Valparaiso, Indiana. Apparently, they learned about me from the man who sat next to me on the plane from Korea.

I understood these men and the dozen men who showed up at the airport in Los Angeles. They needed to find a prospective spouse not only to fill their lonely hearts but they needed each other to complete their lives as a first generation family to establish a lineage for the generations to come and claim their heritage in a foreign land. This was the sacrifice they would have to endure in order for their grandchildren's homeland to be America.

When I thought of the Korean students that way, at the moment, getting married didn't seem like a bad idea for somebody who didn't know where to live in a few more months, but I never wrote either of them back.

In the meantime, Sang-Hie started getting frustrated with my immaturity and that I was still crying all the time and not overcoming my homesickness. After all, she had survived in Los Angeles working part-time and going to graduate school at UCLA before she married Kil-Sup. At the time, I had no idea how much pressure and responsibility she put on herself for my situation.

In January of 1966, Sang-Hie and Kil-Sup took me for an audition for Mr. Fru, the cello professor at Roosevelt University in Chicago, and I was offered a scholarship for the upcoming year. The same week, I received a letter from Curtis Institute in Philadelphia informing me of an audition date. My heart pounded when I read that there was an opening and this would be my last chance to audition for my dream school as Curtis wouldn't accept anyone over twenty-one years of age (I would be 21 the following year).

I felt privileged to have options, because these options gave me hope. It became clear to me that God loved me and he would always see to it that I would make the best choice. In this unbearably lonely place, I would be OK – this I knew for sure.

However, with these pensive and vague hopes, there was a huge barrier in living in a big city all by myself, not to mention the cost of flying out to Philadelphia to audition. Going to Roosevelt University was a possibility, but there was still the matter of having to support myself.

Soon after the second semester began, my prayers were answered. Frances Rogers wrote to Sang-Hie urging her to send me to California. When she heard that I was searching for an opportunity after spending a year at Valparaiso, she decided she knew what was best for me. She said being at Valparaiso even for another semester was a waste of my time and the sooner I came to California and study with Mr. Rejto, the better off I would be. Frances and Bob very generously offered to pay my way through college at USC. She also said that I didn't need to burden Sang-Hie and Kil-Sup, who were students themselves.

Her letter eloquently advised that they had the means of supporting me and that they would be honored to be responsible for me financially and otherwise. She thought that a young girl shouldn't live alone in a big city like Chicago or New York, so California would be the best place for me to be.

When Sang-Hie had asked them to be my sponsor when I was planning on coming to America, it was only to comply with government regulations – every foreign student had to have a responsible party who was financially capable. Neither of us expected them to actually be responsible for me. But Frances sent an airplane ticket along with her letter. I couldn't imagine having to study the required subjects for a bachelor's degree. Music school or a conservatory had always been the only option for me. However, with the predicament I was in, and the Rogers' offer to pay my way, studying at USC seemed to be the answer to all my problems.

31

Bob Rogers stopped his white Buick to pick up a neighbor, walking down winding Hanley Ave. The teenager gave a slight nod to Bob and sat in the front seat, staring quizzically at the black cloth that was laid across the dashboard.

"Your car still not running?" Bob asked.

"No. That piece of shit. Excuse me. Mr. Rogers."

From my window, I had seen him work on his small car in his shorts for days.

"Mr. Rogers, what is this black cloth for?" he asked Bob, pointing his chin at the dashboard.

"To keep the reflection from the sun. In the afternoon, the sun is so bright and it reflects right into my eyes and makes it hard to see," Bob explained excitedly as if he was ready to go into more details on the subject of driving an automobile in the sun in Southern California.

"Oh," the boy nodded quickly and looked out the window. I was comforted to know that someone else got weary of Bob's long dissertations on every subject.

"You see, in the early summer, the sun sets more to this direction," Bob went on.

At this point, I wished Frances were there to cut in and say, "Bob dear, he is not interested to hear your lecture." But then she would have finished his lecture herself. Her poor hearing wasn't an excuse, either, because even if you raised your hand and waved, she would ignore you and go on until she finished whatever she had to say.

Bob enjoyed the freedom to talk when Frances was not around and could go on until you wished you hadn't asked a question at all.

I sat in the backseat as I was instructed. Bob and Frances both thought it would be safer for me to sit in the backseat hugging my cello. I leaned my head back, ignoring the boy and trying to calm my stomach. Ever since I came to California to live in bright sunshine, a sudden spell of carsickness set off every time I was in their car. I never could figure out what triggered this fit but I decided it must have been from the butter-laden, rich food, combined with riding in larger vehicles, which gave smoother rides than the cars I was used to in Korea. When Bob and Frances would take me for a long ride to the beach through Sunset Boulevard or Malibu Canyon, I felt just like I was in a boat riding over violent waves that wouldn't stop.

My stomach was mildly upset tonight but tolerable. I was learning to do away with sour salad dressing or sour cream on baked potatoes. And tonight, knowing I had a lesson, I didn't finish the cheese soufflé. Sitting in the backseat, I yearned for a swig of *kimchee* juice to settle my stomach.

The high school boy took his hand out of his pocket to open the door on the corner of Sunset and Kenter, but as soon as he opened the door the hand went right back into his pocket.

"His father is an airline pilot and he had an affair with a stewardess, so there are just two of them, him and his mom, living across the street," Bob said.

"He has been working on his car in front of his house but I guess he couldn't get it to run yet." I changed the subject. Frances would have never approved of Bob talking about anything gossip-worthy to me. She would have scolded him and said, "Bob, dear, Song-Uun does not need to know such things. And you don't know anything for sure and we don't need to talk about them."

Bob and Frances read more than anyone I knew, and they read on every subject. They explained everything with reason and logic and logical reasons. Once, when our next-door neighbor Mrs. Wilson was pruning a tree, Frances went out to tell her that she was doing it all wrong. The correct way of doing it would be to thin the crown to permit the new growth and to give better air circulation. And it was the wrong time to prune it anyway. Idella Wilson came down the tree, mumbling with embarrassment, "I was rather proud to even tackle the job myself and get on the tree at my age." But Frances didn't hear a word Idella said.

They also knew a lot about classical music. Taking me to my cello lessons every Wednesday was the highlight of Bob and Frances's life. They took turns taking me. Today was Bob's day. It took approximately half an hour to get to the Fairfax area where my teacher Mr. Rejto lived. On Wednesdays they always had dinner early in order to get to my lesson at seven o'clock.

Eating thirty minutes earlier changed Frances's routine. She would set the dinner table around four o'clock and the dinner might be simplified a little. She might not serve salad. Frances insisted on making her own dressing and her salad had many dark green leaves, like spinach and watercress.

For Frances, going out also took a lot of preparation. She put on her support hose and flat laced-up shoes that reminded me of the shoes that waitresses or nurses wore while they were working. Then we would go in her Falcon and I would still sit in the backseat. I was forbidden to talk or comb my hair while she drove. After being in her car a couple of times, I realized she needed to give her full attention to driving since she never quite learned to slow down or stop without nearly giving me whiplash.

When it was Bob's turn to drive me, he stayed in his suit through dinner. At my lesson, Bob would sit with his back hunched over, savoring each note I played and smiling at every comment Mr. Rejto made. Sometimes he would laugh out loud at something that was not at all funny.

"You are a good girl," Mr. Rejto exclaimed.

"You practiced hard. That was beautiful." Mr. Rejto was pleased with the way I played Faure's Elegy. He then looked at Bob with a proud look.

"She practiced, all right. Frances and I love to hear her practice, although we had to stop her one night as she was practicing till eleven o'clock at night. It was one thing to practice melodic pieces, but she started practicing a lot of scales and arpeggios." He sounded high and mighty for knowing all the terms of music and could have gone on for another ten minutes if Mr. Rejto didn't quickly go back to instructing me. *Poor Bob*, I thought. *No one ever let him talk.*

Today was no different. Bob sat there and watched, smiling or nodding his head as Mr. Rejto gave me a full-hour lesson with his strong Hungarian accent.

"Practice until you can find the right notes on the fingerboard like you would on the piano keyboard. Instead of sliding up to the high notes, jump up and hit the right note." It sounded impossible, but it was easy to him.

My lesson never went over an hour and it never went under an hour.

As I was playing that night, I was aware of the lesson; I was aware of the timing. I was counting and consciously jumping up to hit the right notes. Timing, music, and rhythm all seemed so restrictive. "*Relax.*" I said to myself. "*Be creative and sing.*" But the more I said this to myself, the more conscious I became of counting the rhythm. I stopped playing and shook my arms and hands before I played again. "*Shake off the tension and relax.*"

Driving home, I looked out at the dark Wilshire Boulevard, wondering what the heck I was doing in a strange country living with the Rogers. "Do I still want to be a concert cellist?" I wondered. I felt so lonely and confused it hurt to my bones. I sobbed quietly, looking out at the dark empty street.

I bit my lip and assured myself how lucky I was to study with Mr. Rejto and how fortunate I was to have a scholarship to the Music Academy in Santa Barbara that summer and to be able to go to USC in the fall to continue to study with Mr. Rejto. And it was all because of the Rogers. How ungrateful would I be if I only thought of myself and acted childish by crying all the time from homesickness?

"Uncle Bob, I want to tell you how much I appreciate you taking me to my lesson and paying for all the expenses for me," I said softly.

"Song-Uun, it is our pleasure. You know when I was studying in Germany, I saw a lot of poor students there who had no money to pay tuition. And I said to myself, one day I would make enough money to help a foreign student." He smiled and gave me a quick glance and continued.

"And helping you gives us more pleasure than you can imagine. Frances and I think that meeting Sang-Hie was the best thing that ever happened to us. And in turn meeting you, because you have no idea how much joy you have brought to Frances and me." I squirmed around a bit in the backseat. I didn't think I deserved to be such an angelic figure to them.

Frances went to the market twice a week to shop for food after planning her menus. She smelled every jar that had been left in the refrigerator longer than two days, dipping her nose halfway into the jar. Everything they did was down to a science. The location of the pots and the pans with each lid in the cupboard was exact, down to the centimeter.

Every night at her dinner table with all white German dishes and white napkins, Frances became lively and dominated the conversation. Next to Frances's seat was a rolling teacart with an outlet for a teapot warmer. She drank almost a whole pot of tea—nothing special, just the same old Lipton tea. Frances loved telling the same story over and over and when the story got interesting, Bob would repeat Frances's last word then look at me for an approval and they both laughed and laughed, like Ed McMahan would do for Johnny Carson.

Frances declared as she sat at the dinner table one evening that she had something important to tell me. She laid her fork down on her dinner plate, a signal that Bob and I could start eating. "Have you heard of a French cellist named Pierre Founier?" she asked me, pulling in her chair closer to the table.

"Yes, of course. He is probably my favorite cellist. Somehow his tone on the cello is mellower and has deeper volume. His play is so lyrical. I love listening to him play. I saved all my money one time to buy one of his long play records. Do you like him too?"

"Well, he is coming to UCLA to give a recital next week at Royce Hall where Bob and I have season tickets and guess what? I think I am going to get a headache that day, which means you are going to have to go in my place," Frances said smiling mischievously.

"You mean he is coming here in person? He is actually playing here in person and giving a recital in person? He will be here, himself?"

"Yes, yes, and yes to all of them. And you will love our seats, the fifth row on the first floor."

"Wow! Imagine, seeing him in person. He is really alive, huh?" I couldn't believe it. "When I listen to him, with one draw of a bow, I could identify his playing. He is amazing." Before I finished talking, Bob got up and brought one of his LP records to the table from the next room.

"Yes. That's him. I love his playing," I screamed.

To think that my first experience of going to a real concert in America would be to listen to Fournier seemed so incredible, it was almost unnerving.

The night of the concert, Bob and I got into his white Buick, me in my blue suit and Bob in his dark suit with the lustrous green cufflinks.

Fournier walked onto the stage holding a cane in one hand and his cello in the other hand. He laid the cane down gently. There was something so dignified and refined about his mannerisms. When he started playing a Beethoven Sonata, his fingers glided on the strings ever so smoothly. With his vibrato, his hand looked as if delicate butterflies were flying around the fingerboard.

That night, I stayed up and wrote to Eunseong, still feeling unsettled from the excitement. "*I didn't imagine he was a real person until tonight. I thought he was only someone we saw in the record jacket,*" I wrote. "...

he was using a cane. I felt so sorry for him. I don't know what happened to his leg. I am forever grateful to the Rogers for giving me an opportunity to see him. Frances was so kind. She pretended that she was sick so I could go in her place."

My experiences with amazing musicians had just begun. In the following month, Frances' headache occurred again for Rubinstein's recital.

"Next Friday night is the concert night. Would you like to go? Rubinstein is coming," Frances said. The question had become routine. She always let me have the first choice.

"Did you say Rubinstein? You mean Arthur Rubinstein? The Russian pianist?"

"Yes, he is actually Polish but has become a U.S. citizen. He made this place a home. I have seen him perform before. I wouldn't mind at all if you would like to go. In fact, I would feel awful if you'd say no. I know Sang-Hie got to see him and couldn't stop talking about him."

Every lady in the concert hall wore something swanky and glistening on their neck. There were even a few men in tuxedoes and Bob told me that they probably were attending the reception following the concert. Seeing Rubinstein in person was nearly worth all the homesickness. I was still in awe of the privileges I was given by being in America. How is it possible I would be watching Rubinstein perform from the fifth row? I could almost hear him breathing. I was already thinking of what to write to my best friend, Jin-Hee, a pianist. His daring, exotic performance captured me completely. His fingers danced on the keyboard. He jumped off the piano bench when he pounded a chord.

My heart was still resonating to the music when the lights came up, signaling intermission. Bob stood up, glancing at me to see if I wanted to stretch. Just then a woman draped in fur in front of us turned around and introduced a couple, sitting next to me to a woman next to her.

"I would like for you to meet Mr. and Mrs. Gregory Peck."

Gregory Peck? Why does that sound so familiar? The woman's husky voice lingered in my head. Then I realized who it was. I spun my head around to see the well-built man next to me. It was him. The same man who stared at me from the wall of my room in high school was the same gentleman who had his elbow on my side of the armrest all through the first half of the concert, breathing the slight smell of alcohol like Bob's did when he had wine for dinner.

My head spun and my heart pounded for the remaining second half of the concert.

Arthur Rubinstein and Gregory Peck in one night. The word, "dream" was not enough to describe that night. Dreams did come true in America.

32

Bob and Frances never had visitors or invited anyone over for dinner. They also never went out to dinner. Frances did not go out to lunch with her girlfriends, nor did Bob ever have business guests. On Bob's birthday, Frances made a three-layer cake for him with no frosting between the layers or even on top. I still don't know if they didn't have any friends or if they preferred not to entertain.

Each time my brother came to see me, they were cordial and served him tea and sometimes tea and raisin toast, even when it was not morning. They would exchange short, perfunctory conversations.

When he didn't have any plans for the weekends, my brother would come to visit me and take me out to dinner to have Korean food at Ko-Ryu-Jung, the only Korean restaurant in Los Angeles, or to a local movie theater. Even though my feelings about him hadn't changed much, living with the Rogers and not having any social life made me look forward to seeing my brother. It got me out of the house and I got to have Korean food.

Even though the Rogers decided they were undertaking the full responsibility of rearing me, they had not set any limits on how late I could stay out or what movie he was taking me to. But the first time I got in my brother's car, Frances did say, "Sang-In, we are trying to teach

Song-Uun to wear her seatbelt in the car, so would you please make sure she does in your car?"

This was in the '60s when hardly anyone wore seatbelts, and families packed half a dozen kids in the back of their station wagons.

"Of course, Mrs. Rogers, I will make sure," my brother said.

When we got in the car he said, "I have to hand it to you. How do you put up with her?"

"Oh, they are not so bad. Actually, I am learning so much from them. Frances gives me an hour-long English lesson every day. The things they do for me, I will be forever indebted to them. It's hard to imagine what would have happened to me if Sang-Hie hadn't happened to meet Frances at UCLA. For that matter, I owe it all to Sang-Hie. I sure miss her." I sighed.

My brother had also loved having Sang-Hie near him when she first came to UCLA. Sang-Hie was only three years younger than him and he felt it was his personal responsibility to choose the best potential husband for her. In doing so, he found himself to be in the center of attention of all the young men in the Korean community who wanted to date Sang-Hie. As far as he was concerned, no one was good enough for her, and he found faults in anyone who showed an interest in her. So, when Sang-Hie moved to Indiana to be married to Kil-Sup, my brother was not pleased. She had met Kil-Sup at a Christmas party in Los Angeles. Kil-Sup had come to California to visit his sister during Christmas vacation. They wrote to each other for several months and then she moved, in mid-semester to Indiana.

"Huh! I will bet she doesn't miss you. Her and that good-for-nothing husband."

"What do you mean? He is very nice. We all like him very much. He comes from an elite family. He works hard and he is so good to her."

"What do you know about things like that? You are just a little girl. Just trust me. He is just not good enough for her." By then my brother was screaming.

"I am twenty years old. I know a good man when I see one. And I know they are truly in love. I saw them together in Indiana. You are just mad because you wanted to have her around so you can boast about her to your friends. You only care about you. It's always all about you," I screamed just as loud, staring at him. We were in his car, speeding down Wilshire Boulevard when I felt a sharp sting on my face and my forehead hit the dashboard. My mom was wrong about America straightening out a little horror like my brother. He hadn't changed a bit.

"Stop the car. I am getting out of your car. Don't ever come to see me again. I don't want to see you, ever again." I was hysterical, but the more I screamed, the faster he drove. And after each word I shouted, he hit me on my arm, my face, my head, anywhere he could get his right hand while still keeping his other hand on the steering wheel. He was so absolutely maniacal and frantic, I wanted to jump out from the speeding car.

I didn't know how long we drove. He stopped in front of an old apartment building and pulled me out of the car. I looked around, hoping for help. I pulled away from him and stuck my hand out toward the street, hoping someone would stop for me. I would have gone into any car that stopped. But he grabbed me by my arm and dragged me to a door on the first floor and knocked.

Chang-Kyu, my brother's best friend, opened the door. "What are you doing here?" he asked.

"I need to come in and straighten this monster. She thinks she knows better than me. What an impudent little shit she's become."

Sang-In dragged me into the kitchen. From then on I only remember seeing flashes of light. I fell every time he swung his arm. As soon as I got up, he hit me again on the face, on the back, on the stomach, anywhere he could. I yelled and screamed and eventually said that I was wrong and begged him to forgive me. I had to say something he would like to hear to stop his insanity. He then left me in the kitchen and went out to the living room. I heard him say, "What a spoiled bitch she is," to Chang-Kyu, who had been sitting in the living room the whole time.

I followed him out to the living room and asked him to take me home. I had to get away from both of them. I had always known Chang-Kyu was a mild-mannered person from all the days he used come and spend nights at our house with my brother, but I learned for the first time what a coward he was.

"Fighting between the siblings is like severing the water with a knife. You need to forgive each other and forget," Chang-Kyu said, stealing a look at my brother.

"You are right. I would like to go home, please?" I said, quietly looking at the floor. My head was throbbing and my vision was limited. My good eye must have been swollen.

My brother never turned the motor off when he dropped me off at the Rogers'. I ran to the door and knocked and rang the bell.

"Hey, you are back. Did you have a good time? Where did you g-- What happened to you? Your face is all bruised. What happened? Frances, come here. Sang-Eun is injured." He pulled me into the house from under the dim porch light.

"My brother hit me like a madman. He is crazy. I never want to see him. I hate him. Don't let him come here ever again." I plunged into Bob's arms and started sobbing. "I would just like to take a shower and go to bed now, if you don't mind." I finally stopped crying and composed myself.

"Of course, dear. But we need to know exactly what happened. We need to know if there is something that should be done. Would you like us to take you to the hospital?" Frances's lips were shaking.

"No, I don't need a doctor. Let me clean up first and I will talk to you."

I needed to be alone to cry, to get mad, to curse, and to loathe. I knew if I had a gun, I would have shot him.

The reflection of my face in the bathroom made me gasp. My right eye was nearly closed and it was blue all around. The left side was blotchy red. Standing there, I cried some more. All the dreadful memories were coming back. And how did I end up the lucky one to live here with him in the same town?

The next morning, through the window of my room, I saw my brother pull into the driveway. Then I heard Bob saying, "Just a minute, Sang-In," and close the door, leaving him to wait outside.

The night before, Bob and Frances decided that they would only let my brother into their house if I allowed it, and that they would support and honor my wishes of not ever wanting to see him.

"Yes, I will see him, but please don't go anywhere," I said to Bob.

My brother came into my room and handed me a steak.

"I heard that laying a raw steak on the wounds will take the bruise away. I am sorry about what happened last night. What did the Rogers say?"

"Nothing."

"What do you think they are thinking? Do they think I am a violent person? What do you think I should do so they wouldn't think that?"

"They don't," I lied. I wanted to spit at him.

"I am really sorry about what happened last night. It makes me so mad whenever I think of Sang-Hie being married to him."

"So you took it out on me?" I said, looking away.

"I am really sorry. Will you tell the Rogers that I apologized to you?"

I nodded, but in my heart I was thinking that I wouldn't bat an eye if he died tomorrow.

33

Frances kept a simple, neat house with Danish-style furniture. The living room sat diagonally to the street and had a full view of it through the glass panel. Standing at the front door, a large kitchen was visible through the front hallway. Every morning, Bob got up and made us a breakfast of toast and eggs. He made the best drip coffee right on the stovetop. He would boil the water in a teakettle and pour very patiently through a cone until the water was all in the Pyrex coffee pot.

Uncle Bob and I didn't have very much to talk about, but I got up and ate with him anyway, and sat at the table that was set the night before with paper napkins and placemats. Perhaps I felt sorry that he made his own breakfast and ate alone. He sat down to breakfast in his suit and tie and would say, "It's Tuesday, all day."

I didn't quite understand what he meant by that, but it gave me the impression that his life wasn't too exciting. Once I asked him, "All day? What does that mean?"

He said, "It's another day today. It's Tuesday. Can't change that. It's all day."

I guessed he was just making a conversation.

I called them Aunt Frances and Uncle Bob as Frances requested. This was her way of making it clear that even though they loved me, they would never take me away from my mom and try to adopt me.

One day, in her letter, my mom showed me her concern about their possible desire to adopt me. I answered, "There is a reason why this couple is childless, Mom. They don't know how to be parents. I respect them and appreciate them, but if they were to become my parents for any reason, I would come back home to Korea."

The way Frances and Bob enunciated my name was not even remotely close to how it was supposed to sound. Having an American name somehow seemed to make it easier to communicate with English-speaking people. At least they didn't look at you like a rare animal at a zoo before attempting to pronounce your name. I wanted to have a name that was easy to pronounce, like June, because it made me feel like I fit in a little more.

When I first came back to Los Angeles to live with Bob and Frances, I told Frances that I wanted to be called "June," but she adamantly disagreed.

"Dear, Song-Uun is so much prettier than June. Plus, it is your name. So many foreign students abandon their names and their heritage by taking on a new name, which is so unbecoming." She brushed her short, curly gray hair away from her face, showing her frustration. Her flailing arms were so long and awkward, they nearly hit the glass cupboard in the kitchen.

Well, it's not a pretty name, not the way you are saying it, anyway. I wanted to tell her, but I said, "Oh all right." No Korean would have understood what she was saying.

When Mr. Rejto asked if he could please just call me Sang, I said, "That's fine." I decided if he was going to call me by the wrong name, it might as well be easy. Frances wasn't pleased with Mr. Rejto for not even attempting to say my whole name.

One morning when I got up, Bob had already left and I helped myself to coffee and toast. I was studying my English book after breakfast when Frances knocked on my door. "Song-Uun," she said, calling my name in her usual mispronunciation.

"Come in, Aunt Frances," I answered.

As Frances stood by my door, she waved her long, skinny and

wrinkled index finger as she started talking. Everything Frances had was long. Her fingers, her nose, and her arms, and when they were all put together, reminded me of a witch in a storybook. I could tell from her shaky tone and her curled finger something terrible had happened.

"I have something serious to tell you, Song-Uun." She rested her hand on her left hip, which was slightly higher than the right.

"What's the matter?" I jumped out of my desk chair.

"Your Uncle Bob's sister, Edith, lives in Sacramento. She is divorced and has been very unhappy. And early this morning she tried to kill herself. You know? She didn't want to live anymore." Frances waved her long finger again.

"Are you serious?"

"Well, Bob flew up there this morning and he is going to bring her down here to stay. I don't know how long she will be with us, but we will have her for as long as she needs us."

"Of course. Is there anything I can do?"

"Well, yes there is. I need you to understand the situation, but I also want you to know that she will be sleeping in the living room on the couch."

"But I will be happy to let her have my room."

"No, Song-Uun. This is what I wanted to talk to you about. This is your room and we intend to give you your space at all times as we planned."

"But I feel comfortable anywhere. And she might want a little more privacy." I did not want to take the only guest bedroom over a close relative who was having a problem.

"Song-Uun, again, this is why I wanted to talk to you. Bob and I think that her being here should not disrupt our lives. We will do our best to help her while keeping our routine as orderly as we can," Frances said. "She will be here soon and when you meet her I want you to act as normal as possible. And for heaven's sake, don't ask her how she is feeling. They had to pump her stomach to get all the sleeping pills out of her system."

That evening, Bob avoided making eye contact with me as he introduced Edith to me. He looked down and stared at my shoulders and
arms as if he didn't know where to hide. And Edith, poor Edith, stood
behind him like a lost puppy dog. She was pale and thin and had Bob's
looks. I felt like a fifth wheel and a nuisance that was in the middle of
her embarrassing situation. I was not only a stranger to her, but was
placed in a more favorable position at the Rogers' household by taking
the only guest room.

This is how Aunt Edith came into my life. She slept in the living
room until Aunt Frances made an arrangement for her to sleep at Mrs.
Wilson's, next door, for a nominal charge. Every morning, Edith walked
over in her pink terrycloth bathrobe to have breakfast with us. Now I
waited and had breakfast with the ladies. By then, Bob had long gone
to work, and we would sit and have long leisurely breakfasts. Frances
always had lots of stories to tell us from her younger days as a house
mother at the University of Michigan, or stories about her days as an
editor of *Harper's Bazaar* or how she met Bob, the good-looking young
man with an interesting cheekbone who, she said, was a typical New
Englander. She never talked of her age or the fact that Bob was fifteen
years younger than her. Frances talked most of the time, and Edith and
I would nod or get in a few "uh-huh's" here and there.

Edith had sweet and calm disposition. She had a slightly crooked
mouth when she smiled, just like Uncle Bob. She called me Song-Uun
just like Frances and Bob did. But she said it a little slower, and always
with a smile as if she was calling a good friend. There was a soft tone about
it, and it somehow didn't sound as harsh and awkward as Frances.

Like the Rogers, Edith was also a reader. She spent most of the
day reading and watching me practice my cello. She loved taking me to
places like the Bullock's shopping mall in Westwood. We would go and
spend hours looking at purses and shoes. One day Edith asked Frances's
permission to buy me a dress.

Frances replied, "What a perfectly lovely idea. But Edith, I don't
know if you would find anything for her. Everything she owns is custom-

designed and made for her and she is just not used to the ready-made dresses."

"Well, I am sure we could find something she likes. I will ask Idella Wilson for suggestions. She must know where to shop since she raised Suzy right in this area." Edith was firm in her desire to take part in caring for me.

We went to Lanz, a store that Idella Wilson had recommended, and found a lovely dress. It was a fitted dress with black and brown floral print and a large white round collar around the neckline. It pleased her when I told her that I liked the ready-made dresses because I could try them on and make sure that they fit before I bought them. I also told her that I loved the dress my sister bought me in Indiana last year, the black dress with a black and white stripe tie around the neck, which was also off the rack.

"They seem to pay a lot of attention around the neckline here. It's a good idea. It really shows off your face by accentuating the neckline," I said.

"You're so observant," Edith said. "When you get older, I want you to buy a college girl a dress, too."

On our evening walks, she often talked about her stepson, Johnny. Johnny was the same age as me and dropped out of UC Davis shortly after he enrolled. She said, for two young people of same age, Johnny and I couldn't have been farther apart. She said I was good and normal and he was troubled and unsocial. She related all of his problems to his dysfunctional family life and thought it stemmed from having a distant and aloof father.

I figured she was getting some of this information from her weekly visits to the famed Beverly Hill's psychiatrist, Dr. Monk. Every Wednesday after her appointment, she would go out to dinner alone and review her session with him and make notes of what she needed to work on for the upcoming week.

When I wrote to my mom about Edith, I never revealed the fact that she was seeing a psychiatrist on regular basis. I saw no sense in worrying my mom. A mentally unstable divorcee was the last person a Korean mom would want her daughter to associate closely with.

On an unusually warm April day, Edith lay in a hammock on the back patio overlooking the canyon and Frances made us lemonade. I drank the sour lemonade and listened to Edith tell me about her family life, growing up. She said her mother was mentally unstable and nagged at her father incessantly. Her father would leave the house when he could no longer stand his wife's nagging. Her only sister, Marian, was so mean and jealous of her, Edith couldn't wait to go to college. When she finished Cornell University, she married a handsome young widower who could fly an airplane. His first wife committed suicide from loneliness because he was so cold and self-centered. When she saw herself in a similar situation, she quickly got divorced, but only after she was already diagnosed with manic depression. On that day, I instantly felt deep sympathy for her, much like loving a wounded house cat.

Up until then, I had viewed all American people, including the Rogers, as clearly different. The obvious differences were their many different colors of hair and eyes, their taller bodies, and their higher noses. Even their sentiments were bigger. They seemed easily impressed by everything. Everything was amazingly beautiful, incredibly tremendous, fantastic, or unbelievably skillful. Very few things or people were ordinary, yet these sentiments weren't always truthful. In a discussion or argument, they talked in matter-of-fact and unemotional tones. It was hard to see the depth of their hearts. These general impressions of Americans gave me uncertainty and set me apart from them. I couldn't imagine marrying an American.

But now, Edith was showing me an emotional side, and I was intrigued. Very quickly, I fell into a comfortable relationship with Edith. As far as I was concerned, her actions were completely justified.

One day, Edith and I walked down to the San Vicente market and she decided to take Tigertail Road coming back. I loved looking at all the lovely homes on the street. Some had garage doors in the front and some just carports. One house had a full view of the living room through the window and near the drapery were an armchair and a table with a brass lamp. An ebony baby grand piano displayed half a dozen family photographs. Another house had a full view of the dining room with a lovely centerpiece. The dark wood dining table with the high cane-back chairs looked so inviting.

"Wouldn't you love to be invited to dinner in that dining room?" I asked Edith. She smiled and said, "You like nice things, don't you?"

"I think I like pretty things."

Walking up the hill, we became tired and sat on the curb of a front yard that was full of red and pink geraniums. The California sun was so bright and the flowers were showing off brilliant colors. I would never see this in Korea.

I should be happy, I thought. *There is so much I like about Los Angeles. For one thing, it is always bright and sunny. I am taking lessons from a great cellist. I have a wonderful summer planned. And in the fall, I will start school at USC. Why am I not happy?*

I sat there looking at the flowers, and all of a sudden, loneliness whipped through me like a whirlwind, and I was drenched with sadness. I wanted to go home to Korea. What was I doing here in this strange country in the middle of the day wasting my life? I wanted to cry. I didn't belong here.

"What's the matter?" Edith asked.

"I am homesick, Aunt Edith. I want to go home."

"Oh no, Song-Uun, you mustn't cry. I know you must be homesick. I would be too." She put her arm around my shoulders.

"You are so talented and you are such a wonderful young woman. And I know Bob and Frances love you so much and think a world of you." Edith seemed so calm it was hard to think that she attempted to take her life away.

I crumbled completely. Until then, I had tried to be strong and compose myself in front of Bob and Frances. And of all the people, I fell apart in front of Edith. I was supposed to help her with her pain.

"Let me tell you what Bob said to me." Edith handed me a tissue. "When I arrived at Los Angeles Airport with Bob, it was late at night and the airport was dark and wet from the rain. I was looking outside from the windows of the plane, and I had no hopes. I was feeling so depressed. I wished my suicide attempt succeeded," she said. " I didn't know why I was coming to L.A. I had no reason to come here and I had nothing to look forward to." Edith's eyes sparkled from tears. I felt so sorry for her, I almost forgot how miserable I was.

"Then, Bob told me about you." She wiped her eyes.

"About me?" I looked at her.

"He said, 'Edith, just wait till you meet Song-Uun. I am promising you. She will change your life. And when you watch her play the cello, you will know that your life is worth living. She is like an angel.' That's what Bob said."

"He didn't say that, did he really?" I said, embarrassed.

"Do you ever go to church?" I asked. "I know Aunt Frances and Uncle Bob don't."

"I know they don't. I did go from time to time when I was a little girl, but that was about it. Do you want to go? If you do, I will take you. I can drop you off and pick you up after the service."

"No, no, I just thought you might like to go, in which case I will go with you. I still have a hard time understanding the sermon. I went every Sunday in Valparaiso though."

"Well, no. I think going to church and believing in Jesus might give a person some point of reference in the moral and ethical standard in life, but I am an honest person and know not to do unethical things. I don't believe I need to go to church to be a good person."

"We were taught otherwise, Aunt Edith. I went to a Methodist high school and college in Korea. Sometimes it helps to have faith in God, you know. The Bible says He planned your life even before you were born," I stammered.

"Well, Song-Uun, I guess I don't believe that."

Every evening, Frances and Bob read or listened to classical music. I roamed around the house between practicing my cello and joining Bob in the music appreciation, desperately wishing they had a TV set. Their only entertainment or outings were the season tickets to Royce Hall and

Schoenberg Hall at UCLA. They would read up on the pieces before going to the concerts, so they were knowledgeable of the pieces that were to be performed.

Bob had a subscription to the *Audubon Society* and was fascinated by birds. He showed me the books of colorful birds and talked about each of them for hours. One time I was so tired of listening, I told him that I didn't like birds. He asked me why not, and I said because they had such small heads and with such small brains, they must not be very smart. "You must like frogs, then, since they have big heads," he said. I guess he was a little hurt that I had no empathy for his love for birds.

Even with all of their peculiarities, I grew to respect Frances and Bob for who they were. They were intellectual, knowledgeable, considerate, and kind.

When I was about to get into trouble with immigration, she took me to the Korean consul's office and explained why I wasn't going to school even though I was on a student visa. She gathered up all my papers, including the acceptance to Valparaiso University on a full scholarship, acceptance to the Music Academy of the West in Santa Barbara for the summer of 1966 on a scholarship, and the acceptance to USC for the upcoming fall semester, as well as my passport and Bob's sponsorship guarantee while I was studying in the US.

Once we were in front of the consul general, Frances started explaining my whole life story to him. "The bottom line is that she had several scholarships from different universities but Valparaiso University was the only one who gave her a full ride including room and board. She needed to go there since her mom was unable to support her from Korea. She was basically on her own. Unfortunately, the cello teacher at Valparaiso was not able to teach her much since she was already an accomplished concert cellist." I was embarrassed and wished I had waited outside.

I was sure that there were millions of foreign students who skipped and transferred schools every semester, and it wasn't anything new to this gentleman. He was just humoring her naïve jabber, nodding his head and tapping the ashes of his cigarette on his mother-of-pearl inlaid table, missing the ashtray.

As we left his office, he said to me in Korean, "She said that you are too good for the professor. He didn't have anything to teach you, she said."

I winced and bowed when we left, too embarrassed to say anything. I hated bowing in Korea and I still hated it.

Frances then went to the immigration office with all the same paperwork and made sure that they knew I would be attending college full-time as a music major.

Even though she was sometimes overly diligent, I learned to appreciate Frances's impeccable way of handling matters and understood Bob when he said, "Your aunt Frances is always there if anybody in the family needs help. My mother always said that."

Frances also inspected every thank-you note I wrote and made sure I knew the proper way of writing letters. She showed me the differences between ladies' stationary and men's stationary. She checked out textbooks for English as a Second Language and made sure that I studied every day. She also insisted that I wear no make-up and completely stop wearing high heels. I didn't say yes or no, but decided I would wait until I moved out of their house and then do what I wanted.

One thing she didn't have any advice on was my wardrobe. I had brought all my clothes from Korea: dressy suits, casual sweaters, comfortable school clothes, and dressy long and short dresses. I had something to wear for every occasion.

While I was living with the Rogers, I turned 21. Frances and Bob decided to take me out to celebrate at a nice restaurant in Hollywood. Edith came with us, and I got all dressed up in my white and blue flowery dress and white pumps with an open toe. When I came out of my room, Frances looked at my shoes and said, "Oh." Then she said, "You look lovely, dear."

While Bob was driving his white Buick to the restaurant, Frances had the map on her lap.

"Bob, dear, you can take Sunset all the way. You don't need to take Wilshire at all."

"I know, I know," Bob said.

"Bob dear, you missed the turn," Frances said, agitated.

"I thought this would be the faster way. I know where I am going," Bob said.

"You might be able to get there this way. But the traffic is really bad here right now." Frances was waving both of her long arms.

"Frances, let me drive. I am doing fine and the traffic is not bad right now." Bob said without raising his voice.

"Well, it's all yours." Frances threw the map like a bratty little child.

"OK, OK. I will get you there. Don't worry." Bob was a saint, I thought. I knew Edith was thinking the same thing because she looked at me and winked. I smiled.

When we got to the restaurant, we were almost twenty minutes early.

I ordered a steak and salad with Thousand Island dressing. That was the only dressing I knew.

"Can I buy everyone champagne?" Edith looked at Frances.

"I can't stop Song-Uun if she wants it. She is twenty-one today."

Frances's answer made me uncomfortable. And I saw no reason to celebrate.

"I don't care for any, thank you," I said. I didn't feel any different. I didn't feel like an adult. It was just a number.

34

In the backseat of Bob's Buick, I looked out of the window in awe at the Pacific Ocean. As the waves washed along the coast, they left ribbons of stringy kelp ashore. The shoreline curved around the mountains and canyons; I watched rocky cliffs stand bravely through the battering waves. Though I had driven along the Pacific Ocean with them many times, I had never driven this far or for this long, and the largeness of it overwhelmed me. The breathtaking view of the shoreline went on and on to an uncertain destination.

I pressed my heart to keep it from pounding. Anticipating the next two months of playing and studying under the world-famous musicians by this beautiful ocean was turning my stomach with excitement and anxiety. I didn't know what to expect or what it would be like to play chamber music with foreigners. Would I meet their expectations? Would I be able to understand and get along with them? And how would I manage this haunting homesickness that ached to my bones? My anticipation turned into confusion and fearful elation.

The first time I had heard about the Music Academy of the West in Santa Barbara was when Hyo Kang was offered a scholarship there three years earlier. When the renowned violinist Berl Senofsky came to Korea on his concert tour, he was impressed with Hyo's violin playing and offered him a scholarship to the Music Academy for the upcoming summer and told him he should study at Juilliard the following school year. It was every music student's dream come true.

We all envied him and talked about it. "I heard that Heifetz and Piatigorsky give master classes there."

"Did you know that the world-famous conductors come and spend summers there directing the Academy's orchestra?" Our list of dream schools expanded and the Music Academy got on top of the list as a priority summer camp.

The second time I had heard the name "The Music Academy of the West" was from Mr. Rejto, when I first arrived in Los Angeles.

"Mrs. Rogers tells me that you will be spending a year in Indiana. But will it be possible for you to come and study with me in Santa Barbara next summer on a scholarship?" Mr. Rejto asked, laughing cheerily, as if he was a new father, giving out cigars. "You mean you teach in Santa Barbara in the summer?" I was stunned. "I mean where Piatigorsky--I mean, I would like to. Very much."

In Santa Barbara, five of us shared a three-bedroom apartment — designated student housing by the Academy. Laura, who played French horn, and Alison, an oboist, shared a room opposite the hallway, and Holly, also an oboist, had a single room next to theirs.

"Do you think we will meet some cute guys here?" My roommate, Lori, a violinist from Reed College, asked as she threw on her bedcovers carelessly. She then dumped the whole contents of her suitcase into the top drawer, watching me line my drawer with daisy-patterned paper.

"What guys? What do you mean? Who is cute?"

"You know, guys to go out with. I refuse to have two months of lonely nights here."

I was shocked. I wasn't sure if I heard her right. School hadn't even started, and boys were the last thing on my mind, especially white boys, who were still an unfamiliar species to me. They talked differently, walked differently, and laughed more loudly than Korean boys.

"Have you met Dr. Abrabanel?" I quickly changed the subject, only because I had been full of anxiety about meeting our conductor.

"No, I haven't. But I hear he is like a musical genius. He conducts the Utah Symphony, you know? I am really excited to play under him."

"I wonder how they will seat us. I mean, do you think you will be in the first violin section?"

"Oh, I don't care where I sit. I don't mind sitting in the second violin section. I would imagine there will be lots of kids who are tons better than me." Lori shrugged her shoulders. She tilted her head and started combing her long brown hair with her fingers. I wondered why she was wasting her time here.

When Mr. Rejto asked me what pieces I had played in the orchestra in Korea, I told him at Ewha University, being a women's college, we played mostly Baroque pieces that didn't require many wind instrumental players. Girls in Korea didn't play wind instruments, with the exception of the flute. I also told him that seating didn't matter, I would take any seat. This was another Korean way: Always be humble, even if it's a lie. I plopped myself down on the bed, wishing I had exaggerated my orchestral experiences to Mr. Rejto. That's when I heard the doorbell.

"Is Miss Lee here yet? I was told that she would be moving in today."

"Who? Miss Lee? Oh, you mean the Korean girl. Yes, she just moved in. I will get her for you," we heard Holly say in her nasally voice.

Lori and I looked at each other.

"Miss Lee? Is someone looking? Me?"

"Yeah, you, Miss Lee. Tell you what. We can sit here and play a guessing game, or you can go and find out. I would take the latter if I were you," Lori laughed.

Halfway to the door, I came back to drop an armful of underwear on the bed, then I headed out to see who was at the front door.

With the bright sunlight behind him, all I could see was a small young man with dark hair. He spoke, "Oh my gosh, I thought it might be you. Welcome to the Academy. My gosh, how long has it been?" Hyo kept repeating himself and I felt a surge of adrenaline upon realizing it was him.

"I didn't know you still come here in the summer? Don't you live in New York? Going to Juilliard?"

"I am so excited to see you. My gosh. Wait. Go ahead and finish unpacking. But let's go out to dinner tonight and catch up."

As a Juilliard student, Hyo came back to the Academy for the third summer in a row.

After a lonely ten months in a strange place, running into Hyo in Santa Barbara was a hugely unexpected pleasure to me. I felt like a fish that had finally been thrown back into the ocean after barely surviving in a shallow dish of water.

Hyo, Jin-Hee, and I played in a piano trio as high school students, mostly Mozart and Haydn, and when he went to Seoul National University, he became best friends with Eunseong, my boyfriend.

"Oh, but come back in for a minute. I am almost done. I can't believe it's really you." I made no effort to hide my delight in my high-pitched whiny voice, though we didn't touch or hug. We didn't even shake hands.

He sat in the living room and lit a cigarette. I pushed the ashtray toward him on the coffee table.

"Would you like one?" He offered with a slight hesitation. He didn't want to assume that I practiced the unaccepted vice. I wondered if Hyo remembered that Jin-Hee and I were the only girls who smoked at his farewell party three years before.

"I don't know. I am dying for one but I haven't—you know, since I have been living with the Rogers." Smoke clouded Hyo's face and a craving to inhale nearly made me shake. I couldn't resist.

Our voices were two octaves higher and laughter filled the room. Lori came out of the room in her long striped shift.

"What is that?" Hyo made a snide comment in Korean mocking Lori's appearance.

"Oh, I wish I could smoke. It always gives me a headache. Can I just hold one?" Lori sat down and grabbed one from the table. I wanted to tell her that I had a headache too, but it was worth it.

That evening, Hyo and I decided to walk down to State Street to eat at a Chinese restaurant. The slight ocean breeze cooled our bare arms pleasantly. The streets were clean but bleak, not anything like the crowded streets of Myung-Dong where you would almost bump another pedestrian. Walking alongside him made me realize he was shorter than I remembered. Hyo talked excitedly about Wojczeck, the Polish pianist at the Academy.

"Man, he sure has shitloads of talent." I laughed at his casual tone, thinking he wasn't as charming as I remembered.

"When did you start swearing so much?" I rolled my eyes, looking at him.

"When I grew up. I speak and act as I feel. This is the greatest country. No more putting on an act."

"What do you mean?"

"I mean, if I like a girl I take her out, blond, brunette, I don't care. I practice violin a lot. I do everything as my heart desires."

"I still don't know what you are saying? You mean you didn't do what your heart desired in Korea?" Hyo just smiled, and I no longer saw Koreaness in him.

"You sure have changed. For the best, I guess," I said nonchalantly. In Korea, he was quiet and tried to keep somewhat of a mysterious image, hoping to intrigue the girls he was interested in. Now he was open and not afraid to show his true self. Being with him lessened my sense of alienation.

Hyo ate every bit of the mediocre, borderline-awful, Egg Fu Young. He told me that the food was one thing he was having an extremely hard time with in America. He would take any Chinese or Japanese food, unless he happened to find a Korean restaurant, over a hamburger or steak. To him, the worst thing to put in his mouth was a peanut butter and jelly sandwich.

"How anyone would eat that shit, I will never know." He shook his head.

I made a mental note to make him *kal-bi* one night, if I could find the ingredients for the marinade.

Later that week, holding an armful of orchestral music, I leaned on the bed. I spread the music on the bed and started humming and playing the Brahms third symphony on my folded arm. Then I skimmed through Stravinsky's Firebird Suite. In the orchestra rehearsals, I was thrilled to play such great symphonic works, but I made light of it, pretending I could sight read most of them. Letting out a big sigh, I closed my eyes in a desperate attempt to sort out my empty feelings of disappointment. I grabbed a piece of paper and started scribbling.

I have only listened to these great pieces before. Now I am actually a part of making the amazing music. This is the opportunity I had dreamed of. Or is this really what I dreamed of doing? Then why do I feel so dejected? Why? Why? Why?

The apartment on Ladera Street was so quiet that it seemed I could almost hear a spider climbing on the wall toward the ceiling. I stared at the spider and when it got to the top of the window, I opened it slowly and shut it again as soon as the spider crawled outside. At least I got rid of one. According to Lori, the apartment must have been infested with spiders. Our first morning at the Academy, we both woke up with bites all over, Lori was sure that they were spider bites.

"Fine first day at the Academy. With all sorts of spider bites on my arms and legs," Lori grumbled, wetting her index finger and dabbing the red dots on her arms with her saliva. She flung her long, straight hair away from her face, exposing her huge silver hoop earrings.

On the day of the first orchestra rehearsal, Mr. Rejto seated me in the fourth row, outside seat. Jeff Solow was the principal cellist. Mr. Rejto's son, Peter sat in the second row outside seat and Karen and Nina, who were dating Jeff and Peter sat in the third row. My heart sank with pure devastation, disappointment, and complete dismay. I had never sat anywhere but in the first row in the orchestra, mostly at the principal cellist's seat.

Where I sat in the orchestra mattered to me. It was like lining up all the string players in order of strength and showing how many were better than me and how many were behind me. It not only mattered to me – it was a pivotal factor in my conviction about whether or not I

328   SANG-EUN LEE BUKATY

should pursue my career as concert cellist. Competition was everything in music.

Hyo Kang sat next to the concertmaster in the orchestra. In the orchestra, his intense eyes looked as if they would pierce through the music. The first time I had noticed his penetrating stare was during my high school days playing piano trio with him. If our eyes met during a rehearsal, his intensity made me almost uncomfortable. His stare looked like he could see my next notes and he could tell how I was going to play the next phrase. Even though Hyo never participated in music competitions, anyone who listened to his playing understood his proficiency as violinist was on another level. He knew to compare Yascha Heifetz to Isaac Stern in the finest points and depth, while I was just busy following the melody of either of their performances.

For the first week, Hyo and I went out to dinner, had lunch together and spent evenings talking about our mutual friends in Korea. A few weeks into the summer program at the Academy, he came and asked me to walk down to State Street to have sushi dinner. I was flipping through the Bible, the large Korean version Eunseong gave me when I left Korea.

"A Bible? Do you always read that?"

"Not always, but I try to when I have time." This was my usual answer when anyone caught me reading it.

"It comforts me. Have you ever read it? Any part?"

"No, but I grew up Catholic so I know what's in it. Just don't look at me with pitiful eyes like I am a lost sheep."

"I am not. And I don't think you are a lost sheep. But everyone needs God." I shrugged and closed the Bible.

We were walking back to the apartment after having sushi, when Hyo blurted out,

"What happened to you?"

"What do you mean? Nothing happened to me"

"I know you can play well. Why aren't you playing like you could?"

GRACE NOTES

"I don't know. Well, I will soon. For one thing, I just don't like my cello. I need a better cello. I don't even dust my instrument any more. It's got an inch of rosin dust under the bridge."

"That's a load of crap. You have to do the best you can with what you have at each moment. You are a musician. Find beauty in it. And treasure the best you have right now. Do not punish your instrument but cherish it with care. You know music instruments are alive. If you punish it, it will shrivel up."

"I know. It's an excuse. Well, to tell you the truth, Mr. Rejto doesn't think I am that good and it depresses me to know that my teacher thinks less of me than I really am. He sat me in the fourth row in the orchestra. Didn't you notice?"

"So? They seat you by seniority. Do you think I sat in the first row in the first year I was at the Academy? You have to show him you are interested in learning, performing, and playing in the orchestra every chance you have." He shook his head. "Are you playing for the opera?"

"They didn't ask me," I answered.

"Here is another thing you should know. In this country, you have to do your share to get anywhere. No one is going to take you by the hand and lead you. You have to find the way you want to go. You have to find food, bite it, and chew it yourself. No one will chew it and put it in your mouth for you like Korean teachers and Korean parents would."

"But Hyo, you don't understand. You are telling me instruments are alive and it will shrivel up if you don't give enough encouragement. Did you ever think that a live musician might shrivel up too? When it comes to creative art, confidence takes a huge part in expressing it. When you are discouraged and lose confidence, your ability shrivels up. Your creative juice stiffens and dries up. And your tonality shrivels. The other day in our master class, I was playing the Boccherini Sonata No. 6. You know I played the piece in high school and I had played the second movement with fluid and clear spiccato. Well, you should have seen me playing in front of everyone. I choked. My bow wouldn't bounce. My wrist was so heavy, the spiccato became a muddled detache. Even Rejto was frustrated and had me play "At the Fountain," by Davidoff, which required spiccato all through the first half. He had given me that piece only two months before, and he knew I was skillful in the technique. When I played it with ease, everyone shook their heads, perplexed. I don't know why. I just don't. I feel like a failure, a huge disappointment to everyone around me. Just like when I failed junior high. Well, you probably don't understand it," I argued, pleading.

Still, I knew he was right. I had no time to sit in the corner and cry about how much I missed my homeland. Instead of complaining about how little I understood, I should study English and learn to speak, join in all the fun and experiences that were being offered to me, buy bikinis and go to the beach parties with everyone instead of pretending I had something important to do and brooding in an empty apartment. I should tell Mr. Rejto I could play as well as Jeff Solow. I knew Hyo was right, but I was becoming more perplexed about how to do it.

Hyo went on without acknowledging my pleading.

"You also need to learn to speak up. Why would you agree to perform the Requiem for Cello trio with Karen and Nina? You are much better than them. You need to play with better people. Try out for the concerto night. Show them what you can do."

He was firm in his admonishment, and I nodded in amazement at how mature and motivated he had become in the few years he had been in America on his own. I wondered if he had been just as driven and just as quick to recognize an opportunity in Korea. I always wondered how it was that he got to meet Berl Senofsky and I wondered how he managed to go to Juilliard instead of the Peabody Institute of Music in Baltimore where Senofsky was teaching. All of a sudden, I realized that Hyo's talents weren't limited to his violin playing.

"Well, easy for you to say." For some reason I didn't want to acknowledge his newly earned respect. But I knew everything he said was right and wished I had his motivation. Back when we were both in Korea, he sent me a letter when I won the Dong-A competition. In his letter he told me that my cello playing was by far the very best. Remembering that, I felt honored.

The following week, during my cello lesson, I asked Mr. Rejto if I could try out for the concerto night. He gasped. "But Sang, what piece would you play?"

"I studied a number of concertos, Mr. Rejto. I could play Lalo, Saint-Saens, or Hayden concerto. And of course I could play the original version of the Boccherini concerto with my eyes closed."

"You mean you can get any of those pieces ready in a month?"

"I think so. I can certainly try." Mr. Rejto pondered doubtfully for a few seconds and said, "All right. Why don't you play the Lalo concerto for me next week. And we will decide then."

The night of the audition, I played about halfway into the first movement when I heard a clap signaling me to stop. It could have meant either the jurors liked it enough they didn't need to listen to the rest of the piece or they didn't like the way I played so there was no need to waste their time. Either way, I was relieved. I had taken the opportunity to show what I could do and for a short time, the stage was mine. I was able to focus with confidence and came alive on the stage. I had submerged myself into only performing and nothing else. I left the auditorium hoping to find a ride home before the results came in.

"I didn't know you could play like that. You were fantastic."

"Oh my god! You were so good, Sang." A few kids surrounded me outside of the auditorium.

Jeff Solow congratulated me for a flawless performance and said that he hoped I would be performing the following year on the concerto night, assuming he would be playing the Tchaikovsky's Rococo Variations this year. He sounded genuine and somewhat surprised at my performance.

"I knew you would be playing. But I wanted to try out for the experience." I said, humbly, hiding a tinge of hope.

I was lying on top of my bedspread, staring at the ceiling when there was a rap on the front door. Before I could say, "Come in," Hyo walked into my room.

"How did you do?" I asked him, still lying down. He also tried out and I knew he would be performing the Viotti concerto Number 22.

"Well, Jeff Solow made it. And you know Peter Rejto and the concert master are gonna play the Brahms' double concerto."

"Oh I figured that. But I mean. How about you? Did you make it?"

"No, they didn't pick me. Linda Quan made it."

"Ugh! But you are so much better than her." I got up and slumped my shoulders, feeling sorry for him. I wanted to hug him, but instead I crunched my mouth in a complaining gesture. *Why do we put ourselves into this unjustly competitive world?*

I felt a dull ache in my heart.

The town of Santa Barbara was never extremely hot, and the sky was always clear and hardly ever rained. We took the bus to the campus in Montecito. The campus was an old mansion with a huge English garden in the front. The garden provided secluded spots outdoors for us to practice in the cool breeze. On the way to the Academy and on the way back the bus dropped us off for breakfast and dinner at El Patio restaurant. The kids who didn't buy the meal plans cooked their own meals in their apartments.

The parking lot in the apartment building was almost always empty, since there were only a few kids with cars; it was used largely for playing basketball. The ping-pong table was in constant use in the recreation room downstairs, and there was always lots of beer drinking. Most nights, I stayed in my room alone doing laundry or tidying up, waiting for the summer to be over.

It was one of those evenings when Bob Strava, a violinist from Arizona, came to ask me out on a date.

"Just you and I?" I asked innocently, and he nodded.

"Yeah, we will go to a movie and have pizza or something."

I said OK, pulling on my sweater sleeves, as if long sleeves might cover up my fluttering heart. He stood tall and straight in his neatly pressed slacks and shirt. He always looked so prim and proper, showing no emotion. I wondered if he ever got drunk.

Pizza must be date-night food, I figured. I went out with an American boy once in Valparaiso. His name was Jack. He took me to a movie called "Collector." In the show, Samantha Eggar was kidnapped by a psychopathic collector and was kept in a cellar in an old abandoned house.

"Pretty creepy, huh?" he commented on the movie. Then he took me for pizza. He called it a pizza pie. I remembered the grease dripping down on his chubby fingers and how I wished I hadn't gone out with him.

All week, my excitement grew. Saturday night seemed to take forever to come. Lori was going out on the same Saturday night with a trumpet player name Mark. She wore a white cotton dress. Against Lori's advice to wear a blue polka dot cotton summer dress, I wore an off-white sleeveless silk blouse and a tight pink skirt.

"Oh, you look lovely." Bob smoothed his slicked hair.

"What is your last name?" I asked when my heart finally settled in his borrowed Chevy.

"It's Strava. A Czech name." I didn't know what that meant, but didn't want to seem inquisitive so I said, "I see."

In the dark theater, Bob reached for my hand and I automatically squeezed his hand back. I couldn't explain this small exchange of emotions in words. But somehow it was comforting. I didn't know what I was feeling, but I knew I wasn't offended. When he brought me home, we sat on the couch and I offered him some grapes. In our brightly lit living room, he looked less attractive and less polished. He wrapped grape seeds in the napkin and wiped his mouth after each grape.

"So what do you think of the Academy in general?" I broke the silence.

"Oh, it's like an old shoe to me. A bunch of us came from ASU for the second summer. The kids here are pretty immature. But I just do my own thing." He said it like saying it was a nice day today. Nothing about Senofsky, nothing about the music we played, not even the beach parties that went on until the sky was painted orange, yellow, and red. The sunset over the ocean was enchanting in Santa Barbara.

I wondered if he did anything spontaneously. Are all American guys so emotionless? Where are all the Warren Beattys and Paul Newmans?

And the entrancing Gregory Pecks! No wonder Hyo was so popular among girls here.

"What are you thinking about?" Bob put his hand on my shoulder and I wondered if he had rehearsed this move. This was far from what I had imagined for myself on a date with a charismatic young American man.

When Bob left, I tiptoed into my room so as not to wake Lori up. After changing into my nightgown in the dark, I slid into bed quietly and realized my pillow was missing. Then I heard groaning in Lori's bed and saw the silhouettes of two bodies moving fast and rhythmically.

I instinctively ran out of the room and out to the parking lot. I knew I needed to get away as far as I could. I hugged my chest and sobbed. I had witnessed the unforgivable act of sin. In a confusing way I felt worse and guiltier than getting caught in the act myself. I knew kids did it. But they did it discreetly. Not on my pillow. Not in the room we shared together. I ran out of the parking lot onto the street and realized I was in my nightgown, barefoot.

"Kathy, Kathy, let me in." I went upstairs to Kathy Briscoe's, noticing the bright lights in her apartment. She came from ASU and was sharing her two-bedroom apartment with three other girls. Kathy and I had become close friends and she showed me how to bake cookies, and after lunch at the Academy, we often walked over to Baskin Robbins and she always got two scoops.

"I can't stay in my room tonight." I looked at the four girls playing scrabble, still hugging my chest.

"What's wrong, Sang? Did Lori ask you to stay out tonight? Poor Sang." All four of them looked at each other, squinting their eyes. They all knew exactly what was happening.

"No, no, she didn't. Perhaps she should have. Can I just watch you play Scrabble for a while?"

"You go right ahead and stay here until you feel comfortable going back into your room. You may stay here all night if you want. But let me tell you. That stuff goes on here. Lynn is another funny one, you know?"

"Funny one?"

"You know? I mean promiscuous. She stays in Jeff's room next door--you know the singer?--all night and in the morning she comes to our back patio so she could go out of our front door in case someone sees her coming out of Jeff's apartment." Kathy shook her head.

"You are absolutely kidding me. Isn't she ashamed?"

"Well, Sang, you go tell Lori that you need to go to bed. Don't let her take advantage of you. So disconcerting!" Kathy's roommate chimed in.

Their apathetic attitude was just as shocking to me. I wanted to write a letter to my friends in Korea and tell them how incredibly animal-like American kids were when it came to sex. *This stuff goes on, just forget it and move on*, they said. But I knew that I myself was being desensitized by the shocking experience that had happened only half an hour earlier. I wondered if I would just kick them out next time, telling them never to contaminate my pillow.

"So you wouldn't let Bob kiss you, huh?" Hyo snickered on the bus in Korean on Monday morning.

"What? Who? How? What else did he tell you?"

"Just that. Just that you wouldn't even let him kiss you. He said 'even.'"

"I don't want to talk about it. It was the first date."

"But just a kiss? You gotta get off that. Man, that holier-than-nun business."

"I never said that. But I don't understand some of these American girls. Don't they want to protect themselves?"

"Protect what from what?" Hyo shook his head and said, "Forget it. You are way off." He disappeared into the group of girls who were surrounding him as he got off the bus. I watched him kissing and hugging every one of them. He was in the middle of a new environment, in a new world with new customs and ethics. I watched them walking farther and farther away, laughing and giggling. I watched them becoming smaller and smaller, fully aware I wasn't one of them.

Even though she was with Mark every chance she had, Lori still waited for Hyo to ask her out.

"He told me we will go see a movie one night," Lori grumbled.

"I think he is going out with Gay right now. And you are going out with Mark."

"So? It's not like either one of us is engaged or anything. Far from it." Lori leaned back against the wall on her bed.

"I am bored. I miss Mark. I wonder where he is. What are you doing tonight anyway?"

"I better get ready. I am cooking tonight with Hyo at the Rejto's. The Senofskys and the Rejtos wanted to have Korean food and Hyo volunteered me."

Mr. Senofsky's concern for Hyo was noticeably obvious. In the buffet line at lunch, he glanced at Hyo's tray to see what he was eating. He knew that having to eat American food all the time was a problem for Hyo. On Monday, he asked Hyo what he did and what he ate over the weekend. This might have prompted the dinner party that Hyo and I were preparing.

I had never cooked a whole meal for anyone. But I instinctively knew how to make the marinade for the typical Korean *bul-ko-ki* and *kal-bi*. I did, however, call Sang-Hie in Gary, Indiana to learn how to make *chop-chai*.

As I was spreading out all the ingredients for the beef marinade and the vegetables for *chop-chai*, I realized a good part of the preparation should have been done at home in my own apartment. I started getting nervous. I was about to feed two families--nine people.

"You mean you didn't even clean the vegetables?" Hyo asked.

"We will be all right. Would you just find me a pot to fry the shrimp?"

When we looked all over the cupboard, I did find a heavy pot. It was deep enough to keep the splashing oil in.

"Can I use this, Mr. Rejto?" I asked. Mr. Rejto said, "Of course. By all means. You can use anything you find in this kitchen."

The Rejtos rented a large one-story house for the summer in Montecito every year. Pretty soon their country-style kitchen was filled with the smell of soy sauce and garlic and pots were bubbling and steaming.

Mr. Rejto came into the kitchen. "How are you both doing? Is everything going OK?" Just then suddenly he mumbled in panicked voice, "What. What is that? Fire! Fire!"

Only then did Hyo and I notice the pot I had oil in over the stove was filled with orange flame.

"Oh, my god. How did that happen?" I quickly turned off the stove and backed away shaking. "What kind of oil is this? How does this happen?" Shocked and scared I covered my mouth.

"Hyo. What do we do?"

For a few seconds, we all stood there watching the flame grow taller and taller. By then, the doorway to the kitchen was jammed with frightened dinner guests. Peter pushed through the guests and walked over and grabbed the handle of the pot. He dropped the pot full of flames on the floor. The flames spread wildly as soon as it hit the floor. Everyone stepped back, shaking in terror.

I huddled behind Hyo.

Peter grabbed a rag that hung on the kitchen chair and started beating the flame. It all happened like a fast-forwarded movie.

I thought that the whole house was going to burn to the ground. Peter slapped the floor, beating the flames like a madman.

Eventually, he beat them all out. He straightened up, wiping his brow. We all breathed again.

"Sorry about this. Whoever this belongs to." Peter looked at the bluish-gray rag, which now appeared to have once been a sport coat.

"Oh, that's mine." Hyo examined the coat. It was barely recognizable, burned and caked with black stuff.

"I am so sorry, Hyo. Thank you so much, Peter." I was still shaking, and my voice was not even audible.

"Dear, did you know how to use the pressure cooker?" Mrs. Rejto put her hand on my shoulder.

"No. I don't even know what that is." I sobbed, looking at the oddly shaped burnt holes on the linoleum floor. I knew nothing I could do or say would remotely vindicate what just happened. And there was still the matter of the damaged floor of their rented home, and Hyo's torn coat--his favorite coat, he said.

For the following few days, I didn't speak much. My head was hung low. Every day was a struggle. I wanted the summer to end.

"You know, Sang-Eun. It was an accident. Don't you realize that? You can't be walking around like a cow heading for the slaughterhouse. How long are you gonna do this?" Hyo was disgusted with me.

"I am really disappointed in you. When I watched you on the stage at Dong-A competition, I thought you were a gutsy little person. You are not at all. Well, I tell you what. I have had it." He walked away.

My dream summer had turned out to be a nightmare. Was this the destination the beautiful shorelines of the Pacific Ocean brought me to?

My three daughters at Terry's wedding in 1998.
From left, Terry, Sang-Eun, Michelle, Kimmy.

My three sisters and I with our Mother in 1991
From left, Sang-Eun, Mom, Sang-Hie, Sang-Won, Sang-Soon.

Burial ground on the day of father's funeral
Sang-Eun, with cousins, in funeral garb and white rubber shoes.

Politicians of South Korea in late 1940s
My father is sitting on the right of the first president of Korea,
Seung-Man Rhee, middle front row.

In Pu-San, Sang-Eun (front) with Cho-Sun (back) and her brothers
Sang-Eun is wearing rubber shoes.

Sang-Eun, left (age 7 in Pu-San) and Sang-Won.

Valparaiso, reception after the concert with University-Civic Orchestra.
From left, Sang-Eun, Dr. Hoelty-Nickel, Mrs. Hoelty-Nickel, Sang-Hie, Kil-Sup.

Frances and Bob Rogers in 1967

35

For the six months I lived with the Rogers, Frances did her best to groom me to be her ideal foreign student. Every day, she drilled me in simple conversational English until it came out of my mouth as second nature. She taught me not to answer bluntly "yes" or "no" but to say, "Yes, I did," or "No, I have not." She had me write compositions and read books like *Fifth Chinese Daughter* and a personal memoir by Gregor Piatigorsky and give her an oral reports on them.

She also taught me the proper way of setting the dinner table. She was training me to be, in her mind, the model Korean-American college girl. Frances also showed me how to iron a pleated skirt using a two-by-four – even though it only took me a few seconds, using no apparatus. Sometimes I wondered where Frances thought I came from – either deep in the boondocks of Korea or from outer space.

Still, I was immensely grateful, particularly because my English was improving exponentially. "I have the best one from all of Korea," she said to Mr. Rejto and also to Mrs. Wilson. For someone who never had her own child, I satisfied her innate needs to be a female guardian. However, after spending two months in Santa Barbara away from the Rogers, I had forgotten what it was like to live in her shadow. Frances now seemed more preposterous than ever.

For weeks, the topic of conversation at the Rogers' dinner table concentrated on my living arrangement in the fall at USC. All of my Ewha credits were transferred and I was accepted as a music performance major in junior standing.

"She will meet more friends and will get more involved in college life if she lives in a dorm," Frances said.

"On the other hand, it will be less costly if we just buy her a car and let her commute," Bob Rogers refuted.

"Bob, dear, I will be awfully nervous to allow her to drive all the way downtown every day right after she gets her license."

It never occurred to either one of them to ask me what I might want. Owning a car sounded exciting, but driving the freeways sounded frightening. Living in a dorm with a strange roommate with whom I couldn't communicate might be stressful, but it sounded heavenly not to have to deal with Bob and Frances on a daily basis.

After much discussion, they decided I should live in a dorm. Meanwhile, I had decided I would gratefully accept whatever life was laid out for me. I remembered what my father had said to my mom when we received the refugee relief packages in Pu-San: "When you need help, accept it graciously. And when it is your turn to help others, help generously."

Frances was helping me pack when Bob came into my room holding a glass of wine after work. This was a rare occasion.

"I've got news for you two, Frances and Song-Uun. I have accepted the offer."

Frances looked up with a smirk, like a child on Christmas morning who was anticipating a gift she had spied in the closet a few times already.

"These guys seem wonderful to work with. I would be very happy to move. And Song-Uun, Frances loves New England. Here's her chance to go back, and it will give you a chance to visit us. New England is a wonderful place to live. We will have your room ready for you whenever you want to visit us."

Bob had been offered a job at Raytheon in Concord, Massachusetts and he had met with some of his future colleagues that day and accepted the new job. It was a great opportunity because Bob had been working at the Aerospace in El Segundo and engineers were being laid off there.

"Song-Uun, you mustn't worry," Frances said. "You can come visit us in the summer, and I am sure Edith would love to have you for Thanksgiving or during Easter vacation." Edith had recently found a job at UCLA as a graduate academic counselor and then settled in her own apartment in Brentwood.

Even though I had wanted to get out of their shadow and be free from feeling indebted, I felt a tiny bit dejected. But later, I couldn't help but feel relieved.

On the morning I was to move to Birnkrant Hall at USC, Frances started drumming her fingernails against the breakfast table and drank an extra cup of coffee while everyone else finished their breakfast. Then she started her admonishments.

"Now, listen to me carefully, Song-Uun, you will have one room-mate. In this country, especially at a private university, there are lots of spoiled and careless girls. They might mistake your belongings as theirs and before you know it they will be using your hairdryer or they might even want to borrow your blouse or something. And then you may never see it again. You probably should keep your door shut at all times."

Before she finished her sentence, Bob chimed in: "Somebody might spot your alarm clock and they might quickly lift it up. Who knows?"

"Oh for heaven's sake, Bob. You can't be that suspicious of people. I don't ever remember you being that apprehensive when you started college at Cornell." Edith, who came to help me pack, rolled her eyes.

As usual, Frances settled the issue with the last word: "Well, it doesn't hurt to be careful. I am trying to get Song-Uun ready for the worst case. I sure hope she will have a decent roommate."

Frances taught me English well enough that I was able to pass three parts out of the four initial English tests that were required of all foreign students. I passed reading, comprehension, and conversational English, but failed English composition. I was allowed to take the full load of

12 units of any class I wanted, but had to take English composition. Based on these test scores, most of the Korean students were told to take nothing but English as a Second Language for the first year. I was the only one to take a full load of university-sanctioned classes that would apply toward my bachelor's degree.

My first few weeks at USC were hectic with registration, orientation, and other settling-in activities. The representatives from the various Trojan clubs called or paid a visit to each of the new foreign students. The president of the Korean Trojan club, Ty Noh called me and invited me to the picnic to welcome new students.

"The food is catered by Ko-Ryu-Jung, the Korean restaurant in Los Angeles. If nothing else, you should come for *kal-bi* and *kimchee*," he said.

"Did you call Yi-Soon? I will only come if she does," I replied.

Yi-Soon was one of the four new, single female Korean students that fall of 1966. She was a doctoral degree candidate in biochemistry. She had been in the same class with my sister, Sang-Won at Kyung-Ki girls' high school. She moved into Birnkrant Hall on the same day as me. When the housemother introduced us to each other, her bashful smile and shiny black hair drew me to her right away. We began to spend time speaking in Korean and eating meals in the cafeteria together. We talked about using hairspray, deodorant, and Tampax, which were still new to us, and we soon shared every secretive detail of our personal lives.

"What do you think of the single guys here?" I whispered to Yi-Soon standing in the barbeque line at the picnic.

"What do you think?" she asked. "Aren't they all a little dorky?"

"Exactly," I whispered into her ear without moving my lips.

"I know, I know," she whispered. "Well, it's a good thing. We are here to study."

At the beginning of the picnic, Ty Noh, the president of the club, gave an impressive speech in his heavy accent. He welcomed the new students with an added thanks to Dr. Kaplan. Ty was dressed impeccably, down to his shoes and socks. He stood out like a fresh green leaf in a parched pasture.

Ty offered to give me a ride from the picnic back to the dorm in his '59 Chevy. Yi-Soon quickly found a ride with someone else, sensing Ty wanted to be alone with me.

On the way back, Ty Noh asked, "Is this how you play the cello?" gesturing as if he was playing a guitar.

"No, you are playing a guitar. You don't know anything about classical music, do you?"

"Not much. Good major for girls, though," he grinned and continued. "When you made that comment about Koreans at the picnic table, honestly, you killed them. It was such a profound statement."

"What did I say?"

"You know, that bit about Koreans are by and large hardworking, sincere people. You said that you could count on Koreans — that they will always do what they say they would."

"Well, it is true. Don't you think so?"

"Definitely, I do. I just had never seen anyone, especially a girl, who would speak up so clearly in front of an American professor. I thought Dr. Kaplan was really impressed. And your English was perfect."

"He didn't eat any *kimchee*, did he?"

"No. At least he came. He almost didn't. He said that he promised his wife that he would paint their utility room."

"Oh, yeah, that's why he had to leave right after lunch."

"You see, Korean students work and study so hard with their limited language skills and with the lack of social acceptance, most of them have developed poor images of themselves. You know, like an inferiority complex. But I don't see that trace in you." Ty grinned again. "It was the very reason I decided to get ahead academically. I studied until I got straight A's and got a scholarship, which gave me a whole lot of confidence."

"So what are you saying? That you feel superior to them?"

"I know I am." This time he laughed out loud. I wasn't sure if he was being arrogant or embarrassed for the way he was so pleased with himself. Perhaps a little bit of both.

"I have a good part-time job as an accountant and am ready to graduate. I feel good and know that I could compete with any of the American kids."

"So you have been supporting yourself all along? That's pretty admirable."

"Actually no. My *nu-na* supported me for the first couple of years. I am forever indebted to her."

"Your older sister supported you? Wow! She sent you to this expensive private school? Is she married to a Mr. mega-bucks or something?"

"No, she *is* the mega-bucks. She has her own business and does very well."

"Wow. That's pretty nice. I have nice older sisters too, three of them. But none of them are that wealthy. Does your sister do business in Korea? What's her name?"

"Her name is Nora Noh. She is in the fashion industry."

"Wait! What? Your sister is not *the* Nora Noh? No way."

"She is."

"You've gotta be kidding me. Of course I know her. I mean I never met her but a lot of my friends went to her to get their concert dresses made. Everyone knows her name, even the ones who don't know the name of the president. She really is your sister, huh?"

"Yep."

"Tell me. Why is her name Nora Noh? Why doesn't she have a Korean name? I always wondered where she came from."

"It is a long story. She was married to an army officer during the Japanese occupation by an arranged marriage right out of high school. Believe it or not, my family is very conservative. You wouldn't think that, would you? Her smoking in public and all. My mother thought marrying an officer would guarantee her a good life." He shook his head.

"Anyway, her marriage failed and she packed her bag and came to America to pursue her dream of being a fashion designer. She knew she wasn't born to be an ordinary housewife. You know, she was born in the year of dragon. She is a dragon, all right. She succeeded as a fashion designer in America and when she came back to Korea, they welcomed her for, what did they say – 'Back, dressed in gold?' When she left Korea, she thought of Nora in some novel she had read and changed her name to Nora."

"Ibsen's *A Doll's House*?"

"I guess. I don't know. I don't read novels," He said, dismissing it.

"Anyway, that's when she started a new life as Nora."

"Wow. Fascinating! A true success story of – what do they say in Korea? – 'a dragon from a small stream?' Imagine that. I remember wanting to wear her dress so badly, but my mom wouldn't take me to her salon."

"Well, you may have a chance yet. She is coming in the spring."

"You mean I will get to meet her?"

All of a sudden Ty Noh's status went up a notch in my mind. But I was not about to admit it.

Ty and I started dating and he called me "baby doll" freely in front of our friends and the Ehrlichs. The Ehrlichs also called me "baby doll" from the minute I was introduced to them. They loved Ty because he was outgoing but had a polite mannerism. Jerry and Gladys Ehrlich had offered Ty room and board in their posh home on Doheny Drive when they had first met him two years earlier, hoping he would be a good influence on their son, Michael, who was in high school.

"I am telling you, ever since Ty moved in with us, I so look forward to our dinnertime every night. He has some stories to tell us about his father establishing the Korean broadcasting system in Korea. And the stories about Nora. My, how he makes it sound so interesting," Gladys Ehrlich said to me. "And he is always so happy."

Gladys might have thought Ty was always happy, but I knew him otherwise. We dated steadily, but we fought practically every weekend. As we dated, Ty became more possessive of me.

"I will shoot you if you ever happen to go out with anyone else," he threatened half jokingly. He also told me that I irritated him, and that I brought out the worst in him. "I was real temperamental in Korea, but ever since I came to this country, I've changed. Now you are bringing it out again."

Part of me felt outraged, but a part of me also felt challenged to maintain a secure relationship with him. I wanted to make it right. Soon, I began to think it was my fault that we were fighting. His pompous attitude had an eccentric power over me and I couldn't get away from it.

I didn't have a sense of belonging in this country—not even a vague one. And being with Ty made me feel safe. In part, it was the Koreanness we had in common, and also knowing that we both came from an elite social class. So, even though I didn't feel at peace in our relationship or with myself, I continued dating him.

36

My second year at USC, I moved to EVK, a three-story dorm linked by the cafeteria to Birnkrant. Rooms in EVK were a little cozier than Birnkrant's. Rooms were also a little larger and each had its own sink. In the evenings, a few of us often went to the International House of Pancakes across the street to have silver dollar pancakes or just to drink Coke.

As a senior, my college life seemed sufficiently enjoyable. I had a boyfriend who came to pick me up every weekend. Even though I was perplexed with the intricacies of football rules, I was a part of the crowd that loved watching O.J. Simpson run for our beloved Trojans. Also, since I started dating Ty and met Nora Noh, I was always stunningly dressed. Ty was approaching 30 and finding a prospect for marriage gave his family a reason to celebrate. Ty's mom gave birth to him after ten long years of trying to have a son. Among the ten siblings in the family, they considered Ty and Nora as the two who possessed all the talents and brains. Once Nora approved of me, they were anxious to please me and did what they knew how to do best. They sent me the most expensive dresses, suits, and everything imaginable for a college girl's wardrobe. Marrying Ty was becoming a given. It was just a matter of me graduating. In the meantime, it only seemed natural to become physically intimate with him.

At the same time, my projected life as a music student took a huge turn. I spent more time in the library studying than practicing cello. I was buried in piles of books for history term papers, exams, and quizzes. The complexity of *Syllogism in Logic* took a long time to understand, and the pressure of planning a senior recital kept me awake at night. The responsibility I felt to the Rogers and to my mom spurred me to finish my degree as soon as possible.

Oftentimes, I studied all evening at the library and then studied more in the cafeteria so as not to wake up my roommate. Studying so much started to agitate my eyes again. At times they not only became red, they were also painful. I felt like my eyeballs were being pulled. The only relief was eye drops and a good night's rest.

At the same time, my dream of being a concert cellist was becoming farther and farther from a reality. Ty's insensitivity to my life and dream was disappointing, but being with him was still part of my comfort zone. I was no longer homesick, and I knew my student visa status would be switched to permanent resident as his wife.

Then, one day, I received a furious letter from Frances, in response to the bill she had received from my gynecologist. The bill itemized the exam and the birth control pills I was taking.

> *"…And I am stunned to discover that the responsibility lies on me in leading you to face a life that is so different from what you have left behind. It is so very difficult to think Bob and I contributed to something that would cause your mom's heart to overpower with disappointment and fill the Pacific Ocean with her tears…"*

She went on by saying that she and Bob no longer would support me financially or otherwise. I was irate, not at the doctor for making the mistake of sending them the bill, but at the fact that Frances would respond so hysterically.

Dear Aunt Frances and Uncle Bob,

I realize when you help a foreign student, particularly as generously as you have been for me, you should be totally and completely happy with the person you are helping. I understand your decision to terminate your financial contribution to me.

However, I will always be grateful for what you have done and you will always be an uncle and an aunt to me.

With love always,
Sang-Eun

I started actively applying as a freshman counselor, which would enable me to receive free room and board. I also decided to take out a low interest college loan for another year in college and tried to take as many classes as possible, so I could finish more quickly. Getting a "C" in Music History didn't bother me, just so long as I graduated. Going to concerts at the Music Center and writing reviews was required for a music performance major, but I stopped going to all concerts and copied my then-roommate Molly Judson's critiques.

I needed to spend time reading "*Critical Thinking*" for logic, looking up practically every other word in the book. In the time I would have spent to go to a concert, I could have skimmed through a chapter. I even skipped orchestral rehearsals as I already had enough credits for orchestra. My Ewha University credits were transferable.

One Friday evening, as I walked into the dorm after studying at the library, Edith stood up from a vinyl armchair in the lounge and greeted me.

"I figured if I waited long enough, you would show up sooner or later." She hugged me.

"Have you waited long? Why didn't you call me first?"

"Thought I would surprise you?"

"You surprised me all right. I am just glad that I didn't go out tonight."

"Song-Uun, would you come home with me and spend a night tonight?"

"You must have gotten a letter from Frances. It's OK. I am not offended at all. My feelings about them haven't changed. I mean, I am disappointed she reacted in such a way but she told me what she needed to say to me and I accept her decision," I stated firmly, "I would love to come home with you tonight."

On the way, we stopped to have dinner. Over an open sandwich at a Danish café, Edith told me how proud she was of me.

"Aunt Edith, here is the problem. I used to sneak out to drink and smoke in Korea. I am not the angel Bob and Frances think I am. They need to open their eyes and realize I am just a normal college girl." I shook my head. "And don't you think I am from the Garden of Eden either."

"Song-Uun, I want to tell you, Aunt Frances has been sick about the letter she sent you. She got extremely emotional and wrote such a harsh letter to you. She would do anything to take it back if she could."

"Did she say that?" I put my fork down and looked up.

"In fact, she sent me a check for your next semester's tuition," she said.

When we reached her apartment, Edith sat down in the living room and drew a picture of a man's sex organs on a piece of paper. She said that as long as I was sexually active, I should enjoy it fully. She decided that in order to enjoy it, I needed to understand the anatomy of men.

"And you must not be afraid to move when you have sex," she said.

"I am really not comfortable talking about this." I waved my clammy palm.

At the end of the spring semester that same year, I received a letter from Mom informing me that she would be representing Korea at the

International Home Economists' convention in Tel Aviv, Israel. Her extensive itinerary included an after-convention tour of America, with a final stop in Los Angeles. This would be her first visit to America and my first time seeing her in three long years. My heart pounded with excitement. I couldn't wait until she got to the West Coast.

Anticipating my mom's visit to Los Angeles prompted Ty to talk openly about our engagement. Gladys Ehrlich offered to host an engagement/welcoming party for my mom. Gladys, being a socialite, knew how to give elegant parties, and her huge walk-in closet displayed a range of dresses and matching shoes for various social occasions.

Engagements have always been an important prenuptial event for Koreans, one that involves a ceremonial banquet of both families and often an exchange of gifts by immediate family members. Korean protocol was that the banquet be given by the bride's family, as it was understood that the groom's family was largely responsible for the wedding banquet. Traditionally, the engagement ring is a family ring, purchased by the groom's parents. But Ty wanted to pick and buy a ring for me and pay for the banquet himself. There was much to plan in the few days before Mom got to Los Angeles. Gladys Ehrlich's jeweler, Schoenfield, brought an assortment of engagement rings to her house and she and Ty picked a ring for me. She also called their favorite restaurant, Scam, to reserve the small banquet room.

Ever since the Rogers moved away, I stayed away from my brother as much as I could, although when I had an occasion to see him, we were civil to each other. My brother discouraged Ty from coming to the airport to greet Mom. "Tell him he doesn't need to bother going to the airport. He will have plenty of chances to meet her," he said.

My brother arranged it with his landlady so Mom could stay at his boarding house in a vacant room. For the week Mom stayed in Los Angeles, he picked me up from school and brought me to his house so we could all be together. I slept in the same room with Mom across the hall from him.

The first night, after we were in bed, Mom asked, "What is going on with you two? Why were you bickering all along?"

"Nothing. It's just that he hasn't changed. He is just as much of a brat as he was in Korea, Mom. I never wrote to you about the time he went crazy again. He is spoiled and irresponsible, Mom."

"You need not say things to trigger his temper. It would only hurt you."

"I just won't see him. Once you leave I won't see him anymore."

"Why can't the two who are in the same town get along?" Mom sighed and continued. "What about Ty? Have they met?"

"They have."

"Is your brother OK with him?"

"Is he OK with anyone? But I don't care. He isn't the one dating him."

"You have become so insolent. What happened to you?"

"Nothing happened to me. I have grown up and am beginning to understand life."

"So, what do you understand about life?"

"It's just that performing on the stage isn't the only thing that matters in life."

"Well then, what does matter to you?"

"I don't know, Mom. I am just confused. I think going to a university might have been the best thing I did, although it was the Rogers who talked me into coming here. I wanted to go to a music school back East and only concentrate on playing the cello."

"So are you ready to make a lifetime commitment?"

"I think so. What do you think? Do you think it's the right thing? And he is the right man?"

"I don't know. I just hope you will continue your music and Dai-Heung will be supportive." Mom said, using Ty's Korean name. Her words finally snagged my conscious brain. It was like scratching a barely healed wound. I always knew there was a huge difference between tolerating and supporting.

"He told me he wouldn't object to anything I want to do."

"That's what men say when they haven't come across the bridge."

"I don't know, Mom. I just think that devoting your whole life to performing and traveling would eventually make a person feel void. There's gotta be more to life than that." Only years later would I admit that I was justifying an easy way out.

"What about you and your sister, Sang-Hie? What happened to you two?"

"What did she say to you, Mom?" I knew mom had seen her before she came to California.

"She said that Ty might not be the perfect person for you. She said that she tried to tell you and you got impudent with her."

"She doesn't even know Ty. I mean, she knows him from when she was attending UCLA. She said that he was dating a girl, an Ewha graduate and I don't know, Mom. She immediately said, 'Oh, that infamous Ty Noh.' Then she told the Rogers all about how she hoped I wasn't making a hasty decision."

"She was just concerned for you."

"True, she was. But there is more to it. She can't accept the fact that I have grown up and am capable of making my own decisions. It may not be what she wants for me but she is negative about anything I say or do."

"So you are not speaking to her? She told me that's what you said to her in your letter."

"Oh, that's not true. I told her that I would always be grateful for all the things she did for me but I need to separate being grateful and being independent. I am just not going to do everything directed by her anymore. She can be more suffocating than Frances Rogers." I wiped my tears and continued. "I said to her I was no longer a ten-year-old. When I was ten, she was sixteen, a big sister. But now I am a twenty-three-year-old grown woman. I told her that at our age, we should be more like best friends than having big-sister, little-sister relationship."

"Sounds fair."

"That's when she told me, if I wasn't going to treat her like a big sister, she didn't particularly want to have a relationship with me. She didn't care to be my friend, she said."

Mom waited a while and said wistfully, "You have grown in the three years I haven't seen you." Then she pulled a pale pink Korean dress out of her suitcase. "This is for you to wear for your engagement party. You are supposed to wear pink at the engagement."

"Oh, Mom. It's beautiful. Thank you so much." I dried my tears and held the dress up to look in the mirror.

37

Ty decided we should get married on the 15th of December, his birthday. By then, my finals would be over and the only thing I would have left to do in order to graduate was my senior recital, which was scheduled for the week after our wedding.

"I would like to be married at a church. At any rate, that's what you do in America," I said.

"OK, I guess it will be all right, although I have Japanese friends who got married at a Buddhist temple here in Los Angeles. They were both students at 'SC," Ty said.

"So I gather you don't go to church at all," I said.

"No. My family is Buddhist except for my mom. She turned against Buddha ever since her accident. She lost her leg in a streetcar accident on the way to the temple. She figured if her god wouldn't take care of a pregnant woman on her way to worship him, she didn't want to have anything to do with him any more." He shrugged again.

"She was pregnant and lost her leg?" I widened my eyes.

"Yup. She was pregnant with me. She lost it all the way up to her thigh. She has an artificial leg now."

"Oh, I am so sorry. How awful is that?"

"Yeah, it is," Ty said. "She always had a special attachment to me. You know, I have five older sisters. The oldest was a girl, then my older brother was born, and then my mom had four more daughters. My parents had just about given up on having another son. Then I came along after ten years. My mother thought it was a miracle that she and I both survived the streetcar accident. So when I turned out to be a hoodlum in Korea, she cried every night." Ty smiled. "I am going to make sure she will be at my wedding. I want her to be proud of me for once."

"That will be nice. What did you do that's so horrible that you made her cry?"

"I did things like skipping school, taking the tuition she gave me and went hunting and stuff. I would leave a note telling her not to worry. I'd be back in a few days."

I rolled my eyes and shook my head. "You went to Seoul High School, though. It's a good school."

"Yeah, well, I did. But I never studied."

"Well, I am excited to meet her. I bet she is very sweet."

"I know you will like her. Everyone likes her. And I am sure she will bring your wedding dress," he said.

"You are kidding. She really would? Wow! Imagine that. Wearing a Nora Noh wedding gown."

According to Ty, no one knew exactly how old his mother was because she would change her birth date from document to document. But he was pretty sure that she had been born in the last year or two of the 19th century.

The following week, we visited the Congregational Church of Christ in Sherman Oaks to meet with the minister. We decided to be married on the 14th of December because the 15th was a Sunday, and the church did not perform wedding ceremonies on Sundays.

Ty's younger brother, Dai-Young accompanied their mother on her first trip to America. She got off the plane, slightly hobbling while hugging a large box. Once she was on a flat surface, she walked gracefully in a long skirt, taking small steps, and her limp was hardly noticeable. Her oval-shaped face was smooth and wrinkle-free.

"I told her to only mind the box. It's the wedding dress," Dai-Young said coyly, carrying three large carry-ons, one on each hand and another hanging on his shoulder.

When we got to Ty's apartment she pulled out the most beautiful trousseau for me. There were half a dozen dresses, in bouclé with leather collars, a high-neck green and navy dress in light gabardine, and more. There was a pink suit, light green suit, gray pants suit, all with matching blouses, and some hostess pants-and-top coordinates, as well as a few cocktail dresses. Then she stood up holding a long red dress. The rich dark red top of the sleeveless dress had a few elegant, gold-embroidered flowers, which gradually spread out to the bottom of the full skirt.

"This is for you to wear at your recital. Try it on. She worked hard to make sure it would fit perfectly and yet would be comfortable to play the cello in," Ty's mother said.

When I sat in it, holding the cello, I looked like I was sitting in a flower garden.

Before I could fully shake myself from the uncontrollable trance the new clothes had spun over me, she handed me a large box full of jewels. The jewels literally flowed out of the box: a pearl pin with matching earrings, and platinum rings with all kinds of colored gemstones, each with a matching brooch. There were still more necklaces with matching earrings. They were all gifts to me from each member of his family. And in a separate small box was a present from Ty's mother, a delicate watch surrounded by diamonds with three larger diamonds inlaid on the top and bottom of the face. "Oh my gosh, are these all for me?" I thanked my *shi-umoni* (mother-in-law).

"Well, we had to do it. What with you marrying into Nora Noh's family and all. You know, people talk. They always want to know what was in the dowry chest," she muttered. "The watch is in place of the family ring, because Dai-Heung bought your engagement ring himself. Madame Noh sends her regrets for not being able to come. You know, Dai-Heung is her favorite brother."

"Madame Noh?" I looked at Ty.

"I know. She calls her Madame Noh. Mother says Nora has become too important to be called Myung-Ja. It would be disrespectful to her, she says. It's my mother's Japanese upbringing."

"She grew up in Japan?" I asked in English.

"Yea, she was sent to Japan when she was seven years old," Ty explained. "In those days, it was an honor to be sent to Japan. Only the privileged ones got to go to Japan."

"I learned to speak Korean but I still can't write well at all," she said.

My wedding was big and festive. Four of my friends from school played in a string quartet and another friend, a voice major, sang. I had five bridesmaids, all friends from school. Ty maintained that I should have at least one Korean girl in the wedding and invited Booja, his relative, to be my maid of honor. I felt privileged to have Ty's mom and his brother at our wedding. Most of the Korean students who got married in America did not have the luxury of being able to invite their parents. Traveling to America was still a monumental accomplishment for any Korean.

During her month long stay, Ty's mom told us that according to a fortune teller, Ty and I were not a match because I was born in the year of the rooster and Ty was born in the year of the rabbit.

"But because you are living in America, which is the huge diversion in location and because of your birth month, your charts read as compatible," she added. "Also because things are different nowadays. What with women being highly educated and taking part in business world and everything," she added dismissively, "I don't believe any of it anyway. It's Madame Nora Noh who is into all that."

Nora, who claimed to have learned the techniques of reading the charts, told her that Ty and I were a great match even though I would be pecking him with every little detail of our lives and that Ty would be jumpy and hoppy like a rabbit on an impulse. He would always be quick with his sharp criticizing nibbles and I would always be controlling with my loud cock-a-doodle-doos.

Then Ty's mother half-jokingly told us that we were still a match made in heaven and that I was just about the only person who could handle Ty because I was so smart and clever to deal with such a spoiled son.

She openly admitted to spoiling him. They were so happy to have a son after ten long years that they made sure his rice bowl always had pure white rice. When dinner was not to his liking, he flipped the dinner table upside down. "When his school uniform was not ironed crisply, he refused to go to school, yelling, 'Do you really think I should wear this rag to school?'" she told me, almost proudly. "That's how finicky he always was with food and clothes."

There was a huge vacant feeling in my heart leading up to and through the whole matrimonial affair. I thought it was because my mom wasn't there. Or perhaps it was that I was going through the most significant event of my life in a foreign land. I thought these were all blameworthy reasons. After all, I was outfitted with the most luxurious trousseau and dowry, and a Nora Noh wedding dress.

It never occurred to me that I might be marrying the wrong person.

38

Phyllis Hoffman, our neighbor, was fond of Asian girls, specifically me. A few days after Ty's mom left, Phyllis invited me to her apartment for a cup of coffee. Their apartment was spacious with three large bedrooms. A fitted clear plastic sheet covered the back and arms of her beige couch. I got the distinct impression that the couch was only for show, because she sat me at the kitchen table and asked me to get comfortable. The white Formica table was set with two plastic placemats with large daisy prints and two floating camellias in a crystal bowl. Her husband Nat, who was in garment sales, usually left early in the morning and came home late in the evening. Since he took their only car to work every day, this gave Phyllis all day to keep house and fiddle with her bonsai plants. Phyllis also loved Asian décor. She showed me their six-sided Chinese screen with inlaid mother-of-pearl and asked, "You like?"

"I do. I like it. It is absolutely gorgeous!" I answered with a big smile.

"You speak English very well," Phyllis looked at me with a surprised look. "Were you born here?" She looked a little disappointed this time. Perhaps because I had not turned out to be a shy little Asian neighbor girl who would marvel wide-eyed at her Asian collection of arts and bonsai. Not to mention the range of her modern Kitchen-Aid gadgets on her long, white tiled counter.

This was the start of my friendship with this old and wise Jewish woman I came to love. She and Nat had two sons, both married, and as well as a granddaughter named Tammy, short for Tamara, and a grandson named Jason. She told me that she had always thought Asians were smart. She said that the Asians were smart because they discovered soybeans and manipulated them in so many clever ways.

"You know, Sang," she said one day, "My grand son Jason asked me, 'Grandma, if you are going to be stranded on a desert island and you are allowed to have one food item, what would you choose?' You know, Sang, I thought and thought and finally told him that I would pick soybeans because they have all kinds of nutrients you can live on and it would still fill you up, too."

"I'd buy that. What a clever question, though. What did he say he would take?" I asked.

"Oy-vey! He said he couldn't decide between Snickers bars and string cheese." We laughed until tears ran down our cheeks. She poured me another cup of coffee then she clapped her hands as if she had the most brilliant idea.

"What if I bring a list of the toughest and the most unused English words periodically for you to learn?" I didn't know what possessed her to think of such a thing, but Phyllis started flipping through the pages of Webster's dictionary. She thought people would get a kick out of me using words like "osculation" or "recalcitrant."

She loved most of what I cooked even though she could hardly eat any of it. And she apologized for not cooking Jewish food for us; she couldn't eat brisket or corned beef because of her gallstones, but she made us homemade kosher pickles.

One afternoon, she knocked on my door when I was practicing the cello. Looking particularly forlorn, she asked if I could play Kol Nidrei.

"It was my favorite piece. I performed it at least a dozen times in Korea," I said. When I played it by heart, she wiped her eyes and said,

"You know, Sang, you look like an angel playing that. I don't think you know what it means to me to have you play it for me, just for me."

"Oh, thank you, Phyllis. Why is it so moving to you?"

"Do you know what Kol Nidrei is?"

"I thought it was a prayer, isn't it?"

"Yeah, it is an ancient Jewish prayer. It also means a vow. It was to be played on Yom Kippur, the Day of Atonement, the holiest day."

"You mean like repentance for Christians?"

"It makes me think of my past, my present, my life. So much to be thankful for. And so much remorse. You know?" Phyllis kept wiping her eyes.

"Are you OK, Phyllis? Is something wrong?"

"Sang, we will be moving next week, to a two-bedroom apartment. We can't pay the high rent anymore. Nat's business isn't doing so good. The company declared Chapter 11 a while ago. You see, he worked long hours all his life and now at our age we realize we don't have money to live on."

"Oh, Phyllis, I am sorry. What is he gonna do? What are you gonna do? Who am I gonna have coffee with? Is there anything we can do?"

"He will be selling clothes in the swap meet every weekend. We will be like a couple of beggars. I would go to work if I knew how to do anything. You know, when we moved to this building, I said to Nat, 'Nat, I can't live in an apartment. I don't know how. I need a yard.' I was so sad to have to give up my house. But look what God brought me. You made it all worthwhile to live here."

"Oh, Phyllis, where are you moving to? We will still see each other. We are friends. Friends don't give up each other that easy."

"We won't be far. Just up the street on Victory Boulevard. I know I will walk down and see you but it won't be like we can have coffee in our bathrobes, you know?"

Phyllis and I kept up our friendship even after Ty and I moved to another apartment. She would periodically have Nat drive her to our apartment so we could spend a day together. On one of those days, Phyllis asked me why I wasn't starting a family.

"I don't know, Phyllis. I keep thinking I am not ready for a baby yet. I keep thinking I need to do something that's more important."

"Like?"

"Don't know. I need to keep on taking cello lessons and get better at it first."

"Then what?"

"Don't know. I will worry about it when it happens. Whatever it is."

The following week, I made a decision to stop taking birth control pills. I didn't have any specific plans but it seemed right, at the time. More importantly, it seemed right not to have any specific plans.

Then one day, coming home from a dinner party, Ty had to stop the car so I could throw up. And we found out it wasn't food poisoning. It wasn't even carsickness. I was pregnant. When I called Phyllis and told her how bad my morning sickness was, she made me chicken soup and predicted the exact date Terry would be born. She told me that no one dies from morning sickness.

"Just keep drinking the soup," she said.

39

It was more like a celebration cocktail party, but Edith probably would have wanted it that way. In her final letter to Bob she wrote:

Each day is becoming harder and harder to continue living, if you can call it that. I see no hope, nothing to look forward to. It is increasingly more difficult to deal with each person at work; walking into an empty apartment...I see nothing but darkness ahead of me.

She also wrote, *"I would like to leave my record player to Sang-Eun. I know how she likes to listen to her long play records."* She didn't mention anything as far as what kind of memorial service she might want.

It was strange to be in a room full of people Edith had known. I had not met most of them before. It was even more odd that there was no sign of it being a memorial service. No one prayed. No one offered to talk about Edith. No one shared his or her loving memory of Edith. No one cried. No one questioned why she killed herself. No one wanted to recite Psalm 23: *"The Lord is my shepherd, I shall not be in want. He maketh me to lie down in green pastures...."*

Bob and his two brothers, Don and Art, made the arrangements for a small gathering to remember their little sister, Edith and say some final goodbyes. Idella Wilson graciously offered her house. It seemed appropriate since Edith had rented a room at Idella's at such a vulnerable period of her life before she moved into her own apartment.

Idella's living room was modestly furnished for affluent Brentwood. Her brownish floral davenport sat facing the backyard, looking out on the hills. Two faded old-fashioned wing chairs faced the couch. On one of them was the U-shaped pillow that Idella used to support her neck so that her protruding back would fit snugly in the wing chair. With the antique teacart in the corner and odd-shaped tables here and there, it was clear that the owner of the house had to be an old widow.

Art, Edith's older brother who had flown out from Taos, New Mexico, sat on the other wing chair squirming and changing positions every few minutes. He was about the only one sitting in the roomful of well wishers, mostly women.

"Uncle Art, can I get you something to eat or drink?" I put my hand on his shoulder. Even though this was the first time I had met him, it seemed presumptuous if I didn't refer him as uncle.

"No thank you, Song-Uun. I am OK right now." He answered, looking far away. He and his older brother, Don went to meet with Dr. Monk, Edith's psychiatrist, early that day and spent half of the morning trying to figure out just what exactly went wrong. Everyone, including Dr. Monk, thought that Edith was cured. She had seen Dr. Monk weekly for the last few years in accordance with her court-ordered divorce settlement. It was hard for me to comprehend the complexity of chronic or clinical depression. Edith never raised her voice and she never seemed agitated. She possessed a placid and untroubled appearance.

When her ex-husband came to deliver her car from Sacramento, Edith, anticipating his arrival, told me that she was not looking forward to seeing him. It was shortly after she moved in with the Rogers. Yet Edith had greeted him calmly with a smile on her face.

"Thank you so much for bringing my car. I appreciate it. I only wish I could offer you a room to stay, but as you can see I am imposing on Bob and Frances myself." Her ex-husband extended his hand to shake hers and said, "Take care of yourself, dear Edith. And remember, I am always here for you. Don't get ahead of yourself, and take time to get well."

Edith had stopped rubbing the windowsill with her index finger and looked down at their linked hands, with her tightly closed mouth drooping to one side from a forced smile.

I remembered hugging my arms to cover the dull ache in my heart. I felt so closely attached to Edith. I wished I could make her pain go away. When he wanted to take her out to lunch before he headed to the airport to fly home, Edith asked me to come along with them. All through lunch, I bit my lower lip to keep myself from tearing up. Even though there was no exchange of any kind of emotion between them, they each demonstrated genuine concern for each other. As we got up to leave the restaurant, I dropped a large Hershey's chocolate bar in the open duffle bag he was carrying. I wanted him to know he was OK by me.

After he left, sensing that I didn't see much wrong with him, Edith said softly, "He is a nice man. There is no doubt about it. But he sure made me lonely. He is pretty self-centered. I never felt his love. He probably is the coldest man on earth I know."

Maybe Edith was right. He might have been too busy flying or mountain climbing to come to his ex-wife's memorial service. That might have been why he wasn't there. But then again, maybe Bob didn't inform him. In any case, it saddened me to know that there wasn't anyone who was suffering heartbreak over her death—no spouse, no children, no parents.

Bob, the oldest brother, went around the room thanking everyone for coming out on a rainy night. Don and Art didn't say a word, only nodded their heads when Bob introduced them to different people. Marian, Edith's sister, made a full circle of the room, shaking hands and introducing herself to everyone. Her large behind bumped into the person next to her all evening.

"So all your siblings are here tonight. How nice. Now, do you all live in California?" a woman in a bright red suit who introduced herself as Edith's superior at UCLA asked Marian.

"Oh no. Don lives in Philadelphia, Art's from New Mexico, and of course Bob lives in Concord, Massachusetts now. You know he used

to live right next door here. But you know, none of their wives came."
Marian shrugged her shoulders.

"They couldn't come," I interjected. "But we talked to Frances a
few times already. And Dot and Peggy both sent their regrets. I realize it
is hard to get away at a moment's notice, especially when you still have
children at home, I am sure."

"Oh, dear girl, what children? Grown children? Excuse me, but I
always thought my three brothers married their mothers."

Marian's thoughtless remark made me want to get away from her.
"Excuse me. I am needed in the kitchen."

"Are you Song-En Lee?" The woman in red emphasized "En" in a
raspy voice.

"Yes I am. My last name is Noh now. I am here with my husband
and expecting a baby," I added touching my stomach. For some reason
I felt the need to explain why I was wearing a navy and white maternity
dress.

"Oh, Edith was so fond of you. She talked about you incessantly.
And you look exactly as I imagined."

"Do I really?" I smiled. "Excuse me. I am wanted in the kitchen.
But I would like to talk with you some more later." I turned around,
annoyed that everyone was jolly, that the food was disappearing fast, and
that they would show up in brightly colored outfits.

As I turned around, I smelled Yardley, either from Marian or the
woman in red.

The smell took me immediately to a multitude of memories of
Edith. I hadn't known what Yardley smelled like until Bob took me to
the Vincente Drug Store to buy her Yardley soap for her birthday one
year. Bob told me it was Edith's favorite fragrance. I could still see her
full smile – one of the few times she had smiled completely – as she
smelled Yardley through the wrapping paper.

"Oh, Song-Uun, Yardley! You got me Yardley."

Thinking of that night, I let out a convulsing sob. I covered my
mouth and ran into the large bathroom adjacent to all three bedrooms.
Idella's and Edith's bedrooms were next to each other and the guest

room was directly across from the bathroom. I had stayed there one year for Thanksgiving and Christmas vacation after the Rogers moved to Concord. Knowing that Edith's apartment was one bedroom, Idella invited us to come and stay so we could all be together during the holidays.

I smothered my mouth, choking on both a loud cry and vomit. My sobbing was triggering the morning sickness and my mouth filled up with saliva. I bent over the toilet and started heaving. I used to throw up the same way every time the Rogers took me out on a drive either to the beach or to see the night lights. The Rogers never knew that I was prone to carsickness, since I would quietly go into the bathroom to get sick. But when Edith came along for a ride and saw me run into the house to the bathroom, she followed me and rubbed my back, saying, "Poor darling!"

"I will miss you, Aunt Edith," I whispered into the mirror. As vulnerable as she was, she became an important part of my life at the most vulnerable period of my life. Edith always supported me.

"Are you all right?" Ty knocked on the bathroom door.

"I am fine. I will be right out."

I squeezed a dab of toothpaste on my index finger and rubbed it all over my teeth to get rid of the sour taste in my mouth. Then I splashed water on my face and took a swallow out of my cupped hands. The nausea and the upset stomach were making me dizzy. The instinct to protect the baby made me stroke my stomach gently. Edith was so pleased when I told her that I was expecting.

"How wonderful! I am so happy for you, Song-Uun. It's just that it pains me to know I won't be able to hold the baby. I mean, I am just not used to holding a baby. You know, I never had a baby myself. I have no, uh, no experience in holding one of those delicate angels," she stammered.

"So she knew her plan to quit her life all along, before February when my baby is expected to be born," I murmured looking in the mirror.

I left the bathroom and walked over to the food table to pour myself a glass of wine.

"Excuse me. I wanted to introduce myself," Dr. Monk startled me, and I quickly wiped my tears.

"Oh yes, I know who you are, Dr. Monk. So nice to meet you," I smiled and nodded.

"Edith talked about you quite often. I feel like I know you." He pushed his glasses up and I felt like I had to say something to make him feel better. I knew it took a lot of courage to come and face Edith's whole family and me.

"Likewise, Dr. Monk. I know she looked forward to seeing you each week. After her appointment with you, she would go have dinner alone to sort out her thoughts. She used to come home feeling like a million dollars." I looked at the perspiration on his forehead. "I know it meant a lot for her to see you on a regular basis. She was a special person in many ways. Perhaps so special that God thought it was her time to be with Him." I surprised myself when I said this. I never thought of it that way. But it was true that everybody died in God's timing.

When Edith found me reading the Bible one day, she had told me that she admired me for reading it. She said she didn't read it because her depth of faith was questionable. She couldn't imagine leaving everything to God and God alone. But someday she might understand. She also said that she held it in high regard that I was continuing my life as a Christian while living with Bob and Frances. After all, they were atheists, even though Frances' father was a Dutch minister with his own church and his sermon was never skimpy. I wanted to ask Dr. Monk if he thought Edith was in heaven. She was baptized as an infant.

Looking back, her depression could have been easily controlled with medication, if only she had waited another decade. She gave herself four years from the first attempt to the second. In that time, I was lucky enough to have her in my life. But underneath the calm and placid appearance, she still suffered in unmanageable darkness.

A part of me will always feel somewhat responsible for not doing my part to try to deepen her faith, and for not being there.

40

Morrison Street in Sherman Oaks in the fall reminded me of a peaceful town somewhere in the Midwest. The fully established elms lined up along the sidewalk on both sides. Every house showed off flowering hedges on their well-manicured front yard, a sign of comfortable middle-class life. During a stormy season in November, the rain carried the yellow and red fall leaves onto the sidewalk and covered it completely.

Ty and I drove to make the final inspection of the house in the middle of the block, our very first house, in an anticipation of our first baby's arrival in February.

The front door of the house was set in between two windows, with a dining room on the left and a den on the right. Standing across the street, I stared at the window on the right and imagined gingham curtains and a lamp sitting on the table by the curtain. That would make a cozy and inviting corner to cuddle up with a good book by the fireplace, watching the smoky chimney through naked trees or just listen to the tapping of the rain on the roof.

On the left, I pictured a glistening chandelier over a formally set dining table with Christmas dishes and a red centerpiece. I knew it would be my house the first time we looked at it. The wrought iron gate to the detached garage and the wood-shingled roof over the squarely sitting property gave the feeling of a solidly built home.

The two floor-to-ceiling windows on either side of the fireplace in the living room showed a full view of the large backyard, filled with fruit trees. It gave me a feeling of nostalgia as if I had been there before, somewhere else in California. Gazing at the bare trees in the California rain, I hoped this would be a place where I might find the contentment I had been looking for, a place that would fill the emptiness in me.

For the last two years, living in a clean adult apartment, I thought, time and again, that there was something not quite intact about my life. I didn't know what I was waiting for, nor did I know what I wanted. All I knew was that my life was not complete.

Somewhere in that house by the fireplace, under the glistening chandelier, I thought I would find a place for me. A place I had been looking for, a place that would make me whole.

Like most homes, it showed off well with a roomful of Victorian furniture in the soft glow, but as it turned out, the living room was dark and the carpet was dreary. But replacing it with the trendy long shag carpet was out of the question for now.

Underneath the chandelier in the dining room, I placed a Formica table and four vinyl chairs, which were redeemed with Blue Chip stamps. The living room was sparsely furnished in "Thrifty Eclectic," with a blue couch and a Mediterranean coffee table we had purchased at an estate sale. An early American rocking chair faced the couch, which I exchanged for almost twenty "Blue Chip stamp" books.

Ty went to work dressed sharp in his Italian suit every morning. His dozen or so business suits filled half of the closet, while the other half was filled with white dress shirts starched stiff, hung loosely so as not to touch each other. He walked into the house at 5:30 every evening and demanded a full course meal. A full course Korean meal meant lots of side dishes accompanying rice and meat. Homemade soup was also a must-have every night. After dinner, Ty buried himself in the stock chart and read *The Wall Street Journal*.

I got busy setting up a nursery for the first two months. Since I didn't have a car, I spent much of the time ordering nursery furnishings from a catalogue. I learned quickly that a cottage look could be achieved with Sears and Penny's. I scrubbed the kitchen and the bathroom floors with Ajax and vacuumed the flocked wallpaper.

I set up Terry's nursery across the hall from the master bedroom, which gave me easy access to peak at her angelic face a few times a night. There were many nights I would sneak up to her crib and stare at her for hours through the spindles. I would place my hand on the back of her barely five-pound body to feel the tiny waves of ups and downs, listening to her gentle gasps. For the first couple of months, I surrounded her tiny body with stuffed animals as if they were protecting her.

When she napped for a long time, I would go into her room and make noise purposely so she would wake up. I loved being a mother.

For the first time, I knew what it was like to hold something that was more precious than my own life, so precious I would give up anything in the world for. I got up in the middle of the night and put my hand on her back to make sure she was breathing and caressed her tiny fingers. I thanked God for blessing me with this precious miracle. She gave me a reason to be healthy: so I could take care of her.

Phyllis Hoffman brought chicken soup and stayed all day to help for the first few days. "Sang, my goodness, I have a bigger chicken than this," she exclaimed. "Is Ty a good father? You know, Nat was so scared to touch my babies when they were first born, saying they were too tiny."

"He is pretty good. It doesn't seem to bother him to hold Terry."

Ty adored Terry. He did the father's share by changing her diapers and feeding her willingly. We laughed together when she blew bubbles and cooed and Ty and I fought over who got to pat her back until she fell asleep. I rubbed her back quietly but Ty sang a lullaby in his out-of-tune squeaky voice, patting her back to the rhythm much like a victory song. "*Jal-ja-ra uri aga… apdul gua dwit-dong-san ae….*"

When I wondered and doubted about our marriage, Terry made it worth being married to Ty. And I was grateful that we lived in a comfortable house and that I didn't have to go to work. It seemed perfectly all right to give up my dream of being a concert cellist only to be her mother. Still, I constantly had the nagging thought that there had to be more to married life than this.

One day, I approached Ty, hoping he would help me. "I wonder if we should find a church around here and start going on Sundays."

"You are absolutely crazy. I will never go to church, never. Churches are for hypocrites."

"I went to church all my life and went to a Christian school. Are you telling me I am a hypocrite?"

"Just don't ask me to go, ever again. You go if you want. But I will never go to a church. Ridiculous!"

"But we got married at a church and you liked the minister who married us. You followed his directions. Do you think he is a hypocrite?"

"I don't want to talk about it. Just drop it. And don't ever let me see a Bible around the house. Read it if you want but not in front of me."

There was something so threatening about Ty's reaction even though he said that I could go to church if I wanted. Just as he neither objected nor offered to help when I wanted to audition for the Glendale Symphony Orchestra, which was semi-professional at the time, but I had no way of getting to rehearsals and concerts. I wanted a husband who would say, "Why don't we buy a second car so you can continue your cello playing." Ty had a way of thwarting my desires. He made my desires seem insignificant, unimportant.

My life as a mother was busy. In the summer I would place Terry's buggy in the backyard with a mosquito net over it so Terry could enjoy morning naps under a tree, and in the afternoons I took her for walks in her stroller around the neighborhood.

On one of those walks, I met Kathy and Andrea. They lived two doors away from each other and I lived six doors down on the street perpendicular to them. We each had one daughter. We got together in the afternoon between the babies' naps to compare our babies' eating and sleeping habits and discuss menus for dinner. We cooked our special recipes and invited each other for dinner and soon our husbands became friends, although Ty never became as close to either one of them as they were with each other. To Ty, Alan and Bob would never be much more than round-eyed white neighbors.

Kathy and I talked and saw each other daily. When I was sick, she took me to the doctor's and took care of Terry. We pushed our kids in the stroller and walked to Fashion Square to shop.

"How can you be such good friends with Kathy who swears at her husband all the time? And did you notice Alan's manners the other day?" Ty never approved of my friendship with Kathy and Alan.

One afternoon, I walked into Kathy's house when she and Andrea were sitting on the couch laughing and giggling.

"Wait, I have to tell Sang." Kathy pounded the cushion, signaling me to sit down, still laughing hysterically.

"Sang, tell me what your orgasm is like?" I was horrified that she would blurt out such a question.

"Have you guys been smoking pot? If so, I am leaving, 'cause I want no part of it." I headed for the door, holding Terry.

"No, no, we are not. Just come and sit down. But first put Terry in the playpen with Erin." She composed herself.

"Andrea just told me that she's never had a true orgasm."

"What are you talking about?" My face felt hot from blushing. They were not even whispering. "Isn't anything sacred anymore with you two?"

"All she feels is shallow and rapid vibration. She doesn't know what it's like to have the deep satisfaction." Kathy ignored me and went on excitedly.

"I know, I know. I have a problem. My therapist told me that I need to explore myself," Andrea said.

"What? What therapist? Are you telling me that you have a therapist on sex?" I rounded my eyes and picked up Terry. "I am sorry. I need to go. I don't want to talk about this."

"Sang, there is nothing wrong with talking about this. You have a child and you are pregnant now. That means you had sex and enjoyed it. Don't you want to enjoy it fully? How can you sit there and say that you don't care and that you don't want to talk about it?"

"No, I am not saying that. I just know that – I don't know. I just feel uncomfortable talking about such a personal matter." I sat back down.

"I can see that. It's all right if you don't want to talk about it. I am just telling you that Bob and I are both frustrated because I can't seem to have full satisfaction."

Andrea elaborated.

"I am telling you. You have to smoke pot before you have sex. Your orgasm goes on and on. It never ends. I am telling you, it's the weirdest thing," Kathy said, shaking her head in amazement.

"All right, Kathy. Let's change the subject. I know Sang doesn't want to talk about this." Andrea puffed a cigarette swinging her crossed leg back and forth.

"Thank God." I rolled my eyes.

For the rest of the day and evening, I thought about what Kathy and Andrea said, curious and confused. Someday I would have to ask Kathy more about this forbidden subject.

The following month, Kathy gave me a surprise shower for my second baby. She and Ty made the guest list, which consisted of my Korean friends and some people from the neighborhood. My Korean friends were the wives of Ty's high school buddies. The first part of the shower went as planned. I walked into her house not knowing anything, and they all yelled "Surprise." Of course, Alan, being a photographer, took a picture of me walking into the house with the dumbest look on my face, totally confused.

When I started opening presents, Kathy decided to serve the cake and coffee that was percolating on the stove on very low heat. Only when we heard a loud pop did we know something was happening in the kitchen.

"Damn! What the hell!" Kathy walked out of the kitchen covering her face.

Her face was blotchy with red spots all over and a large spot on her forehead was already blistering.

"What the fuck, Kath? What did you do to yourself?" Alan dropped his camera and rushed over to Kathy. Everyone got up to surround her.

"I was going to open the lid to take out the Max Pax. When I barely touched the lid, the whole damn thing blew up. Go look at the ceiling and the walls in the kitchen. The damndest thing is all over everywhere. Not a drop left in the fucking pot. Excuse me. Man, that hurts! I am suing fucking General Foods. Excuse me again."

The room quickly became chaotic and some of the guests left, allowing Alan to rush her to the emergency room. In any case, this was a good time for the party to end, especially for the Korean women, who were putting up with this nonsense American triviality.

I was more confused than anything. I didn't know how a coffee pot could blow up. I didn't know what exactly happened to Kathy's face. And how and why did it happen? I didn't know if it hurt a lot or what to do about it. I felt guilty for some reason. I felt it happened because of me and because of all the work she put on to please me.

Kathy decided she wouldn't go to the hospital, but she wanted to come to our house. Ty was kind and kept supplying ice packs for her.

"Tell me, Kathy. What exactly happened?" Ty interrogated her like an FBI agent.

"I am telling you, I love that Max Pax. It's measured exactly in a mesh bag. I just drop the thing in the percolator and forget about it. Just keep it on real low heat and serve it when you are ready. But today, for some reason the dammdest thing, excuse me Ty, just fucking, excuse me Ty, blew up, all over my face. Not to mention the whole dammed kitchen. Boy that hurts!" Kathy got more and more excited.

"I know a good personal injury attorney if you ever decide to sue. Of course, you need to keep a record of the evidence," Ty said, shrugging his shoulders.

"Say, that's a thought. We will sue the heck out of General Foods. A big company like that? They will probably just want to settle out of the court for maybe like thousands of dollars. Hey, maybe I should take a picture of your blistering face." Alan grabbed his camera.

A few days later, Ty came home from work and walked over to deliver the exciting news to Alan and Kathy.

"Well, it worked exactly like Kathy said. The coffee pot exploded in the lab. The coffee stain covered the entire ceiling." Ty wiped his forehead with a handkerchief.

"No shittin'? He really did it, huh? He really experimented with the Max Pax? I'll be damned. What a good attorney!" Alan's smile was ear-to-ear, as he looked Ty up and down.

"Look at you, Ty. Is that how you go to work every day? You look really sharp. Where do you buy your clothes, tie and all? You look like a Wall Street guy. Ty the tycoon. Any good stock tips today?" Alan rambled.

"He likes to shop at Phelps Meager at the Bullock's Fashion Square," I said.

"Hey, you guys, let's stay with the lawsuit. You need to make an appointment and see him tomorrow. Not wait till blister go away," Ty ignored Alan and went on. His accent seemed more profound when he was excited.

Ty had taken Kathy to an attorney and made sure he understood the cause and the consequences of the accident. And most importantly, he made sure he knew that Kathy didn't misuse the cleverly pre-measured and prepackaged coffee. I looked at Ty proudly. He had one quality I held in high regard and counted on: He was responsible and thorough. And he would see to it that things were done right. Only it always had to be *his* way.

For the first few years of our marriage, Ty never bothered giving me Christmas presents. Nothing shown at the department stores was worthwhile to pay his hard-earned good money for, he said.

The year Terry was born, he decided to take a day off to shop for me. He spent all day shopping and came home in the evening with a black lizard evening purse trimmed with a gold-plated clasp in a Saks Fifth Ave. shopping bag.

"I almost gave up. I thought I wasted all day. I happened to see it at the window as I was walking out of the store. It was the only thing I liked." He handed it to me unwrapped and told me that it was worth every penny of the six hundred dollars he paid.

For some reason, I felt undeserving of his spending all of his precious workday combing through store after store. His days at work were challenging and exciting to him, and his work came before anything else. He got up bright and early and got himself ready every morning with a full breakfast to face a day of manipulative and innovative adventures in finance. I, like a good wife, made him toast and bacon faithfully each morning. And today, he had made up for all the years of neglecting me by giving up a day. I felt so strange and awkward that I couldn't bring myself to thank him. But I appreciated his integrity and I appreciated his way of loving me.

I could see that Ty took this matter personally and made it his mission to make sure that Kathy and Alan were adequately compensated for the accident. After all, Kathy cleaned, cooked, baked, and decorated her house for his wife and her friends. And Alan had waited with his camera, ready to capture the surprise moment.

Kathy's face healed and the grocery stores carried the new packages of Max Pax with the warning labels telling the users not to leave it on low heat for long periods of time. Kathy and Alan's attorney recommended that they accept the generous offer General Foods made to them. Kathy's bangs grew out and she parted her long straight brown hair again when her scars faded.

The week after the settlement, Kathy drove her new yellow Pontiac station wagon over to our house and I hopped in for a ride. The following week, the workers were digging up their backyard for a new swimming pool. These were two things Kathy had yearned to have for as long as I had known her. And while the workers were digging, Alan went shopping at Phelps Meager for the first time.

41

Dr. Robinson thoroughly checked my second baby, Kimmy – all five pounds and eleven ounces of her – immediately after her birth. He listened to her heartbeat. He pricked the ball of her foot. He wiggled her fingers and toes, lifted her arms, checked inside her mouth, eyes, ears, and nose. I watched him with his large hands, pulling and tugging and flipping the baby. "Perfect," he declared.

I now had two perfect baby girls, a year and a half apart. "They will become best friends," I thought. I rested, feeling content and satisfied, though I was delirious from the residuals of the saddle block. The sharp pain from the episiotomy made me twitch sporadically. My lower body felt unattached but gave me continuous dull aches.

I pushed the button to call the nurse and asked her to wheel me to the nursery window so I could see my perfect baby.

"The baby is sleeping and we don't want to disturb her rest, not just yet. Plus, you must lay flat for the next twenty-four hours, or else you'll get a severe headache," the nurse replied through the intercom.

"Can I feed my baby at the next feeding?" I asked.

"I will let you know. We have been feeding her often, you know, because she is so little."

"But I would like to hold my baby. I would like to feed her myself," I insisted.

"Your pediatrician will be here to make his rounds shortly. I will ask him."

I said OK, feeling uneasy that the nurse was so possessive of my baby. *They* will feed her, *they* will talk to the doctor. Whose baby was she anyway?

That evening, a nurse in white-laced shoes brought my roommate's baby, carrying him like a bundled-up football.

"Will you be bringing my baby to me so I can feed her?" I raised my head and asked.

"Dear, we already fed her. Put your head down. The doctor is examining her right now. He will talk to you. I will let you ask him."

"Examine her? For what? Is he here right now?" I asked. The nurse quickly glanced at me and turned her head. "What do you mean you are going to *let* me? Thank you for allowing me to ask *my* doctor about *my* baby."

The nurse stared and grimaced.

When Dr. Robinson came into my room, I immediately felt sick. It wasn't his concerned look, but the way he avoided eye contact.

"Mrs. Noh, your baby seems to be struggling to breathe. We need to do some more tests. Her lung is not functioning right," he said softly. His voice was shaky.

"You need to tell me more, Doctor. I don't know what that means. What do you mean it's not functioning right?" I sat up and looked straight at him.

"It's just that only one lung seems to be working right now. We don't know why and we don't know what to expect," he continued, using terms like "infantile lobar emphysema," something about abnormal blood vessels, and something about obstruction and respiratory distress.

"Doctor. You told me that she was perfect. Did one lung just stop working? And please, doctor. You need to tell me everything in plain English. Explain to me what the symptoms are and what you are doing about it in simple language."

Suddenly, the doctor I had counted on to care for Terry for more than a year looked incompetent. I wanted to shake him.

"We are doing everything we can do to determine why one of her lungs does not work at all. For starters, we are saving all her energy for breathing only. Her healthy lung is being overloaded. It is working very hard. We don't want her to spend her energy sucking. We inserted a catheter through her umbilical cord and fed her through it for the first couple of feedings. So she has been fed and nourished. The nurses here are excellent. For the next feeding we might try a nipple. It could be that her lungs may not have matured fully yet." He looked at me briefly.

"I would like to transfer her to Cedar-Sinai hospital. She needs to be in intensive care and we don't have the facility here at Valley Pres. The main thing is to watch her closely and hope she won't need open-heart surgery. I will still be caring for her, but I would like to take advantage of their facilities. I already talked to their doctor and he is expecting her. Both of us will be taking care of her. But without your permission, we can't do anything."

"Is that what you would do if she was your daughter?" Even though I was enraged, I was in no position to offend him. I needed him.

"Mrs. Noh, the truth is, you have no option. She is very sick. Sick enough to have the best care she needs to have. And of all the hospitals, Cedar-Sinai has what she needs at the moment. In any complication, early diagnosis is the key. And Cedar has all the latest technology. This is definitely what I would do."

"Let's not wait for another second then. What will they do to her over there? Can I hold her before she is transferred?" I bit my lip and asked.

"It would be very hard for you to hold her as she is connected to tubes – a few of them. We have contacted your husband. He is on his way, and you two can decide. You can see her through the window."

I wanted to rage against the doctor, but mostly, I wished I could give Kimmy my lung. Suddenly I knew how my mom must have felt when she pleaded to the Japanese doctor to give one of her eyes to me. She probably resented him too, yet she knelt in front of him.

"They will give her more tests and watch her very closely. If we don't see changes very soon, we may have to go in."

"You mean…."

"Open-heart surgery. Yes."

"But doctor, she's so little. How can you… to such a little one?"

"Let's really hope not. You just never know."

"How will she be transferred with all the tubes? Who will take her?"

"We will heat the incubator to keep her warm and will transport her in an ambulance. The incubator will stay warm for two hours. But it will get there in less than half an hour." Dr. Robinson patted the back of my hand and left the room.

When Ty came, he sat at the foot of my bed and sobbed.

"Sang, I don't want you to see the baby. She is lying down with only a diaper on. She's got tubes hanging out of every orifice of her body. She looks like some kind of an animal ready to be dissected in a lab. It is the saddest sight."

I was grateful that he was protective of me, but I also felt resentment. *Why is he keeping me from seeing my baby? I need to see my baby, especially when she is sick.* He always told me what to do. His sentences always started with, "I want you to…."

I wanted to ask him if he ever considered what I might want to do. But instead, I held his hand and rubbed his back. Though he was not the man I married three years ago and I was no longer sure I wanted to spend the rest of my life with him, I wanted to do something to take away his pain. At the moment, he was the only one in the world who shared my anguish.

"What are the tubes for? What are they doing to her? I want to see her."

"No, don't. It will really upset you. I will be going with her in an ambulance and I will call you as soon as we get there." Ty wiped his tears by rubbing his whole face and left the room.

As I watched him rush out of the room to take care of our baby, I felt, for the first time in a long time, an absolute closeness to him. Sharing concern and love for the baby we made together filled me with the ultimate sense of intimacy. No one else would have had the same intensity of despair. All at once, I experienced a tinge of regret for thinking that he was a self-centered person. And yet I was still on guard. I didn't ever feel free to reveal my true feelings to him.

I lay in my hospital bed, past feeling. My baby, who had been declared perfect a few hours prior, now might not make it. I sat up and put my hands together and started praying.

"Dear God, I have forgotten you for so long. But I do believe you are my Lord, my savior. I know you have control of everything that happens and I know you are the only one who can perform miracles. Please, God, I ask you to heal my baby whatever her problem might be. Make both of her lungs function. Give the doctor's wisdom and skills to cure her, Jesus."

"Mrs. Noh. Time for your pills." The night nurse came in with a small cup of pills.

"Your husband just left to get the nurse who lives around the corner. Don't worry. He should be on the way now."

"What are you talking about? What nurse? He is just now on the way? He left here almost an hour ago."

"The ambulance driver refused to drive the baby to Cedar without a medical professional present. He thought the baby might, you know, not make it. In which case he would be responsible. But 22 babies were born today and there were only two nurses working tonight taking care of 22 babies. So he had to stop to wake up an off-duty nurse who lives five minutes away."

Listening to her long explanation, I felt lightheaded. What else could go wrong?

At one o'clock in the morning, the night nurse informed me that Kimmy was safely at Cedar-Sinai intensive care and Ty would come over first thing in the morning. In between dozing on and off, I prayed all night. I promised God that I wouldn't forget Him. I would teach my kids to know Jesus. Only please heal my Kimmy.

The next morning, Ty told me that when he finally woke up the nurse and watched her get ready calmly, he had begged her to hurry. The baby had been in the heated incubator for longer than an hour by then, and the incubator was getting cool. When they both finally got in the ambulance, the driver asked for a hundred dollars in cash.

"Where am I going to get a hundred dollars in cash at this time of the night? Please, I have my checkbook with me and American Express and Visa card," Ty said, sweating.

"I will take American Express. It's just that our policy is to ask for cash first."

Ty told me that he would have punched him if it were any other time. Kimmy's one lung was pumping up and down so visibly high, he was filled with panic. It looked as though it might burst. He finished the story and sobbed again.

If anyone had asked me what would be the worst thing a mother could go through, I would have said, losing a child. But having a sick child with an undiagnosed illness and no place to turn for even a calculated hopeful answer now topped the worst of the worsts.

I couldn't face the possibility of losing my baby. At least death seemed to be a silent finalization. After death, life goes on, even though there may be sadness or bitterness. But the agony of living with a possibility, knowing that there might be something that I was overlooking, was unbearable.

I gave birth to my baby; I should be able to fix her. It was my responsibility.

When my obstetrician came in for his morning round, I told him to discharge me. I didn't want to stay there without my baby. I needed to go to Cedar and meet with the doctors in the intensive care unit.

With the double dose of pain pills I took and all the adrenaline, my body was fueling me for this crisis, I felt no discomfort as I walked into Cedar-Sinai. Their pediatric intensive care unit was a large, oddly shaped room with incubators on wheels everywhere. A black nurse brought my baby to me so I could bottle-feed her. By then all the tests were done, and they had disconnected the tubes. The test results offered no answers. The doctors were now more perplexed. They were considering open-heart surgery. Open-heart surgery. The words sounded deadly wrong.

I finally held my Kimmy. She only covered half of my forearm. Deep yellow from jaundice, she sucked slowly, with effort, and rested between sucking, then she went back to sucking. She clearly had the instinct to eat and survive. After holding her and watching her eat, I somehow knew she was going to be OK. How can a gracious God take this precious one away from me?

"Can I see the doctor?" I asked the nurse walking by.

"Yes, of course. He will be here a little later. But your main doctor is still Dr. Robinson. Didn't he talk to you?" the nurse asked.

"Yes, he has been talking to me all along. But don't I need to see the doctor at this hospital?" I wanted someone else who just might give me an encouraging view.

"Well, Dr. Robinson is the one you want to talk to, because he will be the one who will perform the surgery. Like I said, he is your main doctor."

"Yes, He mentioned something about the open-heart surgery."

"I have a form for you to sign," she said. "He needs to go in to determine what the problem is."

"When does he want to do this?" I asked.

"What did he say to you? I thought it was scheduled for tomorrow morning, unless there was a huge change by tonight."

"Like what kind of change?"

"You know. Like if all of a sudden they see a sign of improvement. Even the slightest change will require alternate treatment. In any case, doctors won't perform any surgery until they talk to you in person. So don't worry."

"Like what treatment?"

"I don't know exactly. That's something you need to ask the doctor."

I felt helpless. *Why couldn't they figure out what was wrong with her?*

"Can I sign it tonight when I come back for her night feeding? I would like to come back tonight, if that's OK," I asked, feeling ridiculous for asking to see *my* baby.

"Sure. Suit yourself." She said it with a smile, but I knew she didn't want to be bothered with me anymore.

When Ty and I got home, he started mowing the lawn. It was just as well, because all I wanted to do was pray. From the time that Ty told me never to ask him to go to church with him, but to go ahead and go if I wanted to, I never felt comfortable talking to him about God or Jesus, and discussing the Bible with him would agitate his temper.

I prayed in bed all afternoon. I told the Lord that I thought Kimmy was a survivor for the way she was fighting to breathe and eat. I thanked Him for allowing me to have such a survivor for my baby. I hugged Terry and prayed for Terry. I thanked him for sending us Ty's brother, Dai-Young, to take care of Terry while I went to the hospital to have Kimmy.

When Ty and I went back to the hospital for the evening feeding, Kimmy looked rested. Even though she weighed less, her face seemed to have filled up a little. When I held her, she sucked more steadily and fell asleep after drinking two ounces, the most she had eaten to that point.

I signed the paper and left the hospital. I felt somewhat peaceful, knowing she was in God's hands.

In the morning, Ty and I hurried to the hospital as soon as we woke up, although I'm not sure I slept at all. I believe it was the only morning Ty ever skipped his breakfast of bacon and toast.

"Good morning," the nurse said cheerfully. "Your baby had a great night. She started doing better after you left last night. This morning, she looks a thousand times better and is breathing much better. The doctor is waiting to talk to you."

For a second, I thought I was dreaming. Dr. Robinson spoke to us. "Her lungs are much improved. We can see a small pumping of the right lung. I think we should just watch her closely and continue to do what we have been doing. She seems to like the care she is getting here. We have determined she has pneumothorax, and she is pulling out of it like a champ. We do want to keep her here for another week or so to strengthen her and make sure she doesn't relapse."

I didn't think I ever saw Dr. Robinson smile until then. He was always so serious and stately.

"She is a survivor," Dr. Robinson said, smiling again. "You watch, she will have her way in life. She will be one of those kids who will not take the backseat for anyone."

On the way home, I looked at the blue sky and quietly murmured, "Thank you, Lord."

42

Dearest little sister, Sang-Eun,
   It's hard to believe that you are a mother and a wife, my dear baby sister. I can still hear your high heels clicking on the cement steps of our apartment building when you arrived home late from a concert. Here you are living a thousand miles away as a grown woman.
   I miss you so terribly. And I regret we didn't spend more time together.
   I wish I could see you before you turn into a cold and selfish American....

My tears fell on the aerogramme and smudged the blue ink as I read Sang-Soon's letter again and again. I put the letter to my face to inhale the warmth of her silky smooth eggshell skin. Through her tidy Korean handwriting my whole body submerged into the tenderness of each word, and the genuine selfless love I felt from her.

For as long as I remember, she was in charge of our household and supervised the maids. She made sure the house was clean and the laundry was brought in from the clothesline when it rained. The maids would consult her over my mom with questions like what kind of *kimchee* to make, cucumber or cabbage.

When my ears were full of earwax, she put my head on her lap and cleaned it out with a tiny silver ear spoon. Her gentle and soothing way of manipulating the spoon in my ear always put me to sleep. When

Mom was late coming home, she would call Sang-Soon and tell her to instruct the maids with dinner. Sang-Soon managed the grocery funds and while the maids went to the market, she mopped the floor.

She did everything quietly. She learned Korean traditional dance at school for free, so Mom didn't have to pay for lessons. When she started college, knowing that tuition was a burden to my mom, she quietly went for an interview at the Bank of Korea and took a part-time job. When she had her menstrual period, no one knew. I still don't know where she washed the soiled strips of gauze and where she dried them.

Our relatives and neighbors constantly told us that she was the model-perfect *mat-myu-nuri* (oldest daughter-in-law). It was the biggest compliment given to a marriageable age woman. It meant that she would be the love of any mother-in-law's eye and the top on a match-maker's list. To add to her perfection, she moved and danced elegantly and daintily. When she performed Korean traditional dance on the stage while attending Ewha girl's high school, her soft smile and wavy hair lit up the stage.

From the time she was a freshman in college, she was barraged with inquiries from various matchmakers, well-meaning distant relatives and busybody acquaintances, all guaranteeing a perfect husband. They would make official visits to my mother with the potential husbands' detailed particulars, such as the family background, father's occupation, their educational background, and above all, their birth order in the family.

The oldest daughter-in-law holds far more responsibility and she needs to have the wisdom to eventually hold the position of queen of the household. All of this personal information was important because it pertained to the success of their future social standing as married couple. Of the prospective husband's profession, medical doctors and engineers were of the highest value but dentists with a diploma from an elite university were acceptable, too.

The most pertinent information needed by the matchmakers was *sha-ju*, the Four Pillars, which were the year, month, day, and hour of the prospect's birth. A good matchmaker would have already taken the Four

Pillars of both parties to a fortune teller to have their charts read. Marital harmony depended on the Four Pillars both inwardly and outwardly. Outward harmony had to do with prosperity and abundance, and this information was presented openly. But as they examined the written characters of the Four Pillars, they would whisper about their inward harmony, the night time bed harmony. Sometimes matchmakers would suggest herbal medicine to enhance the couple's bedtime harmony. The Four Pillars were written in brush calligraphy on rice paper. It was wrapped in a red silk scarf with blue lining and tassels on the four corners and was sent to the groom's family when the match reached an agreement.

The Aunties – as we called the matchmakers – worked hard in hopes of receiving a pocketful of gratuities in case the match resulted in an engagement.

When Sang-Soon met her husband, three prospectives were waiting for my sister's answer. All the while, their families were sending my family crates full of apples buried in rice husks, boxes of plump dried persimmons, and a surprise delivery of ribs from a local butcher.

I was secretly hoping she would choose the oldest son of the Oh family who lived down the street in a big Western-style house with a veranda overlooking the large front yard full of cosmos in the fall. Their oldest son had just come home from studying in Paris. When they brought their proud son to our house to meet my sister, my dream of having a tall, handsome, almost foreign-looking man with a big nose as my oldest brother-in-law was completely shattered. He was small, dark, and shriveled up.

Sang-Soon never seemed to be in a hurry to be married. Every time she came home from a *miaii* (arranged meeting of an unmarried couple by a matchmaker) she never showed any emotion, other than to say, "He is not my type."

Sang-Soon finally agreed to marry my brother-in-law – not because she was impressed with his doctoral degree in engineering from England, but because my mother insisted it was time she made a decision.

"Afternoon fish will be tossed out of the market or sold for half-price at the most," Mom said.

Once she made her decision, she spent each day preparing for her wedding while other women purchased all the wedding accoutrements. She made quilts for their new home. She made red and blue scarves with tassels to wrap gifts for her new in-laws.

Every night she massaged her face to make it glow for her wedding day. She got a traditional Korean costume with a five-color-striped blouse ready, just in case her new in-laws expected her to wear it as a bride. She did everything to meet the duties of a daughter-in-law. She only thought of serving and helping her new in-laws and her new husband.

Sang-Soon and I had a conversation one day that made me truly aware of her generous heart. I was still in high school, and my life revolved around my music. Everything in my life at the time had to do with performing and competing.

I had been practicing cello and decided to take a break from aching fingers and arms by lying next to her and sticking my cold feet into the quilt. She was reading her French book, sitting on the warm *on-dol* floor of the *an-bang* with a quilt covering her legs. I lay next to her, staring at the ceiling.

"Sang-Soon *unni*, can I ask you something? Do you ever think about what you might be in ten years? Twenty years? I mean, like, do you have a dream? Like, what is the ultimate goal of your life?" I asked, turning toward her.

"I don't know. In ten years? I would probably want to go to America, for one thing. I know I will, one day. Just don't know when it might happen. What about you? What is your dream?" She turned her face to mine.

"My dream? You mean what do I wanna be? I don't know if I wannna tell you. I think that I want to be a real famous cellist. I mean, like world-famous. In the top seven, maybe. What about you?" I gave her a quick glance. I never thought about what her dreams might be, if any. She was a French literature major in college but no one thought

much of what she would do with her degree unless she got a job at the
French Embassy or something. I assumed she had to pick something for
her major and French literature was as good as any. What could be her
personal dream?

"Well, I do have a dream. Do you wanna know what it is?" The
shiny waves of her black hair half-covered her gentle, smiling eyes. "My
dream is to be the oldest sister to one of the best cellists in the world,
maybe in the top seven,"

"Is that really your dream?" Peering at her almost translucent skin, I
felt the bridge of my nose tighten. Of course she would think of someone
else first. I smiled, feeling selfish and embarrassed.

"*Unni*, I know you lived with 'new-house-grandma' when you were
little. Tell me how it happened?"

"You mean you never heard what happened?"

"Well, I have, but not the whole story. I don't know why you were
sent."

She turned to lie on her stomach, supporting her upper body with
her elbows and told me the story.

"I was born in the year of cow, and people always said that I was
as obedient as a cow and worked hard as a cow. I was born only a year
after Mom and Dad's number one son was born. And you know, he had
every kind of infantile disease and needed Mom's full attention. There
wasn't enough milk for both of us and him being the first son, he was too
precious. Mom was weak after having two babies one after the other and
even with the wet nurse, brother's health was on the line. So they sent
me to Grandfather's concubine, you know, the new-house-grandma in
Ham-Kyung province. Grandpa kept his concubine in a silk wardrobe
and the greenest jade hairpins. And I guess I was a beautiful baby with
naturally wavy hair and chubby pinky cheeks and I melted the concubine's heart. She loved dressing and feeding me. I was a live doll to her. I
lived with her for a long time, it seemed. The new-house-grandma even
started collecting my dowry when I was only three years old. She bought
every color of silk fabric for all seasons."

"But then brother got well and became the terror of the Lee

household. I heard that he screamed at cold weather and spit at the maids when he didn't like the meal.

"Father visited me every once in a while and when he came, he would bring leather shoes and sweet candies. You know, they were pretty far away in another province. Then Sang-Hie was born and they started missing their sent-away first daughter and realized that they might lose her to Grandfather's young wanna-be wife." Sang-Soon brushed her wispy bangs.

"In panic, Father started sending letters asking them to send me back. He even sent a servant to bring me. But they ignored the letters and when the servant came home alone he told them that she had said, 'They had better have more babies while they are still young.'"

"Then one day, while the concubine went out to the city for another batch of silk fabric, Father came to their house and snatched me. Father said I was dressed impeccably in a silk brocade suit and black patent leather shoes. You know, I remember being so happy to see father, but I was so sad, I cried. I didn't want to leave the concubine. By then, home to me was with the concubine and I had forgotten Mom. You see, I had been apart from her for over two years." Sang-Soon continued, pensively. "After a long train ride, Father carried me in his arms and presented me to Mom. Mom was so happy to see me. She stretched out her arms to welcome me, her first daughter she dreamed of every night. But before Mom even touched my arms, I guess, I slapped Mom's cheek, screaming, 'I don't want you. I want to go back to Grandma,' of course Mom was really hurt."

I don't know how many times I had heard this part of the story from Mom. I always felt sorry for my mom when I heard it, but today, I felt sorrier for my sister for not ever knowing where her home was, and whom to love. I believed that a permanent distance was formed between my sister and my mom that could never be wholly filled.

My sister continued with a sad look on her face: "I missed the new-house- grandma so much for so long." She stared at a spot on the floor. "About a year ago, I looked her up, after all these years. She was living alone in the countryside. She was so aloof to me, showing no emotions."

Looking far ahead Sang-Soon said softly, "And here I thought of her so often wondering how much she must have missed me."

"She was probably senile by then, don't you think?" I said.

"I don't know. But I heard that she missed me so much and burned the entire dowry she had prepared for me." Sang-Soon looked at the wall. "I want to be loved like that again." She tilted her head, making my heart sting. I wanted to give her the love she was missing and yearning for.

"You want to hear something else?" She turned to lie on her side and told me another story. "It happened during the time when our parents lived in Sin-Kyung, the northern most part of Korea, which was considered a part of China."

"In those days, little girls were hot commodities in China because women did most of the work from the time they were young, and there were not enough women for all the men in China to bed with. Girls were being kidnapped left and right and sold into slavery or to factories for labor during the day and for men's pleasure at night. There was such a scarcity of girls, it was no wonder they bound their feet to keep them from running away." Sang-Soon went on with the story and told me of the time she was nearly kidnapped by a Chinaman on a bicycle.

"He was riding his bike, whistling. He looked like he was busy making deliveries. His black Chinaman's costume had buttons all the way down and his black coolie hat was placed tight on his head."

My sister and the maid went out on an errand, which was one of the maid's fun jobs and my sister's least fun thing to do. As the oldest daughter, she was often expected to be the maid's helper. As the Chinaman, in his jolly mood, passed by my sister and the maid, he stared at my sister, and when he was ahead of them, he looked back and stared some more. Then he stopped his bike, picked up my sister and placed her in the wooden bucket on the back of his bicycle as if she belonged to him.

The wide street was bleak and the severe Siberian wind was sweeping the street clean. In the speeding bike, my sister cried silently. She was scared, but she didn't think she could scream loudly. Somehow, she felt she deserved to be taken away. She covered her face and arms with her coat collar and closed her eyes. She was seeing tigers and ghosts and the scary fire-breathing dragons.

The shriek of the maid made her peek out of her covered coat, and she saw the flailing arms of the maid running after the bicycle with all her might. Finally the Chinaman picked my sister up and placed her on the sidewalk, then went on his merry way, whistling, as if nothing ever happened.

What bothered my sister more than anything was that Mom didn't fuss over her at all when she heard about what happened.

"You know, in both cases, my whole life could have changed. Can you imagine? I could have belonged to a Chinese working-class family, working day and night as their slave. Or I could have been New Grandma's treasured only daughter, never lifting a finger for anything. And here I ended up being the big sister to all of you. I guess I should be thankful."

Clutching her letter close to my heart, I sobbed. My sweet oldest sister. She never made it here. We were destined to live apart.

43

"*Even the mountains and the rivers will alter in ten years.*" So the saying goes.

As the plane approached the tarmac, I couldn't control the thumping of my heart. Ten years had passed since I left Korea. I was home.

The first thing I noticed was the armed guards on each side of the customs inspection line. Terry and Kimmy each clutched the edge of my denim coat and hid behind me at the guards' stiff postures. "Those men are protecting you. They are nice men." I bent down and hugged the girls, forcing a smile.

"The country is still on guard especially at a vulnerable place like the airport, I guess." Ty shrugged his shoulders as he offered an explanation. The next thing we noticed in the airport were uniformed policemen walking around with scissors in their hands. They were imposing a haircut code on men. Long hair was not allowed. The policemen would randomly pick guys with long hair and hack it with no warning or hesitation.

"Mommy, I want to go home. I am scared." Terry and Kimmy started crying at their first threatening impression of Korea. But my heart was still pounding with elation. I was about to step into the homeland where I grew up and had missed so dearly for the last ten years. I was about to be reunited with my family whom I had left as a college girl. I was now

married and a mother of two daughters, four and three years old, with
my teenage dream of being a concert cellist abandoned. Mountains and
the rivers were not the only things that had changed unrecognizably.

Everyone who came to the airport to greet us was invited to the Noh
house for the welcome dinner. Their two-story, modified, Western-style
home was big enough to house Nora and Hyun-Ja, Ty's two divorced
sisters. They lived upstairs and Ty's mother lived downstairs. Our
welcome dinner was in their *an-bang*, his mother's room downstairs.
Sang-Soon and Sang-Won sat with their spouses at the far end of the
long, rectangular table. My mom was seated next to me in the middle of
the table. At one point during dinner, Sang-Soon edged over to where
I was sitting and held my hands, quietly examining my face as if she
couldn't believe it was really me sitting there with two of my own young
daughters hanging onto me, one on each side.

Sang-Soon, knowing Terry had vomited as soon as she stepped into
the Noh house, stroked Terry's back and asked, "Would she drink some
cold *kimchee* juice? It would settle her stomach in half a second."

"I don't know. I have never given it to her. I wonder if it's too
spicy for her. Anyway, I think she is OK now. She's got a very sensitive
stomach, especially when traveling. She gets motion sickness easily." I
smiled and touched her hand. My sweet big sister.

"I know you should stay here. But when do you think you will come
over to Mom's house?" she whispered.

"I will in a couple of days, I promise." I squeezed her hands.

The third morning at the Noh house, I was awakened by the noise
of everyone bustling around the house getting ready for the trip to the
Buddhist temple to express their gratitude to Buddha for Ty's home-
coming and for me, his wife, and Terry and Kimmy, his children. Ty
successfully finished college as an honor student, something his family
never expected, and held a respectable position at work. That alone
made him a "dragon from a small stream." To his family, he came back
as a golden dragon.

"The official prayer worship service will be next week during the week of April 8, Buddha's birthday week. Today is a courtesy visit – you know, a greeting."

"What do we do there?" I asked. "I had never been to a Buddhist service before."

"Nothing. Just be there with your kids."

We climbed at least a hundred steps to the Buddhist temple. It sat high at the end of the street in the residential section of Seoul. The double wooden gates of the temple were massive with their own roof. When we entered the gate, we could see the main temple. It was a large Korean-style hall with a long ledge below the front doors. Through the two open doors above the ledge, we could see the lower part of the Buddha sitting on a pedestal. The roof of the temple was colorfully deco-rated in turquoise, blue, brown, and red and sculptured animals that resembled monkeys lined the ends of the curved roof. *Are they supposed to be guarding the temple?* I shivered with an eerie sensation. I didn't feel right being there.

A couple of pairs of rubber shoes that belonged to the monks, were laid neatly on the rectangular stepping stone underneath the ledge of the doors to the temple hall.

I held Terry and Kimmy's hands and followed everyone into a sepa-rate structure on the right, next to the front gate. As soon as we sat on the *on-dol* floor, as if they had been waiting for us, two of the female monks brought in a table full of food.

"They always serve us lunch first. And we need to eat whether we are hungry or not. You can't insult their hospitality," Hyun-Ja whispered to me.

"This is the best food. I love the temple food," Ty said.

"You've eaten here before? Aren't they all vegetables?" I asked, looking at the table.

"Of course. Lots of times. The head monk made sure they cooked all of my favorites."

Terry and Kimmy ate a little bit of the plain rice and I had some soybean soup. Then the ritual began. We were ushered by another monk into the temple hall where the threshold was so high that it was hard to straddle over it into the hall. The Buddha sat on a high pedestal on carved wooden lily petals, and there were lit candles all around the lily pad. We sat behind a monk who sat with a rosary around her neck and clattered a dried gourd and a stick, all the while chanting something undecipherable.

Terry and Kimmy kept looking at me as if they wanted me to rescue them. I pulled them close to me and put my arms around each of their shoulders. "Lord, I know this is wrong for me to be here. I am sitting here because I was told to do so by my in-laws. I am not worshipping the Buddha," I closed my eyes and prayed.

The night before April 8th on the lunar calendar, Ty's sister, Hyun-Ja explained, to the credit of the generosity of Nora, monks would light a lantern for Terry and another one for Kimmy for the worship service. They donated twice the money for the biggest lantern for Kimmy, because she needed twice the prayers from the monks since she had been born with a weak lung.

"We couldn't buy a smaller one for Terry. So Terry has Kimmy to thank for her double blessings from Buddha," Nora added. "We had to write down their names in Korean so the monks will be able to bid for their health."

"So what are Terry and Kimmy supposed to do with their lanterns?"

"Nothing. The kids just have to be there for the service. The lit lanterns will light Buddha's way for them so they will prosper and have a healthy life. Kimmy needs a lot of prayer."

That night I tossed and turned with the image of myself sitting in the temple hall floor staring Buddha with his one hand open and the other pointing at the open one with a glowing dot on his forehead.

I handed my predicament over to God and prayed, "Dear Jesus, I don't know why I am put in this kind of situation. If I should go tomorrow and bow to the Buddha, please know that my heart is not in it. I am asking you to show me what to do. Show me your wisdom."

A Korean girl, once married, had to obey, follow and do nothing to offend her in-law's wishes. In this modern world, what Nora said was the law in Ty's family. This ritual was also their way of showing how much they loved my kids. No matter how much I tried to justify otherwise, the fact that I was about to take my kids to this ominous place to pray didn't feel right to me.

At the breakfast table, Terry and Kimmy were excited to hear their Auntie Nora explaining the lantern ceremony.

"Your lantern is huge, Terry, and it will be lit in bright red and it will have your name written in big letters in Korean. Monks will sit and chant in their gray suits just for you. And the Buddha will send you all kinds of blessings. All five hundreds dollars' worth."

Terry waved her chopsticks and smiled.

"What about me? What about me?" Kimmy tapped her shoulders with her sticky rice-covered hand.

"Oh, you too, of course. They will bless you more since you were so sick when you were a baby. Buddha knows that you need help from him. He will make you healthy. Wait till you see your big lantern."

"What's a lannun?" Kimmy asked with her nasal voice.

"Oh, you will see. It's got your name on it. It says, 'Kim-ba-ri.' That was the best we could write in Korean. But we don't care. They know it's you."

I watched them with a smile, hiding my predicament.

Then, as if she read my mind, Nora looked at me and said, "I was just thinking, why don't you go and see your mom and your sisters today instead of going to the temple?"

"Huh? Do you really want me to?"

"Well, you have been staying here so much ever since you came, you didn't get to see your family much at all. We will take your kids and take good care of them. Stay there as long as you want. I will call you when I need you for a fitting."

"Fitting?"

"I am going to make at least ten outfits for you to take back to America. I know the stuff they have there. You can't wear that ready-made stuff. You are the Noh family daughter-in-law now."

"If you think it's OK not to go to the temple," I mumbled.

God, how can I not believe you exist? I thanked Him silently.

My sisters, Sang-Won and Sang-Soon, came as soon as I called and picked me up in a compact Hyun-Dai. They lived only fifteen minutes away from each other, and Sang-Won and Mom lived in the same condominium complex, the Han-Kang Mansion.

"We were so excited you called. Mother said that she would get off early today and come straight home," Sang-Won said.

"What do you want to do? Isn't there anything you would like to eat? Something that you have been craving?" Sang-Soon said, sitting in the driver's seat of her car.

"I would just like to go to Mom's house and be with you two. I am still tired from jet-lag and from talking late every night with Ty's sisters."

"You sure have been spending a lot of time with your in-laws. We are so jealous of them," Sang-Won smiled impishly. "You are my little sister. You belong to us."

"I know, I know. You know, for the last ten years, I missed all of you so much and would have killed to see just one of you, any one of you, even for a day. And it's overwhelming to see all of you, such dear ones to me, all at the same time, I just don't even know what to say or anything," I said, dabbing my eyes.

"We missed you too. We did. Missed your wedding and missed your kids' births and all. Gosh, you, having babies all alone with none of us around. And when you were sick with morning sickness and craving dried corbina fish, I wished I could be a bird and fly out there." This time, Sang-Won dabbed her eyes.

"Wow! Sang-Won, crying? You know, she never cries. Did you know that?" Sang-Soon said teasingly, looking at me.

"I am not crying. I just felt pity for Sang-Eun. Why do we have to live so far apart? And having to cook and clean and care for two kids in diapers and everything."

"Well, that's what you do in America. Everyone does. Sang-Hie *unni*, too. Hey, Sang-Hie got to live here for a year a few years ago, huh?"

"Yeah, well, it turned out to be a mistake. Kil-Sup got his doctoral degree but it hurt their marriage to be apart that long. Sang-Hie taught music here at the foreign school and supported her kids so Kil-Sup could concentrate on studying," Sang-Soon sighed. "Her attempt not to have him burdened with supporting his family backfired. It still kills me to know that she is divorced."

"Hey, Sang-Won *unni*? Are you still an audacious tomboy?" I asked, slapping her arm endearingly.

"Never mind me. I want to know if you are still as sensitive and emotional. You cry easy, you laugh easy and you get mad easy, isn't it right? Are you still that way? And happy?"

"I know we were opposite. I guess I am still that way. And yeah, I am happy."

"Tell us, Sang-Eun-ah. What do you love about your husband, Dai-Heung so much? You two look so happy together," Sang-Soon said.

"Aeh, how do you measure happiness? I love my life as a mommy."

"Nora Noh cannot stop talking about you every time we see them. She thinks you are just wonderful."

"What else is she gonna say to you?"

"She doesn't have to lie. They invited us to their house and showed the gifts their mom was taking to you when you two were getting married. Nora Noh said that they didn't have enough for you, that you deserved more."

I smiled sheepishly and didn't respond. A part of me wished I was as happy as they thought I was, and another part of me hoped to become as happy. With all the attention and love I was getting from both families, I could almost see a glimpse of it happening.

44

"**B**ut you were always so happy! My youngest daughter!" Mom waved her arms in frustration.

"No, I wasn't. It hurt too much to talk about it, so I never did. I have kept you in the dark all these years. I am informing you now only because I have made up my mind. The decision is final. I am leaving him," I uttered in one breath to avoid giving her the chance to reproach me – to tell me that I should be more understanding and more obedient, and how it was a wife's duty to put up with it all.

"Mother, my mind is made up. Please just trust me; I will be a lot happier without him."

Convincing my mom that I wanted to leave my husband felt like more of an ordeal than the divorce itself.

"But dear, you have a model family," Mom insisted. "I never suspected that you were unhappy. Even when I lived with you when Michelle was born, when I first moved here from Korea, years ago. It just never occurred to me that you would – you were always acting happy."

"That's right, Mother, I was acting, I was just pretending," I screamed.

"*Eiigu*! You immature thing. What women are happily married? They all put up with their men, don't you know that?" This was a shock to me. I couldn't believe my mom actually said this.

"Well, I don't know about other women but I am not living this way anymore. Not now, not ever. My kids are now big enough to understand, and they are big enough to deal with it."

"But, but what about the money and the house and the kids' education and…"

"What about it, Mother? What about it?" My rage was taking over my power to speak. I had not uttered one word of my eloquently planned speech of how dysfunctional our family was, and how depressed I had been, and how controlling and demanding Ty was. How from the beginning we fought; even when we were dating, we fought week after week. I couldn't help it. Everything I did irritated him for reasons I didn't know.

The anger I was now directing toward my mother was on the verge of exploding. But Mom was only frustrated and bewildered, searching for the appropriate words to pour out on me, which would conclude that I was nothing but a spoiled, immature, and Americanized brat.

"I – I just don't even know what to say to you. I just know that you can't divorce him. What will you do with your kids, all three of them? And what will become of you and what will happen to your husband?" Mom sighed and covered her red face, plopping herself on a barstool in the kitchen.

I wanted to lash out at her. How could she be so blind and insensitive?

"Mother, all I want from you is enough love and trust in me to hear you tell me that I must know what I am doing," I pleaded in a soft voice. As always, I needed her approval. Now I needed to know that she would love me even as a divorcee. I wanted to be accepted and respected for my own decision.

"But you don't know what you are doing. You are just living in a dream world. The real world isn't perfect. Life isn't perfect. If there is anything that is perfect, it is your husband. Think about it. He doesn't drink, he doesn't gamble, he doesn't take a concubine, and he comes home at 5:30 every evening. And if you are a mature woman, you would know what a wonderful provider he is. Look at all the expensive stuff you have. Does he ever complain when you go around writing checks like there is no end?"

Her eyes fixed on me as she rattled off all the things I should be grateful for. She sounded pleased with her articulate admonishment.

My fury rose again. How could my mother of all people – a highly educated woman – be so stupid?

"I don't need your permission, you know. I only wanted to let you know my decision."

Mom said nothing.

"I will not come to you for help." I waited and then added, "I know I will be all right. All I know is that I would rather die than live with him. I really tried, Mother. I did. I stood by him at every stage, whether it was him changing jobs or taking an exam. I supported and encouraged him, told him how smart he was. When we moved down to Orange County, I told him it would be a good move for all of us. Yet I cried for a month because I missed my friends in Sherman Oaks. And Ty never even knew I was lonely. Even all those times he threw tantrums and told me what a horrible cook I was, I held everything in. I tried to be a good wife. You know, a person can only take so much when you get no respect and no recognition."

This was how my first talk with my mother about my divorce went. She had come to spend the 4th of July weekend with us. That night, after everyone went to bed, Mom held my hand across the kitchen table and with tearful eyes begged me to rethink my decision, if only for the kids' sake.

"Mother, I am doing this for their sake. I will not subject my kids to grow up in an environment that will make them fearful of men and lose their self-esteem."

"What could be so bad that you would sacrifice your kids and yourself like this?" Mom wiped her tears with her handkerchief, which was already soaked.

"I stopped loving him altogether. Living with him completely made me lose my identity. I am a decent human being with one mission:

to raise my kids to grow up to be decent human beings. You see, in America, a family is a unit where everyone loves, shares, and respects one another. My kids will grow up to be their own persons with self-respect. I am not raising them to eat well and get good grades and go to Ivy League schools to please me. Every part of their character should be nurtured. If a parent ignores their emotional needs, they will never learn to have self-respect. But of course you wouldn't know that. Did you ever respect me as a child? Did it ever even occur to you to respect me?" I shouted at Mom, letting out what had been bottled up since I was a child, being chased by books.

My mother did not respond. After a moment, she asked quietly, "Have you thought about how you are going to manage financially?"

I sighed. "Mom, in the state of California, all the assets have to be split in half in a divorce. I should have enough to live on. Plus, you know I have been going to graduate school. I was hoping to be able to teach at a junior college. But I realized how little they pay, so I am preparing to take a certification exam to be a court interpreter. And I will be playing in a string quartet on the weekend to make money if I need to. I am also getting a license for design work with Sharon as a partner. I can only freelance because I would like to be home when the kids come home from school. In any case, I am asking you to just trust me and be supportive."

None of this was in my prepared argument. I had not made plans to take the exam and I had not contacted musicians to organize a string quartet, though I did think about all of these possibilities as additional source of income.

Just two days earlier, Ty had threatened me that I would not have the luxury of being a stay-at-home mom anymore and that he was sorry not to ever have taught me how to live on an allotted budget. He further added, "And if you ever see a lawyer on your own or ask me to see a counselor, you will not get a penny from me."

I was amazed how little he knew me after fourteen years of living together as husband and wife. This confirmed, once again, that I was doing the right thing. Did he actually think I might change my mind for financial security? Did he really think that I would stay with him for fear that I might not be able to buy a pair of shoes or a blouse when I wanted to?

"Have you been going to church?" Out of desperation, mom questioned my Christianity.

"No, you know it's hard to go to church with Ty around. It's just hard when you live with a man who mocks Christians." I didn't want to tell Mom that I had grown to need Ty's approval in everything, including going to church. I also knew Mom was a lot more emotionally independent than me. All her life she had no problem doing anything she wanted, with or without my father's support.

"My kids go to church camps in the summer and they are in the Christmas program at church. I try to expose them to the church environment every chance we get. And let me tell you, when we move out, we will go to church every Sunday." At this, Mom's wrinkled eyes widened.

"What do you mean, when you move out?"

"Yes, we are moving out. Ty refuses to move out. He says that I should move out. It's OK. I am ready to move out to a one-bedroom apartment if I need to." I realized I said the wrong thing.

"When you moved into this house, you said that you found your house. You would never move again. That you would die here." Mom shook her head.

"I did, Mother. I died here. Mom, I pray every night and every morning. I think, actually, this is God's way of calling me. He knows I pray when I am in pain. And you know what? I feel so comforted when I pray, like he is giving me permission to leave Ty. And this is what's giving me courage to go through with it. Yes, I am scared, terribly scared. But I know it's the right thing to do. I feel like this huge weight was lifted off my shoulders. I am relieved and, in a way, excited to live the life God has intended for me." I swallowed.

Just when I thought I convinced my mother she said, "Maybe if you really pleaded, Ty might understand you and even go to church with you."

"No, mother. I will not plead to him. I am done with him. D-O-N-E. Done! And I will tell you something else. You are telling me all the wonderful things about him. How he doesn't drink, how he doesn't do this and that and how he makes good money. Well, let me tell you, you can be wonderful at nine factors out of ten and you would think that a person should be overlooked at that one shortcoming. Well let me tell you, Mother. That one thing can infect the whole life, the whole body, the whole marriage. Just like a person can have healthy arms, legs, shoulders and stomach, he appears to be perfectly healthy. But if he has a terribly weak heart and he can barely breathe, his days are numbered. He has nine parts of his body fully functional but one part, his heart, doesn't function. He needs to have a pacemaker put in hoping it would work for a few years anyway. Right? So don't tell me he is a wonderful person."

There was a long silence. Then she asked, "So what exactly is his bad heart?"

"Oh for God's sake, mother. He has a bad temper. He is controlling and demanding and he is self-centered. Every one of the chambers is diseased. When he doesn't like dinner, he throws his chopsticks and walks away from the table. Sometimes he will toss his napkin over the soup. He is a brat and he makes me fearful of him. I simply will not put up with that behavior anymore."

There was another long silence. The clock was ticking and I noticed it was approaching three a.m. I was exhausted, and Mom looked pitiful. She was probably blaming herself for being a failure as a mother because now she was going to have two divorced daughters.

When Sang-Hie got divorced, Mom said to me, "It is my fault. I should have taught her better. I should have taught her a long time ago that there is no 'me' in a marriage. And there is no 'us' either in a Korean marriage. There is only 'husband.'"

What bothered me more than this absurd notion was the fact that she was more concerned how she would look to her friends and relatives as a mother of two divorced daughters. It would be a mortifying embarrassment to her. Still, I was hoping she would begin to have a tiny bit of understanding.

"I suppose I do know what you mean. I see you being so careful and timid all the time like you are walking on thin ice. It always made me feel uncomfortable. But then I thought that was the American-style marriage."

"Hallelujah!" I sighed.

The next morning, as if our conversation had never taken place, Mom grabbed Terry and took her outside to the backyard.

"You mother say she and your father divorce. You go say her 'no divorce, no divorce.'"

"But Grandma, she knows what she is doing. Don't worry, Mommy will be fine," she said. Holding my mom's hands, Terry led her into the house. "Really, don't worry about her. She will be fine." I didn't know what made Terry so sure that I would be fine.

* * *

Years later, I became aware of Terry's keen sense of discernment about our family life when I read an essay she wrote for her English class, titled "A Family Dinner."

"A Family Dinner"

Working hard in the kitchen, my mother knew everything had to be perfect. Although it was just an ordinary night, this continuous worry and stress accompanied my mother with every meal, every night. Her petite body worked vigorously, tending to pots and bowls.

Our kitchen was very beautiful. It was a blue, white, and brick country kitchen. The stove and counter block in the center of the kitchen forced it to look less spacey and not as large as it actually was. Along the counter side of the block were four barstools where my sisters and I sat. We watched my mom cook as we worked on homework our elementary school teacher had assigned us. The darkness of the outside night air contrasting with the bright of the lit and alive kitchen made it appear very homey and warm. One of the French doors in the back of the kitchen was slightly ajar, allowing a subtle wind to drift in and barely chill our skins. Despite all of the food that was being cooked, the only vivid scent was of the steam coming up from a pot of boiling water. Mom always made her own beef broth.

The manly voice of a newscaster is disturbed by the clinking of silverware and pans. My father is watching the early evening news on the small kitchen TV. He is silently staring at it as if each word that trails from the newscaster's mouth holds the world's greatest importance. We all knew not to bother Daddy while he was watching the news. His usual poor posture was unnoticed. His thick black hair was well cut and brushed back. He has a very tan young looking face, which was tired from a long day. His bow-legged legs were linked at the ankles and he looked very comfortable. Not content and far from peaceful, but just there, waiting for his dinner to be served.

When dinner is ready Mom signals us to finish setting the table. We would usually split the job. One of us would do the silverware, one of us would do the water, and the youngest of us would supervise. My father still had not moved from his television viewing position, nor had he spoken one word to any of us.

As we all sat down to begin our meal, the nervousness, or actually the fear my mother felt was unknown to all of us. With each bite of food my father took, my mother waited silently for his screams of the meat being too salty, the soup too hot, the water too wet, and "Don't you know how to cook anyway?" His usual insults did not offend her, she heard it every night. She was never pathetic with her reactions to these remarks though, she was civil. She never apologized. She would usually not say a word, or if she was overly frustrated one day, she might defend herself, or throw back some kind of remark. Then my father would yell at her until she was crying as he would finish his meal, and then retire to the family room to finish watching the news. My sisters and I would remain silent and just finish eating.

After dinner my mom would do the dishes. We would help clear the table and being children we would complain about it. Then we would go upstairs to do our usual nighttime activities — homework, watch television, *bathe, or just play, then off to bed. Our loveable mother would tuck us in, talk with us, laugh with us, until we would fall asleep.*

We wouldn't go to bed upset or unhappy. We grew up thinking this was right. The usuality of this behavior between my parents became normal to us. Of course we became resentful and fearful of my father but we didn't know we were, and we didn't know this was wrong. Perhaps we were too immature to realize the difference between the parents of our friends who would help each other with making dinner and tell each other of their day and our own parents.

This was not a particular night, but a combination of all those nights that I remember from my childhood. Whether they were never in love or a couple who fell out of love, for over fifteen years, and the beginning of mine and my sisters' lives this was how we lived, and although we never knew that this was affecting us, that's what made the effect so bad. We were never aware something was wrong....

My heart ached again knowing what I had put my kids through. But the strangest thing was, as I read it, I felt terribly sorry for Ty. Terry could write about her feelings and share them with me. She dared to see the good and the bad of the situation and learn from it. But Ty had no one he could talk to or share with, except me. But now I was no longer a part of his life.

45

"Stealing Mom's furniture, huh?" the mover, with a mermaid tattoo on his upper arm, snickered as he wiped sweat off his forehead with his T-shirt sleeve. His eyes narrowed, he gave me a slimy smile. The mermaid moved like a hula dancer each time he flexed his muscles to pick up a piece of furniture.

"No," I answered, turning around. I had no desire to have a conversation with him. He was the last person I wanted to discuss my divorce with.

The wrought iron gate to my courtyard was wide open, as were the double doors into the foyer. As I stood at the front door looking out to the country French brick courtyard, loneliness and fear flooded through my whole body. My heart felt as if a ton of bricks were pressed on it, and I felt strangely void, even though there was excitement as well.

Hugging my arms tightly to cover the heaviness of my heart, I took a deep breath and examined every inch of the courtyard. The tall magnolia tree had a few blossoms. The wrought iron balcony off Terry's room upstairs was almost upon a big branch. I looked up at the leaded, beveled French doors to her room through the magnolia leaves.

I fell in love with this courtyard the first time I saw this house. It was so quiet and secluded; I could almost hear a lute playing in the slight breeze. Fallen magnolia leaves were rolling on the bricks. On the opposite end of the triangular yard were Michelle's bedroom window and the round bathroom's frosted glass. The plain blue drapes on her window were drawn and the reflection of the fichus tree leaves danced across the courtyard. I remembered the day when the holly bushes beneath this window were covered with lipstick tubes, eye pencils, foundation, and everything else that had been on my makeup table. In a tantrum, Ty had swiped everything off my makeup table into the trash and flung the whole basket into the courtyard because he couldn't stand the perfume I was wearing. "I should have left the asshole right then," I mumbled.

I shuddered and then turned to continue instructing the movers.

"All of the furniture in the family room goes," I said. "The living room furniture stays, including the piano. Load only the sealed boxes into the truck. "We," I pointed to my friends, Betty and Sharon, "will move the open boxes."

The new house my girls and I were moving to was only a few blocks away. Sharon and Betty had been helping all morning by moving most of my wardrobe, valuables, and dishes. They'd just come back for another load when Betty explained she had a thing against putting dogs in her car, and asked me if there was anything else she could do to help.

"Do you want to run down to Mervyn's and get me a tea kettle?" I asked.

"A tea kettle? Sure, but what for?"

"Well, I am taking the microwave and Ty heats water in the microwave for his instant coffee every day. So, I kind of want to leave a tea kettle so he will have something to boil water."

"You're worried about that? Are you serious?" Betty said.

"Yeah, I am," I said. "He's going to come home to an empty house and I want him to at least be able to have coffee. I'm leaving him the everyday china and pots and pans so the kitchen stays intact. You know how picky he is with food."

"All right. I'll be right back. But don't send me to a Korean market to get his dinner. I won't do it," she said.

"It's the abused wife's syndrome," I apologized, swallowing in disbelief that I'd actually made a remark about my marriage. I had kept silent to nearly all of my friends for as long as we'd had problems, which started shortly after the honeymoon.

"Mental and verbal abuses are the worst," I added. Betty and Sharon didn't respond to that, and I was glad.

I told the movers to take the blue canopy bed in Michelle's room. Then I pointed to the master bedroom.

"Everything in this room stays," I said.

It had been two years since I slept in the same room with Ty. There was a time when I'd loved everything, from the cherry wood headboard, to the lounge chair in matching blue floral polished cotton, to the bedspread and the gleaming blue silk moire wall coverings. But now I couldn't care less.

"He can have the whole fucking thing," I mumbled under my breath.

Two years prior, I left a note on the kitchen counter informing Ty where we would be so he couldn't claim I was kidnapping the kids. I'd packed a few things and told the girls to do the same, and we went to my friend Sonja's house until I could find a place for us to stay.

Ty and I talked of divorce but nothing was ever done, so I decided to physically remove myself in order to start some kind of procedure. When I dropped the kids off at Sonja's, I went to see a friend who was a divorce attorney. When Ty came home and found my note he called me at Sonja's and demanded that I send the kids home, knowing full well that I wouldn't send just the kids back. My attorney friend, John suggested that we go back, but live upstairs in a separate living arrangement.

The staircase off the kitchen led upstairs over the garage, completely away from the main house. It was the builder's brilliant idea to create a room for in-laws or an older kid's wing. He probably never expected it to be a wing for a separated spouse.

Kimmy and Michelle traded their rooms so Michelle, who was the youngest, could be close to me upstairs. I slept in Michelle's room and in the mornings after Ty went to work, I came downstairs to shower and get dressed.

The girls did their homework at the kitchen counter watching me cook dinner every night, and we laughed and giggled upstairs in the evening. Downstairs, Ty watched the news, ball games, made stock charts or watched Wall Street Week, and went to bed.

Kimmy never seemed to mind walking down the long corridor to her room by Ty's downstairs master bedroom at bedtime. But, I always came down with her to tuck her in.

In preparation for moving out of the Bali Circle house, Terry and Kimmy had carefully packed all of their precious possessions. I noticed a box Terry had marked in large red letters: "Fragile, This side up." I knew it held her collection of little perfume bottles that she had once displayed on a shelf. I stroked the box back and forth lightly and told the movers to be careful with it.

My girls didn't wear perfume anymore since one night that we were on our way to a nice family dinner. Ty was unusually quiet; I had no way of telling what was bugging him. His choices of restaurants were usually limited to Korean, Chinese, or Italian, but on this particular day we were headed for El Torito in Newport Beach. He'd found a dish that he liked there by accident a few months before, grilled shrimp wrapped with bacon served over Spanish rice.

My daughters had come home from a day at the pool, showered, and we were off. Outwardly, we appeared perfectly happy. A beautiful house on the golf course, three lovely daughters enjoying country club life on a Saturday, and here we were, going out to dinner as a family.

The girls were quiet in the backseat and I turned around and smiled at all three of them. My precious babies! Terry smiled back with her mouth slightly open. Her long flowing wavy hair complemented her sweet smile. Kimmy tightened her arms on her knees and gave me a grin. Her cheeks were glowing like mahogany, as were her legs and arms, the perfect color to go with her straight silky black hair. Michelle waved, showing her dimples, and said, "Hi Mom."

This little exchange of smiles and loving eyes was my attempt to make them all feel at ease.

All four of us were saturated with tension in the car. *Maybe the market crashed or maybe he is tired*, I thought. *Maybe he's upset there is nothing good to eat anywhere or maybe he is just extremely busy at work. Or maybe there is no good reason.*

"How was swimming at the pool, girls?" I broke the silence.

"Good," all three answered.

"Michelle had two hotdogs, Mom," Kimmy snitched.

"That's ok. She is growing." I winked at Michelle.

"What do you mean she is growing? That's why she can't lose weight," Ty said, finally opening his mouth.

"It's so hard to put a little girl on a diet, Ty," I defended.

"No one said dieting is easy," Ty said, his squeaky voice elevating to a higher pitch. "Have you noticed how fat she is getting?"

"She will lose it when she gets older. It's still baby fat," I snapped at him.

This triggered him, and he screamed, "Are you wearing that horrible smelling perfume again, Sang? That stuff makes me nauseated. Shit!"

"I am not wearing any perfume," I said.

"Well, I smell the fucking thing! Are you telling me that I am smelling things?"

"Well, you might be smelling my body cream. But it's the same thing I have used for years," I said trying not to raise my voice. "And it doesn't smell horrible," I added.

"Dad, I'm wearing perfume," Kimmy said softly, frightened. "Maybe it's me."

"It smells like shit. I can't take it." Without saying another word, he crossed two lanes, got off the freeway and swerved around back toward the house.

"Take a shower and get rid of that smell," he growled at Kimmy as he parked the car in the garage.

I put my arm around Kimmy's shoulders and led her into the house. She looked at me pleadingly, and I gave her a smile and kissed her black hair.

Clenching my teeth, I brushed her wet hair for her after the second shower she'd taken within half an hour. I hated him. I wanted to scream. I wanted to cry. I wanted to leave him right then. Instead, I smiled at Kimmy and gave her another kiss.

"Terry, smell me now. Do I still smell like perfume?" Kimmy's face was full of fear. Terry sniffed all over her face and upper chest.

"Right here, right here," Terry said pointing at her sister's chest. "I can still smell it a little."

I took Michelle out to the backyard to chase Coco and Scooter while Kimmy took her third shower. It was all I could do to keep from sobbing. While Kimmy scrubbed her chest, Terry went through her perfume collection and wrapped each one individually with tissue paper before placing them back on the shelf. They looked like little wounded soldiers all bandaged up. When I questioned her, she said that she was afraid that her dad might smell them.

Suddenly, I felt relieved and excited to leave this awful place; the most beautiful house, with the most dreadful memories. At the new house, Terry would be able to display all her perfumes in her room and they wouldn't have to look like mummies.

Why did it take me so long to leave him?

"You can have the fucking house!" I mumbled again.

"What about these chairs in the living room?" the mermaid arm hollered as he pulled up his pants. No matter how often he pulled them up, his crack showed every time he bent over. Real classy little creep, he was.

"For the second time, everything in the living room stays," I spat out without looking at him.

I took a last walk through the front door to the magnificent foyer of dark parquet wood. Then I walked to the living room to take in the wide-open view of the fairway. I knew I wouldn't miss any of this. The moving truck was loaded. My Mercedes wagon was filled with boxes of fine china and crystal; Coco and Scooter lay between the boxes. When I got to my new home, a two-story colonial house, Sharon was turning the last screw to replace the front doorknobs. She'd opened all the windows to air out the smell of new carpet and stocked the refrigerator with milk and diet Pepsi. The aroma of the freshly brewed coffee was inviting, as was the box of a dozen old-fashioned buttermilk-glazed donuts. My eyes welled up.

"How did you find the time to do all of this and make the trips between the two houses?" I asked.

"It was easy," she said. "I went to the hardware store, then swung by Winchell's and Von's all in one trip. You know, we gotta have coffee."

I looked at the new front doorknobs, wondering.

"They were so rusty and oxidized," Sharon said. "That was one thing I knew how to do. I just replaced them at my house."

By the time the girls came home, all three rooms looked orderly with their own furniture and the beds were made. Terry and Kimmy had a few curious friends following them and I welcomed all of them with donuts. The girls went upstairs to unpack their boxes and I heard lots of laughing and screaming with excitement.

Later, I noticed Kimmy had hung her bulletin board and pinned Ricky Schroeder's picture in the middle of it. All around Ricky Schroeder, she hung awards, schedules and reminders of different activities. Her days were full from being the student body president, doing charity work, and playing on the tennis team.

Terry's room had an alcove off one wall where I placed her bed and promised to make curtains to tie back so she would feel like she was a princess. I watched as she talked on the phone, rearranging her perfume bottles on the dresser on a mirrored tray. She placed Coco's picture on her night table and then plopped herself on the floor, twisting the phone cord with one hand. She sounded so happy that I thought to myself that I would go easy on their phone privileges as long as they brought decent grades home.

Michelle's room was next to my bedroom and had a built-in desk along one wall. She had lined up books all the way from one end of the wall to the other, and then put stuffed animals in front of them. I came in just as she was putting a Hello Kitty doll on her pillow while humming "Tomorrow" from the musical *Annie*.

"Do you need help? Mich?" I asked.

"No, I'm almost done. I like this house, Mom."

Looking at her dimples, I hugged her tightly. I was overwhelmingly comforted and satisfied. I was home. Even though it might be called a broken home, I did not feel shattered. I was free to nurture and love my three daughters, Terry, Kimmy, and Michelle, my true pearls.

46

Michelle looked forward to our Friday night dinners at Coco's when Terry and Kimmy each went out with their own group of friends. Michelle would chomp on her huge hamburger and tell me all about how much she wanted to be on the stage singing and dancing. Sometimes she would hash out girlish squabbles that happened at school. "Such immature girls, they are," she always said. Then, without fail, she would ask me to tell her a story about my childhood. I told her little bits about my mother, my father, and about the Korean War. I told her how beautiful she was and that I would rather hear about her. These Friday nights became precious memories to us, just like the weekly picnics she and I used to have when she was four years old, in the backyard watching the golfers go by every Thursday. She would munch on a peanut butter and jelly sandwich, sometimes two. She didn't talk much then, just twirled her body around holding a sandwich, doing fancy choreographed dances.

Even though the girls and I had moved out, there was nothing legal about our separation. Ty and I still had a joint checking account and used the same credit cards. Ty never questioned any of my spending but I was aware that the bills went to him, enabling him to monitor all of my expenses.

Though I wanted to be free from Ty, I dreaded facing the divorce procedure, which always came with loud yelling and screaming. It was just as easy to stay separated. I was just thankful to live independently without having to deal with him in the same house, and avoid facing the indefinite financial outcome of a divorce settlement.

Every Saturday morning, I would sit by the kitchen window with my coffee and go over my finances, balancing "credits and debits" for the next decade or so. Because I didn't know what might trigger Ty to change his mind regarding the rough division of assets, I decided to look for income possibilities.

Prospects were slim, as my first priority was to be home when the girls came home from school. I also wanted to pick them up from school myself. I contacted a few musicians in the area and organized a string quartet group. Once I dusted my cello off and rebuilt my callouses, we were ready to perform at wedding receptions and special banquets. And it was usually over a couple of hours on the weekend. I collected a few easy string quartet scores of popular wedding music like the Bach's "Jesu, Joy of Man's Desiring" or the Smetana's "Moldau," and we rehearsed for a couple of hours once a job was booked. The most requested piece at the time was the Pachelbel's "Canon in D."

Over coffee, Sharon and I often exchanged ideas about decorating and designing homes while her daughter Amy and my Kimmy were in school. Sharon's husband Bill, a prominent attorney, always supported her ideas and was willing to supply the financial means for her to experiment and be creative, whereas Ty generally opposed most of my ideas.

One day, while sitting in the kitchen at my new house having coffee, Sharon and I decided we'd form a partnership and start a decorating company. Acquiring a license was easy. All we had to do was go down to city hall and apply for it; then we would need to make a public announcement of the company by posting a fictitious name in the paper. We knew finding clients would take time, but in the meantime, we kept busy by taking classes at a local community college and experimenting with different ideas in our own homes. As licensed decorators, we were able to purchase home furnishings at wholesale prices, which was already an advantage.

However, being a court interpreter still seemed like a steadier income. The Korean population in Orange County was growing exponentially and their legal problems followed – from petty theft, to felony assault with a deadly weapon, to divorce. There was a huge demand for certified Korean interpreters. I started going to the courthouse to observe Spanish interpreters and get accustomed to the system. There were very few Korean interpreters to watch at the time and even fewer certified ones. I studied and memorized court terminology, and when two certified U.N. Korean interpreters came from San Francisco to hold the exam, I drove to Los Angeles to take it.

There were only a few Koreans taking the test, and we were placed in separate rooms. When my name was called, a clerk led me to a small room where the two test administrators sat at a round table. My heart started beating quickly and my mouth dried. Any kind of test had become bitter and scary ever since my junior high entrance exam.

For the first part of the exam, the testers presented a document written in Korean. I took a deep breath and translated it into English with ease. For the next part of the exam, they played a recording of a cross examination in a civil case. I was to interpret Korean into English and vice versa, consecutively, after each person spoke. For the last component of the exam, they played the judge's admonishment to jurors before they were to deliberate. The judge's voice was unvaried and his speech was long. I was to interpret this part of the exam simultaneously, as I listened to the speech through the headset. I was extremely nervous and having the giant earpieces over both ears seemed to block my alertness.

"I am sorry, I am having a hard time interpreting as I listen through the headset. I need to hear my voice to interpret. Anyway, could it be played through the speaker?" I asked, timidly but politely.

"But this is the way we present the tests," the female assessor said.

"But this isn't the way a court interpreter would listen to the judge's speech, is it? through a headset?"

"You are right. No problem. Let's just take that off your ears," the male tester quickly intercepted.

When I finished the long speech, I sighed and they both smiled at me. Unlike consecutive interpreting, simultaneous interpreting took more skill because the word order in Korean sentences is the exact opposite of English. In simultaneous interpreting, I had to say, for example, "The documents were brought by me," instead of, "I brought the documents." When interpreted verbatim in Korean it would be said, "I documents brought." I had to start talking as soon as each word was spoken. Waiting until the sentence was over would cause me to get behind and miss an important part of the sentence.

A month after the exam, I received a certification letter from Sacramento informing me that I had passed both parts of administrative hearing and court interpreting successfully.

In a matter of a few months living at my new house I had accomplished an assortment of industrial freelance opportunities. My phone started ringing for court cases as well as arbitrations and depositions in law offices. Jobs were done early enough that I was home by the time the girls came home from school.

Most of the court cases were simple arraignments. Preliminary hearings took concentration on my part so that I didn't miss a word, and trials were the hardest work. My job as an interpreter was to make sure the person I was interpreting for would understand everything that was said in the courtroom as if there was no language barrier. While a counsel and a prosecutor exchanged their cross-examinations and arguments in turn, I had to speak non-stop. No matter who spoke, I had to interpret.

I interpreted two to three days a week at different courts in Orange County. I did an equal amount of depositions in law offices. I packed my briefcase with a notepad and a small law dictionary; I dressed in a suit with high heels like a businesswoman.

Working as a court interpreter, I encountered many kinds of Koreans I had not faced before. A businessman in an Armani suit came, caught for bribing a city official to operate a massage parlor, which was in fact a brothel. I felt no compassion for him when he was sentenced to a few years, but as a fellow Korean, I was ashamed. I interpreted for a young woman who had become a kleptomaniac from the loneliness of living in a foreign country. She came to three different courts for getting caught at three different locations. Her husband owned a large company and she was wearing Gucci shoes.

"I don't know I am stealing. When I come home I find things in my purse," she murmured to me during the arraignment. Neither she nor her husband ever looked up and never looked at the attorney's face. As I interpreted, my heart went out to her. I felt her pain. She could have been any Korean woman who had ever felt unbearably lonely and lost.

One day my agent called me for a job. "This is a million-dollar case, Sang. You have to go. Please. They are desperate, and the attorneys only want a certified interpreter." When I said I had a conflict, she insisted.

"What is the case about?" I asked.

"Divorce dissolution."

"Oh, great. I have to watch a husband and wife fight? Who am I interpreting for? Wife or husband?"

"I am not sure. Husband, I think."

When I got to the fancy glass penthouse office, the court reporter was already there waiting.

"Hi, I am the interpreter. My name is Sang," I introduced myself.

"I am Karen. Ready for the battle?"

"Is this a continuance for you?" I asked, and she nodded, rolling her eyes.

"I don't care. I am just an interpreter."

"It's just this is my fifth divorce disso this week. That's all."

When everyone sat around the oval conference table, the deposing attorney introduced himself to me, "The name is Randy Richardson," and introduced me to the wife's Korean attorney, Mr. Kim. I was interpreting for the wife, a mousy little woman who was carrying a Louis Vuitton purse and wearing a starched white linen blouse and an ankle-length skirt.

"Let me ask you this first: Are you certified?" her attorney asked me in a strong Korean accent.

"Yes, I am. Both in court trial and administrative hearing," I answered smiling, ignoring his rudeness.

"Yeah, she is. I made sure with the agent," Richardson cut in.

"Let me tell you. That doesn't mean anything. I seen lots of certified ones. And they are terrible."

"Well, let's start." Richardson ignored him, and the stenographer winked at me as if to say, "*What a jerk.*"

About half an hour into the questions, Richardson asked Kim to repeat his comment about his client's answer, that he didn't quite understand what he was saying.

"Let me tell you. I am really irritated. If this goes on, I might just walk out of here." Kim waved his arm toward the door. No one knew what he was referring to.

"Do you want to? Or do you want to continue?" Richardson calmly asked.

"Let's just go on," Kim spat out, and they went on.

"No, no, no, no, no. What are you talking about?" This time Kim's interruption was directed to me. "That's not what she said."

"Wait just a second, Mr. Kim. You know and I know what she just said. I am interpreting exactly what she said. If you don't like your client's answer, you need to instruct her more clearly. You do not blame me for it," I said, looking straight at him.

"All I am saying is that she didn't say it came from his family."

"And all I am saying is that's exactly what she said." I stood up. "From the moment you saw me you were rude and combative. In fact, I am going to dismiss myself. I am a good interpreter and will not subject myself to this kind of treatment. Do I need this?" I packed up my notes.

"I was not rude. I just asked if you were certified? There's nothing wrong with asking that?"

"Did I ask you if you passed the bar? Oh, never mind. This is silly. I am done here," I turned to Richardson. "Mr. Richardson, I am sorry this is happening. I will make sure my agency will waive the charges. I certainly won't expect to be paid."

I walked out of the building and once I got in the car, I sobbed all the way home.

It made me sad to know the little woman was being screwed by her devious husband who was manipulating American divorce laws by insisting that all of their assets were his inheritance from his deceased parents, who at one time were wealthy landowners in North Korea before Korea was divided. I knew that the wife's attorney had to know it was impossible to keep assets from the North. It depressed and saddened me to see the woman depended her life on such an incompetent attorney, but as an interpreter, there was nothing I could do to help or advise her. I stormed out for my own pride.

All in all, interpreting was the perfect job for me. There was some reading but not enough to inflame my eyes. I also felt in a vague sense that I was contributing to the Korean community. When a scared and desperate person pleaded with me about his situation, I would advocate for them with their attorney, asking him to lend an ear for some extra knowledge of Korean culture.

Once, a father who held two jobs working as a laborer fourteen hours a day was arrested for hitting his teenage daughter, who was about to flunk out of school. He had been in jail for a month and could not find anyone to defend him. I told the attorney that we have a saying in Korea, "Give an extra rice cake to a child you don't care about and give a whipping to a child you do care about." I knew his spoiled child reported her own father out of resentment.

"Is the bruise on her leg still there?" I asked. "As long as there was no permanent physical mark, I would be willing to be his expert witness if you think he got caught in the legal system. Corporal punishment is very common in Korea. I mean, premeditated spanking is," I said to the attorney.

By the mid '90s, Los Angeles had a large Korea town along Olympic Boulevard and Orange County, on Garden Grove Boulevard. They both stretched for several miles, lined with Korean storefronts and restaurants. Many successful corporate businessmen, as well as many who hadn't quite made it in Korea, moved their families to America. For those unfortunate ones, it was still a dream to prosper in the land of opportunity. They owned dry cleaners, coffee shops, restaurants, karaoke bars and such. They learned barely enough English to operate businesses, but ended up buying homes next to American medical doctors. And their children grew up having their parents' goal drilled in their heads: going to an Ivy League school.

The possibilities were limitless in the land of opportunity.

47

I picked out half a dozen plump chicken wings from the pot and arranged a dinner plate with glazed carrots and white rice. I wrapped the plate tightly with foil so the juice from the chicken wings wouldn't run out. I've been told I make the best chicken wings.

"I'll be right back. And dinner will be served in fifteen minutes," I yelled from the bottom of the staircase.

"Where are you going?" Terry yelled back.

"Out. Will be back in a few."

My first stop was Conroy's flowers, where I bought a single red rose. I parked on the side street next to Dan's apartment building and took the shortcut to his unit on the third floor. I left the dinner plate at his doorstep and carefully placed the rose on top. I dashed down the stairs, afraid I might run into him. We had only been dating for a couple of months. I smiled with deep satisfaction, tingling all over; I had the overwhelming desire to cook for him every night.

Through the sheer white curtains of our kitchen window, the girls and I could see the neighbors strolling down the sidewalk for their after-dinner walks. People would often stop and admire the flowers that lined the brick path to our front door. I loved having a window by the table and loved hearing my girls talk as we sat around the glass table.

My daughters loved all the food I made. There were many things I couldn't make when we were living with their dad, because the dinner menu was limited to Asian food, and he insisted that each evening meal begin with a homemade soup.

Now that we were on our own, I could make curry rice, tacos, New Year's Eve chili with carrots, pan-fried hamburgers, spaghetti, and, like tonight, chicken wings. Sometimes I would even make deep-fried ice cream for dessert.

Our dinner conversations were lively and full of laughter.

"I could have died today. I saw John Drake and he smiled at me. Do you think he likes me?" Terry was not shy about a senior she had a crush on.

"Mom, he really is cute. Actually, I think he likes *me*," Kimmy said and giggled. "I wonder who he is taking to the prom. When I am ready to go to the prom he will have graduated. How is he going to ask me?" She giggled again.

"Does he even know you, Kimmy?" Michelle rolled her eyes as she scraped mounds of chicken bones into the trash. "I can't believe you both have a crush on him. I don't even think he is that cute."

The phone rang and Coco and Scooter, who sat in the garage by the kitchen door, turned their heads toward the phone. They were not allowed in the house, as they were never properly potty-trained. But we always left the kitchen door open so the dogs would feel like part of the family. I picked up the phone and Terry and Kimmy narrowed their eyes, letting me know that we weren't supposed to answer the phone during dinner. I ignored their looks, saying it was important.

"I didn't leave any dinner. It wasn't me," I laughed.

"I hope it was you. In fact, I know it was you. The soy-sauce base was a dead giveaway," Dan laughed.

"Well, I guess you are right. Who else would make that?" I was still looking at the kids, trying to sound casual.

"Is this a trick question?" From his laugh, I felt a warm intimacy. I wished I could see him. Maybe I would drive over after dinner. *But what would I tell the kids? Where would I tell them I was going? No, I shouldn't go. Try to keep a little distance*, I thought. I hung up the phone, aware of my daughters' watchful eyes. I tried to get involved in the dinner conversation but I only heard half of what the girls were saying.

The first time I went out on a date after Ty and I separated, I came home with my date and all three girls were sitting on the top step of the staircase, with their chins resting on their palms.

"Isn't it a little late, young lady?" All three narrowed their eyes.

"It's – uh – it's not even midnight," I stammered. And the guy never called again.

Dan was different. After our second date, he wanted to take the girls out to dinner with us. Ty and I used to play couples' tennis at the same club as Dan and his ex-wife before we were both divorced. My daughters knew Dan from hanging out at the tennis lounge after their tennis lessons.

He was a good listener and always had something interesting to contribute to their conversations. He knew more trivia than anyone I knew. Pretty soon, the girls started saving their questions about cars, airplanes, or even how long they should wait for the clear beach weather, for Dan when he came over. Dan loved to barbeque in our backyard with the girls, and he even cranked up the old-fashioned ice cream maker.

"I brought plenty of food, ribs, tri tip, and corn on the cob. So if anyone wants to invite friends, the more the merrier. The only rule is, everyone has to take turns cranking the ice cream maker," said Dan.

"Can Danny and Amy come and eat with us?" Michelle asked.

"Oh, my kids? They think they are too old to hang around the cheerleaders on the weekend. That's what happens when your kids get old." Dan laughed playfully. "Actually they are at the river this weekend with their friends. Maybe the next time."

Before he finished his sentence, all three girls trampled upstairs and fought over the phone to invite their friends. My daughters loved having him around, and Dan loved inviting the girls out to dinner on weekends before the two of us went out to movies.

But despite all their fondness for Dan, I realized that my dating affected them emotionally. I didn't realize it until one day when Terry wrote me a letter after she and I had an argument.

"...It hurt me to see that you just wanted to get out of here and go out with Dan....I am also sorry that I said I hated you. You know that I don't. I love you more than anything in the world. I won't ever say it again to you....I guess it's just hard to share your love with Dan. I like Dan a lot and I wouldn't want you to see anyone else. It's just never been like this before and I guess it finally hit me. I promise I will try to be more understanding. I love you. Love always, Terry."

I cried and thanked Terry for being honest and open about her feelings. I promised her I could never separate them from me no matter how much I was in love with anyone. I also promised her that they would always come first. I wouldn't give my soul to anyone without their approval.

More and more, I appreciated all the little things Dan did for me, like leaving the air conditioner on while he stopped at the ATM. I liked the way he always remembered my favorite salad dressing and ordered for me at restaurants. He never neglected to open the car door or ask what I would like to do. On my birthday, he came to pick me up all dressed up in a suit. Sometimes, he would show up at the tennis court on my regular Thursday night game just to surprise me. And most of all, my kids adored him.

Dan appreciated the kind of mom I was. I got involved in all of their activities, volunteered at their schools, and always drove their friends when they went to roller skating parties. He understood my girls' importance to me and placed them at the same level of importance in his life. In turn, my girls looked forward to his visits and called him freely. When Coco and Scooter got in a fight with possum, they called Dan to save the dogs. Terry called him to teach her how to drive a stick shift, knowing he was patient.

Marriage was not a priority for Dan or me when we started dating, but after six months, being united in marriage seemed right to us.

"I feel like I was jipped," Dan said one day, stroking my hair. "Why didn't I meet you twenty years ago?" I felt a knot in my throat.

"I used to play football in high school, thinking, 'One day, I will marry a little cellist from Korea,'" he laughed.

"And I grew up in Korea thinking, 'One day when I go to America, I will marry a Polish-American man with a big nose.'" We both laughed.

Before we could get engaged, however, there was much that needed to be worked out. My divorce procedure hadn't even started. My mother showed an obvious reluctance about me dating a "foreigner." While my daughters liked Dan, I didn't know how they would accept him as the head of the household and how they would accept their mom as someone other than their father's wife.

But, being with Dan was like coming home. He always made me feel comfortable and special. And when he came over, the laughter filled the house and my daughters began to show their genuine desire to be around him. I knew then Dan was the kind of Dad my daughters longed to have and I also began to believe he was the man God had blessed me and my daughters with.

48

Michelle and I followed the crowd into the subway. I held a half-open city map in one hand and clutched the shoulder strap of my purse in another. We sat next to a young woman whose eyes were fixed on the fashion magazine spread on her lap. Her leather backpack was on the floor against her ankle. Her ankles were well protected with gathered wool socks over ballet sweats, the same kind Michelle wore after her dance rehearsals. Half of her hands were covered by her long sleeves. Her hair was pulled back and intertwined sloppily with a Burberry cashmere scarf over a large gray chenille sweater. I felt as if I was looking at a caricature on the cover of *The New Yorker* magazine.

New York is still the most exciting town, I thought to myself, staring at her.

"Mom, stop staring at her," Michelle whispered, nudging on my back. "You are acting like a tourist."

"I am not," I said.

"Look at you, Mother. You've got a map in your hand wide open and look around. Do you see anyone in a bright red coat? You've got a huge sign all over you saying 'I am a tourist.'" Michelle laughed and rolled her eyes. This was her first trip to N.Y. since she was three years old, but she was already an expert on New York fashion.

Michelle had applied to NYU's Tisch School of performing arts as an acting major and I was accompanying her on her audition trip. She finished the audition the day before, and we were now on our way to visit my high school friend, Myung-Soon on West End Avenue—wherever that was—and we decided we would take the subway like all the other New Yorkers.

Michelle and I argued back and forth, each insisting on our own conjectured route. The fact is, neither of us knew where we are supposed to get off, and one stop seemed as good as another.

At each stop, a few people got off and a few more came on board. A couple of men in business suits, rarely seen in California anymore, were engrossed in business magazines and newspapers. No one seemed to care about our perplexity with the subway system or my bright red coat.

The New Yorker caricature stood up, gathered her magazine, her backpack, and flung one end of her scarf behind her. She dropped her head slightly to the side, looking tired, but showed no expression in her face. Michelle caught me staring at her again and shook her head.

As soon as she got off, I said to Michelle, "Do you think she is a dance major? Going to college? Maybe she is coming home from a studio."

"I don't know, Mother. Who knows? And who cares? You are just so weird." Michelle shook her head again giving me the same mischievous smile she would give a five-year-old. I shrugged my shoulders and told her that she should carry energy bars in her backpack when she goes to dance or to acting studio.

"I have to tell you these things when you are so far away. It's not like your sisters who went to college in Los Angeles. I am going to worry about you knowing I can't just drive up with a package in an afternoon."

The subway arrived at the final destination and everyone got off. "I think we are lost. We'd better get back on the subway and go back to where the hotel is. Or just grab a cab and forget this nonsense of exploring the city on foot," I mumbled, climbing the stairs to the street level.

As we came up into the bright daylight from underground, I saw a huge sign ahead of us that read, "East Harlem Swap Meet." My heart sank. We took the wrong subway and went northeast rather than northwest. We were right in the middle of Harlem. I pulled Michelle's arm through mine, told her to stay close, and walked fast across the street to catch the subway to the opposite direction. I turned my ring around on my left hand so the diamond would be hidden inside my hand and shoved my hand deep in my pocket to cover my watch.

Unlike busy midtown where our hotel was, the streets in Harlem were bleak and eerie. The few seconds we spent waiting for a green light seemed like an eternity. I kept quiet and didn't look at Michelle so as not to frighten her more. I didn't know if she was as scared as I was. I didn't even know if Michelle had ever heard of Harlem. To Michelle, I was an unsophisticated worrier and she--a typical nineteen-year-old--knew everything. But then, she may be right, I didn't actually know if we should be scared.

I still felt responsible for putting us in this predicament, just like the time I ended up in the middle of Watts in my brand-new BMW because I missed the turn off Harbor Freeway. That's when Dan installed a compass in my car and told me never to go south on the surface roads if I ever got lost in L.A.

We were still waiting for the signal to change when a black stretch limo with a dent on one side stopped in front of us and three tall black men in black suits and ties jumped out. A chill whipped through my body and my heart started pumping so fast I could hear it in my head. I clutched Michelle's arm tightly, sped around the broken taillight of the limo, and crossed the street as quickly as our little steps would carry us. I whispered, "Don't look. Just keep walking fast." We never turned to see what the men were doing. We ran for out lives all the way to the southbound subway.

Still clutching Michelle's arm, I sat, gasping, and gaped at her flushed red face.

"What just happened? Boy, that was close." I sighed.

"Those guys were probably minding their own business. I think you overreacted, Mom," Michelle said calmly. I unwillingly nodded my head.

When we came to our hotel room, Michelle admitted that she was just as scared as I was. I made her promise me never to take the same line all the way again. I refrained from the urge to go on for a few more minutes with guidelines about living in New York.

I called Myung-Soon and apologized for being late and told her that we would take a cab this time. The cab dropped us in front of a light gray edifice that resembled an old office building. Their apartment was right off the elevator on the second floor. At the first knock Myung-Soon opened the door and screamed with excitement.

"Sang-Eun-ah! Oh my God! How long has it been? How long? Over thirty-five years, maybe?" She kept hugging me and forgot her husband standing behind her.

"You must be Albin. A violinist, right?" I extended my hand to shake his hand.

"That's right. And you must be Sang-Uun, A cellist, right?" We both laughed.

"Well, I used to be anyway," I said, glancing around their apartment.

Their apartment was small and plain but airy and pleasant. Both the living room and the kitchen were in full view from the front door. An Indian-patterned blanket was thrown on the couch in the living room. Books, unopened mail, sheet music, and pencils were stacked on a table next to an armchair across the couch. The wall-to-wall bookcase behind the armchair was filled with sheet music. It could have been a college kid's den. I looked at Michelle to see her reaction, but she was already in a deep conversation with Albin. Michelle had never been one to feel socially uneasy with older generations.

"So, you both play in the New Jersey Symphony?" I asked.

"Oh my gosh! Yes, that's all we do. And that's all we know."

It was a world that was so foreign to me now. I felt a touch of envy.

"Do you still practice quite a bit?"

"We do, because we perform a lot of modern music. And it requires practice."

"Are you the principal cellist?" I asked.

"No, are you kidding me? Who cares where I sit?"

"Really?" I smiled nonchalantly.

"What about you? Do you ever play?" I shook my head.

"You should. Even half an hour a day just so you don't lose it. Your techniques were so amazing. It's a shame." Myung-Soon and I were rivals growing up. Saying that I had great techniques would be the last thing she would have admitted when we were in high school.

"Trust me. I lost it all a long time ago," I said. "You know, the brown spot in the middle of your chest from playing the cello? Disappeared years ago. My fingers are soft. No more callouses – and my nails are manicured. I even wear my wedding ring in my left hand." I shrugged my shoulders to show I didn't care.

It was approaching dinnertime and Myung-Soon and Albin took us out to a nearby Chinese restaurant. Across the table, Myung-Soon and I and Albin and Michelle got into two different conversations. As Myung-Soon and I reminisced about high school days, we gradually switched to Korean.

"Do you remember how we fought over seats in the orchestra?" I asked.

"Of course I do. Can you believe we were that juvenile? Why was it so important? I remember one time at the amphitheater, you got there before me and claimed the first seat by leaning your cello on the chair and went to the bathroom. While you were gone I put a chair outside of yours, making my chair the principal's seat. I can still see your face when you came back from the bathroom." She giggled and we both laughed, genuinely happy to see each other.

"Did you ever play Beethoven's Triple Concerto?" I asked. That was one piece I always wanted to play but never had an opportunity.

"The cello part in that piece is pretty tough. It's not an easy piece," she said, not answering my question.

"I loved it. It is the most Beethovenesque piece to me," I said softly. She didn't respond.

I wanted to tell her that I had become an important figure to my three daughters. Each one had hugely different personality, yet they interlaced with each other in their love. They are content with what they each possess, yet they look for each other for completion. Like the Beethoven Triple Concerto, they ask, answer, compare, and advice loudly and softly. They have grown and still grow in perfect harmony. And when they feel lost, they look for me, the orchestral part. They are more precious to me than the string of notes I used to deliver and submerge myself into. But I didn't tell her, because I knew it would bore her, or she wouldn't understand. They never had any children, nor had a desire to.

"Do you go to church?" Myung-Soon asked.

"I do. Do you?"

"No. It's just that I see so many fanatical Korean Christians, you know? You are not that way, are you?"

"What way? I do walk with Jesus and read the Bible every day."

"Oh, but you don't go around preaching all the time, do you? You don't look like a Bible beater. I think that's better."

I wanted to ask her, "Better than what?" but I changed the subject.

"We sure had a good time when we were young, didn't we?"

"We did. And when I came to visit you in Los Angeles – going to Disneyland with Ty – gosh, how time flies. It's so good to see you so happy in your new marriage." She smiled.

"We each married twice," she said nonchalantly. "Hey, do you ever hear from your old boyfriend Eunseong? You know, Kang Hyo's friend?"

"I have no contact with him. I heard he became a conductor. Who told me that? I think my sister did. Speaking of Hyo, what happened to him?"

"Oh, he became big. He teaches at Juilliard. He is pretty popular. Good old days – those days when we were all music students, thinking we knew the destiny of our lives. We live so differently now. Can you imagine?" She shook her head.

It took less than half an hour for us to feel like a couple of teenagers again. We grew up in the same neighborhood and went to the same elementary school. We both failed junior high school, which motivated us to play the cello. We dreamed the same dreams. But our current lives couldn't be farther apart. A few decades of separation limited our conversation to only reminiscing about the olden days. There was nothing else we had in common, other than each of us being married to a Caucasian. Back in the day when we were both in love with Gregory Peck after seeing "Guns of Navarron," we had wondered what it would have been like to marry an American. It was such a far-fetched idea we could not even imagine.

Myung-Soon was always a little more worldly and a little more sophisticated than the rest of us. She dated older men when the rest of us longed for uniformed high school boys. I wanted to ask her if she remembers the beautiful little park in Sung-Book-Dong where she had her first kiss. But I didn't ask any of these things. She seemed so close yet so distant. We were no longer connected by anything but memories.

Reuniting with her, even for a short while, brought back many fond memories from my teenage years. But I felt somber like I had just lost a valuable that was so precious and dear to me. I felt all alone – like I didn't belong anywhere.

Coming back to our hotel at sunset, my heartbreak grew deeper and deeper. I missed those teenage days. I missed the streets of Seoul, the dusts, the smell, going to concerts on the bus, my house. I missed all those days I would never have again.

Days inundated with thoughts of music. No matter what I did or thought, it was related to the music. The amazing intricacies of life and the purist joy we felt from the brilliant harmonization and dynamics of concertos, piano trios, Bach suites, romantic pieces of Saint-Saens, Lalo, Tchaikovsky trios – all of which were never stingy about capitalizing the enchanted energy of the mysterious cello. I was no longer a part of it. I was an alien now. I had grown old.

In the cab home I looked at Michelle's dimple and smiled. "Do you think I should play the cello again?"

49

"What happened to the little trails between the trees?" I said. "This place is nothing like what I remember. It lost its charm." Through the window of my sister's Hyundai SUV, I looked at the stone walls bordering the winding road to Nam-San. "Are you sure you know where you are going?"

This was my fifth trip to Korea since I left thirty-eight years earlier. My sister, Sang-Won was driving me to the restaurant on the top of Nam-San hill, where I was to meet Eunseong, my old college boyfriend.

The road to Nam-San was nicely paved but had lost its quaintness. Whatever happened to the little dirt paths with stepping stones, linked together by the randomly growing clovers?

"Wow, it's changed," I whispered to myself. *Whatever happened to the poplar trees on both sides that used to canopy the paths and nearly block the sky?*

As a young college girl, coming up here was the most romantic rendezvous – like Mulholland Drive for kids in Los Angeles. We didn't have cars, so we didn't park, but we held hands and enjoyed hours of romantic walks. At night, from the top of the hill, we could see the magnificent city lights that looked as though the stars were sprinkled across Seoul.

In high school, we were not allowed to date or go to the movies. When we went out, we were not allowed to wear anything but our school uniforms. But dating and sneaking into the movie theaters in regular clothes gave me a thrill; I was doing something forbidden. I was never able to understand why we had to suppress our feelings anyway, so I went right ahead with romantic pursuits every chance I got.

When it came to romance, the "good kids" used to wait to graduate from college, depending on a matchmaker to fix them up to be married. For many of them, it wasn't uncommon to marry a man after meeting him just a few times.

But in high school, I used to sneak cigarettes, sneak out for dates and had a steady boyfriend. Smoking as a high school girl was considered bad enough to get you expelled from school – if you were caught. But it never stopped my group of four friends from going to a Chinese restaurant where we would get a private room and stay for hours. We enjoyed feeling naughty by doing something no other kids did, but we knew how ludicrous it was, since all we did was smoke and talk about the guys we liked.

"At least Sang-Eun seems to date kids with good grades and with good family backgrounds," Mom used to say.

Once she approved of the boyfriends we had, Mom even encouraged us to bring them over to the house so we could spend time together, which was highly unusual by Korean standard.

Memories were fast-forwarding through my mind. We were always together. He used to carry my cello and I carried his violin. If we didn't go to a movie or a concert, I would go over to his house or he would come over to my house. We would visit old palaces or just walk around the city, stopping at teahouses or beer halls. We talked about how he would become a conductor and I would become the principal cellist in his orchestra.

I wondered how much of that my sisters knew. They knew we dated but no one ever knew that we were secretly promising to be together

forever. And I made sure that my mom thought that we were only casually dating.

I had seen my older sisters go through many nights of crying and
fighting with my mom over not-so-desirable boyfriends. Music students
were not the best potential sons-in-law material to Korean parents. I
knew my mom would want me to marry a doctor or an engineer. Dating
a musician would not satisfy a Jewish mother of the Orient (that's what
I used to call her). I was equally quiet about our relationship to my
girlfriends.

"We are just good friends," I used to say. But I let him believe
otherwise. I now felt terribly guilty for leading him on. The thought of
marrying him was exciting when we were together, especially if he was
going to make it as a conductor. But inside, I was clearly struggling with
the deeply cemented idea that a husband had to be someone powerful
and successful – at least a college professor. A violinist would never give
my mom a chance to boast over her prospective son-in-law.

Looking at the sky, I murmured silently, "Dear Lord, I was so
dishonest and so immature. Forgive me for hurting him."

Then I thought about my miserable days in Valparaiso when I first
left Korea. I had felt like I couldn't breathe. I was so lonely and missed
everything I had in Korea: my mom, my sisters, my friends, Ewha
University's campus, the streets of Seoul, the concerts, and especially
him. How I regretted coming to the United States. And how I wished I
could talk to him just once. I prayed every night that God would allow
him to come to the United States so we could be together. I missed his
lips, I missed his arms, and most of all, I missed his gentle eyes that
always seemed to plead, "Be nice to me. I love you so much." All I ever
wanted then was to be with him. All of my dreams of becoming a world-
famous cellist didn't mean a thing without him.

My stomach felt a little inflated from nervousness. I was going over
each word of our phone conversation from two days ago.

"Hello, is this Professor Park's residence?" I asked softly.

"Yes, it is." I knew it was him, though his voice was no longer familiar.

"Is he there?"

"Speaking." His answer was polite and for a second, I wished I could come up with something clever and witty to say. I nearly said, "Guess who this is?"

"Is this Eunseong Park?" My voice raised an octave from nervous excitement.

"Yes, it is."

"It's me, Sang-Eunee."

"What? Are you – is this for real? Could this day be really happening?" For a second, I thought he dropped the phone.

"Where are you calling from?"

"I came to Korea on a visit."

Our conversation went on for a while, but I was not fully aware of what was being said. Then he asked, "Can I see you?"

"Of course, I would love to see you."

"How are you doing?" he asked, as if he didn't know what else to ask.

"Well, I don't play the cello anymore."

"Why not?" He sounded shocked. "But you were so good at it. You do have the cello though, don't you?"

"Well, I traded it in for a set of golf clubs." I slurred in a high-pitched nervous giggle.

"You are kidding, right?" He was laughing.

For a few brief moments, I was back in my teens. I was full of mischief and he was always so gentle and serious. I had forgotten how much I had complained about his being so proper and so predictable. I had wanted him to be more spontaneous and more carefree and most of all, more passionate. He had put up with every one of my bratty behaviors and I knew I could get away with just about anything with him.

"Yes, I am kidding. I still have the cello."

We ended the phone conversation by promising to meet at a Chinese restaurant in the Tower Hotel in Nam-San for lunch.

I was amazingly calm, although my breakfast was still sitting like a wad of clay in my stomach. My oldest sister, Sang-Soon, who sat in the backseat, seemed more excited than anyone. The three of us were spending as much time as we could together during my visit to Korea.

"You look great. I will bet he will be surprised to see you haven't changed a bit. Do you realize how young you look?" My sister poked me on my arm from the backseat. To my big sister, I was perfect. She loved everything about me.

My sisters dropped me off in front of the hotel and drove off.

It was a nice and cool August day. I was dressed casually in a short red skirt and open blouse with a black top underneath. I thought, *how am I going to react when I see him? Should I give him a hug? Should I just look at him to see if I recognize him? Would he recognize me after thirty-eight years—nearly four decades?*

As I walked into the restaurant, three hostesses greeted me. In the middle of the long red counter where they stood was a huge vase full of flowers that was much too big for the counter. The large and airy restaurant was packed with round tables with white tablecloths and painted aluminum legs. I felt a tinge of disappointment in his choice of restaurant. Things like that were never important to him. I thought of Dan back at home. Dan would have picked a quaint little place with lace curtains.

I told the hostesses that I was meeting a gentleman for lunch and one of them took me to a table in the front, the only one occupied. My heart was flapping like a giant bird in a small cage. Just then I thought I saw the familiar smile. Could it be him? He didn't look anything like I remembered. He looked like he could have been one of my uncles. He looked old. I don't know what I expected. He couldn't stay as nineteen-year-old forever.

I smiled back fully, with my mouth open. I wanted him to know that I was happy to see him. His face looked wider, and his nose looked flatter. But it was him. I could see the same eyes and the same expressions. He had the same sweet, shy smile with his mouth closed and his eyes – the same tapered eyes – were full of yearning.

"You can't be Eunseong?" I said loudly as I approached him; he was already standing up. I hugged him and I felt him hugging me tightly. His outfit, a dark gray sport jacket over a button-down shirt and no tie, was something I could have expected of him. He was never a navy-suit-with-snow-white-dress-shirt kind of guy. He smiled like he was a little unsure and doubtful about something – the same as I remembered. Yes, it was him. It was my guy! I felt at home right away, as if we were there on one of our dates as two nineteen-year-old kids again.

We sat down and he offered me a cigarette. I shook my head.

"Do you still smoke?" I asked.

"No, not really. But after your phone call I …"

I noticed he was smoking a Korean cigarette. Not the minty Salem we used to buy in the smuggler's black market.

I told him about my three daughters and he told me about his two daughters. The older one played the violin and the younger one didn't want anything to do with music. His wife was a pianist out of Juilliard and his days were generally busy with concerts and recordings. During the school year, he also held a professorship at Han-Yang University.

"Tell me about your husband. How old is he?" he asked.

"Fifty-eight, same as me," I answered. "My husband doesn't know much about classical music," I said it apologetically. "But he would love it if I picked it up again."

"When is his birthday?" I sensed he was comparing Dan to himself. I remembered that Eunseoung was a few months younger than I was.

He remarked that I looked young for a grandmother. "Just as cute," he said.

"I didn't grow, that's for sure." I winked as I smiled.

I told him briefly about how I went through a divorce and started a few freelance jobs, like decorating and court interpreting, in preparing myself to be financially independent.

"But I don't work at all now. I play golf and bridge." I surprised myself, realizing I didn't mind making my life sound unimportant. I was a lot more interested in hearing about how his life had gone. There were so many things I wanted to know – all the things that happened after I left almost four decades ago.

He put his index fingers on his lips figuring out what to talk about first. I sensed there was a whole lot he wanted to pour out, which was fine with me, since I mostly wanted to listen. Strangely, I felt like I was in a position to make amends for whatever his heavy heart desired, maybe for leaving him, and maybe for not feeling as nervous as him even now.

"On the day you left – it still hurts to think about. I was so so upset – more sad than upset, I suppose. Kim Min and I went to my house from the airport after seeing you off. I remember telling him how strange, how so strange it was to be in a world where there was no you. And Min said he understood; it was strange for him too. He knew I was so in love with you. Then we went out for beer and drank. It seems like it was yesterday."

He sighed.

"I took a semester off in my senior year. I started drinking heavily. I missed you desperately, and couldn't keep up with the schoolwork. I knew I couldn't have you back. I had heard that you were engaged to be married to someone else, and I was wasting my life away. Every time I looked up in the sky, I would see your face. For years, when I was driving, your face would appear on the windshield."

He looked far away and took a drag.

"Then one Sunday during a church service, I realized I had to snap out of it. I was still hurting so much that I needed strength from the above, you know – Jesus."

He palmed his hands together as if he was praying and took a deep sigh. As I was watching him I remembered his name meant: "By the grace of God."

At this point, I felt so terribly guilty I had to interrupt. "I was so lonely; I probably missed you a thousand times more than you did. At least you had your family and your friends here with you. I was alone in a strange country."

It was my meek attempt to give an excuse for sending him a "Dear John" letter shortly after meeting Ty.

He kept trying to catch his breath. Even though I felt empathy for him, I took my eyes off of him, feeling like a child trying to cry at a grandparent's funeral. Even so, I felt like we could pick up where we left off thirty-eight years ago. There was a clear soothing feeling like I was home. That's exactly how we started our relationship, with not much passion on my part. But I grew to love him. I wanted to bury my face in his chest and pound it for not coming to America when I was so lonely.

"So, how long did you study in Vienna?" I blurted out and looked at him with envy.

"Eight years." He tapped the cigarette on the edge of the ashtray and went on.

"Then I went to New York one summer where my parents had moved and met my wife there and got married."

Somehow his being married to someone else seemed unfair. I didn't want him to stay single forever, but the thought of him belonging to someone else still didn't seem right. As I struck a match and held it up for his second cigarette, I could see his hand was trembling.

"So, I hear you are a famous conductor," I said as I blew off the flame.

"I don't know if I am famous, but I am doing what I had dreamed to do all my life."

"I knew you had talent all along." I looked at him with a smile a mother would send to her son. He became a conductor. He did it.

Oh, how I wanted to see Vienna and how I wanted to study there. I had dreamed that I would get my degree in America and then go on to Europe to further my music education. It never entered my mind which slot of my life I would put family planning into.

Whenever I thought about the word "Vienna," I would imagine myself with him walking on the rainy streets of the city toward the conservatory with my cello under my arm. I knew then I was truly envious. My life as a cellist was still very much alive in me. I wanted to tell him how proud I was of him. I felt guilty for not ever telling him that he had a God-given gift and that I knew that he would be successful one day. I was always the one who was performing and winning the competitions, and he was the one who never stood out. He talked about being a conductor, not a violinist. And I sometimes took it as an excuse for not excelling in violin.

"I heard that you went to see Mr. Lim at the hospital the other day and took a whole choir to sing hymns for him."

He was surprised that I knew this.

"That was so wonderful. I heard that he got better and became very alert for the following few days."

Mr. Won-Sick Lim, probably the most prominent figure in the music society in Korea, was dying of stomach cancer.

"Mr. Lim was my mentor. He adored me and when I performed in Japan, I surprised him by mentioning his name as my greatest teacher and brought him out on the stage. I don't speak Japanese so I spoke in English."

I complimented him on his proficiency in both English and German. "I also heard that you have become a true Christian," I said, looking straight into his eyes. "You know, truly walking with the Lord, having a close relationship with Jesus?"

"I am. But I don't talk much about it. Who told you?"

"Oh, I just heard. I think that's wonderful. Do you remember giving me the Bible when I left Korea?"

"Yes of course, do you still have it?"

"I still do. Along with sacred memories," I said softly.

Even though he had become everything I would ever want from a man, successful and a Christian, I was only happy for his wife and his children because they had him, a gentleman with the purist heart.

"When you were in New York, why didn't you call me?" I asked.

"By then you were a mom and someone else's wife. I knew I couldn't have you back."

"I mean, just to say hi?"

He just smiled. Again one of those doubtful smiles. I wanted to tell him that I got married because marrying my first husband solved all of my problems. And after all, it turned out to be the best thing that we didn't marry each other. In many ways, we might not have been right for each other.

But somehow it didn't seem appropriate to whine about how terrible my first year in America was. Reluctantly, I let him keep the image of me as an unfaithful betrayer.

"You were my first love. You will always be special to me." He looked far away and reached to hold my hand without any hesitation. For a moment, the thirty-eight-year gap was completely closed. It was the same hand I had held every day. His hand felt warm and I thought I nearly conjured up the smell of Dial soap. I was getting increasingly uncomfortable not knowing where to look or what to say with my face hot from blushing.

"Do you still use Dial soap?" I blurted out as I pulled my hand away.

He just smiled again.

"But you are happy though, aren't you?" I added.

"Yes, actually I am, very. I do love my wife very much." He nodded. "I do think that maybe we were not meant for each other. If we ended up together, you would have walked out on me one day anyway. I know it. Maybe it was a good thing you left after all."

"Really? Why do you say that?" I asked as if trying to justify my unfaithfulness.

"You were always so dissatisfied with me. Full of complaints. I never thought you really loved me."

Even though he was determined to victimize himself, I was glad for him. I wanted him to have a wonderful family. I even wished he had a lovely wife and that they shared a special connection through music. Something I didn't have in either one of my marriages.

It was a strange feeling as if I came home from college, but without a degree. I was having the same intimate feelings that I had thirty-eight years ago. It seemed as though he should rightfully belong to me. But he didn't. And what's more, I was not a musician. Music was so much of our lives then. But then, somehow it all seemed right. We had a precious thing together, but it all became a precious memory as we each went on to separate lives that couldn't be farther apart.

Peering at his face, in the confusion of strange and familiar feelings, things were becoming slowly clear to me. I didn't feel complete with him. That was it. Somehow there seemed to be an inadequate blankness. He never knew how to fill that hollowness I was feeling when I was with him. It had been there then, and it was still there now. That's what made me always wonder if I really loved him when I was seeing him day after day. I had known it then, that he was not for me, and I knew it now.

I missed my husband Dan, in California. After being married to him for fifteen years, I still waited for him to come home from work and got excited to see him every night. With him, I had a place that I didn't want to leave.

Dan always remembered my favorite food when we went out to a restaurant. When he ran into a drugstore, he would leave my favorite station on in the car so I could enjoy classical music. And he loved my kids simply because they are mine. What was important to me was important to him. He would have picked a restaurant that had ambiance because he knew things like that were important to me. And I loved the feeling I had when he held me and called me "Sugar." There was no void with Dan; his love made me feel true and whole.

The thought of him made me feel warm all over. I wondered what he was doing right then. He made me want to come home to him and he made me excited about my life. I wanted to be a good golfer for him and a good wife to him. I was thankful to God for blessing me by sending him to me.

"I never thought this day would happen in my lifetime."

Eunseong's voice brought me back to reality as I took a bite of spicy tofu.

"When we were young, it used to really bother me that you were not totally happy with me. You thought that I was not manly enough for you. I wanted to make you love me as much as I loved you," he added.

"But I did love you."

"Did you really?"

"Of course I did. And I feel very blessed to have been loved by you. I mean it."

"Can I call you from time to time?" he asked.

"Of course," I said with a smile and added, "I will call you, too. I promise."

We must have talked for a few more hours about his family and my family and our friends; we shared many friends who all had the same goals and dreams.

In front of the hotel, he hailed a cab for me. As I got into the cab, he whispered to me, "Remember, I love you."

Sitting in the backseat of the cab, I felt like I just had a dream. Did I really see him? We had somewhat resolved the unfinished matters. At least he did. He told me how he felt, how he had done, and what happened to him.

I still had a lot I wanted to tell him. I wanted to tell him how very sorry I was. There was something elite about him, a quality I loved in a man. But he was only my boyfriend because he was so good to me, even though I always had the haunting image of a powerful man with impeccable taste as my husband in the back of my mind. I wanted to be completely honest with him for once, that he was never for me. He never belonged to me. But I had lived thirty-eight years without telling him anything. What was another ten or twenty years?

But one thing was clear: I did love him. He was there when I needed a date to go to a concert. He was there so I could say I had someone who loved me. He loved me because as far as he was concerned, I could do no wrong. I loved his gentleness. I loved him for his kind, loving, and pure heart. I loved him for being a genuinely good person. He made me feel good about myself.

I stared at the CD he gave me and looked at his picture on the cover and said softly, "I did love you."

50

The dim light in the underground parking lot of the Sixth Street convalescent hospital in Los Angeles revealed suspicious puddles on the cement floor. Wiping my tears, I clicked open my red BMW, entered, and locked the doors before turning on the motor. This had become my routine for the last month. I made daily trips, driving up in the afternoon and back home late at night when the traffic cleared.

Every afternoon, I walked into the sordid one-story building that smelled of urine and into Mom's room, calling, "*Umma*, I am here." Some days she looked as if she was trying to open her eyes, some days she wiggled her fingers slightly. On those days, I continued to hope that she recognized me, even though my gut instinct told me her movements were just reflexes.

As Mother's condition worsened, I made sure her single room on the first floor was clean and that the nurses changed her diapers promptly. Mother had stopped speaking or eating nearly a month earlier, and no matter how much I wiped the furnishings with Clorox, the room still reeked of silent death. Her slightly open mouth was dry and the tip of her tongue was split and dark from dried blood. I asked the nurse to moisten it with a wet cotton swab.

I pushed her chin up to close her mouth but it sprang right back open. When I held her hand, she didn't squeeze mine back. Her peaceful face twitched involuntarily. I jumped to see if she was coming around.

I put her hand against my cheek. Her wrinkles were soft and warm. I repeated this day after day until a nurse came in last week with a warning sign saying, "Keep away." She explained that an unidentified bacteria was growing in Mother's body. "How do they know?" I thought. "And what the hell is the unidentified bacteria?" But I was reluctant to touch her, so I felt guilty.

I was tired, and going home at ten o'clock was scary. Kimmy, who worked at Paramount Studios, would come to see her grandmother after work with an armful of flowers. On the way home, we would stop and have a late dinner at a Korean restaurant, and I looked forward to it. Sometimes I cried at dinner and she whimpered with me. Then she followed me onto the freeway and when I safely moved over three lanes to the 110 South, she would ride alongside me until she turned off at the 105 freeway and waved goodbye.

"Drive faster than fifty miles an hour, Mom," she said every time.

Two days ago, the doctor pressured me to make a decision to exercise my "power of attorney," so he could stop force-feeding her. She was eighty-eight years old, her heart was barely functioning with an extra supply of oxygen, and she was only kept alive in an incoherent state by a feeding tube.

"I know she wouldn't want to be remembered as pathetic as that," he said.

I called my sisters, one in China, one in Florida, and another one in Korea, and cried some more to each one of them. I told them that I would decide tomorrow. I resented that my sisters left it up to me to make the decision to starve Mom to death.

As I left the parking lot and weaved through the traffic on Wilshire Boulevard, I wondered what it would be like to live in a world without Mom. I knew my life would go on. I had lived without her for over a decade before she immigrated to America. I would always have my precious daughters to fill my heart, and I would always have my loving husband. But I knew there would be a permanent empty spot that only Mom could fill: a great void. I burst into a convulsing cry and the windshield grew foggy from my sobbing.

The final night, Kimmy was held up in a meeting and did not meet me at the convalescent hospital. I stayed with Mom, watching her passive face. I made sure the nurses changed her and gave her a sponge bath for another senseless night's rest.

Dan greeted me at the door.

"You are home a little early today."

"The drive home was a breeze," I said. He poured me a glass of Chardonnay and asked where I wanted to go for dinner.

"Would any place be open this late? It's almost ten o'clock."

As soon as we come back from a salad dinner at Coco's, I pushed the blinking message button on the phone. My heart pounded.

"*Yu-bo-se-yo*, hello, this is your Uhmonim's doctor at the hospital. Your mother just passed a few minutes ago. She went peacefully with her eyes closed."

His deliberately slow voice reminded me of a funeral. Stupid doctor! Her eyes had been closed for the last month. So what was so peaceful about that?

I called my three daughters and my sister-in-law, my brother's wife, Young-Ja. She regularly brought prepared Korean meals to my mom and cared for her every chance, even after my brother died from a heart attack.

Terry quietly sobbed and told me that she and Thad were leaving immediately. Kimmy howled, and like a sergeant, ordered me not to drive, but to have Dan drive. Michelle bawled and told me to be strong, that Grandma was in a better place. Dan silently hugged me and kissed my forehead.

All of us arrived about the same time. Terry and Thad from Costa Mesa, Kimmy from Manhattan Beach, Michelle from Los Angeles, and my brother's wife from Woodland Hills. In spite of the nurse's warning about not going too close to Mom, Terry caressed Mom's forehead and brushed her wispy hairs away as she tenderly said, "Grandma, now go ahead and breathe all you want. You don't need the oxygen and the breathing machine anymore. And you have no more pain now. Go ahead and be free to be with Jesus. You are in a much better place now. Go ahead."

I cried, watching Terry's love for my mom, a grandmother whom she could barely talk to. I cried some more, seeing the loving connection I had provided between them, or rather, that Mom had provided through her broken English.

Terry was wearing a sweater my mom gave her. She had admired the blue, pearl-embroidered sweater Mom was wearing one day, and Mom remembered and wrapped it in pink tissue to give it to her for Christmas that year.

Kimmy paced the room, wailing. Michelle held Mom's hand and silently sobbed.

I felt a part of me leaving along with my mother.

Over the course of forty years of living in America, I had become less and less of a Korean. The last few times I went back to Korea, the place seemed foreign. People were using a new vocabulary. They no longer covered their mouths when they laughed. Traditional dishes were hard to find at restaurants; there were more fusion dishes now. Everyone looked straight into your eyes when they talked. They no longer bowed to their waist. They were not afraid to ask questions. Even the girls walked around showing off their tan, healthy-looking bodies. It wasn't the same Korea that I remembered. I didn't belong there. The only connection I had left with Korea was through my mom. And I now felt that flickering light go out. I felt lost.

Even though I have no problem communicating or living in America as an American, I will always have black hair and brown eyes and I will always have an identifiable speech pattern. I have adapted artfully to live in America as a competent mother, wife, and friend. But my English is an acquired language. My first words were not Mommy and Daddy. They were *Umma* and *Ahpa*. I have acquired social skills. I have learned to adjust my thought process to be like an American. But it didn't come naturally like growing hair. I don't truly belong here. But I don't belong in Korea, either. This melting pot of experience is what makes me who I am. But now, without my mom, there are few elements in me.

I feel partially empty.

I miss Mom.

Epilogue

I don't remember when or how it happened. Progressive lenses have become a permanent fixture on my face and Citrucel, an essential part of my diet. Traveling now requires an extra bag to hold vitamins and a large bottle of estrogen. Putting on makeup in the morning takes an extra hour of effort to smooth out and cover up the wrinkles and liver spots.

I make endless lists of things to do, but then forget to look at the list. Doctor's appointments are becoming more frequent in order to keep my body well oiled. Acupuncture no longer scares me. Rather, I look forward to an opportunity to get pricked by the fine needles to be relieved from achy symptoms that have been impossible to diagnose by doctors.

My life has reached its summit of blessed being. Dan and I live a quiet life, and enjoy a magnificent view of the sunset over the ocean. He recently made his son, Danny his partner in the company he started shortly before we started dating, and he now enjoys the luxury of choosing how to spend his time. When he is away from the golf course, he makes time to plant and tend to the wisterias I had yearned to have in our backyard, and we both look forward to babysitting our grandkids. To me, having grandkids nearby is a God-given privilege because holding a grandchild in my arms is the closest thing to being in heaven. Dan's

humor keeps me laughing, and growing old along with him reminds me
how blessed I am.

Many memories still haunt me painfully, and others, joyfully. But I
find myself constantly trying to recapture a small shred of bygone days.

After Bob Rogers retired, he and Frances moved to Santa Fe, New
Mexico, where the cost of living was more manageable and the town
offered cultural advantages as well. I visited them in New Mexico shortly
after Ty and I separated. Seeing the same Danish furniture, including
the dining table, on which Bob had served me the odd-looking *kimchee*
the first day I arrived in America, gave me a melancholy sense of coming
home. Bob looked aged in his loose khakis, and Frances looked tired and
faded, like their furniture. The enclosed backyard in their two-bedroom
house provided a patch of dirt where Frances could plant spring bulbs.
On my first night there, Frances splurged and roasted lamb to welcome
me – the one meat I didn't eat. I swallowed a few tiny pieces and quickly
washed them down with the wine Bob served.

And the next day, Bob made us leftover lamb sandwiches for lunch.
Over lunch, I told them that I just finished making my house comfortable for the girls and their constant visitors, and Frances showed me the
letter Kimmy wrote to her when she was a third-grader. Kimmy wrote,
"My mommy told me if it weren't for you, I wouldn't be here. Thanks."

That night, I took them out to dinner and Frances pensively said to
me, "Maybe you might think of playing the cello now that the girls are
a little older."

Shortly after Dan and I got married, we packed our golf clubs and
made a long weekend trip to Santa Fe. Before we explored the golf courses,
we drove our rented car and took Bob and Frances out to lunch. It was
a treat to them because they hardly ever went out to eat. At lunch, after
acknowledging how wonderful it was that Dan and I found each other,
Frances asked me about my brother. "How did he die?" she asked.

"Of a heart attack – alcoholism related," I said. "He did leave a wonderful legacy, though. His son is a wonderful boy – the opposite of my brother in every way. When you see him, you see nothing but good in him.

After living in Santa Fe for nearly a decade, Bob drove his 1965 Buick LeSabre and dragged all their Danish furniture in a U-Haul to an assisted living facility in Hood River, Oregon. Dan and I had the occasion to visit them in Oregon when Frances was in her nineties. Bob's back was hunched over and he depended on a wheelchair to get around most of the time. Frances looked the same except she had lost nearly all of her hearing. To communicate, we spoke through a contraption. Bob adjusted a large headset on her and handed me the egg-sized microphone to speak into. She was able to converse with me, but she still had a hard time hearing my delayed voice through the outer-spacey apparatus.

At one point, she got up and searched through the cupboard and gave me a Paul Revere silver candy dish and said, "This is for Terry. We live a simple life and don't have much now, but I would like to give this to her." It was the dish she had used for marzipan on Hanley Avenue, on the ledge between the kitchen and the living room.

In 1999, Frances Rogers turned 104 years old at their apartment in Hood River, Oregon. I had no idea how old she was until Sang-Hie suggested that we fly up to celebrate her birthday.

Frances had written her memoir, "Footfalls, Echoes of the Life of My Time" in early 1990s. Since she had told her story, she was no longer afraid to disclose her age, and she now wanted to celebrate her long life while she was still able-bodied. I agreed to go and bought an airplane ticket, but an emergency sinus surgery kept me from attending. To my knowledge, it was the only celebration that Frances had in her 104 years of life.

In the event, I spat out the pearl and did not become a concert cellist. I did not succeed in life's competition. But I accepted my life the way God intended for me. He has created me exactly the way I am. I have made the best of both worlds. Nothing was lost. Rather, my life has been enriched in my constant search of the almighty, compassionate, and gracious God.

Reading the Bible has become a priority in my daily life. Being married to Dan has allowed me the freedom to search for a deeper love for God. He not only encouraged my spiritual growth, but he also joined me in learning the word of God so we would share the same purpose in Christ. As far as I am concerned, knowing the Lord together with your loved one is the biggest accomplishment in life. And every day, we are growing a little closer to God.

"I have been thinking, for our twentieth anniversary, would you like to be married again? This time by the pastor of our church?" Dan asked. Our big anniversary was approaching. After watching me read the Bible and seeing the changes in my life, he knew how important it was for me to be obedient to God. When we were originally married, it was by our friend John Torribio, at our country club. We were both forty-one years old, young and vulnerable, and it seemed appropriate, at the time, to be married by a judge.

Renewing our vows in God's presence, in front of our children and grandchildren and making our commitment right in the eyes of God was the ultimate gesture of our love for one another and, more importantly, our love for God.

My vague understanding of and search for my grace notes became clear to me only after I became a grandmother. The song of life was already written. It is my lifelong assignment to decorate and complete the song with grace notes. I was born an imperfect being and only the fruit of the Spirit will complete my character and align it with Christ's character.

My precious pearl was not my music, not my children, not the fame, or any other worldly desire, but Jesus Christ, the Lord who dwells in my heart. I am at peace with myself now, because it gives me joy to polish my true pearl, the Holy Spirit.

When I invite the Holy Spirit into my heart and live in the Spirit, strengthening and polishing it each day diligently, I will grow to have spiritual intimacy with God. Intimacy with God allows me to love with God's kind of love and allows me to grow to embrace the fruit of the Spirit. Only then will my imperfect being radiate.

I don't belong to a Western world or Eastern world. I only belong to and want to be accepted by God. When I eventually gain full knowledge of His truth, I will shine from the most valuable treasure, the precious pearl.

God has blessed me with three daughters who taught me how precious life is just by being themselves. And by His grace, I have learned that true success in life is to know Jesus and have a personal relationship on a day-to-day walk with Him and share the joy with the loved ones.

God's grace is truly sufficient.

Writing this book was my small way of glorifying God.

"For the fruit of the spirit is love, joy, peace, patience, kindness, goodness, faithfulness, gentleness and self-control".

Galatians 5:22